Agile Modeling:
Effective Practices for eXtreme Programming and the Unified Process

Scott Ambler

Wiley Computer Publishing

John Wiley & Sons, Inc.

Publisher: Robert Ipsen
Editor: Theresa Hudson
Development Editor: Kathryn A. Malm
Managing Editor: Angela Smith
New Media Editor: Brian Snapp
Text Design & Composition: D&G Limited, LLC

This book is printed on acid-free paper. ♾

This publication is designed to provide accurate and authoritative information in regard to the subject matter covered. It is sold with the understanding that the publisher is not engaged in professional services. If professional advice or other expert assistance is required, the services of a competent professional person should be sought.

Library of Congress Cataloging-in-Publication Data:

ISBN: 0-471-20282-7

Printed in the United States of America.

10 9 8 7 6 5 4 3 2 1

To my fellow black-belt candidates,

Ed Maloney, Marc Desroches, and Tyler Colisimo

We made it.

Contents

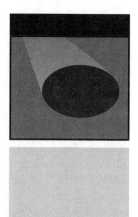

Foreword

When Scott asked me to write the Foreword for this book, I was both pleased and surprised. I was pleased for several reasons: it's always nice to be thought of, it's great to be associated with a book as well-written as this one, and agile methods (specifically eXtreme Programming) are my own focus these days. I was surprised because I was one of the first and most vocal in "suggesting" that Scott *not* address his attention to this topic. "I will explain. No, it is too much. I will sum up."

Software development, to me, is best done with as little specialization as possible. I teach and believe that the best results are obtained with a team of individuals who contribute wherever and however they can, without regard to who is the architect, the modeler, the designer, the programmer, or the tester. Not that we all have to be some kind of godlike software Renaissance man or woman, but that we should all come together and contribute as much of everything as we can.

Furthermore, software development (again, to me) is best done with as little modeling as possible. The point of software development is to develop software. Too much time is taken up in getting ready, leaving too little time for the important part—actually producing solid, well-designed, high-quality software. The quality of the software isn't always correlated with the quality of the models that are drawn with the latest modeling tools before building the system.

So when Scott proposed and started his Agile Modeling forum and Web site, I was opposed to the idea. Too much concentration on modeling, I feared, would take away from the focus on bringing together the team and the skills necessary to build good software. I said so, in no uncertain terms, on Scott's forum and in private e-mails.

Well, it turns out that Scott recognized something that I did not. If people are going to come together in cooperation to build software in the agile fashion, it is not enough that they only bring love, understanding, and passion. They must have skill. The team must have skill in analysis, modeling, design, programming, testing—all of the things that are the basis of good software. And they must apply those skills consistently with the values of agile development, one of which is to focus on "individuals and interactions over processes and tools," as we wrote in the Agile Manifesto.

That's what Scott set out to do in his forum, with his Web site, and in this book. He shows us how to perform effective, light-weight modeling in the context of an agile project. He shows us how to do modeling in non-agile projects, with an eye to helping them become more agile. Most importantly, he does this based on a set of values, principles, and practices that can inform an individual's, and a team's, approach to modeling. He keeps his eye on the game of software development at all times, while focusing on the particular modeling skills and practices you'll need.

Scott addresses the use of simple tools, the kind of workspace required, the way the team needs to be constituted, and how it should work together. I particularly like the quote from Sergeant Rasczak of *Starship Troopers*, "I only have one rule, everyone fights and nobody quits or I'll shoot you myself." Scott relates modeling to everything from eXtreme Programming to the Unified Process, and does a good job of it.

One of one's duties in writing a foreword is to indicate who should read this book. Here's my take: read this book if you are a software developer who needs modeling skills as part of your development—that is, if you are a software developer. Read this book if you are a modeler who needs your work to be applicable to software development in these days of rapid change—that is, if you are a modeler. And read this book if you are a software development manager who needs to figure out what agile development means to your projects—that is, if you are a software development manager. If you're engaged in any way in software development today, this book can help you out.

Scott's book, *Agile Modeling*, describes the skills necessary to do effective modeling as part of software projects that need to move quickly to deliver quality software to their stakeholders. Well done, Scott!

Ron Jeffries

Preface

If you're reading this Preface, then you are very likely trying to determine whether or not you should buy this book. I like your attitude! To help you make this decision I'll quickly answer a few very important questions that you most likely have.

What Is Agile Modeling?

Agile Modeling (AM) is a practices-based process that describes how to be an effective modeler. Current modeling approaches can often prove dysfunctional. In the one extreme, modeling is non-existent, often resulting in significant rework when the software proves to be poorly thought through. The other extreme is when excessive models and documents are produced, which slows your development efforts down to a snail's pace. AM helps you find the modeling sweet spot, where you have modeled enough to explore and document your system effectively, but not so much that it becomes a burden that slows the project down.

The techniques of AM can and should be applied by project teams that wish to take an agile approach to software development, in particular those that are following an agile process such as eXtreme Programming (XP), DSDM, SCRUM, or FDD. AM can also be used to improve and often simplify your modeling efforts on projects where you don't take a purely agile approach.

What Does This Book Cover?

The book starts by exploring the values, principles, and practices of AM and describing techniques to improve your productivity as a modeler. You are likely to discover that you are already following several of these practices, although may have been afraid to admit it to others, and are likely to discover new ways to model effectively. The book also rethinks several important issues that pertain to software development, such as how to write documentation, how to organize modeling sessions and modeling teams, and where UML fits in. As the title of the book suggests, it explores in detail how to model effectively on an XP project. Contrary to what you may have heard, modeling is an important part of XP. This book shows how to simplify your modeling efforts on projects taking a Rational Unified Process (RUP) or Enterprise Unified Process (EUP) approach.

What Doesn't This Book Cover?

This book does not tell you how to create models. For example, it does not describe procedures for writing user stories, use cases, or business rules. This book is not meant to be an introduction to the UML, data modeling, or usage-centered design. This book looks at the bigger picture, at the process of modeling, not the minute details. This is very similar to XP that describes the process for developing software but not how to actually program.

Furthermore, this book is different than any other that you've read about software modeling before. Previous modeling methodology books described several modeling artifacts such as use cases, sequence diagrams, and class diagrams—and described a methodology for using these artifacts to model your software. AM takes a different approach; it describes techniques for modeling but doesn't insist on the types of models that you create. Instead it suggests that you learn how to apply a wide variety of modeling artifacts and that you strive to add more to your intellectual toolbox over time. Where other modeling methods disappear as the underlying technology changes, I believe that you will discover that the principles and practices of AM will stand the test of time because they are truly fundamental.

Who Am I?

Even though I live just north of Toronto, I'm a Senior Consultant and President of Denver-based Ronin International, Inc. I've been developing software since the mid-1980s and building object-oriented software since the early 1990s. I actively work with clients to create mission-critical software and in my spare time write about my experiences in books, magazines, and online white papers. For several years now I have focused on software process issues, including prescriptive processes such as the Unified Process (UP) as well as agile processes such as eXtreme Programming (XP), helping organizations to become more effective in their approach to software development. I also like to take an active role on software projects, getting my hands dirty whenever I can in the role of senior developer or team lead.

Who Are You?

You are very likely a developer or modeler that wants to improve their effectiveness as a software professional. You're curious about how to model on an XP project or how to simplify your modeling efforts on a RUP project. You might even be a project manager or process expert who's trying to figure out what this "agile development stuff" is all about.

Who Helped Me?

I would like to thank the following people for their insights that have gone into this book:

Glen B. Alleman	Martin Fowler
James Ames	Martin Gainty
Dave Astels	Adam Geras
Bruce Bacheller	John Goodsen
Kent Beck	Leonard Greski
John Bennett	Lionell Griffith
Larry Bernstein	David Hecksel
Howard Bolling	Mats Helander
Terry Bollinger	Jim Highsmith
Grady Booch	Luke Hohmann
Larry Brunelle	Gerry Hummell
Scott Clemmons	Ron Jeffries
Alistair Cockburn	Peter Lappo
Anthony DaSilva	Mark Levison
Rachel Davies	Dave Lubinsky
Craig Dewalt	Robert C. Martin
Bryan Dollery	Lynn H. Maxson
Sara Edwards	Bill Meakin
Dale Emery	Drew Mills
Michael C. Feathers	John Nalbone
Rick Fisher	Miroslav Novak
Peter Foreman	Larry O'Brien

Tom Pardee

Erich Pawlik

Neil Pitman

Charlie Poole

Mary Poppendieck

Gareth Reeves

David M. Rubin

Marcelo Lopez Ruiz

Jeff Ruley

Alan Shalloway

Doug Smith

Mike Smith

Roger Smith

Jim Standley

Dr. Gernot Starke

Dan Sterling

Brian Tarbox

Dave Thomas

Neil Thorne

John Welch

Geri Winters

Klaus Wuestefeld

Ed Yourdon

PART

One

Introduction to Agile Modeling

This part sets the foundation for the book through a detailed discussion of the values, principles, and practices of Agile Modeling (AM). This section includes the following chapters:

- **Chapter 1: Introduction.** This chapter outlines the challenges faced by software developers today and how Agile Software Development and Agile Modeling address those challenges.
- **Chapter 2: Agile Modeling Values.** This chapter discusses the five *values* of AM.
- **Chapter 3: Core Principles.** This chapter describes in detail the core *principles* of AM, those of primary importance to agile modelers.
- **Chapter 4: Supplementary Principles.** In this chapter we discuss the supplementary principles of AM that support and enhance AM's core principles.
- **Chapter 5: Core Practices.** This chapter presents the critical *practices* of AM, all of which you must adopt to claim that you are truly doing Agile Modeling. These practices describe how to take an incremental and iterative approach to modeling, how to support and enhance teamwork, how to keep things as simple as possible, and how to validate your efforts in an agile manner.
- **Chapter 6: Supplementary Practices.** These practices describe the motivations for creating an agile model, how to keep your documentation efforts agile, and how to improve your productivity as an agile modeler.
- **Chapter 7: Order from Chaos: How the AM Practices Fit Together.** This chapter presents an overview on how the practices fit together in a synergistic whole.

Introduction

To change your fate, you must first change your attitude.

The current software development situation is less than ideal. Systems are regularly delivered late or over budget if they are delivered at all. Systems often don't meet the needs of our customers and we must develop them again and again and again. Our customers are angry because of these problems and are neither willing to trust us nor work with us because they've been burned too many times in the past. To make matters worse, our customers don't have a very good understanding of what we do, how we do it, or why we do it—the end result is that they put unrealistic demands on us and don't give us the support that we need to accomplish their goals.

It isn't much fun for software developers, either. We work long hours, typically 50, 60, or 70 hours a week and quickly become burned out. When projects run into trouble, often before they've even started, we point fingers at others. Convenient targets include our "pointy-haired bosses" whom we believe are barely competent enough to tie their own shoes, the "paper-pushing fools" in the department down the hall from us that demand excessive amounts of documentation, and our "stupid users" who often don't know what they want, and when they do tell us what they want, it never makes sense anyway. Naturally, we never blame ourselves; we're perfect after all. So what do we do when we realize that a project is in trouble? Sometimes we give it our all, working excessive hours in a futile attempt to meet the unrealistic demands placed on us, embarking on a death march (Yourdon 1997). Sometimes we disconnect from the project entirely. Knowing that it's doomed, we decide that we should at least learn something useful to pad our resumes, so we download some new development tools from the Internet and start playing with them.

Why have we gotten ourselves in such a sad state of affairs? First, I believe that many people have lost sight of the fact that the primary goal of software development is to build systems, in the most effective and efficient manner possible, that meet the needs of their users. For the sake of our discussion, a system includes the software, documentation, hardware, middleware, installation procedures, and operational procedures. Similarly, organizations have lost sight of the end-to-end process of delivering software to customers and have unfortunately organized IT departments into teams with specialist roles that often don't see the overall picture. I suspect that this has happened because one, if not two, generations of IT professionals believe that they must follow a predefined set of activities in order to develop software. We can describe these activities by what is known as prescriptive processes, also referred to as heavy-weight software processes. Prescriptive software processes such as the Unified Process (Kruchten 2000; Ambler 2001b), the OPEN Process (Graham, Henderson-Sellers, and Younessi 1997), and the Object-Oriented Software Process (Ambler 1998; Ambler 1999) all have their place. It is just that they may not be as appropriate as their supporters consider them to be. The problem with these approaches is that they typically focus on prescriptive procedures and the artifacts that should be created, approaches that are often implemented by organizations who consider people to be "plug and play compatible." In other words, their belief is that, with the right process in place and with the necessary number of artifacts, you can swap people in and out of a project with relative ease. My experience is that this is only true when the person you are replacing isn't very productive, something that is often the case in organizations following a heavy-weight process. The reality is that replacing a productive person is difficult regardless of the process you follow, so the "plug and play compatibility" goal is questionable at best.

The interesting thing about prescriptive processes is that they are attractive to management but not to most developers. Prescriptive processes are typically based on a command-and-control paradigm that puts management in control of things, well, at least makes them perceive that they're in control of things. It also has a tendency to make management think they can minimize the role of project stakeholders in software development, bringing them in for a few quick requirements sessions and then ignoring them until they're needed for user acceptance testing. Another problem is that when the going gets tough, developers quickly abandon the process, unfortunately throwing out the good with the bad when they do so, and then they often find themselves in an even bigger mess than before. My experience is that short cuts often lead to quagmires, not salvation, making your death march even worse.

I also believe that the way that developers learn their trade has a few unique dysfunctions. For the most part our colleges and universities are doing a reasonable job of educating developers for entry-level jobs. However, even if the schools were doing a perfect job and everyone was getting a degree or diploma, I suspect that we'd still have a problem due to the inherent nature of software developers. When software developers are young, in their teens or early twenties, they typically focus on learning and working with technology. They describe themselves as PERL programmers, Linux experts, Enterprise JavaBeans (EJB) developers, or .NET developers. To them the technology is the important thing. Because the technology is constantly changing, younger developers have a tendency to just barely learn a technology, apply it on one or two projects, and then start over again learning a new technology or the latest incarnation of what they worked with previously. The problem is that they keep learning the same different flavors of the same low-level, fundamental skills over and over again.

Luckily, many developers become aware of this after several rounds of technologies—once you've written code for transaction control in COBOL, Java, and C#, you start to realize that the fundamentals don't change. The same is true of database access in various environments, user interface design, and so on. Before long, developers begin to realize that many of the fundamentals, which they may or may not have been taught in school, remain the same regardless of the technology. This realization often comes when developers reach their late twenties or early thirties, typically the time when people start to settle down, get married, and buy a house. This is fortuitous because these new demands mean that developers can no longer afford to invest vast amounts of time learning new technologies; instead, they want to spend that time with their families. Suddenly higher-level roles such as project lead, project manager, and (non-agile) modeler become attractive to them because these roles don't require the constant and intensive effort needed to learn new technologies. So, by the time that developers begin to truly learn their craft they're in the process of transitioning out of their roles as developers. Luckily, new "young punks" come along and the cycle repeats itself. The end result is that the majority of people actively developing software are typically not the ones best qualified to do it, and they don't even know it.

Things aren't much better on the business side of things. Our customers don't understand how software is developed, which is actually quite reasonable when you stop and think about it. My experience is that few software developers could tell you how software is developed from end-to-end as well as show a reasonable understanding of the implications of various options along the way simply because software development is spectacularly difficult. Furthermore, our customers generally aren't really interested in participating in complex processes that they don't understand well, and in these situations, they'd rather leave the details to us so that they can get back to doing their jobs. They accept that their involvement is limited to being involved in a requirements workshop or two at the beginning of the project, reviewing key documents throughout the project, receiving glowing (albeit sometimes falsified) status reports throughout, getting involved with acceptance testing just before delivery, and finally receiving the system, often late and over budget. This is the way that it's always been, this is the way the IT professionals tell them it has to be, and they often don't think to question what's happening. What's strange is that they tolerate this situation. What they're asking for is software that meets their needs in an effective manner, but what the developers are giving them is a bunch of documents to review, some status reports, some tests, and then finally some software if things go well. In other words, current practice is to deliver what we want to deliver, not to deliver what customers are asking of us. As you'll see in this book, it is possible (and required) for our project stakeholders to be actively involved; we just have to ensure that the development process is acceptable to them.

Whew! I'm glad that I've gotten all that negativity out of me. Now let's take a positive approach and investigate what we can do to address these problems.

Enter Agile Software Development

To address the challenges faced by software developers, an initial group of 17 method-ologists formed the Agile Software Development Alliance (www.agilealliance.org), often referred to simply as the Agile Alliance, in February 2001. An interesting thing about this group is that they all came from different backgrounds, yet were able to agree on issues that methodologists typically don't agree upon (Fowler 2001a). This group of people defined a manifesto for encouraging better ways of developing soft-ware, and then, based on that manifesto, formulated a collection of principles that defines the criteria for agile software development processes such as Agile Modeling.

The Manifesto for Agile Software Development

The manifesto (Agile Alliance 2001a) is defined by four simple value statements—the important thing to understand is that while you should value the concepts on the right side, you should value the things on the left side (presented in bold) even more. A good way to think about the manifesto is that it defines preferences, not alternatives, encouraging a focus on certain areas but not eliminating others. The Agile Alliance values are:

Individuals and interactions over processes and tools. Teams of people build software systems, and to do that they need to work together effectively with programmers, testers, project managers, modelers, and customers. Who do you think would develop a better system: five software developers with their own tools working together in a single room or five low-skilled "hamburger flippers" with a well-defined process, the most sophisticated tools available, and the best offices money could buy? If the project was reasonably complex, my money would be on the software developers, wouldn't yours? The point is that the most important factors to consider are the people and how they work together, because if you don't get that right, the best tools and processes won't be of any use. Tools and processes are important, don't get me wrong, it's just that they're not as important as working together effectively. Remember the old adage, a fool with a tool is still a fool. This can be difficult for management to accept because they often want to believe that people and time, or men and months, are interchangeable (Brooks 1995).

Working software over comprehensive documentation. When you ask a user whether they want a 50-page document describing what you intend to build or the actual software itself, what do you think they'll pick? My guess is that 99 times out of 100 they'll choose working software. If that is the case, doesn't it make more sense to work in such a manner that you produce software quickly and often, giving your users what they prefer? Furthermore, I suspect that users will understand any software that you produce much more easily than they will understand complex technical diagrams describing its internal workings or describing an abstraction of its usage, don't you? Documentation has its place; written properly, it is a valuable guide for people's understanding of how and why a system is built and how to work with the system. However, never forget that the primary goal of software development is to create software, not documents—otherwise we would call it documentation development, wouldn't we?

Customer collaboration over contract negotiation. Only your customers can tell you what they want. Yes, they likely do not have the skills to exactly specify the system. Yes, they likely won't get it right the first time. Yes, they'll likely change their minds. Working together with your customers is hard, but that's the reality of the job. Having a contract with your customers is important, and having an understanding of everyone's rights and responsibilities may form the foundation of that contract, but a contract isn't a substitute for communication. Successful developers work closely with their customers; they invest the effort to discover what their customers need, and they educate their customers along the way.

Responding to change over following a plan. People change their priorities for a variety of reasons. As work progresses on your system, your project stakeholder's understanding of the problem domain and of what you are building changes. The business environment changes. Technology changes over time, although not always for the better. Change is a reality of software development, a reality that your software process must reflect. There is nothing wrong with having a project plan. In fact, I would be worried about any project that didn't have one. However, a project plan must be malleable, there must be room to change it as your situation changes; otherwise, your plan quickly becomes irrelevant.

The interesting thing about these value statements is they are something that almost everyone will instantly agree to, yet will rarely adhere to in practice. Senior management will always claim that its employees are the most important aspect of your organization, yet insist they follow ISO-9000 compliant processes and treat them as replaceable assets. Even worse, management often refuses to provide sufficient resources to comply with the processes that they insist project teams follow. Everyone will readily agree that the creation of software is the fundamental goal of software development, yet insist on spending months producing documentation describing what the software is and how it is going to be built, instead of simply rolling up their sleeves and building it. You get the idea—people say one thing and do another. This has to stop now. Agile modelers do what they say and say what they do.

The Principles for Agile Software Development

To help people gain a better understanding of what agile software development is all about, the members of the Agile Alliance refined the philosophies captured in their manifesto into a collection of twelve principles (Agile Alliance 2001b) that Agile software development methodologies, such as Agile Modeling (AM), should conform to. These principles are:

1. Our highest priority is to satisfy the customer through early and continuous delivery of valuable software.

2. Welcome changing requirements, even late in development. Agile processes harness change for the customer's competitive advantage.

3. Deliver working software frequently, from a couple of weeks to a couple of months, with a preference to the shorter time scale.

4. Business people and developers must work together daily throughout the project.

5. Build projects around motivated individuals. Give them the environment and support they need, and trust them to get the job done.

6. The most efficient and effective method of conveying information to and within a development team is face-to-face conversation.

7. Working software is the primary measure of progress.

8. Agile processes promote sustainable development. The sponsors, developers, and users should be able to maintain a constant pace indefinitely.

9. Continuous attention to technical excellence and good design enhances agility.

10. Simplicity—the art of maximizing the amount of work not done—is essential.

11. The best architectures, requirements, and designs emerge from self-organizing teams.

12. At regular intervals, the team reflects on how to become more effective, and then tunes and adjusts its behavior accordingly.

Stop for a moment and think about these principles. Is this the way that your software projects actually work? Is this the way that you think projects should work? Read the principles again. Are they radical and impossible goals as some people would claim, are they meaningless motherhood and apple pie statements, or are they simply common sense? My belief is that these principles form a foundation of common sense upon which you can base successful software development efforts. Furthermore, I believe that they define high-level requirements for an effective software methodology, requirements used to formulate the values (Chapter 2, "Agile Modeling Values"), principles (Chapters 3, "Core Principles," and 4, "Supplementary Principles"), and practices (Chapters 5, "Core Practices," and 6, "Supplementary Practices") of Agile Modeling.

Agile Modeling

Agile Modeling (AM) is a chaordic, practice-based methodology for effective modeling and documentation of software-based systems. The AM methodology is a collection of practices, guided by principles and values, for software professionals to apply on a day-to-day basis. AM is not a prescriptive process. In other words, it does not define detailed procedures for how to create a given type of model, instead it provides advice for how to be effective as a modeler. AM is chaordic (Hock 1999), in that it blends the "chaos" of simple modeling practices and blends it with the order inherent in software modeling artifacts. AM is not about less modeling; in fact, many developers will find that they are doing more modeling following AM than they did in the past. AM is "touchy-feely," it's not hard and fast—think of AM as an art, not a science.

Why do we want to be effective at modeling? Because modeling is an important part of any software process. Agile software processes such as Extreme Programming (XP) (Beck 2000), SCRUM (Beedle and Schwaber 2001), and Dynamic System Development Method (DSDM) (Stapleton 1997) include modeling activities. Yes, even XP includes modeling techniques such as user stories, Class Responsibility Collaborator (CRC) models, and sketches. Contrary to what XP's detractors will tell you, XP does not abandon modeling. Instead, it minimizes modeling efforts by taking a test-first approach to design in which you develop your tests before you develop your code. This forces you to think through how you will build your software before you actually build it, exactly as traditional design modeling does. XP fulfills some of the goals of modeling, understanding what it is you're building, in different ways and therefore requires less modeling. There is absolutely nothing wrong with that. Prescriptive software processes also include modeling activities. In the case of the Unified Process (UP), three of the six core process disciplines (formerly called workflows) focus on modeling, and my own OOSP has a project stage simply called "Model."

There are two primary reasons why you model: to understand what it is you are building or to aid your communication efforts within your team or with your project stakeholders. You may choose to model the requirements of your system, perhaps with a use case diagram (common modeling artifacts are described in Appendix A of this book) or a collection of business rule definitions. Similarly, you may choose to develop models to analyze those requirements, or to formulate a high-level architecture or a detailed design for your system. In each of these cases your goal is to gain a better understanding of one or more aspects of your system. In other words, you use models to help you to explore what it is you are working on. Furthermore, you may use models to communicate within your team or with individuals or groups external to your team. A data model helps to communicate the structure of your database to people writing Java source code that interacts with that database. A user interface flow diagram communicates the overall structure of your system's user interface to the people working on individual screens, web pages, or reports. An activity diagram communicates the business processes that your system proposes to support to the project stakeholders providing funding to your project team. In short, modeling is critical to your project team's success. But how do you model in an effective and agile manner? That is the fundamental question that AM addresses.

AM has three goals:

1. To define and show how to put into practice a collection of values, principles, and practices pertaining to effective, light-weight modeling. What makes AM a catalyst for improvement aren't the modeling techniques themselves—such as use case models, class models, data models, or user interface models—but how to apply them.

2. To address the issue of how to apply modeling techniques on software projects taking an agile approach. Sometimes it is significantly more productive for a developer to draw some bubbles and lines to think through an idea, or to

compare several different approaches to solving a problem, than it is to simply start writing code. There is a danger in being too code-centric—sometimes a quick sketch can avoid significant churn when you are coding.

3. To address how you can improve your modeling activities following a "near-agile" approach to software development, and in particular, project teams that have adopted an instantiation of the Unified Process such as the Rational Unified Process (RUP) (Kruchten 2000) or the Enterprise Unified Process (EUP) (Ambler 2001b). Both of these processes are flexible enough to be tailored so that on the one extreme they are very prescriptive or on the other extreme agile enough so that AM will work with them. Although you must be following an agile software process to truly be agile modeling—more on this in a moment—you may still adopt and benefit from many of AM's practices on non-agile projects. This is similar to non-XP teams benefiting from adoption of some of its practices such as pair programming or refactoring—they aren't truly doing XP but have still improved their productivity by adopting a portion of it.

An important concept to understand about AM is that it is not a complete software process. AM's focus is on effective modeling and documentation. That's it. It doesn't include programming activities, although it will tell you to prove your models with code. It doesn't include testing activities, although it will tell you to consider testability as you model. It doesn't cover project management, system deployment, system operations, system support, or a myriad of other issues. Because AM's focus is on a portion of the overall software process, you need to use it with another, full-fledged process such as XP, DSDM, SCRUM, or UP as indicated above. Figure 1.1 depicts this concept. You start with a base process, such as XP or UP or perhaps even your own existing process, and then tailor it with AM (hopefully adopting all of AM) as well as other techniques as appropriate to form your own process that reflects your unique needs. Alternatively, you may decide to pick the best features from a collection of existing software processes to form your own process. To simplify the discussion throughout this book, I will assume that you have taken the first approach and started with a base process.

Although AM is independent of other processes, such as XP and the UP, it is used to enhance those processes. In Part Three of this book I will show how to tailor AM into XP, and in Part Four I will discuss how to tailor it into the UP.

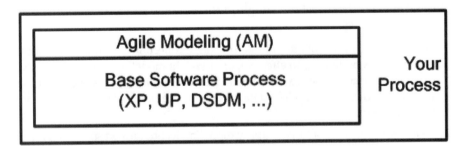

Figure 1.1   AM enhances other software processes.

Who Are Agile Modelers?

An agile modeler is anyone who follows the AM methodology, applying AM's practices in accordance with its principles and values. An agile developer is someone who follows an agile approach to software development. An agile modeler is an agile developer. Not all agile developers are agile modelers.

Now I'm going to confuse you a bit, something for which I am sorry. Throughout this book I will use the term "agile modeler" whenever I want to indicate an activity pertinent to someone taking an agile modeling approach. I'll use the more generic term "agile developer" to discuss an activity that is not only pertinent to AM but to agile software development in general. In other words, when I say that an agile developer does something, you should assume that it is something that agile modelers do, too.

A Brief Overview of Agile Modeling

In Chapter 2 you will see that AM adopts the values XP (Beck 2000), which are *communication, simplicity, feedback,* and *courage* and adds a fifth value, *humility.* It is critical to have effective communication within your development team as well as with and between all project stakeholders. You should strive to develop the simplest solution possible that meets all of your needs and to obtain feedback regarding your efforts often and early. Furthermore, you should have the courage to make and stick to your decisions, and to have the humility to admit that you may not know everything, that others have value to add to your project efforts.

AM is based on a collection of principles (Chapters 3 and 4), derived from the principles of the Agile Alliance, such as the importance of *assuming simplicity* when you are modeling and *embracing change* as you are working, because requirements do in fact change over time. You should recognize that *incremental change* of your system over time enables agility and that you should strive to obtain *rapid feedback* on your work to ensure that it accurately reflects the needs of your project stakeholders. Agile modelers realize that *software is your primary goal,* although they balance this with the recognition that *enabling the next effort is your secondary goal.* You should *model with a purpose.* If you don't know why you're working on something, then you shouldn't be doing so. You also need to recognize that you need *multiple models* in your development toolkit to be effective. A critical concept is that models are not necessarily documents, a realization that enables you to *travel light* by discarding most of your models once they have fulfilled their purpose. Agile modelers believe that *content is more important than representation,* that there are many ways you can model the same concept yet still get it right. To be an effective modeler you need to *know your models.* To be an effective teammate you should realize that *everyone can learn from everyone else,* that you should *work with people's instincts,* and that *open and honest communication* is often the best policy to follow to ensure effective teamwork. Finally, a focus on *quality work* is important because nobody likes to produce sloppy work, and *local adaptation* of AM to meet the exact needs of your environment is important.

To model in an agile manner you will apply AM's practices (Chapters 5 and 6) as appropriate. Fundamental practices include *creating several models in parallel, applying the right artifact(s)* for the situation, and *iterating to another artifact* to continue moving forward at a steady pace. *Modeling in small increments* and not attempting to create a magical "all encompassing model" is also fundamental to your success as an agile modeler. Because models are only abstract representations of software, abstractions may not be accurate. You should strive to *prove it with code* to show that your ideas actually work in practice and not just in theory. *Active stakeholder participation* is critical to the success of your modeling efforts because your project stakeholders know what they want and can provide you with the feedback that you require. There are two fundamental reasons why you create models, either you *model to understand* an issue (such as how to design part of your system) or you *model to communicate* what your team is doing (or has done). The principle of *assume simplicity* is supported by the practices of *creating simple content* by focusing on only the aspects that you need to model and not attempting to create a highly detailed modeling, *depicting models simply* via use of simple notations, and *using the simplest tools* to create your models. You travel light by *discarding temporary models* and *updating models only when it hurts*. You enable communication by turning models into information radiators (Cockburn 2002), by *displaying models publicly*, either on a wall or on an internal web site, through *collective ownership* of your project artifacts, through *applying modeling standards*, and by *modeling with others*. You greatly enhance your development efforts when you *consider testability*, *apply patterns gently*, and *reuse existing artifacts*. Because you often need to integrate with other systems, including legacy databases and web-based services, you will find that you need to *formalize contract models* with the owners of those systems.

At its core, AM is simply a collection of techniques that reflect the principles and values shared by many experienced software developers. If there is such a thing as agile modeling, then are there also agile models? Yes.

What Are Agile Models?

To understand AM you need to understand the difference between a model and an agile model. A model is an abstraction that describes one or more aspects of a problem or a potential solution addressing a problem. Traditionally, models are thought of as zero or more diagrams plus any corresponding documentation. However, non-visual artifacts such as collections of CRC cards, a textual description of one or more business rules, or the structured English description of a business process are also considered models. An agile model is a model that is just barely good enough. But how do you know when a model is good enough? Agile models are good enough when they exhibit the following traits:

Agile models fulfill their purpose. Sometimes you model to communicate; perhaps you need to communicate the scope of your effort to senior management; and sometimes you model to understand; perhaps you need to determine a design strategy to implement a collection of Java classes. For an agile model to suffice, it clearly must fulfill the purpose for which it is created.

Agile models are understandable. Agile models are understandable by their intended audience. A requirements model will be written in the language of the business that your users comprehend, whereas a technical architecture model will likely use technical terms that developers are familiar with. The modeling notation that you use affects understandability—UML use case diagrams are of no value to your users if they don't understand what the notation represents. In this case you would either use another approach or educate them in the modeling technique. Style issues, such as avoiding crossing lines, will also affect understandability—messy diagrams are harder to read than clean ones. The level of detail in your models, see below, can also affect understandability, because a highly detailed model is harder to comprehend than a less detailed one. Simplicity (see later in this chapter) is similarly a factor that affects understandability.

Agile models are sufficiently accurate. Models often do not need to be 100 percent accurate; they just need to be accurate enough. For example: If a street map is missing a street, or it shows that a street is open but you discover it's closed for repairs, do you throw away your map and start driving mayhem through the city? Likely not. You might decide to update your map. You could pull out a pen and do it yourself or go to the local store and purchase the latest version (which still might be out of date). Or you could simply accept that the map isn't perfect but still use it because it is good enough for your purposes—you can use it to get around because it does accurately model most of the other streets in your town. The reason you don't discard your street map the minute you find an inaccuracy is that you don't expect the map to be perfect, nor do you need it to be. Similarly, when you find a problem in your requirements model, or in your data model, you can choose to either update the model at that point or accept it as it is—good enough but not perfect. Some project teams can tolerate inaccuracies, whereas others can't. The nature of the project, the nature of the individual team members, and the nature of the organization will decide this. Sufficient accuracy depends on both the audience of the model and the issues that it's trying to address.

I was working on a project using Enterprise JavaBeans (EJB) (Roman et. al. 2002) technology and needed to explain how EJB's invocation of entity beans worked. In the process of doing this I drew a sketch explaining how EJB's concepts of home and remote interfaces worked and a couple of sketches walking people through the lifecycle of an entity. As I did this I forgot the exact details of bean activation and passivation, I even mislabeled the name of one of the operations, but I still got the general idea across to the audience. The audience was composed of people, not computers; therefore, they didn't require a perfect specification, they just needed a description that was good enough to provide a basic explanation from which they could fill in the blanks and correct any mistakes.

Agile models are sufficiently consistent. An agile model does not need to be perfectly consistent with itself or with other artifacts to be useful. If a use case clearly invokes another in one of its steps, then the corresponding use case diagram should indicate that with an association between the two use cases that is tagged with the UML stereotype of <<include>>. However, you look at the diagram and it doesn't! Oh no, the use case and the diagram are inconsistent! Danger, Will Robinson, Danger! Red alert! Run for your lives! Wait a minute; your use case model is clearly inconsistent, yet the world hasn't come to an end.

Yes, in an ideal world all of your artifacts would be perfectly consistent, but no, it often doesn't work out that way. When you're building a simple business application, you can tolerate some inconsistencies. For example: On a use case model you could have an actor called "Customer," yet in your class model a class called "Client." Is it customer, client, or both? If it's important, you can look into it and address the problem appropriately, but if isn't important, you can simply move on and live with the inconsistency. Granted, sometimes you can't tolerate inconsistencies—witness NASA's recent learning experience regarding the metric and imperial measuring systems when they accidentally slammed a space probe into Mars in 1999. The point is that an agile model is consistent enough and no more; you very often do not need a perfect model for it to be useful.

Regarding accuracy and consistency, clearly there is an entropy issue to consider here as well. If you have an artifact that you wish to maintain, what I call a "keeper," then you will need to invest the resources to update it as time goes on. Otherwise it will quickly become out of date and effectively useless to you. For example: I can tolerate a map that is missing one or two streets, but I can't tolerate one that is missing three quarters of the streets in my town. A data model that is missing a few recently added columns still provides very good insight into your database schema, and a deployment diagram that still indicates you're using an old version of an EJB application server is likely good enough for now. There is a fine line between investing too much and not enough effort to keep your artifacts sufficiently accurate to be effective.

Agile models are sufficiently detailed. A road map doesn't indicate each individual house on each street. That would be too much detail and thus would make the map difficult to work with. However, when a street is being built, I would imagine the builder has a detailed map of the street that shows each building, the sewers, electrical boxes, and so on in enough detail to make the map useful to him. This map doesn't depict the individual patio stones that make up the walkway to each building; once again, that would be too much detail. Sufficient detail depends on the audience and the purpose for which they are using a model—drivers need maps that show streets, builders need maps that show civil engineering details.

Consider an architecture model. Depending on the nature of your environment, a couple of diagrams drawn on a whiteboard and updated as the project goes along may be sufficient. Or perhaps several diagrams drawn using a CASE tool is what you need. Or perhaps the same diagrams supported with detailed documentation are what is required. Different projects have different needs. In each of these three examples you are in fact developing and maintaining a sufficiently detailed architecture model. It's just that "sufficiently detailed" depends on the situation.

Agile models provide positive value. A fundamental aspect of any project artifact is that it should add positive value. Does the benefit that an architecture model brings to your project outweigh the costs of developing and (optionally) maintaining it? An architecture model helps to solidify the vision to which your project team is working, which clearly has value. But, if the costs of that model outweigh the benefits, then it no longer provides positive value. Perhaps it was unwise to invest $100,000 developing a detailed and heavily documented architecture model when a $5,000 investment resulting in whiteboard diagrams that you took digital snapshots of would have done the job.

Agile models are as simple as possible. You should strive to keep your models as simple as possible while still getting the job done. Simplicity is clearly affected by the level of detail in your models, but it also can be affected by the extent of the notation that you apply. For example: Unified Modeling Language (UML) class diagrams can include a myriad of symbols, including Object Constraint Language (OCL), yet most diagrams can get by with just a portion of the notation. You often don't need to apply all the symbols available to you, so limit yourself to a subset of the notation that still allows you to get the job done.

Therefore, the definition for an agile model is that it is a model that fulfills its purpose and no more; is understandable to its intended audience; is simple, sufficiently accurate, consistent, and detailed; and investment in its creation and maintenance provides positive value to your project.

A common philosophical question is whether source code is a model, and more important, whether it is an agile model. If you were to ask me outside the scope of this book, my answer would be yes, source code is a model, albeit a highly detailed one, because it clearly is an abstraction of your software. I would also claim that well written code is an agile model. Nevertheless, in this book I will distinguish between source code and agile models for the simple reason that I need to treat the two differently—agile models help to get you to source code.

What Is(n't) Agile Modeling?

I am a firm believer that when you are describing the scope of something, be it a system or in the case of AM a methodology, you should describe both what it is and what it isn't. The following points describe the scope of AM:

AM is an attitude, not a prescriptive process. AM comprises a collection of values that agile modelers adhere to, principles that agile modelers believe in, and practices that agile modelers apply. AM describes a style of modeling, when used properly in agile environments, that results in better quality software and faster development while avoiding over-simplification and unrealistic expectations. AM is not a cookbook approach to development—if you're looking for detailed instructions for creating UML sequence diagrams or drawing user interface flow diagrams, then you need to pick up one of the many books listed in the references section at the back of the book.

AM is a supplement to existing methods; it is not a complete methodology. The primary focus of AM is on modeling, and its secondary focus is on documentation. That's it. AM techniques should be used to enhance modeling efforts of project teams following agile methodologies such as XP, SCRUM, and Crystal Clear (Cockburn 2001b). AM can also be used with prescriptive processes such as the Unified Process, although its success will be determined by the agility of the process.

AM is complementary to other modeling processes. Modeling methodologies such as ICONIX (Rosenberg and Scott 1999) and Catalysis (D'Souza and Wills 1999) focus on the details of how to create certain types of artifacts, explaining in detail how to go about applying artifacts such as use cases, robustness diagrams, or component models. What they don't focus on are the high-level practices for effective modeling that AM does. My experience is that AM and other modeling methodologies work very well together, and I have no doubt that we will one day see books such as "Agile Modeling with ICONIX" and "Agile Modeling with Catalysis" on the market.

AM is a way to work together effectively to meet the needs of project stakeholders. Agile developers work as a team with their project stakeholders, who in turn take a direct and active role in the development of the system. To paraphrase a well-known saying about teamwork, there is no "I" in "agile."

AM is effective and is about being effective. As you read more about AM, one of the things that should become poignant to you is AM's ruthless focus on being effective. AM tells you to maximize the investment of your project stakeholders, to create a model or document when you have a clear purpose and understand the needs of its audience, to apply the right artifacts to address the situation at hand, and to create simple models whenever you can. Do no more than the absolute minimum to suffice.

AM is something that works in practice; it isn't an academic theory. The goal of AM is to describe techniques for modeling systems in an effective manner, one that is both efficient and sufficient for the task. My co-workers and I at Ronin International, Inc. (www.ronin-intl.com) have applied many of AM's techniques for several years, techniques that we have honed at a wide range of clients in various industries. Furthermore, since February 2001 several hundred modeling practitioners on the Agile Modeling mailing list (www.agilemodeling.com/feedback.htm) have examined and discussed these techniques and found them to be effective.

AM is not a silver bullet. Agile modeling is an effective technique for improving the software development efforts of many professionals. That's it, nothing more. It isn't magic snake oil that will solve all of your development problems. If you work hard, if you stay focused, if you take AM's values, principles, and practices to heart, then you will likely improve your effectiveness as a developer.

AM is for the average developer, but is not a replacement for competent people. AM's values, principles, and practices are straightforward, many of which you have likely been following or wish you had been following for years. You don't have to walk on water to be able to apply AM's techniques, but you do need to have basic software development skills. The hardest thing about AM is that it prods you to learn a wide range of modeling techniques, a long and continuing activity. Learning to model can seem difficult at first, and it is, but you can do it if you choose to learn a technique at a time.

AM is not an attack on documentation. Agile modelers create documentation that maximizes their investment in its creation and maintenance. Agile documentation is as simple as possible, as minimal as possible, has a distinct purpose that is directly related to the system being developed, and has a defined audience whose needs are understood. Agile documentation is described in detail in Chapter 14, "Agile Documentation."

AM is not an attack on CASE tools. Agile modelers use tools that provide positive value by helping to make them more effective as developers. Furthermore, they always strive to use the simplest tool that gets the job done.

The SWA Online Case Study

Throughout this book I will present models for a common case study called SWA Online. This section provides a brief management vision for the system, the type of high-level vision statement that you might receive at the start of a project.

SWA Enterprises is a distributor of high-margin goods throughout the United States, supplying specialty retail stores with unique goods that are difficult to find elsewhere. SWA Enterprises prides itself on identifying an eclectic and ever changing mix of products. Although the company has been successful to date, it wants to expand its presence to the Internet. The following is the initial vision that senior management has for the new system, called SWA Online, which it wants developed.

SWA Online will offer the entire range of physical products sold by SWA Enterprises for now, and we may want to sell virtual products such as online music and videos at some point in the future. Our target market will remain the United States for now. At one point we considered all of North America, but we consider that too aggressive for our first release—far better to focus on our existing market and get it right before venturing into new territory. Eventually, selling products internationally is our true goal.

We'll use our current distributor, Fly-By-Night Shipping, but we're concerned that they may not be able to handle our business in the future. They have proven very effective shipping to retail stores within the United States; overnight shipping is no problem as are lower cost options such as multi-day ground shipping. We're not sure how effective they are shipping internationally, and we eventually want to not rely on a single vendor for key services such as shipping.

We believe that our system, a commercial off-the-shelf (COTS) package that we purchased several years ago, which calculates taxes and handles inventory-related functionality, should be sufficient for the first release of SWA Online, although that is something that the development must confirm.

SWA Enterprises currently employs 87 people. Major focuses of the organization include sales to retail stores, buyers focused on identifying new products to carry within our catalog, and shipping and returns. We have just hired a Vice President of Online Sales, Sally Jones, who will be responsible for building the organization required to support and operate SWA Online. Sally will be actively involved with your project team and will help you to obtain access to other business staff within SWA

Enterprises as you need them. The primary responsibility of these people is naturally their full-time, day-to-day jobs, but we have instructed them to find a way to participate with your development team as much as required.

The software process that SWA Enterprises has adopted is a stripped-down version of the EUP that has several of the practices of XP tailored into it and also includes the full collection of the practices of AM.

A Brief Overview of this Book

This book is organized into five parts:

Part 1: Introduction to Agile Modeling. The foundation for the book is set in this part through a detailed discussion of the values, principles, and practices of AM.

Part 2: Agile Modeling in Practice. This part explores critical issues such as effective communication and documentation practices, using simple tools to model, and the organizational and cultural aspects that support AM. Advice for organizing modeling work areas, modeling teams, and modeling sessions is provided and an examination of the UML is presented in light of agile development.

Part 3: Agile Modeling and eXtreme Programing (XP). This part presents a detailed discussion of how to enhance XP with the principles and practices of AM. It begins by setting the record straight regarding modeling and documentation within XP. It then focuses on modeling portions of the SWA Online case study with an XP/AM approach.

Part 4: Agile Modeling and the Unified Process (UP). This part presents a detailed examination of how to simplify modeling within the UP by following the principles and practices of AM. Once again, modeling portions of the SWA Online case study are provided.

Part 5: Conclusion. This part describes important organizational and management issues that pertain to Agile Modeling.

Agile Modeling Values

Modeling is similar to planning—most of the value is in the act of modeling, not the model itself.

When I first read *Extreme Programming Explained* (Beck 2000), one of the most poignant things about XP for me was how Kent first defined a foundation for his methodology. He did this by describing four values: communication, simplicity, feedback, and courage. This fascinated me because he had found a way to describe some of the fundamental factors that lead to success at the software development game, and he managed to do it in such a way as to personalize it for individual developers. Bravo! Therefore, when I began putting Agile Modeling (AM) together, I decided to take an approach similar to that which Kent took with XP. I would start with a set of high-level values, define a collection of concrete principles (Chapter 3, "Core Principles") based on those values, and then formulate practices (Chapter 4, "Supplementary Principles") from those values and principles that agile modelers should apply on the job.

Because I fully agree with XP's values, I have adopted all four of them—why reinvent the value wheel when you can reuse it? However, I felt that there was something missing, something that I just couldn't put my finger on. Then one day I was working at a client site and found myself in a discussion with another developer about requirements. Our users had described how they performed their jobs, and this developer disagreed with what they outlined. He insisted that they couldn't work that way even though our users had explained to him several times that yes, indeed, they could and did. He had another way to do things, which he claimed was better, and technically it probably was, but the users simply weren't interested and wanted to do things their way (users can be strange like that). Fair enough I thought, but not for this developer. He was right, the users were wrong, even though they were arguing about user requirements. Yikes. I eventually had to insist that we go with what the users told us, and then later spent some time mentoring him in the concept that project stakeholders, *not* developers, are the source of requirements. Although this had been a growing pain for our team, it revealed to me a value that agile modelers need: humility. Therefore, the values of AM are:

- Communication
- Simplicity
- Feedback
- Courage
- Humility

Communication

What is communication? *Merriam Webster's Collegiate Dictionary 10th Edition* defines communication as "a process by which information is exchanged between individuals through a common system of symbols, signs, or behavior." Communication is a two-way street: You both provide and gain information as the result of communication. My experience is that effective communication—between everyone involved on your project, including both developers and project stakeholders—is a requisite for software development success. Problems occur when communication breaks down on a software project. For example, a developer doesn't tell her co-workers that her code doesn't work properly, resulting in extra work on the part of another developer to track down the problem. A user doesn't explain the relative importance of their requirements, and the developers focus on low-impact features while ignoring several that are critical to your organization. Your project manager downplays the importance of having new workstations for your development team and as a result doesn't get funding for needed upgrades. Developers show project stakeholders a user interface prototype that simulates the working system, but the stakeholders mistakenly believe they are seeing the real system and insist that you deliver six months earlier than initially agreed upon. Many problems experienced by software development teams can trace their causes back to miscommunication.

When you stop and think about it, one of the primary reasons you model is to help improve communication. When your users describe a complex business process, you can help to improve your understanding of the process by sketching a data flow diagram that depicts its logic. You can often learn more in five minutes drawing a diagram with your users than you can in five hours discussing it or reading about it in corporate manuals. When you try to explore the design of a portion of your system with another developer, you may choose to model portions of it together, perhaps drawing a UML class diagram to understand the structure of your classes. Together you will work through the design, talking about the implications of various approaches and negotiating how you intend to build it. Modeling helps you to communicate your ideas, to understand the ideas of others, to mutually explore those ideas to eventually reach a common understanding. In Chapter 8, "Communication," I explore the importance of communication within the software development process and how it is enhanced by AM's practices.

Simplicity

I believe you would be hard pressed to find a software engineering book that didn't mention the KISS rule (Keep It Simple Stupid!) at least once. The IT industry has preached simplicity for years, but for some reason the choir hasn't been listening. These same software engineering books then advise you to take actions that invariably complicate your software, making it harder to develop, test, and maintain. Common complications include:

Applying complex patterns too soon. If you need to implement telephone numbers for your customers, applying the Contact Point analysis pattern (Ambler 2001a) is very likely overkill. Yes, implementing this pattern is interesting, but its class hierarchy is much harder to build, test, and maintain than a simple telephone number class. You're better off waiting until you also need to implement email addresses and surface addresses to justify application of the Contact Point pattern. Don't get me wrong, I'm a firm believer in patterns, and I am often the first to admit that sometimes applying a pattern is in fact the simplest approach available to you. The point is that this isn't always the case.

Over-architecting your system to support potential future requirements. Maybe the bank information system you are currently working on may one day need to support the selling of insurance policies, so wouldn't it be better to architect a generic way to deal with financial instruments? Yes, modeling that would be very interesting, but you would be making your software more complicated than it needs to be today. Developers who are insecure about their ability to handle future change, or whose egos motivate them to produce the "ultimate" system, will often architect their software. Agile developers do not overbuild their software. They bet that they can build it as simply as they possibly can today and then add new functionality, once again as simply as possible, when they actually need it. How does this work? Martin Fowler (2001b) describes it best with his discussion of the YAGNI (*You Ain't Gonna Need It*) principle. He points out that you can't always predict what you'll need in the future and you're just as likely to be wrong about it as you are to be right. Therefore, why develop, test, and maintain that extra functionality, functionality that you definitely do not need right now and may never need? Wouldn't it be better to focus on fulfilling the current needs of your project stakeholders today, thereby keeping them happy (always a good thing), and instead have the courage to assume that you can solve tomorrow's problems tomorrow? If you focus on building the simplest thing possible today, then when you go to add new functionality tomorrow, you know that you'll be working with a simple system. Wouldn't this system be as simple to modify tomorrow when you actually need the new functionality as it is to modify today when you don't know yet if you need it?

To develop a complex infrastructure. A common mistake that project teams make is to invest the first portion of their project developing their infrastructure—typically components, frameworks, and class libraries—that they intend to use as the building blocks for their system. The idea is that their initial investment will pay off sometime down the road. However, this approach has several serious drawbacks. First, you're investing your project stakeholders' resources without giving them something in return that they can actually use. Your stakeholders have likely asked you for specific features to help them do their jobs, and the first thing that you deliver is an error-handling subsystem. The result is that you're putting your project at risk by not delivering useful functionality quickly. Second, you're very likely ignoring the YAGNI principle and developing features in your infrastructure that you very likely won't need. A better approach is to simply develop your infrastructure as you need it throughout the project. For example: Build the error-handling subsystem over time when you discover that you actually need a subsystem to do so.

So what does all this have to do with agile modeling? The fundamental point is to keep your models as simple as possible, model today to meet today's needs, and worry about tomorrow's modeling needs tomorrow. In other words, don't over model—follow the KISS rule and not the KICK (Keep It Complex Kamikaze) rule.

TIP **Don't "What if" Yourself to Death**
I often see software developers divert themselves from their true task, to build software that meets the needs of their users in an effective manner, with wacky "what if scenarios." They start to over-model their software to meet all imaginable problems, problems that their project stakeholders very likely aren't concerned with or believe are so unlikely to happen that they are willing to go at risk on them. Then because they over-model, they also overbuild it. Yes, you don't want to be completely naïve in your efforts. It's reasonable to expect that some problems such as database problems or network glitches do occur, but you need to be realistic when you're modeling.

Models are critical for simplifying both software and the software process—it's much easier to explore an idea, and to improve upon it as your understanding increases, by drawing a diagram or two instead of writing tens or even hundreds of lines of code.

Feedback

The only way that you can determine whether your work is correct is to obtain feedback, and that includes feedback regarding your models. Models are abstractions. For example: A collection of use cases is an abstraction of how people will work with your system, whereas a component model is an abstraction of the internal structure of your software. How can you know if your abstractions are correct? There are many ways that you can obtain feedback regarding a model:

Develop the model as a team. Software development is a lot like swimming; it's dangerous to do it alone. When you work with other people, you quickly obtain feedback about your ideas.

Review the model with your target audience. Ideally, members of your target audience should be involved with the development of the model. Requirements models should be developed in conjunction with your users; detailed design models should be developed with the people who will be doing the programming. If this isn't possible, then the next best alternative is to sit down with them and walk them through your models, perhaps working through usage scenarios. Informal reviews can occur on an informal basis; perhaps you hold a quick meeting with someone to get their feedback regarding your work, whereas formal reviews (Gilb and Graham 1993) take more effort to organize.

Implement the model. The surest way to obtain feedback is to implement your model in software and have your project stakeholders work with the software. The proof is in the pudding.

Acceptance testing. Fundamentally your models should reflect your project stakeholders' requirements for your system. Your stakeholders validate those requirements during acceptance testing, so by implication you are also validating your models.

It is interesting to note the timescale for each feedback technique. When you work together as a team, feedback is relatively immediate, on the scale of seconds or minutes. With informal reviews, feedback can occur within minutes or hours, although if someone is available for an informal review then, why aren't they available to work on the model to begin with? On the other hand, formal reviews may not occur for days, weeks, or even months depending on the availability of the reviewers. With implementation, feedback ideally occurs within several hours or at least days (remember, you're taking an agile approach to development). Acceptance testing typically provides feedback weeks or months later.

Why is timescale important? Because the more immediate the feedback is, the less likely your models are to deviate from what you actually need. Although all forms of feedback have their place, given the opportunity you should prefer the feedback provided through teamwork because it is immediate. Having said that, there is something to be said about proving your models with code because everything looks good on paper until you actually try it out.

Courage

> **Courageous people walk through the door;**
> **they don't stand there and wonder what's on the other side.**
>
> **-Sempai Rick Micucci**

Agile Modeling, and agile software development in general, is new to most people as well as to the organizations in which they work. As you saw in Chapter 1, "Introduction,", agile software development principles challenge the status quo, and that's threatening for many people. It is a lot easier to sit back and accept the current situation, to not try to improve things, or to wait until someone else comes along and fixes things. This paralysis by fear is a primary contributor to the current sad state of the IT industry.

I once worked for an organization whose data administration group had a death grip on the software development group. Developers couldn't do work with corporate data without first going through the data group, they couldn't set up their own development database without going through the data group, and they certainly couldn't release software into production without the blessing of the data group. This wouldn't have been bad if the data group worked effectively, but unfortunately that wasn't the case. My team was working on an Enterprise JavaBeans (EJB) project, the first one for this company, using an Oracle database on the backend. When we heard that it would take several weeks to have someone from the data group set up our development database, we decided to do it on our own, initially spending a couple of hours doing so and then spending time over the next few days to tweak things as we needed. The reason the data group would have taken several weeks is they insisted on following their own procedures to size the database (work we had already done), ensure that our machines had sufficient disk storage (we had already maxxed out the box), and of course, fill out a myriad of forms that nobody but them wanted. They were incensed, and the manager of the group chewed out my manager, who then chewed us out. We held our ground, saying that we didn't have the time to cater to the bureaucratic whims of the data group. Nobody had successfully stood up to this group. People on my team were worried, but our priority was to build our system on time, so we fought it out. This took courage. To smooth things over, we said that we would be more than happy to work with them to administer our database and to evolve our data schema over time, which was completely true. This was where we ran into our second problem. Instead of providing us with a single database administrator (DBA), they instead wanted to put several people on our team: one to administer the database, one to work on a logical data model (which has absolutely no value when developing object-oriented software), and one to work on a physical data model (we wanted this). Furthermore, they wanted to do this in parallel with our development activities, instead of as an active part of the team. In other words, most of what they proposed was make-work. It would have been more of an effort for us to work with this separate group of people than it would have been to do the physical data modeling ourselves. We had several people more than qualified to do this, and to generate and apply the schema to the database (something several of us had done for years). Once again we fought it out with them, another courageous act considering nobody had ever done so in the past and they were already gunning for us. Everything eventually came to a head in a big meeting involving our managers and their managers. We actually had a good relationship with several of the DBAs within the data group who agreed with us privately and were hoping that we could break the deadlock within the organization. At the meeting, the head of the data group claimed that our concerns regarding our productivity slowing down were unrealistic, that his people could quickly get us moving forward in several weeks and continue helping us for the next few months. It was at that point that I said we had our database up and running and offered to show the working database to anyone in the room. We had the courage to do the right thing, to stand up to a clearly dysfunctional group, and to show everyone involved that there was a different way to do things. It was hard but in the long run, not only did our project benefit but the whole organization did, because it gave other teams the courage to stand up to the data group as well, eventually motivating them to streamline (albeit not enough in my opinion) their processes.

Agile methodologies ask you to closely work with other people, to trust them, and to trust yourself. This takes courage. Methods such as XP and AM ask you to do the simplest thing that you can, to trust that you can solve tomorrow's problems tomorrow. This takes courage. AM asks that you create documentation only when you absolutely need it, not just when it feels comfortable to do so. This takes courage. XP and AM ask that you let business people make business decisions, such as requirements' prioritization, and let technical people make technical decisions, such as how the software will fulfill individual requirements. This takes courage. AM asks that you use the simplest tools possible, such as whiteboards and paper, and that you use complex modeling tools only when they provide the best value possible. This takes courage. AM asks that you not dally making your diagrams pretty in order to put off difficult tasks such as proving your models with code. This takes courage. AM asks that you trust your co-workers, trust that programmers can make design decisions, and therefore you do not need to provide them with as much detail. This takes courage. AM asks you to choose to succeed, to end the cycle of near-disasters and outright failures within the IT industry. This takes courage.

I believe that courage is a fundamental requisite of agile software development. First, courage is important because you need to choose to take an agile approach, and then stick with that approach when the going gets tough (and it always does). There will be people in your organization with other visions—you need to adopt the XYZ tool, you need to adopt a heavy-weight process, management needs to exert greater control, you need to outsource all of IT, you need to follow the dictates of this other department— and they will fight your efforts every step of the way. That's what politics are all about. Second, during development you need courage to make important decisions, such as choosing one architectural approach over another or deciding which development language to work in. During development you also need courage to change direction when some of your decisions prove inadequate, by either discarding or refactoring your work.

Third, you need courage to recognize that you're fallible and will make mistakes.

Fourth, you need courage to trust that you can overcome tomorrow's problems tomorrow. Courage, it's not just for breakfast anymore.*

Humility

The best developers have the humility to recognize that they don't know everything. Frankly, it isn't possible. You could be the best Java coder there is and still not know every single detail about every single Java API. Furthermore, just because you're a great Java coder, it doesn't mean that you're a great user interface designer, or a great database designer, or a great musician—it just means that you're a great Java coder. Just because you're a great Java coder, it doesn't mean that you can't learn something new from other Java coders, including the junior person on your team. In fact, I often learn more from junior people than I do from senior people, because the junior will ask

---

*This is a modification of a North American advertising campaign from the mid-1990s–Eggs aren't just for breakfast anymore.

me why things work and will likely challenge my own beliefs with new ways of doing things.

Agile modelers understand that their fellow developers and their project stakeholders have their own areas of expertise and have value to add to a project. Some developers will be better at coding than you are, or better at testing, or better at requirements modeling, or better at architectural modeling. Your users likely understand various aspects of the business better than you do: Senior managers have a better grasp of where their industry is headed, and operations staff know what may or may not work in production. Agile modelers have the humility to admit that they need help to do their jobs successfully, to work together with others.

Humility also comes into play in the way that you interact with people. Agile modelers have the humility to respect the people that they work with, realizing that others likely have different priorities and experiences than they do and therefore will have different viewpoints. They don't denigrate their managers by calling them "pointy-haired bosses," people in other departments "paper pushers," or their users/customers "stupid" or "totally screwed up." Denigrating people isn't an act of humility; it's an act of arrogance. Arrogance leads to communication problems that in turn lead your project into trouble, because it motivates people to stop collaborating with you. Agile modelers are humble and more effective as a result.

Beyond Motherhood and Apple Pie

Agile modelers are courageous: They seek out simplicity, they seek feedback, they communicate well, and most of all, they're humble. It almost seems that if you become an agile modeler, you'll be nominated for sainthood. The reality is that agile modelers are people. They're fallible, they have other concerns in their lives beyond effective modeling practices, and they think and act of their own accord. The reason I defined these values is not to get overly sappy, I may not have achieved this goal, but instead, to build a foundation from which individuals may build an agile mindset, and teams and organizations may build a culture that supports agile and effective development efforts. These values are also used, along with the values and principles of the Agile Alliance (2001a, 2001b) presented in Chapter 1, as a base from which to define the principles of AM in Chapters 3 and 4.

CHAPTER 3

Core Principles

Principles only mean something when you stick to them when the going gets tough.

Agile Modeling's values (Chapter 2, "Agile Modeling Values")—communication, simplicity, feedback, courage, and humility—in combination with the values and principles of the Agile Alliance (2001a, 2001b), are used to define AM's principles. When applied on a software development project, these principles set the stage for a collection of modeling practices (Chapters 5, "Core Practices," and 6, "Supplementary Practices"). AM's values, while important, are somewhat abstract and too high-level to provide much guidance to your software development efforts; hence the need for AM's principles—concepts that are far more concrete. Some of the principles have been adopted from eXtreme Programming (XP) (Beck 2000), which in turn adopted them from common software engineering techniques. Reuse! For the most part, the principles are presented with a focus on their implications to modeling efforts and as a result, material adopted from XP may be presented in a new light.

This chapter overviews AM core principles; principles that you must adopt in full to be truly able to claim that you are agile modeling (more on this later). Chapter 4, "Supplementary Principles," overviews AM's supplementary principles that define important concepts that help to enhance your modeling efforts. AM's core principles are:

- Software is your primary goal
- Enabling the next effort is your secondary goal
- Travel light
- Assume simplicity

- Embrace change
- Incremental change
- Model with a purpose
- Multiple models
- Quality work
- Maximize stakeholder investment

Software Is Your Primary Goal

The primary goal of software development is to produce high-quality software that meets the needs of your project stakeholders in an effective manner. This principle is effectively a re-wording of the Agile Alliance's (2001b) principle that "working software is the primary measure of progress." Like it or not, the primary goal is not to produce extraneous documentation, extraneous management artifacts, or even to produce models. Creating extraneous documentation can be comforting because you can fool yourself into believing that you are making progress when in fact you're not. Instead, you're actually avoiding a difficult task, likely writing and testing code that may show that your chosen approach isn't working as well as you thought it would. Writing status reports, trumpeting your successes to everyone, or even worse, covering up your failures, may make you feel good, but it isn't getting you any closer to your end goal. Have the courage to focus on what is important, the creation of a system for your users. We're not documentation developers, or even model developers; we're software developers. Think about it. Any activity that does not directly contribute to the goal of producing quality should be questioned and avoided if it cannot be adequately justified.

Enabling the Next Effort Is Your Secondary Goal

Your project can still be considered a failure even when your team delivers a working system to your users—part of fulfilling the needs of your project stakeholders is to ensure that your system is robust enough so that it can be extended over time. As Alistair Cockburn (2001b) likes to say, when you are playing the software development game, your secondary goal is to set up to play the next game. Your next effort may be to develop the next major release of your system or it may simply be to operate and support the current version that you are building. To enable it, you will not only want to develop quality software but also create just enough documentation so that the people playing the next game can be effective, transfer skills from your developers to others, motivate existing staff to stay and develop the next release of your system, or simply motivate team members to stay with your organization. Factors that you need to consider include the nature of your developers, the nature of the next effort itself, and the importance of the next effort to your organization. In short, when you work on your system, you need to keep an eye on the future. This principle supports the AM value of Communication.

Travel Light

Traveling light means that you create just enough models and documentation to get by. Every artifact that you create, and then decide to keep, will need to be maintained over time. This includes models, documents, and project management artifacts such as schedules, test suites, and source code. For example: You decide to keep seven models. Whenever a change occurs—such as a new or updated requirement, your team takes a new approach, or adopts a new technology—you will need to consider the impact of that change on all seven models and then act accordingly. If you decide to keep only three models, then you clearly have less work to perform to support the same change, making you more agile because you are traveling lighter.

Similarly, the more complex/detailed your models are, the more likely it is that any given change will be harder to accomplish (the individual model is "heavier" and is therefore more of a burden to maintain). Every time you decide to keep a model, you trade off agility for the convenience of having that information available to your team in an abstract manner (hence potentially enhancing communication within your team as well as with project stakeholders). Never underestimate the seriousness of this trade-off. Jim Highsmith (2000) points out that someone trekking across the desert will benefit from a map, a hat, good boots, and a canteen of water. They likely won't make it if they burden themselves with hundreds of gallons of water, a pack full of every piece of survival gear imaginable, and a collection of books about the desert. However, it is possible to travel too light—clearly, it would be foolish to try to cross a desert without a minimum of supplies. Similarly, a development team that decides to develop and maintain a detailed requirements document, a detailed collection of analysis models, a detailed collection of architectural models, and a detailed collection of design models will quickly discover they are spending the majority of their time updating documents instead of writing source code. A good rule of thumb is to not maintain a model until it is very clear that you need it.

You need good communication among your team to be able to effectively travel lightly; if developers don't understand your requirements or your architectural approach, or at least if there is no one that they can work with to get their questions answered readily, then you are in serious trouble. Clearly, good communication is a requisite to support traveling light. To travel light requires courage, to trust that you're not going to need a certain artifact but are prepared to create it if you are proved wrong in your assumption. Traveling light enables simplicity in your approach to development because your artifact maintenance efforts during development are dramatically decreased.

Assume Simplicity

As you develop, you should assume that the simplest solution is the best solution, and as the title suggests, this principle is clearly derived from AM's value of *Simplicity* as well as the Agile Alliance's principle of simplicity (2001b). As Kent Beck (2000) points out, the vast majority of the time the simplest solution works well, and because it is simple, it is easy to implement. The advantage is that you aren't investing extra time implementing difficult solutions, approaches that take more time and effort to put in place. The advantage is that in the few times where the simplest solution proves not to work, you have time to implement a more difficult solution because you haven't wasted resources elsewhere. Furthermore, the simplest solution is also the easiest to maintain and to enhance.

An implication of this principle is that you don't want to overbuild your software, or in the case of modeling, don't depict additional features in your models that you don't need today. Don't over-model your system today; model based on today's existing requirements and then refactor your system in the future when your requirements evolve. The implication is that you should keep your models as simple as you possibly can. This principle is the Occam's Razor of modeling—when in doubt take the simplest approach possible.

Will taking the simplest approach work every time? Likely not, but it will work the vast majority of the time. When it doesn't work you will have learned something and will very likely have failed very early in your efforts. Contrast that to taking a complicated approach—complicated approaches fail as well—where you've invested significant resources to discover that your ideas didn't work.

Embrace Change

Accept the fact that change happens. Revel in it. Change is one of the things that make software development exciting. Requirements evolve over time. Your project stakeholders' understanding of their requirements changes over time. Project stakeholders can change as your project moves forward, new people are added, and existing ones leave. Project stakeholders can change their viewpoints as well, potentially changing the goals and success criteria for your effort. Furthermore, your business and technological environments change as your project evolves; things occur that are often beyond the scope of your control. The implication is that your project's environment changes over time.

Agile modelers embrace change. They understand that change is a common occurrence on software projects. The Agile Alliance (2001b) advises that you welcome changing requirements even late in the project lifecycle. Agile modelers know that their work will be affected by changes; they actively strive to communicate with their project stakeholders, to seek their feedback, so they can identify changes and then act accordingly. They do not blame their project stakeholders for change; instead they actively work with them to understand and communicate the implications of the changes to enable their stakeholders to make effective decisions as to if, how, and when the change will be supported by their development efforts. Furthermore, agile modelers understand that their models are only models, that developers will tear them apart and reassemble them into something better; they accept that their work will be improved upon by others.

Agile modelers also recognize an inherent danger in embracing change—the tendency to get sloppy when doing up-front work such as requirements modeling. Why invest a lot of time understanding requirements if they're only going to change? Far better to simply bang some code out and wait for your project stakeholders to tell you to change it? Right? *Wrong!* You'd be much better off investing the time to understand the requirements to the best of your ability now and implement software based on those requirements. Some requirements will change, and you need to embrace this fact, but many requirements won't change (at least not soon). Note that AM's principles of *Quality Work* and *Maximize Stakeholder Investment* counteract the tendency to get sloppy.

Incremental Change

To embrace change you need to take an incremental approach to your own development efforts, to change your system a small portion at a time instead of trying to get everything accomplished in one big release. You can make a big change as a series of small, incremental changes. In fact, the Agile Alliance's (2001b) third principle states that you should deliver working software frequently, from a couple of weeks to a couple of months, with a preference to the shorter time scale. An important concept to understand when agile modeling is that you don't need to get everything right the first time. In fact, it is very unlikely that you could do so even if you tried. Furthermore, you do not need to capture every single detail in your models; you just need to get it good enough at the time. It is futile to try to develop an all-encompassing model at the start of your project. Instead, put a stake in the ground and develop a small, detailed model, or perhaps a high-level model, and evolve it over time (or simply discard it when you no longer need it) in an incremental manner. It takes humility to accept that you can't get it right the first time, or even the nth time, and courage to admit it. Kent Beck (2000) said it well, "Make it run, make it right, then make it fast."

Model with a Purpose

If you cannot identify why and for whom you are creating a model, then why are you bothering to work on it at all? Many developers worry about whether their artifacts—such as models, source code, or documents—are detailed enough or if they are too detailed, or similarly if they are sufficiently accurate. What they're not doing is stepping back and asking why they're creating the artifact in the first place and whom are they creating it for. This requires humility; you aren't modeling solely for the personal satisfaction of modeling; instead you are modeling to fulfill the needs of your project stakeholders.

What are valid reasons to create a model? Often you need to understand an aspect of your software better, perhaps you need to communicate your approach to senior management to justify your project, or perhaps you need to create documentation that describes your system to the people who will be operating, maintaining or evolving it over time. You model to understand, or you model to communicate.

The following aren't valid reasons:

- Your prescriptive process tells you to, so you dutifully do so without considering whether it makes sense to.
- Someone else has requested the model but is unable to explain why they need it, other than because they told you to create it.
- Instead of having a face-to-face conversation with someone, and have the option to do so, you instead want to create a model to give to them.

Your first step when modeling is to identify a valid purpose for creating a model and the audience for that model. Once you identify the purpose and audience, develop the model to the point where it is both sufficiently accurate and sufficiently detailed. Once a model has fulfilled its goals you should stop working on it—you are finished! Move on to something else, such as writing some code to show that your model works. This has the advantage that your models will remain simple because you won't clutter them with needless detail. This principle also applies to a change to an existing model: If you make a change such as applying a known pattern, then you need to have a valid reason to make that change, such as to support a new requirement or to refactor your work to something cleaner. An important implication of this principle is that you need to know your audience, even when that audience is yourself. For example: If you create a model for maintenance developers, what do they really need? Do they need a 500-page comprehensive document or would a 10-page overview of how everything works be sufficient? Don't know? Go talk with them and find out.

Another way to look at it is this: The point at which a model just barely fulfills its purpose is also the point of diminishing returns for that model. When you first work on a model you most likely have a sense of accomplishment because you're thinking something through, gaining a better understanding of what you need to do, or gaining improved insight into how you should build it. As you continue to work, you get closer and closer to your goal for developing that model, whatever that goal is, until you finally get to the point where you've reached your target. It's at this point that further work on the model is providing less and less benefit. Yes, you may be filling in some details. Yes, you may be improving its consistency and accuracy, but you could have moved on; you could have found something else to work on, ideally, source code that provides greater benefit to your project.

Multiple Models

You have a wide range of modeling artifacts, many of which are summarized in Appendix A, "Modeling Techniques," available to you. These artifacts include the diagrams of the Unified Modeling Language (UML) (Object Management Group 2001), structured development artifacts such as data models, and low-tech artifacts such as essential user interface models. Each artifact has its strengths and weaknesses; each one is appropriate for some situations and not others. Because modern software is complex, no single artifact, even in the case of the UML family of artifacts, is applicable for all situations. The implication is that to be effective, you need to use multiple models to describe software systems, because each model describes a single aspect of your software. For example: Figure 3.1 shows the logic for placing an order online, whereas the user interface (UI) flow diagram of Figure 3.2 describes how users navigate around the UI of SWA Online. It is interesting to note that the sequence diagram is an artifact prescribed by the UML, whereas the UI flow diagram is not (yet), and that both diagrams depict different but important aspects of the SWA Online system.

By using each model for what it is good for, and not trying to use them when it isn't appropriate, you can describe the complexities of what you are building using several

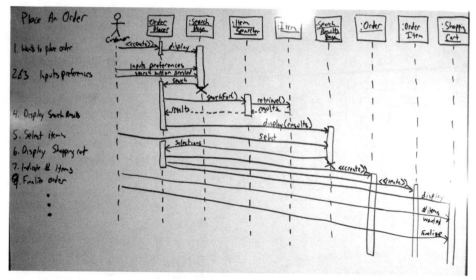

Figure 3.1   A UML sequence diagram for placing an order.

simple models instead of one or two very complex ones. This is easier for you as a developer, when you're working on the database for your system use data models, when you're working on the UI use UI-oriented models such as user interface flow diagrams. It's also easier for anyone that you need to communicate with because they can focus on one model at a time instead of trying to understand everything at once. This principle clearly supports AM values of *Simplicity* and *Communication*.

Note that although you have a wide range of models available to you, you don't need to develop all of them for any given system. Depending on the exact nature of the software you are developing, and the software process that you are applying AM with, you will require at least a subset of the models. For example: An XP project team will apply user stories as its major requirements modeling artifact, whereas a Unified Process project team will likely apply a combination of use cases, business rules, constraints, and technical requirements. An EJB application will need object-oriented design artifacts such as those described by the UML, whereas a data warehouse project will need data models. Different types of projects require different subsets of artifacts. To be effective as an agile modeler you will need to learn a wide range of models to be able to apply the right type of model based on your situation. To continue to be effective you need the *Humility* (another AM value) to admit that you can always learn new techniques, often from junior developers fresh out of school or from project stakeholders who understand the business.

You Need an Intellectual Toolbox of Techniques

An analogy that I use throughout this book is that developers should have an intellectual toolbox (McConnell 1993) of techniques that they can apply when needed, just as

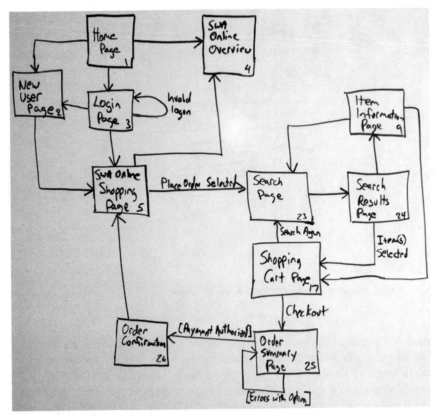

Figure 3.2   A user interface flow diagram for SWA Online.

a carpenter has a toolbox of tools. The more tools you have, and know how to apply, the more effective you will be as a developer, because you are more likely to have the right tool for the job when the need arises. Just as every fix-it job at home doesn't require you to use every tool available to you in your toolbox, every development task won't require you to apply each technique that you know. The variety of fix-it jobs you perform at home will require you to use each of your tools at some point, and similarly, the development projects you are involved with will, over time, require you to apply all of the various modeling techniques that you know. Finally, just as you use some tools more than others, you will apply some types of models more than others.

Quality Work

Nobody likes sloppy work. The people doing the work don't like it because it's something they can't be proud of. The people coming along later to refactor the work, perhaps yourself a few weeks later when your requirements change or perhaps a maintenance developer who has been assigned to evolve your system, don't like it because sloppy work is harder to understand and therefore harder to update. In other words, quality work improves communication on your project. Your end users won't like your sloppy work because it's typically fragile and/or doesn't meet their expectations. Senior management won't like your sloppy work because they will feel they aren't getting good value for their investment in your efforts.

Agile developers understand that they should invest the effort to make permanent artifacts, such as source code, user documentation, and technical system documentation (documentation is described in detail in Chapter 14, "Agile Documentation") of sufficient quality. It takes guts to stand up and say that you need the time to do a good job. Similarly, agile developers don't invest much effort in artifacts that they intend to discard, particularly sketches or low-fidelity artifacts such as essential user interface prototypes. In other words, they have the humility to spend their time wisely because they realize they would be wasting their project stakeholder's resources otherwise. Is this advice contradictory? I don't think so. If something is worth keeping, then it's worth building properly; otherwise, invest minimal effort in creating it.

Rapid Feedback

Feedback is one of the five values of AM, and because the time between an action and the feedback on that action is critical, agile modelers prefer rapid feedback over delayed feedback whenever possible. By working with other people on a model, particularly when you are working with a shared-modeling technology such as a whiteboard, CRC cards, or essential modeling materials such as Post-It notes, you are obtaining near-instant feedback on your ideas. This gives you an indication of whether or not your approaches are likely to solve the situation at hand, as well as provides opportunities to evolve and improve your model(s). Working closely with your customer to understand their requirements, to analyze those requirements, or to develop a user interface that meets their needs provides opportunities for rapid feedback. Writing code based on your models is another opportunity for feedback because it shows whether your model is feasible and very often reveals flaws in your approach because you simply can't think all of the issues through. Obtaining feedback on your work is a humbling but informative experience, one that you want sooner rather than later so you can act on any issues before they become serious problems.

There are two reasons why rapid feedback is important: We make most of our mistakes in the "early" aspects of development and the cost of fixing defects increases exponentially the later they are found. Technical people are very good at technical things such as design and coding—that is why they are technical people. Unfortunately, technical people are often not as good at non-technical tasks such as gathering requirements and performing analysis—probably another reason why they are technical people. The result, as shown in Figure 3.3, is that developers have a tendency to make more errors during requirements definition and analysis than during design and coding. Furthermore, on a non-agile project the cost of fixing these defects rises the later they are found as shown in Figure 3.4. This happens because of the nature of software development—work is performed based on work performed previously. For example: Design modeling is performed based on your requirements. Programming is done based on the design models, and testing is performed on the written source code.

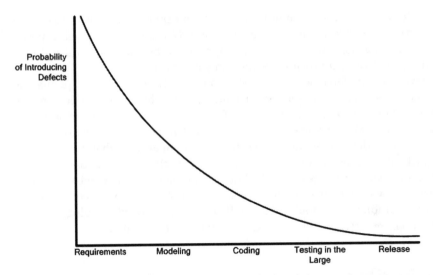

Figure 3.3 The decreasing probability of introducing defects.

If a requirement was misunderstood, all modeling decisions based on that requirement are potentially invalid, all code written based on the models is also in question, and the testing efforts are now verifying the application against the wrong conditions. If the only feedback you receive is the errors detected late in the lifecycle of your project, during testing in the large, or after the application has been released, they are likely to be very expensive to fix. However, if you receive feedback quickly, just after

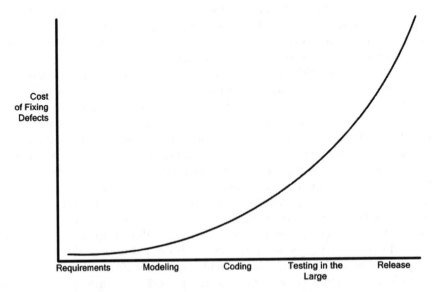

Figure 3.4 The rising costs of finding and fixing defects.

misunderstanding what you were originally told, it will be much less expensive to address the misunderstanding.

Maximize Stakeholder Investment

Your project stakeholders are investing resources—time, money, facilities, and so on—to have software developed that meets their needs. Stakeholders deserve to invest their resources the best way possible and to not have them frittered away by your team. Furthermore, stakeholders deserve to have the final say in how those resources are invested or not invested. If it was your money, would you want it any other way?

> **TIP** **System Documentation is a Business Decision, Not a Technical One**
> It is important to recognize that every time you decide to keep a model or document, you are making a serious trade-off—you are forgoing new functionality in order to write documentation. When you stop and think about it, this is a trade-off that is a business decision, not a technical one. You are trading business functionality for the potential risk-reduction benefits of having permanent artifacts that describe your system. Therefore, you should go to your project stakeholders and ask their permission to invest their resources in this manner, presenting the advantages and disadvantages of doing so. Sometimes they will choose to keep the artifact(s) that you suggest, and other times they will choose to accept the risks of not having them and instead travel light. That's their decision, not yours.

Why Core Principles?

Why do I stress the need to adopt all of AM's core principles to truly claim that you're doing AM? I want to avoid the problem that XP has faced—people who claim to do XP but who really aren't, then blame XP for their failure. Like XP, the principles and practices of AM are synergistic, and if you remove some, the synergy is lost. By failing to adopt one of the core principles or practices of AM, you reduce the method's effectiveness. Yes, you can benefit by only adopting a portion of AM, but you likely won't obtain dramatic improvements in your effectiveness because of the drop in synergy. In short, feel free to adopt whatever aspects of AM that you see fit, just please don't claim that you're doing AM when you've only partially adopted it.

Supplementary Principles

It is easier to fight for one's principles than to live up to them.

—Alfred Adler

Agile Modeling's supplementary principles define concepts that increase your effectiveness as an agile modeler. Although these principles support AM's core principles, described in Chapter 3, "Core Principles," their adoption is not required for you to be truly agile modeling. These principles are all very good ideas and you should adopt them if they fit well into your organizational culture. AM's supplementary principles are:

- Content is more important than representation
- Everyone can learn from everyone else
- Know your models
- Local adaptation
- Open and honest communication
- Work with people's instincts

Content Is More Important Than Representation

Any given model can be represented in several ways. For example: AUI specification could be created using Post-It notes on a large sheet of paper (an essential or low-fidelity prototype); as a sketch on paper or a whiteboard; as a "traditional" prototype built using a prototyping tool or programming language; or as a formal document including both a visual representation as well as a textual description of the UI. Depending on the reason you're creating the model, the various representations may be equivalent. If your goal is to explore the layout of an HTML page, then all three representations are sufficient. In fact, making the specification prettier using a drawing tool and documenting it comprehensively does not add anything to further this goal. The content is more important than its representation in this case.

An important implication of this principle is that you don't need to jump into using a complicated CASE tool right away. Yes, CASE tools can be very useful if they generate code for you or if they can reverse engineer an understandable model from existing code, but at first it is better to work with simple, flexible tools. I discuss this in detail in Chapter 10, "Using the Simplest Tools Possible?"

Consider another example. A UML class diagram could be drawn as a sketch as shown in Figure 4.1, using a drawing tool such as Microsoft Visio as shown in Figure 4.2, or created using a sophisticated CASE tool. It's still the same class diagram, just depicted differently. The sketch may be sufficient for its purpose—it helped the people that drew it to understand an initial approach to designing the software they were working on. Could you use the sketch of Figure 4.1 in your official documentation (assuming that it captures critical information that you want to persist)? Why not? It's

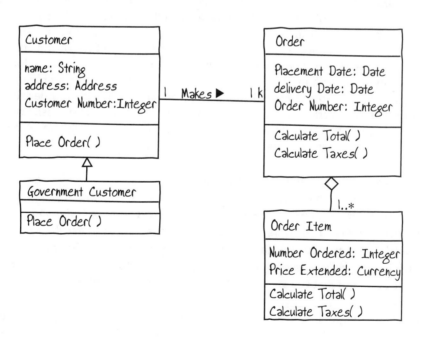

Figure 4.1 A UML class diagram sketch.

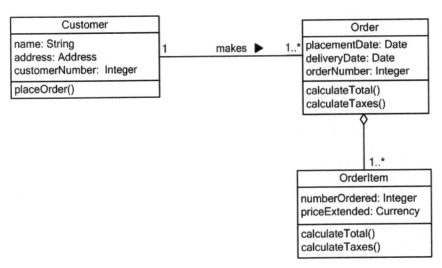

Figure 4.2   A UML class diagram using Microsoft Visio.

not as pretty as the tool-drawn diagram in Figure 4.2, but the sketch took one-third the time to draw. Remember, agile modelers *Maximize Stakeholder Investment*, so it's a serious decision to invest time simply to make something look nice. I suspect that the world isn't going to end if you use a hand-drawn sketch as part of your official documentation. I often use scans or digital pictures of sketches in official documents or presentations—the sketch captures the idea that I want to communicate and I don't want to waste time transcribing the sketch into a more sophisticated tool simply to make it look pretty. It's OK to show people imperfect work and to defend your decision to do only the minimal work required and then move on. This model clearly isn't complete, and frankly, my handwriting is a disaster, but remember, an agile modeler models with a purpose and stops as soon as that purpose is fulfilled.

TIP **Meet the Expectations of Your Audience**
Whether it is a viable strategy to include hand-drawn diagrams in your documentation depends on the audience: if your readers are "prim and proper," then you'll likely be required to invest the time to transcribe your models using an electronic tool. There's nothing wrong with this; after all it's their money you're spending, but recognize that you do have an option to be more agile and that you should make them aware of this option.

Similarly, the same structure of classes presented in Figures 4.1 and 4.2 could be depicted using a different type of artifact, such as a Class Responsibility Collaborator (CRC) model or using a different notation, perhaps the OMT notation (Rumbaugh et. al. 1991). Having said that, I would not choose the OMT notation over the UML notation for the simple reason that the UML is an industry standard, whereas the OMT notation is not. Yes, there may be technical reasons why OMT is superior to UML, but chances are good that the communication loss from not using a common standard is more significant.

An interesting implication is that a model does not always need to be a document. I could have drawn the sketch in Figure 4.1 simply to understand the structure of the classes that I was working on, proceeded to code and test the classes, and then discarded the model once I was finished with it. Even a complex set of diagrams created using a CASE tool may not become part of a document; instead they are used as inputs into other artifacts, very likely source code, but never formalized as official documentation. The point is that you take advantage of the benefits of modeling without incurring the costs of creating and maintaining documentation. This principle is motivated by AM's values of *Simplicity* and *Communication* and the Agile Alliance's (2001a) preference for working software over comprehensive documentation.

Everyone Can Learn from Everyone Else

Agile modelers recognize that they can never truly master something; there is always an opportunity to learn more and to extend your knowledge. They take the opportunity to work with and learn from others, to try new ways of doing things, to reflect on what seems to work and what doesn't. Technologies change rapidly; existing technologies such as Java evolve at a blinding pace, and new technologies such as C# and .NET are introduced regularly. Existing development techniques evolve at a slower pace, but they still evolve. As an industry we've understood the fundamentals of testing for quite some time, although we are constantly improving our understanding through research and practice. The point is that we work in an industry where change is the norm, where you must take every opportunity to learn new ways of doing things through training, education, mentoring, reading, and *working with each other*.

An implication of this practice is that everyone should expect to work with others to help them learn new skills. In fact, I believe that you are responsible to help others increase their intellectual toolkit. This principle is motivated by the values of *Communication* and *Humility*.

Know Your Models

Because you have multiple models that you can apply as an agile modeler, you need to know their strengths and weaknesses to be effective in their use. Furthermore, modeling techniques evolve all the time to reflect the changes in technology. As aspect-oriented programming (Xerox 2001) becomes more mainstream, if it ever does, I fully expect to have to learn one or more aspect-oriented models and/or aspect-oriented extensions to existing types of models. This enables you to keep your models as simple as possible as well as improve the quality of communication on the project that you're applying the modeling techniques to.

Local Adaptation

It is doubtful that you will be able to "apply AM out of the box." Instead, you will need to modify it to reflect your environment, including the nature of your organization, your co-workers, your project stakeholders, and your project itself. When you adapt AM to meet your unique needs, you will definitely need to consider the modeling techniques that you plan to apply. For example: Your users may insist on concrete user interfaces instead of initial sketches or essential UI prototypes. The tools that you use will have an effect on your approach. Perhaps there isn't a budget for a digital camera but you already have licenses for an existing CASE tool. AM can be modified to reflect the software process where it is applied. Part Three discusses applying AM on an XP project, and Part Four describes applying AM on a Unified Process project.

You will adapt your approach at the individual level as well as at the project level. For example: Some developers prefer one set of tools over another. For instance, when I'm Java coding, I prefer a sophisticated code editor and the JDK, whereas my co-workers may prefer a Java IDE. Some people focus on coding and do very little modeling, whereas others are more visually oriented and prefer to invest time sketching before they write code—different people, different applications of AM. It's important to note that the values, principles, and practices remain the same, but their application varies.

Also, remember that AM isn't going to work in all situations, as I indicated in Chapter 1, "Introduction." It may not be realistic to try to adopt AM in full, at least not right away, so you may find that you can tailor a portion of AM's principles and practices into your existing software process. As long as you improve your effectiveness as a developer, that's perfectly fine.

Open and Honest Communication

People need to be free, and know that they are free, to offer suggestions. This includes ideas that pertain to one or more models. Perhaps someone has a new way to approach a portion of the design or has new insight regarding a requirement, or simply a new method to present the current status of their work. Open and honest communication enables people to make better decisions because those decisions are based on more accurate information.

Open and honest communication requires commitment on everyone's part and an understanding that effective communication is a critical success factor for software development projects. People who dare to speak their mind must also be open to hearing something they may not like. It requires humility on everyone's part to be willing to abandon their pet ideas upon hearing that they may not be as good as they originally thought.

Work with People's Instincts

When someone feels that something isn't going to work, that a few things are inconsistent with one another, or that something doesn't "smell right," then there is a good chance that that is actually the case. As you gain experience at developing software, your instincts become sharper, and what your instincts are telling you subconsciously can often be an important input into your modeling efforts. If your instincts tell you that a requirement doesn't make sense or it isn't complete, investigate it with your users. If your instincts tell you that a portion of your architecture isn't going to meet your needs, build a quick technical end-to-end prototype to test out your theory. If your instincts tell you that design alternative A is better than design alternative B, and there is no compelling reason to choose either one of them, then go with alternative A for now. It's important to understand that AM's *Courage* value indicates that you can remedy the situation at some point in the future if you discover your instincts were wrong.

Benefiting from These Principles

The principles described in this chapter and Chapter 3 are little better than well-intentioned exhortations unless you internalize them. Agile modelers adopt and act in accordance with these principles, something that is easy to say and hard to do. I don't know how to ensure that you actually internalize these principles; all I can do is ask that you think about them and try to follow them whenever you can. I've put together a pamphlet summarizing Agile Modeling—it includes a list of AM's values, principles, and practices—that you can download from the AM web site at www.agilemodeling.com. Perhaps printing this document, the three lists appearing on a single page, and tacking it on the wall in your work area will help your efforts. It's worth a try at least.

Core Practices

Perfect practice makes perfect.

–Sensei Rick Willemsen

The heart of Agile Modeling is its practices. It is AM's practices that you will actually apply on your projects, practices that are guided by AM's values and principles. As with AM's principles, its practices are also organized into ones that are core and those that are supplementary. As I indicated in Chapter 3, "Core Principles," you must adopt all of AM's core practices to be able to claim that you are "doing AM." Of course, you can benefit from adopting only some of the practices, but it is better to adopt all of them if they fit well into your organization's culture. Adopting AM into your organization is discussed in detail in Chapter 28, "Adopting AM on an UP Project."

AM's core practices are organized into four categories that are described in detail in Chapter 7, "Order from Chaos: How The AM Practices Fit Together." These categories, and the core practices within them, are:

1. Iterative and Incremental Modeling
   - Apply the Right Artifact(s)
   - Create Several Models in Parallel
   - Iterate to Another Artifact
   - Model in Small Increments
2. Teamwork
   - Model with Others
   - Active Stakeholder Participation

- Collective Ownership
- Display Models Publicly

3. Simplicity
   - Create Simple Content
   - Depict Models Simply
   - Use the Simplest Tools

4. Validation
   - Consider Testability
   - Prove it With Code

TIP **None of These Practices Are New**
As you read this chapter and Chapter 6, "Supplementary Practices," you will very likely recognize many if not all of the practices that make up AM. That's because the individual practices of AM aren't new, they are techniques that effective modelers have been following for years. What is new is that I have packaged them together for the first time and described them in a single place. Furthermore, they are the distillation of hundreds of "best practices" that modelers follow, and as you'll see in Chapter 7, they fit together into a synergistic whole, something that I call Agile Modeling.

Practices for Iterative and Incremental Modeling

AM defines four practices that support an iterative and incremental approach to modeling:

1. Apply the Right Artifact(s)
2. Create Several Models in Parallel
3. Iterate to Another Artifact
4. Model in Small Increments

Apply the Right Artifact(s)

This practice is AM's equivalent of the adage "use the right tool for the job." In this case, you want to create the right model(s) to get the job done. Each artifact—such as a UML state chart, an essential use case, source code, or data flow diagram (DFD)—has its own specific strengths and weaknesses, and therefore is appropriate for some situations but not others. For example: The UML activity diagram (Rumbaugh, Jacobson,

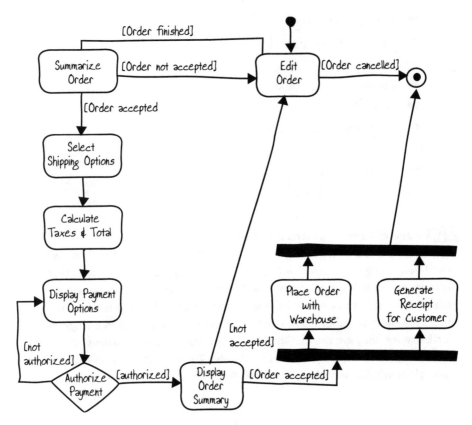

Figure 5.1   A UML Activity diagram for order processing.

and Booch 1999) in Figure 5.1 is useful for describing a business process, whereas the static structure of your database is better represented by a physical data model (Reingruber and Gregory 1994) such as the one presented in Figure 5.2. Similarly, a diagram is a better choice than source code. If a picture is worth a thousand words, then a model is often worth 1024 lines of code when applied in the right circumstances, an idea borrowed from Karl Wiegers (1999). This is because you can often explore design alternatives more effectively by drawing a couple of diagrams on whiteboards with your peers than you can by sitting down and developing code samples.

An important implication to agile modelers is that they need to gain an understanding of when and when not to apply each type of artifact, information that is presented in Appendix A, "Modeling Techniques," for a wide range of modeling techniques. Learning the nuances of each type of artifact can be difficult, a problem that is compounded by the numerous artifacts available to you.

TIP   Start By Learning a Subset of Artifacts
Overwhelmed by the number of modeling artifacts described in Appendix A? Don't worry, that's normal. A serious downside about AM is that it explicitly asks you to learn how to apply a wide range of modeling artifacts, and that's

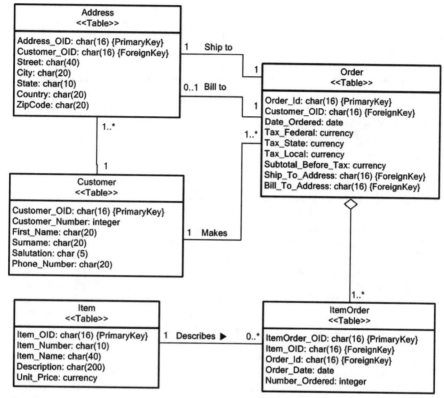

Figure 5.2 A start at a physical data model for SWA Online.

something that takes time and effort. A good way to start is to focus on a core subset of them at first, and then learn new techniques one at a time as needed. Methodologies such as ICONIX (Rosenberg and Scott 1999) and Catalysis (D'Souza and Wills 1999) will often recommend several artifacts and describe how to apply them in practice, and then as you discover missing aspects of the methodology you can supplement it with the appropriate modeling artifacts.

Create Several Models in Parallel

Because each type of model has its strengths and weaknesses, no single model is sufficient for your modeling needs. For example: When you are exploring requirements, you may need to decide to develop a use case (Jacobson et. al. 1992; Cockburn 2001a) as you see in Figure 5.3; an essential UI prototype as you see in Figure 5.4 (Constantine and Lockwood 1999); and Class Responsibility Collaborator (CRC) cards (Cunningham and Beck 1989) as you see in Figure 5.5. The use case describes how someone places an order, the UI prototype specifies the requirements for a screen or page to support order entry, and the CRC cards capture conceptual information about the business domain.

- The use case begins when a customer chooses to place an order.
- The customer searches for items via the use case "Search for Item(s)."
- The customer adds an order item to their order.
- The customer indicates the number of a given item they wish to order.
- The system calculates the subtotal for the item by multiplying the unit price by the number ordered.
- The customer repeats steps 2 through 5 as necessary to build their order.
- The customer finishes adding items to their order.
- The customer provides their ship to and bill to information, including their name, phone number, and surface address.
- The system calculates the subtotal for the entire order by adding the subtotals of the individual line items.
- The system calculates the taxes applicable for the order according to the business rule *Calculate Taxes for an Order*.
- The system calculates applicable discounts for the order according to the business rule *Calculate Discounts for an Order*.
- The system displays the applicable taxes and discounts.
- The system calculates the grand total for the order by adding the applicable taxes to the order subtotal and subtracting the discounts.
- The system displays a summary of the order.
- The customer verifies that the order is what they want.
- The system schedules the order for fulfillment (see the use case Fulfill Order).
- The system produces a receipt for the customer summarizing the order.

Figure 5.3   The basic course of action for placing an order.

As you work with your project stakeholders to explore their requirements, you would update each of these models appropriately, capturing information in the artifact in which it makes the most sense. Similarly, when you are designing Java software, you may discover that you need to develop a UML class diagram to formulate its structure, a UML state chart diagram to explore the inner workings of a complex class, a UML sequence diagram to determine how to implement the logic of a flow within a use case (as you see in Figure 5.1) or a business rule, and a physical data model to understand the structure of your relational database as you see in Figure 5.2. In combination with the practice of *Iterate to Another Artifact* (see next section), agile modelers will often discover that they are far more productive working on several models simultaneously than if they are focusing on only one at any given time.

An interesting implication of this practice is that it brings into question two common antipatterns in the IT industry. The first one is something that I call Single Artifact Developers, someone who specializes in the development of one kind of

Figure 5.4 An essential UI prototype depicting the requirements for a screen/page.

deliverable. Examples of this are people who want only to write code, low-end coders who believe that everything of importance is in the source code and nothing else matters, and data modelers who believe that the most important thing is data and everything else pales in comparison. The reality is that modern software is far too complex for anyone with such a narrow focus to be effective. My advice is to become very adept at creating several types of artifacts, source code and data models are actually good candidates, but to have at least a passing understanding of a wide range of techniques. In other words, fill your intellectual toolbox as best you can. The second antipattern is Single Artifact Modeling Sessions. Use case modeling sessions are the most common example, where you work on one type of model. A requirements modeling session makes sense to me, a use case modeling session just doesn't make any sense in an agile environment.

Creating several models in parallel will be difficult at first for some people, particularly those who prefer to focus on a single task at a time and those who currently exhibit the Single Artifact Developer antipattern. If AM is new to your organization,

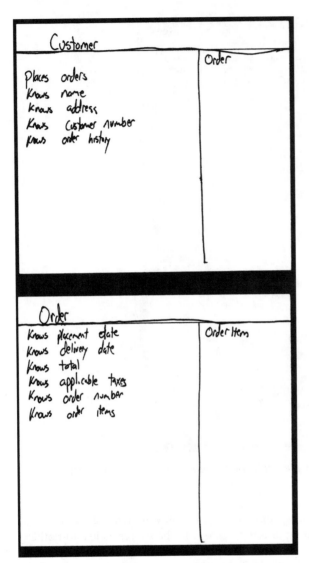

Figure 5.5 Two CRC cards for SWA Online.

then you need to be prepared to help people get used to practices such as this one. I have found that the first step to overcome these difficulties is to work on two models at once, following the practice *Model with Others* discussed later in this chapter and having someone involved who is comfortable with this approach work with the person who is uncomfortable. I will usually focus on an artifact they are familiar with and one that they would usually consider "downstream" that they are also familiar with. Perhaps I would choose a use case and a UML sequence diagram in combination, or a UML class diagram and a physical data model. The goal is to help them build up their confidence in the practice, to prove to them that it does in fact work well.

Iterate to Another Artifact

Perhaps you are working a use case, CRC card, sequence diagram, or even source code and discover you are struggling with it. This is an indication that you should consider working on another artifact for the time being. Each artifact has its strengths and weaknesses; each artifact is good for a certain type of job. Whenever you find you are having difficulties working on one artifact—perhaps you are working on a use case and find that you are struggling to describe the business logic—then that's a sign that you should iterate to another artifact. By iterating to another artifact, you immediately become "unstuck" because you are making progress working on that other artifact. Furthermore, by changing your point of view you often discover that you address whatever it was that caused you to be stuck in the first place. Besides regaining momentum, you get the added bonus of getting meaningful work accomplished, a key concept for agile software development.

The hardest thing when applying this practice, after recognizing that you are in fact stuck, is to identify a likely candidate to iterate to. Experience will guide your choice, but if you are short on experience, then in Appendix A I provide an indication of likely candidates to iterate to when you are working on a modeling artifact. For example, if you work on an essential use case, then you may want to consider changing focus to start working on an essential UI prototype, a CRC model, a business rule, a system use case, or a change case.

Model in Small Increments

The principle *Incremental Change* indicates that an incremental approach to development is a fundamental of AM. In fact, you saw in Chapter 1, "Introduction," that it is a fundamental aspect of agile software development in general (Agile Alliance 2001b). The basic idea is that you organize a larger effort into smaller portions that you release over time, ideally in increments of several weeks or a month or two. This increases your agility by enabling you to deliver software into the hands of your users faster, and thus obtain concrete and rapid feedback from them throughout your project. Because you are taking an incremental approach to development, you will also be taking an incremental approach to modeling.

With incremental development you model a little, code a little, test a little, then deliver a little. No more big design up front (BDUF), where you invest weeks or even months creating models and documents. Instead, the majority of modeling sessions, impromptu gatherings of people to explore one or more issues, last on the order of 10 or 20 minutes. Agile modelers model in small increments, just long enough so they can return to working on software as outlined in the principle *Software is Your Primary Goal*. Longer modeling sessions, sometimes lasting several days (particularly at the beginning of a project), can occur but they are the exception, not the norm. The longer you go without concrete feedback, the greater the chance that what you are modeling won't be what is actually needed and therefore will be wasted effort. Furthermore, you run the risk of violating the practices of *Depict Models Simply* and *Create Simple Content*, described later in this chapter, when you focus for a long time on your model(s).

The hardest part of following this practice is to stop modeling once you've fulfilled your goal. You often want to model the things that you'll need to work on tomorrow, next week, or next month. Your subconscious goal is to think things through as best you can. Stop doing this. Have the courage to solve today's problem today, and trust that you can solve tomorrow's problem tomorrow (Beck 2000).

Practices for Effective Teamwork

AM defines four practices that enable effective teamwork and communication within your team and with your project stakeholders:

1. Model with Others
2. Active Stakeholder Participation
3. Collective Ownership
4. Display Models Publicly

Model with Others

Software development is a lot like swimming, it's very dangerous to do it alone. When you model with a purpose, you often find that you are modeling to understand something or that you are modeling to communicate your ideas to others to develop a common vision regarding your project. These are best suited as group activities because you want the input of several people working together effectively. You will often find that your development team needs to work together to create the core set of models that are critical to your project. For example: To develop the metaphor or architecture for your system, you will often need to model with a group of people to develop a solution everyone agrees on, as well as one that is as simple as possible. Most of the time the best way to do this is to talk the issue through with one or more people. There's nothing wrong with drawing a simple sketch to think something through on your own, but once you are finished, talk about your ideas with someone to see if you're going in the right direction. Two or more heads are better than one. This practice helps to improve communication on your project, helps to build a common vocabulary among the people you are working with, increases the chance that you'll do quality work, and provides opportunities for people to learn from their co-workers.

This practice can be difficult to adopt at first within organizations that have a "divide and conquer" culture where the focus is on assigning work to individuals, or that have highly competitive cultures that pit individuals against each other. To counteract the problem you will need to communicate the benefit of working together, perhaps taking the approach that "new methodologies imply new ways of working so let's just try it for now and see what happens." You also need a work area, see Chapter 11, "Agile Work Areas," that supports people working together as a team. This may be something as simple as a whiteboard on the wall of someone's cubicle or a dedicated workspace for your team.

Active Stakeholder Participation

A project stakeholder is anyone who is a direct user, indirect user, manager of users, senior manager, operations staff member, support (help desk) staff member, tester, developer working on other systems that integrate or interact with the one under development, or maintenance professional potentially affected by the development and/or deployment of a software project. For the sake of AM, in this definition I exclude developers who are working on the project—even though developers clearly have an important stake in the projects that they work on for AM, the term "project stakeholder" will be used to refer to everyone with a stake in a project except for the developers working on it. Hence I refer to developers and project stakeholders as separate groups of people. The alternative is to have terms such as developer project stakeholders and non-developer project stakeholders (yuck).

AM's practice of *Active Stakeholder Participation* is closely related to its practice *Model with Others*. Furthermore, it is an expansion of eXtreme Programming (XP)'s *On-Site Customer* (Beck 2000) practice that describes the need to have on-site access to people, typically users or their representatives, who have the authority and ability to provide information pertaining to the system being built and to make pertinent and timely decisions regarding the requirements and prioritization thereof. While this level of participation is required to make your software development efforts effective, it often isn't sufficient in many organizations, particularly those where politics and not a true commitment to building working systems are the order of the day. Project success often requires a greater level of involvement by project stakeholders: Senior management needs to publicly and privately support your project, operations and support staff must actively work with your project team towards making your production environment ready to accept your system, other system teams must work with yours to support integration efforts, and maintenance developers must work to become adept at the technologies and techniques used by your system. This practice is motivated by the principles of *Rapid Feedback* and *Open and Honest Communication*.

It is clear that in order to be successful, all project stakeholders must actively work with your team to achieve these goals. There are several implications of this practice:

■ Users must be prepared to share business knowledge with the team and to make both pertinent and timely decisions regarding project scope and requirement priorities.

■ For senior managers to effectively support your project, they must first understand the benefits and added value of the technologies and techniques that your team is using, understand why your team is using them, and understand the implications of using them. With this knowledge, their efforts within your organization's political arena are far more likely to be effective at the right times in the right ways. Senior managers won't be able to gain this requisite knowledge by reading a weekly project status report or by attending a monthly project steering meeting. Instead, they need to invest the necessary time to learn about the things that they manage; they need to actively participate in the development of your system.

■ Your operations and support organization must invest the resources required to understand both your system and the technologies that it uses. Your support staff must take the time to learn the nuances of your system; the implication is that they need to work with your system as it is developed and/or your team will need to provide them with training. Furthermore, your operations staff must become proficient with both the installation and operation of your system. You may choose to include one or two operations engineers on your development team or once again to invest project resources to train operations staff as required. Regardless of your approach, both your operations and support organizations will need to be actively involved with your project team.

■ Other project teams need to work with you if your system needs to integrate with other systems. For example: Perhaps your system needs to access a legacy database, interact with an online system, work with a data file produced by an external system, or provide an XML data extract for other systems. Integration often proves difficult if not impossible without the active participation of these developers. Imagine how difficult it would be to access the information contained in a large legacy database if the owners of that database refuse to provide any information about it. Remember that communication is a two-way street; you'll also be sharing information about your system with other teams.

■ Maintenance developers need to work with you to learn your system. When the intention is to either partially or completely hand off the maintenance of your system to other developers, it is common to bring in software professionals skilled in maintaining and enhancing existing systems to free up members of the original development team; then your team must work with these people so they can take over the system from you. Even when some original team members are still involved, you must make an effort to transfer the knowledge to the new members of the team. A good example of this is having original team members mentor new members or simply pair up with them when working on new aspects of the system.

Collective Ownership

Everyone can work on any model, and ideally any artifact on the project, if they need to. For example: If I draw a data flow diagram (DFD) on a whiteboard, there are several advantages to this approach. First, the more people who get involved with the development of an artifact, the greater the opportunity to identify potential issues with it, supporting the principle of *Rapid Feedback*. Second, it provides people with opportunities to gain experience developing various types of models, expanding their intellectual toolbox, and thus making them more effective as agile modelers—supporting the principle that *Everyone Can Learn From Everyone Else* because they can see each other's work and even improve upon it. Third, it reduces the temptation for team members to say things like "*Your* model is wrong," because if they discover that something is wrong, they should fix it, not complain about it. Fourth, it reduces the chance that people will personalize certain artifacts, such as: "This class model is my baby and nothing could possibly be wrong with it," because no single artifact is only theirs. Fifth, it promotes understanding of the system among team members, improving communication within your team and reducing both your need to maintain extensive documentation and your reliance on a single person or subset of people. There is a project management concept called truck number. The idea is that it is an estimate of the minimum number of people you would need to lose from your team before you find yourself in trouble (for example, the number of people that would need to be hit by a truck). A truck number of one is a serious problem; a truck number greater than or equal to the number of people on your team is ideal. Collective ownership increases your project's truck number.

This practice can be challenging to adopt within organizations where the individual is more important than the team, and/or that have a focus on narrowly defined roles on a project team. People need to accept that the artifacts that they work on are the property of the team. They also need to work on a wide variety of things—not work just on the user interface, or just on a single subsystem, or just on system integration code.

Display Models Publicly

You should display your models publicly, often on something called a "modeling wall" or a "wall of wonder" (Gottesdiener 2001). This supports the principle of *Open and Honest Communication* on your team because all of the current models are quickly accessible to them, as well as with your project stakeholders because you aren't hiding anything from them. Your modeling wall is where you post your models for everyone to see; the modeling wall should be accessible to your development team and other project stakeholders. Your modeling wall may be physical, perhaps a designated whiteboard for your architecture diagram(s) or a place where you tape a printout of your physical data model. Modeling walls can be virtual, such as an internal Web page that is updated with scanned images.

A further benefit of this practice is that it shows to your project stakeholders that you are doing valuable work—it's right there in front of their eyes. This is particularly good when you are developing simple models for the first time and are afraid that you might not be adding the same value (due to lack of quantity) that you did in the past. Having several simple models displayed on the wall that are publicly being used goes a long way to showing the worth of your contributions.

This practice can be difficult to implement in firms where wall space is at a premium, where the project team is working in a relatively public area that has your firm's customers or even competitors walking through it and you don't wish them to see your work in progress, or in an environment where significant investment has been made in wall decorations (such as a law firm with oak-covered walls) that you don't wish to harm. If any of these problems are the case, you may wish to consider moving your team to another location. Furthermore, cultural issues such as the unwillingness to share information with people outside your group can also hamper this practice. If this is the case, then my advice is to find the courage to adopt this practice.

Practices That Enable Simplicity

AM defines three practices that enable simplicity within your modeling efforts:

1. Create simple content
2. Depict models simply
3. Use the simplest tools

Create Simple Content

You should keep the actual content of your models—your requirements, your analysis, your architecture, or your design—as simple as you possibly can while still fulfilling the needs of your project stakeholders. The implication is that you should not add additional aspects to your models unless they are justifiable. For example: The UML class diagram (Rumbaugh, Jacobson, and Booch 1999) in Figure 5.6 does not indicate the visibility of the attributes and operations of the classes, presumably something that whoever will be programming these classes (hopefully the people who drew the diagram) will determine when they get to it. This is along the lines of XP's practice of

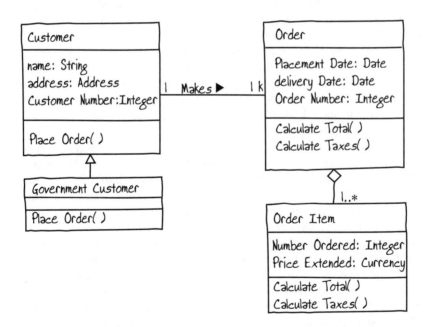

Figure 5.6 A UML class diagram.

Simple Design (Beck 2000). This practice is also applicable to non-model artifacts such as source code, project plans, and user documentation.

So how do you know when the content of your models is simple? I believe the following factors, modified from Kent Beck's (2000) simplest design advice, for determining when a model is simple:

- The model communicates everything that you want to communicate. In other words, it fulfills its purpose.

- The model must contain no duplicate information.

- The model should have the fewest possible elements.

The most common stumbling blocks to adopting this practice are your tendency to want to over-model, something that you can overcome by recognizing the problem and stopping yourself when your model has fulfilled its immediate purpose, and the tendency of others within your organization to equate progress to detailed models and documentation. You'll often find significant organizational peer pressure to conform to existing standards of documentation and modeling detail, particularly in firms with prescriptive processes that are new to agile approaches. If this is the case, you will need to communicate your approach to others within your organization, explaining the reasons behind what you are doing. You should even consider lending them your copy of this book or, better yet, suggest that they buy their own copy!

Depict Models Simply

When you consider the potential diagramming notations that you could apply (UML diagrams, user interface diagrams, data models, and so on), you quickly realize that most of the time you require only a subset of the diagramming notation available to you. For example: A simple model that shows the key features that you are trying to understand, perhaps a class model depicting the primary responsibilities of classes and the relationships between them, often proves to be sufficient. Yes, you could model all the scaffolding code that you will need to write, all the getter and setter operations that your coding standards tell you to use, but what value would that add? Very little for an agile modeler.

Although this practice complements *Create Simple Content*, the two concepts are orthogonal. *Create Simple Content* focuses on the subject matter of the model, whereas *Depict Models Simply* focuses on how you present your models. Common techniques (Ambler 2002) to simplify your diagrams include:

- Avoid crossing lines

- Avoid curved lines

- Avoid diagonal lines

- Avoid different size bubbles

- Avoid too many bubbles (no more than 7 +/- 2)

- Avoid unnecessary detail

Use the Simplest Tools

The vast majority of models can be drawn on a whiteboard, on paper, or even on the back of a napkin. Whenever you want to save one of these diagrams, you can take a picture of it with a digital camera or even transcribe it onto paper. In fact, you've seen several models created with simple tools. Figure 5.1 was created using flipchart paper, sticky notes, and markers; Figure 5.2 was drawn on a whiteboard; and the CRC cards of Figure 5.3 were created with index cards and a pen. Using the simplest tools works because most diagrams are throwaways. Their true value comes from drawing them to think through an issue, and once the issue is resolved, the diagram doesn't offer much value. As a result, a whiteboard and markers are often your best modeling tool alternative. Use a drawing tool to create diagrams to present to important project stakeholders and occasionally use a modeling tool if and only if they provide value to programming efforts such as the generation of code. Think of it like this: If you're creating simple models, often models are throwaways because if you are modeling to understand, you likely don't need to keep them once you do understand the issue; therefore, you don't need to apply a complex modeling tool.

Chapter 10, "Using the Simplest Tools Possible?" explores this practice in detail. Although I explicitly pointed this out in Chapter 1, I'm going to do so again: AM has nothing against CASE tools. If investing in a CASE tool is the most effective use of your resources, then by all means do so, and then use it to the best of its ability. My experience is that there are many CASE tools on the market but that few of them are worth the bother. If a simple tool is sufficient for your needs, then use it.

This can be a hard practice to adopt within organizations that are accustomed to models created using sophisticated tools. Many developers equate modeling with using an expensive CASE tool, and it's very difficult for them to accept that a stack of index cards can be effective. The best way to address this situation is to get them actively involved with using the simple tools, giving them experience in techniques such as CRC modeling and essential UI prototyping.

Practices for Validating Your Work

AM defines two practices that pertain to the testing and validation of your work:

1. Consider testability
2. Prove it with code

Consider Testability

When you model, you should constantly ask yourself, "How are we going to test this?" If you can't test the software that you build, you shouldn't build it. Modern software processes include testing and quality assurance activities throughout the entire project lifecycle, and some even promote the concept of writing tests before writing software, an XP practice called Test-First Design (Beck 2000). Agile developers test early and test often, ensuring that they are producing quality work. The hardest aspect of adopting this practice is to learn the habit of constantly thinking "in the background" about how you're going to test your work.

Prove It with Code

A model is an abstraction, one that should accurately reflect an aspect of whatever you build. To determine if it will actually work, you should validate it by writing the corresponding code. You've developed a sketch of an HTML page for accepting billing address information? Code it and show the resulting user interface to your users for feedback. You've developed a UML sequence diagram that represents the logic to implement a complex business rule? Write the testing code, the business code, and then run the tests to ensure that you've gotten it right. Never forget that with an iterative and incremental approach to software development, the norm for the vast majority of projects, modeling is only one of many tasks that you will perform. Do some modeling, do some coding, and do some testing (among other things). Although the focus of AM is on modeling, never forget that there is far more to development.

There are several common impediments to this practice.

- It works best when the people doing the modeling are also the ones writing the code, implying that an agile developer needs a wide range of skills. In Chapter 12, "Agile Modeling Teams," I argue that agile developers need to be generalists with one or more specialties. Remember, there is far more to software development than modeling.

- Second, many developers have a "big modeling up front" (BMUF) mindset that leads them to model for greater periods of time than they need to, putting off coding for a while.

- Third, many developers are accustomed to a process where you create a model, review and rework it, then code it. With AM you are much more likely to do a little modeling and then do a little coding. The need to review your model goes away because you're proving your model with code and because you are usually your model(s)' customer and therefore are the one directly affected by any problems with it (motivating you to do quality work to begin with).

Supplementary Practices

The practices are not the knowing. They are a path to the knowing.

—Ron Jeffries

Agile Modeling includes supplementary practices that support its core practices, described in Chapter 5, "Core Practices," practices that your team may optionally decide to adopt. Similarly, AM's supplementary practices are organized into categories that are described in detail in Chapter 7, "Order from Chaos: How the AM Practices Fit Together." These categories, and the practices within them, are:

1. Productivity
   - Apply Modeling Standards
   - Apply Patterns Gently
   - Reuse Existing Resources

2. Documentation
   - Discard Temporary Models
   - Formalize Contract Models
   - Update Only when It Hurts

3. Motivation
   - Model to Communicate
   - Model to Understand

Practices to Improve Your Productivity

AM defines three supplementary practices that focus on productivity enhancements for modeling:

1. Apply Modeling Standards
2. Apply Patterns Gently
3. Reuse Existing Resources

Apply Modeling Standards

This practice is the modeling version of XP's *Coding Standards* practice (Beck 2001), the basic idea is that developers should agree to and follow a common set of modeling standards on a software project. Just like there is value in following common coding conventions, clean code that follows your chosen coding guidelines is easier to understand and evolve than code that doesn't, there is similar value in following common modeling conventions. The most common standard is the UML (Object Management Group 2001) that defines the notation and semantics for common object-oriented models.

TIP **The UML Is Not Complete**

The Unified Modeling Language (UML) (Object Management Group 2001a) provides a good start for standard modeling notation but it isn't sufficient. As you can see in Appendix A, "Modeling Techniques" there are many non-UML artifacts described there. At the time of this writing, the UML does not include any sort of model for user interface design nor does it include any sort of data/persistence model. When was the last time you built a system without a user interface or data storage? Don't listen to the marketing rhetoric of the vendors trying to sell you their CASE tools or the self-appointed gurus (oops, guess that includes me) trying to sell you their books, training courses, and consulting services. The next time someone claims the UML is sufficient for real-world development, challenge their claim. I doubt they've actually thought it through. I explore this issue in detail in Chapter 15, "The UML and Beyond."

Your standards should include descriptions of notation for any non-UML models you intend to create; simple hand-drawn sketches are often sufficient. For example, the notation summary for robustness diagrams (Jacobson et. al. 1992; Rosenberg and Scott 1999) presented in Figure 6.1 gives modelers enough information about the accepted notation for robustness diagrams to create the diagram shown in Figure 6.2. Figure 6.1 also provides basic information so that others can quickly grasp the notation being applied. Furthermore, you may want to adopt modeling style guidelines to help you to create consistent and clean-looking diagrams. What is the difference between a

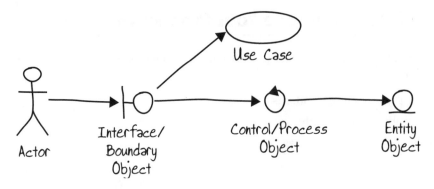

Figure 6.1   A summary of the notation for a robustness diagram.

style guideline and standards? For source code, a standard would be to name attributes in the format *attributeName,* whereas a style guideline is to indent the code within a control structure (an if statement, a loop, ...) by three spaces. For models, a standard would be to use a square rectangle to model a class on a class diagram and a style guideline would be to have subclasses placed on diagrams below their superclass(es).

> **■TIP■ Understandability Is More Important than Following Standards**
> **Don't let the desire to conform to a standard or guideline blind you to the practical reasons why you model—to explore an issue further or to help you to communicate with other people. I've seen people get upset because I've used a filled-in arrowhead on an association between use cases instead of the "official" UML notation, which is an open-headed arrow. Yes, it would have been nice if I were to memorize the 500 plus page specification for the UML (Object Management Group 2001a), but unfortunately I haven't gotten around to it. Loosen up a bit; you'll be far more effective that way.**

The greatest impediment to adopting this practice is lack of existing standards and guidelines within your organization. I prefer to start by introducing notation summaries, such as the one shown in Figure 6.1, because they are immediately useful. I'll then introduce modeling guidelines as needed, evolving the guidelines over time. You should also search the web for existing standards and style guidelines, www.uml-style.org is a good start, and adopt what you think is appropriate.

Apply Patterns Gently

Effective modelers learn and then appropriately apply common architectural, design, and analysis patterns in their models. However, both Martin Fowler (2001b) and Joshua Kerievsky (2001) believe that developers should consider easing into the application of a pattern, to apply it gently. This reflects AM's value of *Simplicity.* In other words, if you SUSPECT that a pattern is applicable, you should model it in such a way as to implement the minimal functionality that you need today but that makes it easy to refactor/rework later if required. When it becomes clear that applying the full-

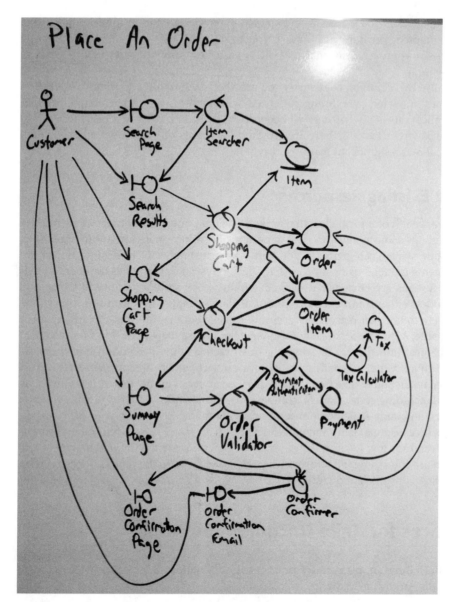

Figure 6.2 An example of a robustness diagram used in practice.

fledged pattern is the simplest approach possible, refactor your work. In other words, don't over-model.

For example: You may recognize a good spot in your design to apply the GoF's *Strategy* pattern (Gamma, Helm, Johnson, and Vlissides 1995), but at the moment you only have two algorithms to implement. The simplest approach might be to encapsulate each strategy in its own class and build an operation that chooses them appropriately and passes them the appropriate input. This is a partial implementation of

Strategy that leaves you in a position to refactor your design if more algorithms need to be implemented, yet does not require you to build all the scaffolding that *Strategy* requires—an approach that enables you to ease into applying the pattern when it makes sense to.

There are two common challenges you are likely to run into adopting this practice. First, many modelers who are experienced with patterns will often jump right into their application—it's what they've been doing for years, so they'll need to learn to rein themselves in. Second, there are hundreds of very good patterns available to you. Clearly, there is a significant learning curve.

Reuse Existing Resources

There is a wealth of information that agile modelers can take advantage of by reusing them. Perhaps some analysis or design patterns are appropriate for you to apply gently to your system. Or perhaps you can take advantage of an existing enterprise requirements model, business process models, physical data models, or even models of how systems are currently deployed within your user community. It's true that these models either don't exist or are out of date in many organizations, but you're often likely to uncover reasonably accurate models with a bit of research. Remember the principle, *Maximize Stakeholder Investment,* and reuse the wheel; don't reinvent it.

The biggest impediment to adopting this practice is the perception that there are few high-quality items applicable to your project which are available for reuse. However, when you realize that there is a wide variety of things that you can reuse on a project, including code, models, components, frameworks, patterns, documentation templates, and large-scale domain components (Ambler 1999), then your list of candidate resources dramatically increases. The "not invented here" (NIH) syndrome is often blamed for low levels of reuse, but my experience is that agile developers will readily reuse something if it addresses a problem relevant to the project they are working on and is of sufficient quality.

Practices for Agile Documentation

AM defines three supplementary practices that pertain to the creation of permanent models and/or documentation:

1. Discard Temporary Models
2. Formalize Contract Models
3. Update Only When It Hurts

Discard Temporary Models

The vast majority of the models that you create are temporary/working models—design sketches, low fidelity prototypes, index cards, potential architecture/design alternatives, and so on—models that have fulfilled their purpose but no longer add value. Models quickly become out of sync with the code and with each other, and there is nothing wrong with that. You must then make the decision to synchronize the models, if doing so adds value to your project, or to simply discard them because the investment to update the models won't be recouped by the value of having done so (there's negative payback).

A complementary practice is *Update Only When It Hurts* (see that section later in this chapter) because if you found that you haven't needed to update a model for a long time, then it was likely a temporary model but you didn't realize it at the time.

WARNING **Not Discarding Temporary Models Puts You at Risk**
If a model is temporary, then discard it the instant you are finished with it. This has several benefits. First, it reduces the clutter within your workspace. Second, it reduces the chance that someone will make a decision based on the (likely) out-of-date information that it contains. Third, it reduces the temptation to invest time updating the model.

This practice is often hampered by fear. Developers are afraid to discard a model because they believe they might need to go back to it at some point to determine what they were thinking at the time. So they'll put their models into a file, or into a pile on their desk, or take digital pictures of everything and store them in a directory. The interesting thing is that they rarely go back to review their models: Either they can't find them or they simply don't run into a situation where their older models help. If saving your temporary models is easy to do and it somehow makes you feel safe, then by all means do it, but at some point I strongly advise that you take the time to reflect on the value of doing this. I suspect you'll realize that saving your temporary models isn't worth the effort, so you might as well discard them at the first opportunity.

Formalize Contract Models

Contract models are often required when an external group controls an information resource that your system requires, such as a database, legacy application, or information service. A contract model is formalized with both parties mutually agreeing to it and ready to mutually change it over time if required. Examples of contract models include the detailed documentation of an application programming interface (API), a file layout description, an XML DTD, or a physical data model describing a shared database. As with a legal contract, a contract model often requires you to invest significant resources to develop and maintain the contract to ensure that it's accurate and sufficiently detailed. Your goal is to minimize the number of contract models for your system to conform to the XP principle of traveling light. Note that you will usually use an electronic tool to develop a contract model because you must maintain the model over time.

The Internet is a perfect example of the success of formalized contract models. The basis of the Internet is a collection of well-defined protocols, such as File Transfer Protocol (FTP) and Hypertext Transfer Protocol (HTTP), and file formats such as Extensible Markup Language (XML) and Hypertext Markup Language (HTML). These protocols are file formats that are defined by standards bodies, in particular the World Wide Web Consortium (W3C), and documented at publicly available web sites. Each definition is effectively a contract model between tool vendors. The HTTP protocol defines how web browser software will interact with web server software—a multi-billion dollar effort whose basis is formalized contract models.

The biggest challenge when adopting this practice is the people issues involved with the effort—getting people from different groups to work together to create the model(s). Over-documentation can also be a problem, although one you can deal with by following the advice presented in Chapter 14, "Agile Documentation."

Update Only When It Hurts

You should update an artifact such as a model or document only when you absolutely need to, when not having the model updated is more painful than the effort of updating it. With this approach, you discover that you update a smaller number of models than you would have in the past, because the reality is that your models don't have to be perfect to provide value. Too much time and money is wasted trying to keep artifacts in sync with one another—in particular, models with each other and with source code—time and money that could be better spent developing new software. Software evolves too quickly, making synchronization of artifacts a nearly an impossible task to begin with. Remember the principle, *Maximize Stakeholder Investment* and the Agile Alliance's (2001a) preference for working software over comprehensive documentation.

For example: Compare the UML class diagram (Rumbaugh, Jacobson, and Booch 1999) in Figure 6.3 with the data model shown in Figure 6.4 (Reingruber and Gregory 1994). They're not perfectly consistent with one another; the class diagram indicates that a customer has an address, yet the data model indicates that customers have one or more addresses. The data model also indicates that two relationships exist between orders and addresses, orders have a ship to address and potentially a different bill to address, yet we don't see any indication of that sort of relationship in the class diagram at all. Should we update the diagrams so they are consistent with one another? The class diagram is simple, so it's likely that it has already been superceded by another artifact (likely source code), and it's hand-drawn, so it may have already been discarded. If the model has been superceded by code, it's likely that the programmer(s) have already figured out that the class diagram wasn't perfect, if for the simple fact that it was inconsistent with both the user interface requirements captured by the essential UI prototype (Constantine and Lockwood 1999) in Figure 6.5 and the data model—which appear to be in sync with each other. It's likely that developers quickly sketched the class diagram as they were exploring a potential implementation strategy for the business classes to support placing an order. They very likely never intended to update the diagram, or keep it once they had written code from it, so they only made

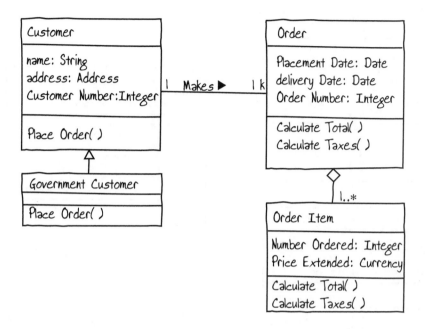

Figure 6.3 A UML class diagram.

it accurate enough for their needs and didn't bother to update it when they got into the details of the source code and database schema. Therefore, it doesn't hurt enough to justify updating this class diagram, so I wouldn't recommend investing any time in doing so.

Figure 6.5 shows an essential UI prototype that depicts the requirements for a screen/page. If, however, developers who were unfamiliar with the existing code and database schema were making decisions based on the class diagram, perhaps they are working on order fulfillment functionality; then you might want to update the class diagrams. Having consistent models and documentation is the best way to ensure that the two groups of developers are developing to the same vision, right? *Wrong!* If you want various groups to work to the same vision, they need to communicate effectively with one another, to collaborate with each other to define and work to their shared vision. Yes, documentation is one way for people to communicate, but as you'll see in Chapter 8, "Communication," it is one of the least effective ways to do so. You'd be much better advised to get the two groups of developers talking with one another than you would be to synchronize your artifacts—not only will you come to a common understanding faster, you'll likely invest fewer resources doing so. As you saw in Chapter 1, "Introduction," one of the principles of the agile development methodologies such as AM is that the most efficient and effective method of conveying information to and within a development team is face-to-face conversation (Agile Alliance

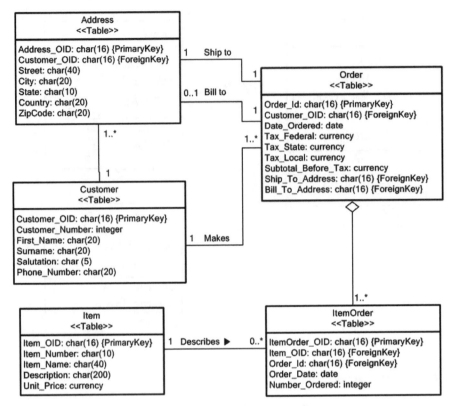

Figure 6.4   A start at a physical data model for SWA Online.

2001a).

   When you first adopt this practice, the most difficult part of it is to become comfortable with artifacts getting out of sync with one another, to wait until it really does start to become inconvenient for you. Many organizations, particularly ones with strong review cultures or ones with sophisticated prescriptive processes, have difficulty adopting this practice at first as it goes against their current tendency to keep artifacts up-to-date with one another. The good news is that this practice is enhanced by the principle of traveling light—the less permanent models and documentation that you choose to maintain, the less painful it is to update them when changes are required.

Practices Concerning Your Motivation

AM defines two practices that explore your potential motivations for modeling:

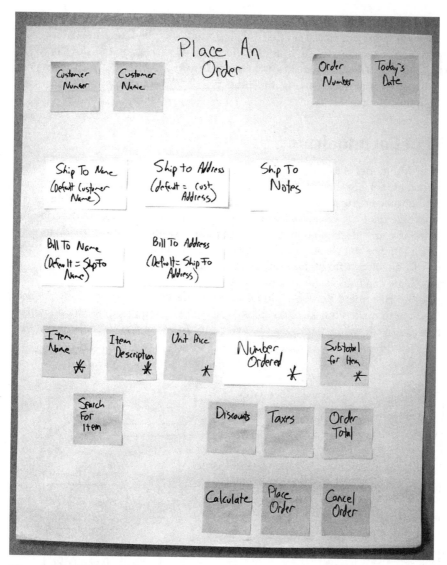

Figure 6.5   An essential UI prototype depicting the requirements for a screen/page.

1. Model to Understand
2. Model to Communicate

Model to Understand

The most important application of modeling is to explore the problem space, to identify and analyze the requirements for the system, or to compare and contrast potential

design alternatives to identify the potentially simplest solution that meets the requirements. Following this practice you often develop small, simple diagrams that focus on
one aspect of your software, such as the life cycle of a class or the flow between
screens, diagrams that you often throw away once you are finished with them. You
will do this with others, following the practice *Model with Others*, often in quick
impromptu modeling sessions.

Model to Communicate

One reason you model is to communicate with people external to your team or to create a contract model (see the practice *Formalize Contract Models*). For example, you may
need to communicate the intended scope of your project to senior management, using
a UML use case diagram or a workflow diagram. You may also need to describe the
architecture of your system as part of the system documentation you provide to your
system maintenance developers (a topic discussed in detail in Chapter 14). Or you
may want to develop a flow chart, an example of which is shown in Figure 6.6, to
explain the logic of a use case to a co-worker.

Because the customers for some models are outside your team, you may need to
invest the time to make your model(s) look "pretty" by using electronic tools such as
word processors, drawing packages, or even sophisticated CASE tools. However,

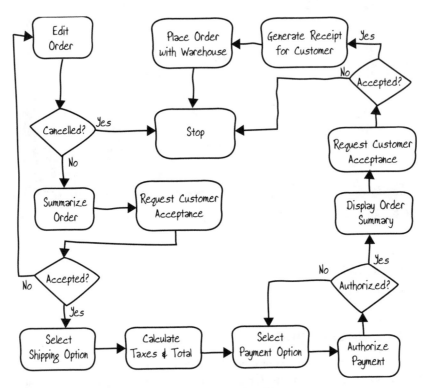

Figure 6.6   A flow chart that depicts the Place-An-Order use case.

remember the principle *Model with a Purpose* and first identify why you are creating this model and for whom. By knowing your audience and through working closely with them, you will be able to determine the most appropriate format for your model (remember the principle *Content is More Important Than Representation*).

An interesting side effect of this practice is that it helps to build a common vocabulary within your team and with your project stakeholders. It also helps to set expectations with your project stakeholders and provide an opportunity for you to build support for your project efforts.

Really Good Ideas

There are several practices that are not officially part of Agile Modeling, but when applied to a project can improve your efforts immensely. In particular, in Part 3 of this book you will see that refactoring (Fowler 1999) and test-first design (Beck 2000) are important aspects of eXtreme Programming that can be used to enhance AM's practices. These additional practices are:

- Know Your Tools
- Refactoring
- Test-First Design

Know Your Tools

Software development products, such as diagramming tools or modeling tools, have a wide variety of features. If you are going to use a modeling tool, then you should understand its features, knowing when to and when not to use them. The implication is that we should give developers adequate training in a tool and the opportunity to learn how to use their tools effectively on the job.

Refactoring

Refactoring (Fowler 1999) is a coding practice in which you make small changes, called refactorings, to your code to support new requirements or to keep your design as simple as possible. An important thing to understand about a refactoring is that it preserves the semantics of your code—in other words, you make a change and your code still works. For example: If you change the name of an operation of a class, all the other code within your system that invokes that operation will now refer to the new name, not the old one. The best way to think of refactoring is that it is a disciplined way to improve both the quality of your code and your detailed design. Refactoring is an enabler of AM practices such as *Create Simple Content* and *Model in Small Increments* and is discussed in detail in Chapter 18, "Agile Modeling Throughout the XP Lifecycle."

Test-First Design

Test-first design is an XP practice (Beck 2000) where you write your testing code before you write your business code. Always. From the point of view of AM, the primary advantage of this approach is that it forces developers to think through their code before they write it, to consider the detailed design of the code. When developers follow this practice, they can spend significantly less time working on detailed design models because their test-first design efforts effectively replace this style of modeling. Following this approach, agile developers quickly discover whether or not their ideas actually work—the tests will either validate their models or not—providing rapid feedback regarding the ideas captured within the models. Test-first design and its relationship with AM are discussed in detail in Chapter 18.

How to Schedule AM Practices on Your Project

Gotcha! Developers apply AM practices minute-by-minute; you wouldn't see tasks such as "Create Simple Content" or "Model to Understand" on your project schedule. Yes, you may include the occasional modeling session, described in Chapter 13, "Agile Modeling Sessions," on your schedule but these are activities, not AM practices.

TIP Read Adaptive Software Development (ASD)
In the book *Adaptive Software Development* (Dorset House Publishing 2000), Jim Highsmith rethinks the process by which software should be developed. If you had hoped to include AM practices as tasks in your project schedule, then I strongly suggest reading this book because he has some very interesting and relevant things to say about the current state of project planning practices, many of which are spectacularly dysfunctional.

Order from Chaos: How the AM Practices Fit Together

So much of what we call management consists in making it difficult for people to work.

—Peter Drucker

The practices of AM are synergistic in the fact that they support and often enable one another. They are chaordic (Hock 1999) in that they define behavior that harmoniously blends order and chaos—more on this at the end of the chapter. To make AM work effectively you need to have an understanding of how its practices fit together. Figure 7.1 depicts the relationships between AM's practices, organizing them into seven categories. The first four categories—Validation, Iterative and Incremental, Teamwork, and Simplicity—consolidate AM's core practices described in Chapter 5, "Core Practices," the ones that you must adopt in full to be truly able to claim that you are agile modeling. The supplementary practices, described in Chapter 6, "Supplementary Practices," in turn are consolidated by the Documentation, Motivation, and Productivity categories. Let's start by considering how the core practices relate to one another within each category, then we'll examine the supplementary practices within each category, then we'll discuss how the categories enable one another.

The Core Practices

AM's core practices are organized into four categories:

1. Teamwork
2. Iterative and Incremental

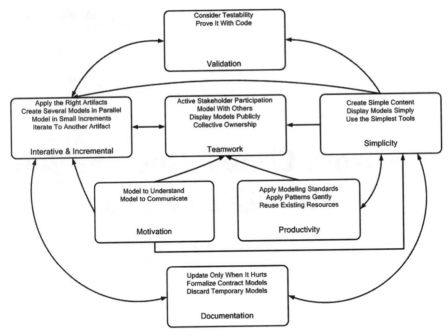

Figure 7.1   How AM's practices relate to one another.

3. Simplicity

4. Validation

Practices for Effective Teamwork

There are four practices in the Teamwork category—*Active Stakeholder Participation, Model with Others, Display Models Publicly,* and *Collective Ownership.* The practice *Active Stakeholder Participation* is critical to your success because it is your project stakeholders for whom you are building your system. They are the people whose requirements you need to understand and fulfill. In other words, you need to work closely with your stakeholders—something that is supported by the practice *Model with Others.* Your stakeholders are included in this "others" category. When there are several people involved in a modeling effort, at least one of which should be a project stakeholder and another a developer, you are in a position where you can work together synergistically by benefiting from each others' strengths and counteracting each others' weaknesses. An agile modeler whose expertise is in business process modeling and business rule definitions may miss information that someone with a focus on structural modeling techniques such as UML class diagrams or data models would pick up on. Similarly, a direct user of your system would provide different information to your team than would senior management. The point is that not only do you want to actively work with your project stakeholders, you also want to do so in a team environment so that multiple points of view and expertise are taken into account.

The practice *Collective Ownership* enhances teamwork because when a single person "owns" a model, that person quickly becomes a bottleneck for your modeling efforts; however, when anyone is allowed to work on a model, people can easily work on it together as a team. The practice *Display Models Publicly* makes it easy for people to look back and forth between the models, considering the information that the models convey all at once, enhancing collaborative efforts between them. This of course assumes that the models are within sight of each other, or at least the ones that you are currently working on are close to one another, a topic that I cover in detail in Chapter 11.

Practices for Iterative and Increment Development

The Iterative and Incremental category of AM practices includes *Apply The Right Artifact(s)*, *Create Several Models in Parallel*, *Iterate to Another Artifact*, and *Model in Small Increments*. Each artifact, no matter what it is, has its own strengths and weaknesses and no single model is sufficient to describe major aspects of your project such as its requirements or its architecture. For example: You often need a combination of use cases, business rule definitions, and technical requirement definitions to explore the requirements for your system. It is very unlikely that your project stakeholders will tell all of their usage requirements at once for your use cases, then switch gears to tell you about all of their business policies to be captured as business rules, then switch gears again to tell you about all of their nonfunctional needs that should be captured as technical requirements. Instead, they'll tell you their requirements as they think of them and will often go back to what they said earlier to provide details or even to change their minds. Your requirements identification efforts can often be very dynamic, and similarly so can your analysis, architecture, and design efforts. I believe the dynamism is the result of the way that people think; our brains seem to connect information in an apparently chaotic manner. The result is that ideas seem to "pop out of thin air" or we have an "a-ha! experience." Agile modelers recognize that people think in this dynamic manner, particularly collaborative groups of people, and act accordingly. They *Create Several Models in Parallel* to collect the wide range of information they are gathering. This practice is clearly supported by the practice *Apply The Right Artifact(s)* as well as *Iterate to Another Artifact*. You may be capturing information about a usage requirement in a use case when your project stakeholder(s) begin discussing their needs for an editing screen, something better specified by an essential user interface (UI) prototype or traditional UI prototype. Iterating back and forth between artifacts, one of which may very well be program source code, is enabled by the practice *Model in Small Increments*. You will typically work on a little bit of one artifact, then another, then another, and so on.

Practices That Promote Simplicity

The *Simplicity* category contains the core practices of *Create Simple Content*, *Depict Models Simply*, and *Use the Simplest Tools*. The two practices *Create Simple Content* and *Depict Models Simply* focus on model simplicity, and often go hand-in-hand during modeling. By focusing on how to depict something simply, modelers often discover how to make whatever it is that they are modeling simpler. For example: I have been involved in the development of several persistence layers (Ambler 2001d), software conceptually similar to an Enterprise JavaBeans (EJB) persistence container that encapsulates persistent storage from your domain objects, and as a result have been involved in some very complex architecture and design efforts. During one of them we were trying to figure out how to create a simple diagram that we could provide to application developers to help explain how to work with the persistence layer. In the process we discovered a refactoring to make our design easier to understand. Simplicity of process is enhanced by the practice *Use the Simplest Tools*. The simpler a tool is, the easier it is to work with. This decreases the barriers to entry for working on your models and thereby increases the chance that other people will in fact do so, including your project stakeholders. By using simple tools, you increase the chance that you will depict those models simply. Furthermore, when you use simple/low-fidelity tools such as index cards, Post-It notes, and whiteboards, you actively experience the effectiveness of simple tools—subconsciously reinforcing the concept that the simplest solution can work very well, a mindset that will reveal itself in a simpler design for the system that you are building.

Practices To Validate Your Work

The Validation category consists of two core practices: *Consider Testability* and *Prove It with Code*. A philosophy that I have always benefited from is if you can't test it then you shouldn't build it, and that "anything you can build you can test." This philosophy leads me to not only consider testing when I am modeling systems, but also to actively seek feedback about my models. I actually generalize this to consider testability of all the artifacts that I create and to actively validate all types of artifacts, but that's beyond the scope of AM. By considering testability when I am modeling, I am far more likely to model something that is testable, and by actively seeking to prove a model with code as soon as possible, I quickly show that my system is testable.

The Supplementary Practices

AM's supplementary practices are organized into three categories:

1. Documentation
2. Motivation
3. Productivity

Practices Relevant to Documentation

The Documentation category consists of three supplementary practices: *Discard Temporary Models*, *Formalize Contract Models*, and *Update Only When It Hurts*. Your requirements, your understanding of those requirements, and potentially even your understanding of your solution change throughout your project (remember the principle *Embrace Change*). Many of your project artifacts, including models and documents, will need to evolve to reflect these changes. As you'll see with the discussion of agile documentation in Chapter 7, one of the best ways to ensure that you are taking an agile approach to your models and documents is to update them only when it hurts. When following this practice, if you find that a model isn't being updated, it is an indication that the model may not provide your team with much value. If the model doesn't provide value, then it should be considered temporary and discarded. However, remember that contract models, models that define an interface between your system and another, are not likely to change much over time, but because of their importance they are not candidates for disposal. In short, if a noncontract model isn't being updated over time, it is a good indication that you don't need that model.

Practices of Motivation

The two practices *Model to Communicate* and *Model to Understand* fall into the Motivation category. These two practices are not closely related. Sometimes you create a model to explore or understand an issue, sometimes you create one to communicate your ideas to someone else, and sometimes you create a model for both purposes. However, as you saw in Figure 7.1, these two practices together enable two other categories of practices, a topic discussed later in this chapter.

Practices That Increase Productivity

Finally, the Productivity category is composed of the practices *Apply Modeling Standards, Apply Patterns Gently,* and *Reuse Existing Resources.* The *Reuse Existing Resources* practice is in many ways a mindset, one that says I want to take the good work of others and benefit from it as best I can. This mindset promotes a willingness to apply patterns, which in my experience is one of the most productive forms of reuse available to developers because you are reusing the proven solutions of other developers (Ambler 1999). This mindset also promotes a willingness to follow modeling standards and guidelines; in fact standards and guidelines in general, promote consistency within your work. Yes, you write your own set of guidelines, and sometimes you do need to because of some unusual factor within your environment, but with a little bit of searching on the Internet, you can quickly turn up development guidelines such as those described at www.modelingstyle.info and www .codingstyle.info.

How the Categories Relate to One Another

Consider the practices of the Teamwork category. *Active Stakeholder Participation* is supported by the practices of the Simplicity category because simplicity lowers any barriers to participation. Participation is also enabled by the Iterative and Incremental practices, particularly *Create Several Models in Parallel* because it opens up more opportunities for stakeholders to get involved. The practices *Collective Ownership* and *Model with Others* are supported by the Motivation practices—your need to understand or communicate an issue often motivates people to work together—as well as the Simplicity practices, once again because they lower barriers to participation. *Display Models Publicly* is enhanced by the Productivity practices, following standards and applying patterns increases consistency and readability, and reuse of existing resources such as common architectural models provides a familiar base from which people can start with your models. *Collective Ownership* is supported by the Iterative and Incremental practices; in particular, *Create Several Models in Parallel* and *Iterate to Another Artifact* seem to promote several people working together on whatever models are appropriate at the time.

The practices of several other categories support the practices of the Simplicity category. The practice, *Depict Models Simply*, is enhanced by *Apply Modeling Standards* and *Apply Patterns Gently,* because both of these practices support modeling in a common language (your chosen standards and well-understood patterns). Simplicity practices are enhanced by the Documentation practices—when you *Update Only When It Hurts,* you are more likely to *Depict Models Simply* and *Create Simple Content* because you aren't needlessly adding information to your models.

Now consider the Iterative and Incremental practices. The Teamwork practices clearly support these practices. With several people involved, there is a greater chance that someone will know what the right artifact is to apply to your situation, enabling you to iterate it as needed. The Validation practices give you the courage to take an incremental approach, particularly when you *Prove It with Code.* And by keeping testability in the back of your mind, you are more likely to want to work on several models at once, and iterate between them, because testing issues will likely need to be captured in a variety of views. The Documentation practices also promote an incremental approach, particularly *Update Only When It Hurts,* although *Formalize Contract Models* often goes against the incremental grain because you want to baseline interfaces with other systems as early as possible. *Iterate to Another Artifact* and *Discard Temporary Models* are complimentary because you often want to work on a model and then move one once it has served its purpose. The Simplicity practices are also important to this category. When you *Use the Simplest Tools,* it makes it easier to iterate back and forth between artifacts. You use minimal time starting the tool, and a focus on simple content and simple depiction ensures that you have a minimal learning curve remembering what the model communicates. Finally, the Motivation practices lead you to work on several models at once because you typically require several views to communicate or understand the complexities of a system, and you will need to iterate back and forth between appropriate artifacts to do so effectively.

The Validation practices are supported by the Simplicity practices—when you *Create Simple Content* and *Depict Models Simply,* you make it much easier to *Consider Testability.* The Iterative and Incremental practices also promote the Validation practices. For example: When you *Iterate to Another Artifact,* a likely candidate to iterate to is source code, so that you can show that your model actually works.

The Productivity practices are enhanced by the Simplicity practices: It is easier to *Apply Patterns Gently* when you are working with simple models; it is easier to *Apply Modeling Standards* when you *Depict Models Simply;* and it is easier to *Reuse Existing Resources* such as enterprise requirements models or common architectural models when those models are simple and easy to understand.

The Documentation practices are supported by both the *Simplicity* and the *Iterative and Incremental* practices. The simpler your documentation is, the easier it is to work with. If your documentation is easy to understand, it gives you the courage to *Update Only When It Hurts* because you know that you will be able to do so easily. Documentation that is harder to understand is a greater risk to your project because you can't be sure that you can update it as required. The practices *Update Only When It Hurts* and *Discard Temporary Models* clearly work only in environments promoted by practices such as *Iterate to Another Artifact* and *Model in Small Increments*.

Chaos and Order: Chaordic

Here we are at the end of the seventh chapter, and the process of Agile Modeling (AM) has been fully described to you, yet there isn't a defined process for you to follow. There has been no advice along the lines of "Create diagram A, then write this documentation, and fill out form B. Your next step is to create models C, D, and E ensuring that they are consistent with one another and that you maintain full traceability between them. Finally, use these models to create diagram F which is what your programmers need to do their jobs." That's a prescriptive process fit for someone with a cookbook mindset, not someone who aspires to be an agile developer. In Chapter 1, I specifically stated that AM is not a prescriptive process, instead I defined it in the following manner AM is a chaordic, practice-based methodology for effective modeling and documentation of software-based systems. The AM methodology is a collection of practices, guided by principles and values, that is applied by software professionals on a daily basis. Chaordic? Practice based? Let's examine these two concepts in detail, because they are clearly different than the vast majority of other modeling methodologies that you are accustomed to.

Dee Hock (1999), founder of VISA, provides the following definition for the term chaordic:

> **chaordic** [kay'-ordic], *adj. fr. E. chaos and order.*
> 1. the behavior of any self-governing organism, organization, or system that harmoniously blends characteristics of order and chaos. 2. patterned in a way dominated by neither chaos nor order. 3. characteristic of the fundamental organizing principles of evolution and nature.

In his book, *Birth of the Chaordic Age*, Hock provides advice for designing chaordic organizations. His experience is that forming a chaordic organization begins with an intensive search for purpose, then proceeds to principles, people, and concept, and only then to structure and practice. I've taken a modified approach to Hock's; after all, I am defining a methodology and not an organization, starting with the goals described in Chapter 1, "Introduction," and the values of Chapter 2, "Agile Modeling Values." These were used as a foundation for the principles of Chapters 3, "Core Principles," and 4, "Supplementary Principles," which drove the practices of Chapters 5 and 6. The concepts of organizational concept and structure are clearly outside the scope of the AM effort, although I will touch on the types of people that are well suited to become agile modelers and even agile developers in Chapter 12, "Agile Modeling Teams," when I discuss agile modeling teams.

Why is the concept of chaordic important? Because it provides a conceptual framework for a practice-based framework such as AM. On the surface AM appears chaotic, unable to produce anything of substance. Frankly, if you were to apply AM's practices at random this would very likely be the case. But you wouldn't do that, would you? AM's principles provide insight as to when and how to apply its practices effectively, and the material presented in this chapter described how the practices fit together in a synergistic whole. Yes, you still have to apply each practice when it is appropriate and in a manner that makes sense, and my discussion in the previous two chapters should provide sufficient background for you to get started. Over time, as you gain experience agile modeling you will gain greater insight into AM's practices, discovering nuances that aren't readily apparent at first.

A practice-based methodology such as AM can appear chaotic at times, particularly to people unfamiliar with it or who are not actively involved with the project. But chaotic isn't the right word because, when followed properly, AM produces significant results. AM supports a good form of chaos, one that is steered, rather than directed, by people working together guided by common values and principles—one that promotes a focus on effective and efficient work habits. Thus AM supports order within your project. Chaos and order: Chaordic.

Looking Ahead

In Part Two I cover issues relevant to successful application of AM within your organization. I start by exploring communication, an important success factor in software development, and follow with a discussion of how to build an effective cultural environment to support AM. Issues such as the use of simple tools and how to be effective at writing documentation are also covered. Other factors important to the success of AM that I discuss include how to create an agile work area, how to build an agile development team, and how to hold agile modeling sessions. I also examine the UML to dispel some very harmful misconceptions that fester within the IT industry and finally, examine modeling with a generic agile software development process.

Agile Modeling
in Practice

This part explores critical issues that pertain to the practical application of Agile Modeling within your organization. This section includes the following chapters:

- **Chapter 8: Communication.** Because modeling is an activity that depends on, and supports, communication, this chapter explores the nature of communication and how to become an effective communicator.

- **Chapter 9: Nurturing An Agile Culture.** This chapter examines cultural and organizational issues that pertain to the successful application of AM.

- **Chapter 10: Using the Simplest Tools Possible?** AM implores you to use the simplest tool(s) to get the job done. However, the simplest tool may not always be a simple one. This chapter discusses the potential modeling tools that are at your disposal.

- **Chapter 11: Agile Work Areas.** Your work environment can greatly affect your productivity as an agile modeler, and this chapter discusses how to organize a workspace conducive to AM.

- **Chapter 12: Agile Modeling Teams.** This chapter explores critical personnel issues pertaining to AM.

- **Chapter 13: Agile Modeling Sessions.** As an agile modeler you still need to hold modeling sessions, and this chapter presents strategies for doing so in an effective manner.

- **Chapter 14: Agile Documentation.** Documentation is an important part of software development, and this chapter describes how to take an agile approach to writing documentation.

- **Chapter 15: The UML and Beyond.** This chapter examines several of the misconceptions and misunderstandings that surround the UML and presents a realistic and practical viewpoint regarding this important industry standard.

Communication

Don't spec the heck out of it.

Communication is one of the fundamental values of AM, although it would be more accurate to say that *effective communication* is what AM deems critical to your success. What is communication? With respect to AM, communication is the act of transmitting information between individuals. Why is communication an issue worth discussing? Because the need to communicate effectively pervades software development, operations, and support. Developers and users must communicate. Developers and operations staff must communicate. Developers and management must communicate. Developers and . . . well, you get the idea.

In this chapter, I explore the issues that surround communication and, in particular, focus on how to become more agile in your documentation efforts. For many people, modeling and documentation go hand in hand, a concept that I argue is questionable at best. This practice is a topic that needs to be addressed. This chapter is organized into the following sections:

- How do we communicate?
- Factors that affect communication
- Communication and Agile Modeling
- Effective communication

How Do We Communicate?

In *Agile Software Development*, Alistair Cockburn (2002) describes various modes of communication that people may choose to apply when working together. Figure 8.1, modified from that book, shows a graph that compares the effectiveness of these modes of communication with the richness of the communication channel employed. The two arcs are interesting; the left-most one lists communications options for documenting (paper includes electronic media such as HTML that could be rendered to paper) and the other communication options for modeling. The relative value of these options is of course dependent on the situation—perhaps video conversation (video conferencing) is more effective between you and John than a face-to-face conversation, whereas the exact opposite is true between you and Sally.

Cockburn contends that the most effective communication is person-to-person, face-to-face, particularly when enhanced by a shared modeling medium such as a whiteboard, flip chart, paper, or index cards. As you move away from this situation, perhaps by removing the shared medium or by no longer being face-to-face, you experience a drop in communication effectiveness. As the richness of your communication channel cools, you lose physical proximity and the conscious and subconscious clues that such proximity provides. You also lose the benefit of multiple modalities, the ability to communicate through techniques other than words, such as gestures and facial expressions. The ability to change vocal inflection and timing is also lost; people not

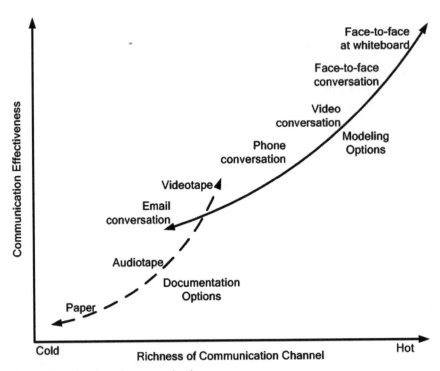

Figure 8.1   Modes of communication.

only communicate via the words they say, but how they say those words. Cockburn points out that a speaker can emphasize what they say, thus changing the way they communicate, by speeding up, slowing down, pausing, or changing tones. Finally, the ability to answer questions in real time, the point that distinguishes the modeling-options curve from the documentation-options curve, is important because questions provide insight into how well the information is understood by the listener.

Factors That Affect Communication

There are several factors that affect communication, including:

Physical proximity. The closer people are to one another, the greater the opportunities for communication. At one end of the spectrum, two people can work side-by-side, pair programming at the same workstation, and at the other end of the spectrum, two people can be in different buildings.

Temporal proximity. Whether or not two people are working at the same time affects communication. You may be separated from some of your co-workers by several time zones; it is quite common for North American firms to outsource development work to Asian or European companies or even simply by different personal schedules. I once commuted from Toronto to San Francisco to work on a development contract, spending four days a week in San Francisco, although keeping my internal clock on Toronto time. As a morning person, I woke up at 3:00 in the morning San Francisco time; however, many of my co-workers were night people and would typically work until 3:00 or 4:00 in the morning. We found this quite effective. I would work during the day and stay at the office until they started to arrive, talking face-to-face with them as needed. I then left for my hotel, slept, and started dealing with email immediately upon waking. This allowed me to find out what they had worked on during the night and then input via email where needed. It wasn't ideal, but we made it work.

Amicability. Cockburn (2002) believes that amicability, someone's willingness to hear the thoughts of another person with good will and to speak without malice, is an important success factor. The greater the amicability, the more high-quality information can be shared and less information is concealed. Amicability is closely linked to the trust that people have for one another and the sense of community they share. Cockburn reports that sometimes amicability can run too high; people can be so worried about offending their colleagues that they are afraid to disagree with them or afraid to take the initiative for fear of being perceived as glory seekers.

Tools. Simple tools—including whiteboards, sticky notes, flip charts, and index cards—are easy to work with and are both flexible and non-threatening. As a result, they are likely to be used in team situations, because there is little opportunity to embarrass yourself by revealing you are not adept with the tool. More complicated tools often prove to be barriers to communication, particularly those CASE tools that are single-user because one person is separated from the conversation when using the tool. (There are some collaborative CASE tools, as shown in Table 8.1.) Furthermore, tools that require significant training reduce the opportunities to work together with others because they may not know how to work with the tool.

Anxiety. Individuals may experience anxiety about certain types of communication. Some people love to speak on the phone; others avoid it. Some people prefer email; others avoid it because their writing skills are not very good. When people collaborate, they need to find techniques that they are comfortable with or, at a minimum, can learn to tolerate for the duration.

When people work closely together, both physically and temporally, they have an opportunity for what Cockburn calls *osmotic communication*—indirect information transfer through overhearing conversations or simply noticing things that happen around them. Osmotic communication can often be beneficial. I've lost track of the number of times I have been working away and subconsciously picked up valuable information. For example, I've discovered that someone had finished their current task, that something wasn't working as expected, or even that management was thinking about canceling the project. Osmotic communication can often be harmful, particularly if another group of people is being rowdy nearby or if you're picking up false rumors, like the one about management canceling the project.

TIP **Can't Get a Dedicated Space? Rent a House**
Many organizations are short on working space, particularly those that are growing quickly or those that are established in expensive areas. I once worked at an Internet startup that was doubling in size every two months. They were so tight for space that my desk, along with those of several others, ended up in the kitchen area for two months. I worked for a company in the business district of London that was so short of space that we often traveled for several miles to find an available meeting room (it often took hours for us to hold a one-hour meeting which was often unnecessary). Although both of these organizations made do, they weren't effective doing so. Another organization, run by a friend of mine, needed dedicated space for a software development effort. Realizing that he didn't have sufficient space at his current office, he started searching for a temporary location for his team. He needed space for nine months for this effort and discovered that he could lease a house for one year for a fraction of the cost of real office space. He installed whiteboards and better lighting in the unfinished basement. Throughout the house, desks were set up that had fully networked workstations and phones. The lesson to be learned is that if you think outside the box, you can get the workspace that you need. Choose to succeed.

Communication and Agile Modeling

Effective communication is a fundamental requirement for agile modeling. You need to recognize that you have several communication options available to you, as Figure 8.1

Table 8.1 Communication Technologies

TECHNOLOGY	DESCRIPTION	EXAMPLE(S)
Collaborative modeling tools	CASE tools that enable several developers to simultaneously work on one or more models with real-time updates of those models.	• Cittera by Canyon Blue (www.canyonblue.com) • Describe by Embarcadero Technologies (www.embarcadero.com)
Collaborative writing tools	Word processing tools that enable several people to simultaneously write a document with real-time updates of that document.	• NetPerfect by Corel Corporation (www.corel.com)
Discussion tools	Tools such as email, newsgroups, mailing lists, instant messaging, and chat rooms that enable transmission of text messages, and other attachments.	• The Agile Modeling mailing list (www.agilemodeling.com/feedback.htm) • IRCPlus (www.ircplus.com)
Personal video	A camera and software is installed on your workstation to enable video conversation between you and someone with a similar video setup.	• LogiTech QuickCam (www.logitech.com)
Version control tools	Software tools used to check in/out, define, and manage versions of project artifacts.	• Microsoft SourceSafe (www.microsoft.com) • Concurrent Versions System (CVS) (www.cvshome.org)
Virtual meeting tools	Tools that enable communication between several people in different physical locations.	• eRoom (www.eroom.com) • Click to Meet (www.cuseeme.com)

shows. You must choose the best communication option for your current situation. Sometimes that will be email, sometimes it will be face-to-face communication, and sometimes it will be writing a document. Furthermore, you want to use technology effectively; as always, the principle to *Use the Simplest Tools* applies. Table 8.1 describes several communication technologies available to you. Web sites such as www.collaboration-tools.com are an excellent resource if you're looking for new collaboration tools and techniques.

Effective Communication

When is communication most effective? When people are willing to work together and do what it takes to get the job done. AM's principle of *Open and Honest Communication* is important. If you don't trust the information that you receive or, for that matter, the people who provide it to you, then your goal of effective communication is lost. The principle that *Everyone Can Learn from Everyone Else* is critical to your success, because it defines a mindset that enables communication. Those who believe they can learn something from the person(s) they are communicating with are much more receptive than those who believe otherwise. This principle has its roots in AM's value of *Humility*, a value that time and again proves to be a significant success factor for developers.

Effective communicators realize that the goal is to share information, and that this information sharing is typically a two-way street. For example, I recently attended a meeting where members of my development team met with members of a team that operated another system that we needed to integrate with. Our goal was to define a contract model that described the interface to this system, something that ended up being a simple file transfer. For the most part, we talked and drew diagrams on the whiteboard. My team had brought a deployment diagram with us that depicted how we currently believed the two systems would work together, and as a group, we negotiated changes to the overall approach. Both teams came to the meeting with the desire to work together. We knew that we needed the other team, and the other team knew that their job was to support groups like mine. Everyone was focused on working together. That meant that we needed to communicate well. Attitude counts.

Another important success factor is your ability to pick the right mode of communication. In the preceding example we chose to get the right people in a room to discuss the issue face-to-face and work things out together. When necessary, we drew on the whiteboard, even drawing our deployment diagram. Most importantly, we talked and we listened. Yes, we could have taken a different approach. I have no doubt that we could have emailed back and forth to one another. We could also have written documents and sent them back and forth. The point is that we chose not to. We had the opportunity to use a superior form of communication—face-to-face communication at a whiteboard—and we used that technique. It was fast, it was effective, and it was agile.

Finally, you need a positive view of documentation. Documentation can either be good or bad. You should stick with the good and avoid the bad. Documentation can come in many forms, including both paper and video recordings, as you saw in Figure 8.1. The point is that you shouldn't forget that documentation can be versatile and not painful to create. As you'll see in Chapter 14, "Agile Documentation," Agile Modeling's fundamental message on documentation is that you should write it only when it's your best choice and only when it adds the best possible value to your project.

Nurturing an Agile Culture

You can be agile or you can be fragile.

Your organization's culture, and in particular your department's culture, must be conducive to Agile Modeling for your team to be effective. If your culture doesn't support agile development methods like AM and, even worse, if it is hostile toward them, then your chances of success at applying AM on your project are greatly diminished. What can you do to nurture an "AM-positive culture" within your organization? My advice is to:

- Overcome the misconceptions that surround modeling
- Think small
- Loosen up a bit
- Rigidly support project stakeholder rights and responsibilities
- Rethink presentations to stakeholders

Overcome the Misconceptions That Surround Modeling

Many software professionals, developers and managers alike, have serious misconceptions about modeling that reduce their effectiveness. Let's discuss these issues and explore how they are addressed by the values, principles, and practices of AM.

Misconception #1: Model = Documentation

This is very likely the most devastating misconception about modeling. It provides developers with an excuse not to model under the guise that they don't want to waste time writing useless documentation. This decision has the unfortunate consequence that many otherwise excellent software developers become little more than programming hacks, producing low quality, brittle systems. Furthermore, this issue has resulted in modeling being perceived as uninteresting. As a result, many developers avoid learning the modeling skills required to be successful. The reality is that the concepts of "model" and "document" are orthogonal—you can have models that aren't documents and documents that aren't models. A sketch on the back of a paper napkin is a model, as is a drawing on a whiteboard, a collection of Class Responsibility Collaboration (CRC) cards, or a low-fidelity user interface prototype built from flip chart paper and sticky notes. These are all valuable models, yet questionable as official documents. My experience is that modeling is a lot like planning: Just as the value is in the planning effort and not the actual plan itself, most of the value is in the modeling and not the model itself. The implication is that you can create a model that isn't part of your system's official documentation; instead you discard it once it has fulfilled its purpose. In reality you will discover that there are few models that you actually need to keep. You can safely follow the practice to *Discard Temporary Models*. Agile documentation practices are covered in detail in Chapter 14, "Agile Documentation."

Misconception #2: You Can Think Everything through from the Start

This misunderstanding is a holdover from the serial mindset prevalent in the 1970s to the mid-1980s, very often the period during which today's managers learned how to develop software. The impact is that projects often invest significant time trying to model everything up front in an effort to get it right, an effort often referred to as big design up front (BDUF). There is often a motivation to "freeze" requirements before coding starts, (see misconception #4) and "analysis paralysis" often sets in—the fear of moving forward until your models are perfect. Project teams that suffer from this myth often produce significant amounts of documentation instead of what their users actually want—working software that meets their needs in accordance to AM's principle—*Software is Your Primary Goal*. How do you overcome this problem? First, recognize that you can't think all the minutiae through. Second, recognize that in these environments, your coders likely have little respect for the efforts of your modelers anyway. A reasonable position considering that your modelers are often doing little of actual value. Your coders will likely take their own approach, claiming that the models don't reflect the realities of your environment. Third, recognize that no matter how good your initial specification is, it is destined to quickly become out of synch with your code and out of synch with itself even if you do evolve your models over time. The fundamental reality is that only your code is ever truly in sync with your code. Fourth, recognize that an iterative approach to software development—one in which you do a little modeling, some coding, some testing, and perhaps even deploy a small working version of your system—is the norm for software development. It's a fundamental principle of modern, heavy-weight software processes such as the Enterprise Unified Process (EUP) (Ambler 2001b) as well as agile processes such as eXtreme Programming (XP) (Beck 2000).

Misconception #3: Modeling Implies a Heavy-Weight (HW) Software Process

This misunderstanding is often related to misconception #1, that models imply documentation. Its impact is that project teams often abandon modeling altogether because the HW process becomes too complex or too burdensome for them. This assumption clearly does not have to be the case, as I hope this book shows. The reality is that you can model in an agile manner by developing simple models using simple tools. Your modeling efforts can be as light or as heavy as you choose to make them. You tailor your modeling process to meet the needs of your environment in accordance with the principle of *Local Adaptation*.

Misconception #4: You Must "Freeze" Requirements

This request often comes from senior managers who want to ensure that they know exactly what they're going to get from a project team. The good news is that by freezing your requirements early in the lifecycle they are likely to get exactly what they asked for. The bad news is that they likely won't get what they actually need. Change happens. As development progresses, your project stakeholders' understanding of the problem domain changes, their priorities change, and their vision of the solution also changes as they see the system evolve. It is a fundamental aspect of most software development efforts, in particular business application software development, that requirements change. AM advises that you accept this fact with its principle *Embrace Change*. Instead take an iterative and incremental approach to software development where you can act appropriately when your requirements evolve—you are much better advised to follow AM's practice *Model in Small Increments* than you are to freeze requirements.

Misconception #5: Your Design Is Carved in Stone

This misunderstanding is similar to the desire to freeze requirements. In this case, management wants to ensure that every developer marches to the same tune by following "the design." By freezing your design in place, you are unable to take advantage of knowledge gained as the project evolves. The result is that developers either build the wrong things, or they build the right things the wrong way to conform to "the design." Alternatively, they may simply ignore "the design" negating any possible benefits of the design efforts. Furthermore, developers are motivated to write significant amounts of documentation instead of actual software and to use documentation-oriented CASE tools instead of ones focused on implementation that are likely to provide real value to your project. Agile modelers expect to evolve their designs, often based on the feedback from following the practice *Prove it with Code* when your programming or database efforts show that your design isn't ideal. The reality is that nobody is perfect, even the best designers and neither is their work. Do you really want to carve imperfection into stone and not allow yourself to fix mistakes? Furthermore, if you don't freeze your requirements, by implication you cannot freeze your design—changes to your requirements will force changes to your design. Remember that your design isn't finished for a given release until you've shipped the code.

Misconception #6: You Must Use a CASE Tool

Modeling is often seen as a complex effort, and in many ways it is, but you can create effective yet simple models that only show critical information and not irrelevant details. Throughout this book I present examples of models created using simple tools such as index cards, sticky notes, flip-chart paper, and whiteboards. Figures 9.1 and 9.2 provide examples of such models. These models fulfilled their purpose and provided significant value to the efforts of the project team, showing that you can be successful following the practice, *Use the Simplest Tools*. Chapter 10, "Using the Simplest Tools Possible?" explores in detail how to use modeling tools effectively, including both low-technology tools and sophisticated CASE tools.

Misconception #7: Modeling Is a Waste of Time

Many novice developers entertain this misunderstanding, often because their education focused on how to write code and not on the full software development process. Their experiences as junior programmers focused solely on implementing code. These developers are forgoing an opportunity to dramatically increase their productivity as well as to learn skills that they can easily transfer between projects and organizations. The reality is that you are very often more productive sketching a diagram, developing a low-fidelity prototype, or creating a few index cards to think something through before you code it—you are following the practice *Model to Understand*. Productive developers often model before they code; they think and then they act. Furthermore, modeling is a great way to promote communication among team members and project stakeholders because you're talking through issues, coming to a better understanding of what needs to be built, and building bonds between everyone involved with the project in the process. In other words, you are following the practice *Model to Communicate*.

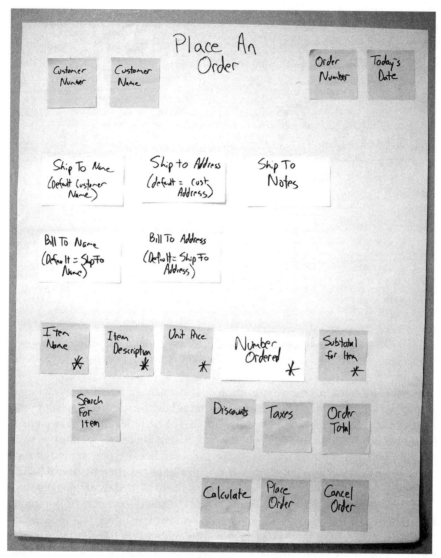

Figure 9.1 A low-fidelity prototype of a data input screen.

Misconception #8: The World Revolves Around Data Modeling

Many organizations hobble their new development efforts by starting with a data model. There are several reasons why this happens: Your organization has operated this way for years and has difficulty imagining that another way exists; the data community effectively has a political death grip on your IT department and, therefore, does everything in its power to ensure that it controls your software development projects; or your legacy database(s) are such a mess that you have no other choice. My

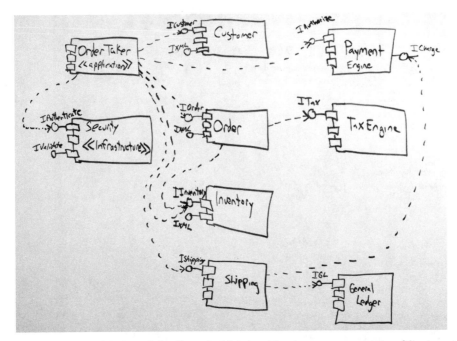

Figure 9.2   A whiteboard drawing of a high-level business component architecture.

experience is that for most business application development efforts, data modeling is an important but secondary modeling task, one that is best performed to design your physical database schema based on your software design (Ambler 2001a). The same is true of data-oriented efforts such as data warehousing projects—without a solid understanding of how people intend to use the data warehouse (something that data models don't show), these projects often end up as failures. As the principle *Multiple Models* tells you, the reality is that you have a wide variety of models at your disposal —use cases, business rules, activity diagrams, class diagrams, component diagrams, user interface flow diagrams, and CRC models to name a few—and data models are merely one such model. Each model has its strengths and weaknesses. You should follow the practice *Apply the Right Artifact(s)* as appropriate instead of blindly following the same prescriptive modeling process over and over. If you find yourself in a situation where someone tells you to base your system on a data model, I would investigate how well they truly understand software development. Ask them when to, and when not to, apply the models listed on the preceding pages. If they can't explain, or if they simply wave the questions off as "something the programmers worry about," then they clearly do not have sufficient grasp of the fundamentals to advise your project.

Misconception #9: All Developers Know How To Model

A serious problem that our industry faces is that most nondevelopers, including senior management and users, do not understand how software is built. As a result, they cannot distinguish between skilled developers and hack programmers, and certainly not between extreme programmers in the XP sense of the term and hack programmers claiming to do XP. They have a tendency to assume that all developers have the necessary skills to develop a system from end to end. This simply isn't true. Modeling skills, for one, are gained over years of experience and only when a developer chooses to gain them. Programmers, as highly intelligent people, often believe they can do anything—they're programmers after all. The result is that people get in over their heads; in their arrogance, they take on tasks that they simply don't have the skills to follow through on. The reality is that software development is too hard and too complex for a single individual to have all of the skills required to successfully develop and deploy even a reasonably complicated system. Instead people need to work together, to balance one another's strengths. People with modeling skills should work together with people who have hard-core implementation skills. Everyone should have the humility to understand that they don't know everything and that they can always learn something important from everyone else: Modelers can learn details of a certain technology from programmers, and programmers can learn valuable design and architecture techniques from modelers. My personal philosophy is that everyone is a novice, including myself, underscoring the importance of AM's principle *Everyone Can Learn From Everyone Else.*

Think Small

To overcome many of the misconceptions listed on the preceding pages, your organization will discover that it needs to change its overall philosophy toward software development. In the early 1990s, it was common to hear the phrase "small is beautiful" when it came to organization size. Now we're hearing that "small is agile" within the software development world. For example, you should prefer:

Short (small) modeling sessions. Short modeling sessions enable you to focus on one part of a system, to work on it, and then quickly obtain feedback on the results. Longer modeling sessions generally result in more functionality being addressed at once. Longer sessions increase the amount of functionality that you are motivated to attempt at one time, thereby decreasing the likeliness of obtaining early feedback on your work and increasing the risk that you will inadvertently get off track. Modeling sessions are discussed in detail later in this chapter.

Small teams. Smaller teams require less management overhead, such as status reports and meetings, than do larger teams. It is easier to colocate a small team than a large one, thereby decreasing barriers to communication within your project.

Small models. Small models are easier to create and understand than large ones. The architecture, requirements, and detailed design of your system are often better communicated by several small diagrams than one all-encompassing one.

Small documents. Small documents allow you to travel light—a 5-page document is easier to maintain than a 500-page document.

Simplicity is one of the five values of AM. By keeping things as small as possible, you are very likely keeping them simple as well.

Loosen Up a Bit

An important part of adopting a more agile mindset is accepting the fact that agile models just need to be good enough; they don't need to be perfect. For example, I've often felt that too much focus is put on whether or not you apply the "official notation" properly, or if you're "allowed" to create a certain type of model right now. I once worked on a project where we spent hours discussing the appropriate use of the <<uses>> and <<extends>>, now <<include>> and <<extend>>, stereotypes on UML use case diagrams. The problem was that different people used the stereotypes in different manners. Yes, you certainly want to follow a common set of modeling guidelines if possible, as the practice *Apply Modeling Standards* advises, but sometimes you need to bend the rules a bit. In a few cases, people applied the stereotypes inappropriately. I resolved the problem by giving a short briefing. But in other cases, the stereotypes were in fact used in a manner that made sense for the situation. We came to the conclusion that our modeling guidelines needed to be malleable. However, up to that point, we had developers wasting time arguing back and forth because they unfortunately thought that there could only be one interpretation of the guidelines.

I've had people get into heated arguments over when the most appropriate time is to apply a certain model. A classic example is the insistence of some people that data models should be created throughout the project lifecycle as part of your requirements, analysis, and design efforts. During requirements, data models can be developed to depict a domain model; during analysis, they can be developed for conceptual modeling; and during design, they can be developed for modeling your physical persistence schema. Yes, understanding the major domain entities as part of your requirements efforts can prove valuable, but do you need a data model for that? Hmmm . . . you are working on requirements. Your project stakeholders should be actively involved. They likely aren't data modeling experts, so a data model may not be your best option. A better option, in some cases, is to use CRC cards for domain modeling, something that I show how to do in *The Object Primer 2/e* (Ambler 2001a). What about an analysis-level conceptual model? Once again data models work well for this task, but is it your best option? My experience, at least when developing systems that take an object-oriented or component-based approach to development, is that UML class diagrams are a better option. Class diagrams enable you to capture both data and behavioral aspects of your system, effectively a superset of what can be captured by data models. They fit in better with the other diagrams of the UML that you are also likely using. The point is that you don't need to slavishly follow a process that tells you that to achieve goal X you need to produce artifact Y. First, question whether you need to achieve goal X and, if you do, then ask yourself what the best artifact is. In other words, follow the practice *Apply the Right Artifact(s)*.

The bottom line is that the modeling police won't hunt you down if you bend the rules. So loosen up a bit and experiment with your models.

Rigidly Support Rights and Responsibilities

One of XP's strengths is its clear and explicit definition of the roles that customers and developers have on a project. Customers are responsible for describing what they want the system to do and to prioritize the resulting requirements. Developers in turn are responsible for fairly estimating those requirements and developing the system based on the prioritization of the requirements. In other words, customers are responsible for business issues, and developers are responsible for technical issues, and each group acts accordingly.

I believe the concept that project stakeholders and developers each have a defined role and scope of influence is critical to the success of your project. Because your project stakeholders are paying you to develop systems for them, a good way to define those roles is from their point of view. In *Software Requirements* (1999), Karl Wiegers summarizes what he believes to be the rights and responsibilities of users. I have modified them here to extend to project stakeholders within the scope of AM. In my opinion, these rights and responsibilities effectively define a contract between a development team and its project stakeholders. You are effectively following the practice *Formalize Contract Models* when you choose to negotiate such a list with your stakeholders, creating a contract that must be honored for the team to be successful.

The rights of project stakeholders are:

- To have developers learn about their business and objectives
- To expect developers to learn and speak their language
- To expect developers to identify and understand their requirements
- To receive explanations of artifacts that developers use as part of working with project stakeholders, such as models they create with them (for example, user stories or essential UI prototypes) or artifacts they present to them (for example, UML deployment diagrams)
- To expect developers to treat them with respect
- To hear ideas and alternatives for requirements
- To describe characteristics which make the product easy to use
- To be presented with opportunities to adjust requirements to permit reuse, reduce development time, or to reduce development costs
- To be given good-faith estimates
- To receive a system that meets their functional and quality needs
- To determine how the project team will spend their resources, including the extent of the investment in permanent documentation (see Chapter 14)

The responsibilities of project stakeholders are:

- To provide resources (time, money, and so on) to the project team
- To educate developers about their business
- To spend the time to provide and clarify requirements

- To be specific and precise about requirements

- To make timely decisions

- To respect a developer's assessment of cost and feasibility

- To set requirement priorities

- To review and provide timely feedback regarding relevant work artifacts of developers

- To promptly communicate changes to requirements

- To own your organization's software processes, to both follow them and actively help to fix them when needed

TIP **Post these Rights and Responsibilities Publicly**
The practice *Display Models Publicly* can be applied in this situation. Post your negotiated rights and responsibilities list where everyone has access to it—to ensure that your team is aware of its rights and responsibilities.

Rethink Presentations to Project Stakeholders

I once worked on a project where the project manager insisted on putting together a formal presentation to the project stakeholders once a month. The project stakeholders loved the presentations. Not only did we summarize the current status of the team, we also described the technical details of whatever it was that we had worked on since the last presentation. One day I was working with a couple of user representatives. They were explaining the details of some complex business rules, and they offered to be available to me the following day to continue with the effort. I declined, saying that I had to work on the presentation slides for the following Monday. They then offered to work with me the next day, but once again I declined saying that the rest of the week was going to be spent working on the slides. They were astounded that one of the senior developers on the project would need to spend that much time working on slides and were particularly upset when I pointed out that I also had several other developers involved on a part-time basis to get the technical details of what they were working on. My project stakeholders were incredibly upset that we would invest that much effort in a status presentation, but unfortunately my manager insisted on it. Needless to say, the next status meeting didn't go very well for him—the meeting agenda was changed to allow the project stakeholders and the project manager to rework the project's priorities to focus more on software development and less on paper pushing. From then on, his presentations relied less on pretty slides, freeing up the developers to focus on the creation of a working system.

Presentations to project stakeholders are a reality on most software projects: senior management wants to keep track of your status, stakeholders who are not directly involved on a day-to-day basis need demonstrations of the current version of the system, and other development teams working on systems that integrate with yours need to understand how it works. You could provide documentation for these groups, but documentation often isn't very effective—if you're traveling light, you may not currently have the documentation that they need. As you'll see in Chapter 6, documentation is a very ineffective approach to communication. The bottom line is that you need to be prepared to give presentations to project stakeholders. Not only do you have to deliver the presentation, you need to prepare for it and often follow-up after it. As a result, presentations quickly become a leading cause of wasted time on your project. Here's how to be more agile:

Minimize the number of presentations that you give. The best presentation is the one that wasn't held. Presentations should have a clear purpose, a well-defined audience (it should be clear why each person is there), and a justification for why it is required. Just as you don't want to give a presentation, chances are good that many of your project stakeholders have more important things to do than attend yet another meeting. Work with them closely to reduce the number of presentations.

Try to find an alternative. Perhaps a quick telephone conversation, a face-to-face conversation in the hallway, or an email will do. It is easier, and often more effective, to find an alternative when you only need to communicate to a small group of project stakeholders—presentations are better suited for large groups, not small ones.

Turn the presentation into a working session. When you have project stakeholders in the room, put them to work. Work with them to identify new requirements, delve into existing requirements, or prioritize your upcoming efforts.

Make project stakeholders aware of the costs. Everybody loves fancy slides, but do they realize how much effort it takes to put them together? Do they realize that the time invested in making fancy slides could have been spent on developing software?

Project stakeholders decide whether they wish to have a presentation. Like producing documentation, the decision to hold a presentation to project stakeholders is a business one that is the responsibility of your project stakeholders.

Keep it simple. Are your stakeholders interested in the system that you are building for them or in your Microsoft PowerPoint skills? Many people make the mistake of investing significant time preparing "pretty slides" for their presentations. I used to spend hours transcribing hand-drawn diagrams into a drawing tool to make them suitable for presentations. Then, one day, I ran out of time and was forced to simply include a scanned drawing in a presentation. Nobody cared. The world didn't end. Since then I've included more and more hand-drawings in my presentations and invested less effort in transcribing the diagrams. The world still hasn't ended. The few times that I've received any comments regarding this approach, I tell my project stakeholders point blank that I had to decide between spending my time drawing pretty pictures and building software, so I naturally chose to build software. Nobody has ever complained. In short, apply the principle, *Maximize Stakeholder Investment* and be smart about what you do.

Minimize the number of people involved in preparation. Do not distract the entire team with the creation of a presentation; it doesn't have to be a committee-based effort. Instead have one or two people create the presentation, drawing on the expertise of others as need be. Note that AM's practice of *Collective Ownership* makes it easier for one or two people to put together a comprehensive presentation. Chances are good that they have worked on a wider range of the system than they normally would on non-AM projects. They have ready access to the current versions of project artifacts as input.

Minimize the number of people that attend the presentation. Everybody on your team doesn't have to attend every single presentation. The best approach is to identify the minimum number of people who need to attend the presentation, ideally only the person giving it, and have them report back to the rest of the team.

There is more to making AM work than simply adopting its values, principles, and practices. You need to nurture an environment that is conducive to AM, one in which you have reworked your attitudes toward modeling. This change includes overcoming common misperceptions about modeling, thinking small, and for the most part, loosening up a bit. It is also important to define and support the rights and responsibilities of project stakeholders. Finally, because presentations can be a significant drag on project teams, I implore you to streamline these activities. Remember that any time you invest preparing for, holding, or following-up on a presentation is time taken away from software development. It is possible to be successful at adopting AM within your organization, but you must choose to succeed.

CHAPTER 10

Using the Simplest Tools Possible?

**Stick with simple tools, like pencil, paper, and whiteboard.
Communication is more important than whizbang.**

–Kent Beck and Martin Fowler in *Planning Extreme Programming*

In Chapter 5, "Core Practices," you discovered that one of AM's core practices is *Use the Simplest Tools*. For ease of discussion, AM distinguishes between two types of modeling tools: simple tools and computer-aided software-engineering (CASE) tools. Simple tools are manual items that you use to model systems, including but not limited to, flipchart paper, sticky notes, paper napkins, sheet paper, string, thumb tacks, whiteboards, and index cards. The vast majority of models can be created using simple tools. CASE tools are software packages that you use to model systems. Common CASE tools include TogetherSoft's (www.togethersoft.com) Together Control Center, Canyon Blue's (www.canyonblue.com) Cittera, Embarcadero's (www.embarcadero.com) ER/Studio, Gentleware's (www.gentleware.com) Poseidon, and Rational Corporation's (www.rational.com) Rational Rose. Each of these CASE tool products has its strengths and weaknesses, and each is a potential candidate for use on a project following the AM methodology.

Wait a minute. Aren't you supposed to use only simple tools with AM, not CASE tools? Not exactly. The practice says to use the *simplest* tools, not just *simple* tools—an important distinction. However, you should use simple tools whenever possible. This distinction makes sense when you are following practices such as *Create Simple Models* and *Depict Models Simply*. The models that you are creating don't have a lot of residual value once they have fulfilled their purpose, which is typically to explore/understand an issue or to communicate an idea to someone else. Furthermore, because you should be following the AM practice *Discard Temporary Models,* investing the extra time modeling with a CASE tool doesn't make a lot of sense. If a simple tool such as index cards or a whiteboard is sufficient for your needs, and according to the principle *Model with A Purpose,* you should know what your needs are, otherwise you shouldn't be modeling, then you should prefer the simple tool. Sometimes, though, simple tools aren't sufficient. Perhaps you need to create a "pretty" diagram to present to important project stakeholders or you want to generate source code based on your models, in which case, more complicated CASE tools make sense. In short, you want to use the simplest tool possible that meets your needs. Sometimes that tool is a whiteboard and some markers, and sometimes that tool is a leading-edge CASE tool.

In this chapter, I explore the following issues regarding modeling tools:

- Agile Modeling with simple tools
- The evolution of a model
- Agile Modeling with CASE tools
- Use the media
- The effects of tools on models
- Using the simplest tools in practice

Agile Modeling with Simple Tools?

What are simple tools for modeling? The eXtreme Programming community (Beck 2000) swears by the use of standard index cards for a wide variety of modeling techniques, in particular CRC modeling, user stories, and tasks. Sticky notes are a common tool used to develop a low-fidelity/essential user-interface prototype on large sheets of paper (Constantine and Lockwood 1999). Sticky notes can be used in combination with whiteboards—the sticky notes are used for the bubbles and the relationships between the bubbles are drawn on the board. I've drawn UML use case diagrams and UML class diagrams like this many times. Similarly, pieces of paper or index cards can be tacked onto a corkboard, connected by strings, and used to create a wide variety of models. For example: The individual sheets of paper can represent database tables and the lines can represent relationships between tables on a physical data model. The sheets can represent screens and the strings can represent navigation flows between screens on a user interface flow diagram. Or the sheets can represent use cases and actors, and the strings can represent associations between the use cases and actors on a UML use case diagram. Other simple tools include a paper napkin that you draw on, a whiteboard for sketching on, and a digital camera to make copies of sketches that you want to keep.

The Advantages of Simple Tools

Why simple tools for modeling? I always advise that you should ask yourself why you are modeling. My philosophy is that you should have an exact purpose in mind when you develop, otherwise you shouldn't model. If you are modeling to understand something, then the value isn't in the model that you create but in the modeling itself. You don't need to invest significant effort using a CASE tool to make your model look pretty or to add comprehensive documentation to it. Instead you're better off using a simple tool, such as index cards or a whiteboard, to get your modeling done quickly and get back to developing software.

Simple tools are inclusive. Everyone can work with simple tools, even your project stakeholders. They need to actively participate because they are responsible for providing the requirements.

Simple tools provide tactile feedback. You can easily manipulate simple tools. Index cards can be moved around on a table. They can be touched. They can be shared with others. By working directly with simple tools, people gain a better understanding of what they are modeling.

Simple tools are inexpensive.

Simple tools are flexible. You can easily write on index cards, sticky notes, napkins, or sheets of paper. You can move them around, and when you find you no longer need them, simply rip them up. Furthermore, simple tools can be used to create a wide variety of models. Appendix A, "Modeling Techniques," suggests at least one simple tool for each type of artifact described there, including all of the ones defined by the UML.

Simple tools are non-threatening to users. In short, nobody is afraid of losing their job to a stack of cards, a collection of sticky notes, or a whiteboard sketch. Many people are afraid, however, of computers. When people are afraid of losing their jobs, they are not very open to using software-based tools. By using a non-threatening analysis technique, you decrease the probability of having to deal with recalcitrant users.

Simple tools are quick to use. When was the last time you needed to wait for a stack of index cards to load into memory?

Simple tools are portable. You can simply throw a package of index cards and a pen in your briefcase and go.

Simple tools can be used in combination with more complex ones. Agile modelers will often start out using simple tools to create many models. Then when they discover that they want to keep the model or take advantage of the features that a CASE tool has to offer, they will migrate their work to another tool. The section, *The Evolution of a Model,* describes this concept in greater detail.

Simple tools promote iterative and incremental development. Developers taking an iterative and incremental approach to development will tackle a problem a small portion at a time. Luckily, simple tools are very useful for exploring small problems, including portions of a larger problem. For example: You could easily explore the internal structure of a component, perhaps comprised of twenty or more classes, using index cards. Could you create an all-encompassing model, perhaps representing hundreds of classes, using index cards? Maybe. But creating the model would likely be clumsy. Exploring the requirements for a report is easy to accomplish using flip chart paper and sticky notes. But exploring every single screen and report within your system? Likely not.

Simple tools promote traveling light. When you don't invest much effort in something, you can easily discard it.

The Disadvantages of Simple Tools

Simple tools also have their weaknesses:

Simple tools aren't acceptable to many people. Developers have become accustomed to creating models using complex CASE tools. They find it difficult to accept that whiteboard sketches or a stack of index cards are often sufficient for their modeling needs. Users have become accustomed to sophisticated and detailed requirements documents describing their systems. They find it difficult to accept that the requirements for their system are described in a little box of cards.

Simple tools are limited.

Simple tools aren't well suited for permanent documentation. Although a box of cards might sufficiently capture the requirements from the point of view of the people that created the cards, most likely the cards aren't sufficient for people outside of the team or people trying to understand the system several years later. You will find that you still need to use more complicated tools, such as word processors or CASE tools, to create permanent documentation. Agile documentation is described in detail in Chapter 14, "Agile Documentation."

Simple tools do not support distributed teams easily. Simple tools are physical. As a result, everyone needs to be in the same location at the same time to work with simple tools. Yes, electronic whiteboards enable people at different locations to work together on diagrams, and you could conceivably teleconference people into your working session. But distributed communication isn't the same. Chapter 8, "Communication," discusses the challenges involved with distributed communication.

When Should You Use Simple Tools?

When should you use simple tools? Whenever you can, which is most of the time. My rule of thumb is that the greater the amount of uncertainty surrounding the issue that you are modeling, the greater the flexibility you will want in your tools. Therefore, you should use simple tools. You can draw on a whiteboard faster than you can draw with a drawing tool, such as Microsoft Visio or a more complicated CASE tool. You can explore the requirements for a screen or report using sticky notes and flip chart paper faster than you can with a software-based prototyping tool. Do you have to limit yourself to simple tools? No. As you gain a greater understanding of an issue, you can migrate to more complicated tools as required, assuming that the tools provide the best value possible for your investment. I discuss this topic in *The Evolution of a Model.* In short, agile modelers typically start by discussing an issue, and they use simple tools to aid their discussion if appropriate. Then, they choose to either manually write source code or to migrate to a CASE tool, which will hopefully generate code for them.

Supporting Simple Tools with Technology

To get around the deficiencies of simple tools, you may choose to use technology-based tools to support your efforts. Commonly, you use one of these tools to create a permanent record of your work or to share information with people at other physical locations. Common technology-based tools used to support simple tools include:

Digital cameras and scanners. One of the easiest ways to "transcribe" the information captured using simple tools is to simply take a picture of it using a digital camera or scanner. You have seen several examples throughout this book of whiteboard sketches and essential user interfaces captured using a digital camera, as well as sketches drawn on paper or index cards that were scanned in. These tools, in particular digital cameras, are quick and easy to use.

Picture software. There are several tools available to you to work with digital pictures. I use products such as Adobe Illustrator (www.adobe.com) and Corel Photo Paint (www.corel.com) to manipulate pictures. I crop the pictures to focus on just the information that I need and to reduce the file size, which reduces storage and transmission overhead. I also use a product called Whiteboardphoto from Pixid (www.pixid.com) to clean up the pictures and to convert them to a format suitable for optical character recognition (OCR) software. For example: With Whiteboardphoto, I generated Figure 10.2 from Figure 10.1 in less than one minute. As you can see, the clean version of the diagram is much easier to read.

Wikis. A Wiki (Leuf and Cunningham 2001) is a collaborative environment that people use to co-author HTML-based information. Think of a Wiki as a web site that comes with its own tools for editing, adding, and removing pages. Wikis are often used in place of email-based discussion groups, particularly when the discussion is relevant to the entire team. Development teams use Wikis to grow their group memory (Ambler 1998) by recording their requirements artifacts, key architectural and design decisions, and shared documents. Wikis support AM's principle of *Open and Honest Communication* and the practice *Display Models Publicly*. For more information about Wikis, visit www.wiki.org.

Word processors, text editors, and HTML editors. These tools are useful at capturing text-based information, particularly when you want sophisticated editing capability. The resulting documents are easy to share with others and to convert to HTML to be displayed on a shared web.

Electronic whiteboards. Electronic whiteboards range in capability. Some boards simply scan your whiteboard and produce a paper copy of your sketches such as Panasonic's (www.panasonic.com) Panaboard product line. More sophisticated tools include TeamBoard (www.teamboard.com) and PolyVision's

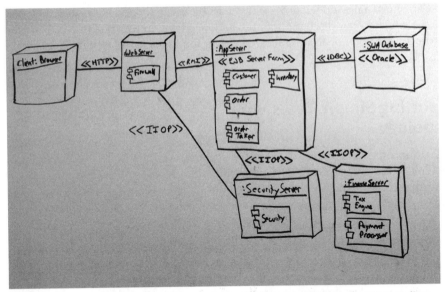

Figure 10.1 A whiteboard sketch of a UML deployment diagram for SWA Online.

Webster (www.websterboards.com). These tools integrate with a computer and potentially collaborative software such as Microsoft's NetMeeting so you can share your work with distributed team members. Note that instead of purchasing a new electronic whiteboard, many organizations opt to enhance existing "manual whiteboards" with products such as Mimio (www.mimio.com).

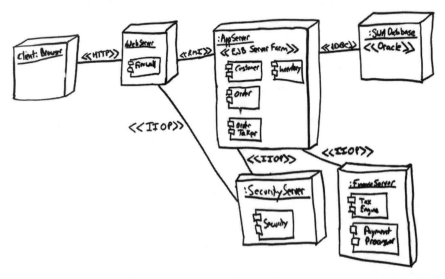

Figure 10.2 A "cleaned up" sketch.

The Evolution of a Model

How do agile modelers use simple tools and CASE tools in combination? Figure 10.3 depicts a flow chart that indicates how modeling tools are used by developers. Agile modelers typically start by discussing an issue that they are working on. If that discussion is sufficient, they can move forward and start writing code. Other times, they realize that they need to *Model to Understand*, so they choose the simplest tool possible to get the job done and begin modeling. The majority of the time, they will choose a simple tool. XP developers often choose index cards, although whiteboards are also a popular choice, and they will work together (following the practice *Model with Others*) to explore the issue they are working on. Agile modelers may change tools as they see fit, perhaps starting with index cards but then migrating to a CASE tool once their understanding of the issue stabilizes. Regardless of the modeling tool they are using, they may choose to start producing code at any time. They will either write the code or generate it with their CASE tool(s), in accordance with the principle *Software Is Your Primary Goal* and the practices *Model in Small Increments* and *Prove It with Code*.

When agile modelers are initially exploring an issue, they need a very flexible tool to quickly change the model they are working on. They don't want to invest too much time at the start because a lot of their initial work is likely to be discarded as their understanding evolves. For example: when I am first exploring how to build a screen, I will often use sticky notes. I stick them to the nearest flat surface that I can find—a desktop, whiteboard, flip chart paper, and so on (see Figure 10.4). Sticky notes are easy to work with. I can write brief descriptions on them or make little sketches, and they are easy to move around. Furthermore, they stay where I put them because of the glue on their backside. This approach allows me to get a feel for the layout very quickly, adding and removing widgets as I need.

As Figure 10.3 implies, you should either move straight to coding the screen or choose to continue modeling using another tool such as a whiteboard or CASE tool. Base this decision on your initial purpose for developing the screen layout model. If your goal was to simply determine a strategy for organizing the major widgets that will make up the screen, then you're very likely satisfied with that purpose, and you can start coding. If your goal is to determine how to organize the screen and to identify the widgets that you intend to use, then you should move to a whiteboard next. With

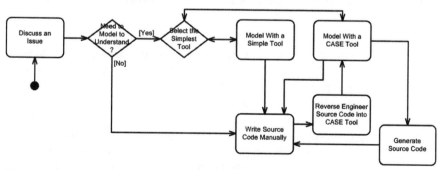

Figure 10.3   How simple tools and CASE tools are used.

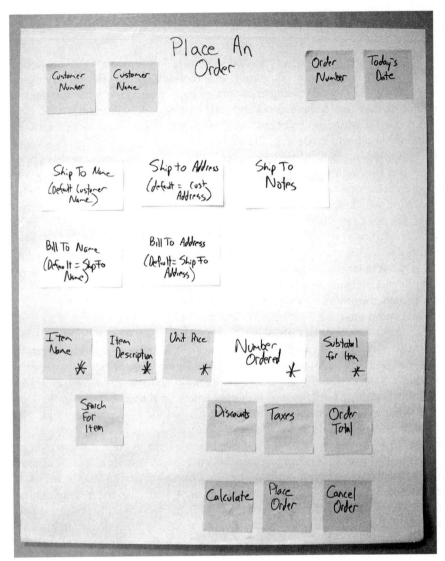

Figure 10.4   An essential UI prototype depicting the requirements for a screen/page.

a whiteboard, you can draw the widgets with greater accuracy, drawing them to their relative size as reasonable facsimiles of the actual type of widget (check box, single-line entry field, multiple-line entry field, and so on), see Figure 10.5. Note that the screen design has evolved from Figure 10.6: A few items have moved around. We realized that we needed to display the number and name of an order item instead of the name and description; we needed to add the ability to remove individual items via checkboxes; and we needed to show shipping charges as part of the total. However, whiteboards aren't as flexible as sticky notes. If you discover that you need to move several widgets, then you may have a lot of erasing and redrawing with a whiteboard.

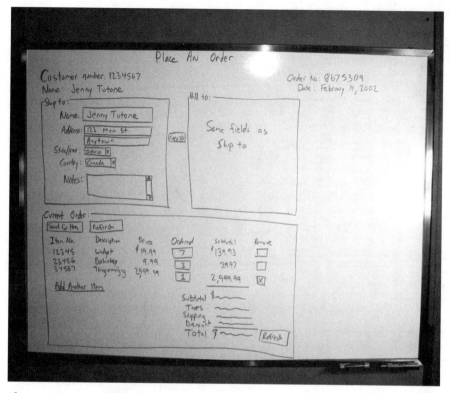

Figure 10.5   A whiteboard sketch of depicting an HTML page for placing an Order.

But with sticky notes, you simply move them around. What you gain in fidelity by moving to a whiteboard you can lose in flexibility.

Should we use picture software to clean up Figure 10.5 as we did to convert Figure 10.1 to Figure 10.2? Or should we leave the figure alone? Depends on the situation. If we want to show the picture to someone else, perhaps we want to email it to a few people to obtain feedback, then we should invest the minute that it takes to run the figure through the software. If we're just using the diagram ourselves, then why bother? The figure is readable as it is, and because we believe in AM's principle that *Content is More Important Than Representation,* we decide to not waste a minute when we don't have to. Just because you can clean up the diagram easily doesn't mean that you have to.

Our next step is to once again consider coding or to transition to yet another tool, in this case, a user interface prototyping tool. Figure 10.6 depicts a full-fledged UI prototype, based on Figure 10.5, for placing orders. Notice that the model has evolved. When our project stakeholders worked with the screen, they realized that manipulating the order items was far more important than editing address information, and they asked us to move this section higher on the page. Our model has increased in fidelity once again. Our users clearly know what we intend to build. We have applied corporate UI development standards (remember the practice *Apply Modeling Standards*) using corporate colors and aligning fields effectively. In the case of HTML, we've arguably coded part of our page, at least the visual aspects of it,

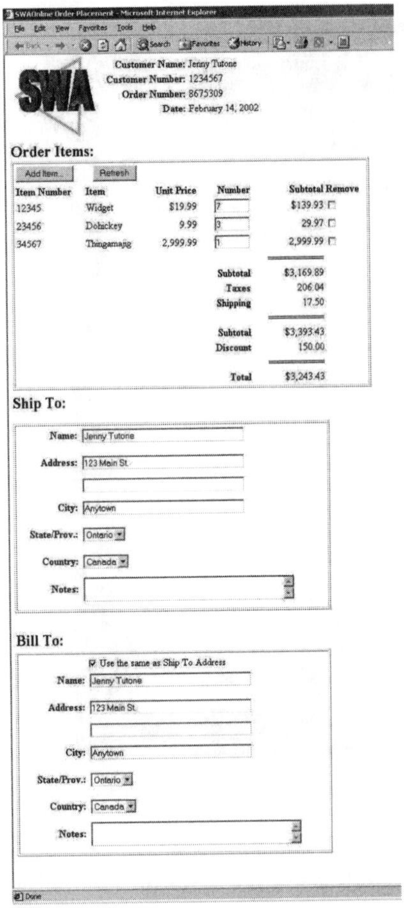

Figure 10.6   An HTML-based user interface prototype for placing orders.

although we may decide to refine our work further by hand-coding Javascript or to tweak our page using a text editor to accomplish something that our HTML prototyping tool couldn't.

Had you been working on a data model, you would want to consider using a data-modeling tool. If you were working on a UML class diagram, then you would want to consider using a tool that supports that kind of diagram, and so on. In other words, pick the right tool for the job. An important aspect of the *Use the Simplest Tools* practice is that you should only use a tool if it provides positive value. Often you will find that you have already gained most of the value by modeling with index cards or a whiteboard and that typing the model into a CASE tool only provides sufficient value when you use that tool.

Why use tools at all? Why not jump straight to code? First, code isn't as flexible as either sticky notes or whiteboard sketches. We can't move things around in code as easily as we can with sticky notes, and we very likely can't change widget types as easily as we can sketch. In short, a few minutes working with sticky notes and possibly drawing some sketches will likely pay for itself, several times over in saved coding time. Second, sticky notes and sketches are more inclusive than code. Non-developers such as our direct users can become actively involved with the UI design effort—we're working on something, the user interface of the system we're building for them, that they can directly relate to and are clearly interested in.

Agile Modeling with CASE Tools

On the surface you can easily assume that if you're an agile modeler, you aren't going to use a CASE tool. Poppycock! An agile modeler uses a tool, any tool, when that tool makes the most sense for that situation. Just as a carpenter will use a manual screwdriver sometimes and other times an electric screwdriver, sometimes an agile modeler will use an index card and other times a complex software design tool. In this section, I address the following issues regarding CASE tools:

- Choosing CASE tools
- Overcoming CASE tool misconceptions
- Generated source code
- Generated documentation

Choosing CASE Tools

Any tool, including a CASE tool, should be used only when it provides the maximum value for your investment—in accordance with the principle, *Maximize Stakeholder Investment*. The following is basic investment theory: If you can invest your money one way and get a 10 percent overall return, or you can invest your money another way and get a 15 percent overall return, everything else being equal, you're better off with the second investment. With respect to modeling tools, you always have several choices: Use simple tools such as index cards and white boards, use a diagramming tool such as Microsoft Visio, or use a more complicated tool such as TogetherSoft's Together Control Center or Computer Associate's ERWin data modeling tool.

How do you calculate the expected value for your investment in a tool? I suggest that you don't, at least not in the strict accounting sense of the idea. Yes, you could prepare a complex spreadsheet listing all the costs, both quantitative costs that have a clear dollar value and qualitative costs that need to be fudged into a dollar value. Then you could compare the costs with the expected benefits, both quantitative and qualitative (see Table 10.1 for a listing of potential costs and benefits). Naturally, you'd have to calculate the net present value (NPV) of those figures to ensure that you're comparing apples to apples. I've got a very good write-up of how to do all this in my book *Process Patterns* (Ambler 1998) if you're really interested, but I highly advise against this sort of lengthy analysis. Why? Because this analysis is a lot of work that is more often than not a façade used to justify a political decision anyway.

How do you select CASE tools in an agile manner? You could fall back on the principles and practices of agile modeling. The principle *Develop with a Purpose* tells you

Table 10.1 Potential Advantages and Disadvantages of CASE Tools

ADVANTAGES	DISADVANTAGES
• Forward engineering (code generation)	• Initial training and education
• Reverse engineering of existing code	• Evaluation costs
• Support for changing levels of abstraction (for example, from requirements to analysis to design to code)	• Maintenance of the model over time (it's even worse when the model has outlasted its usefulness but you're still maintaining it for posterity)
• Testing of the consistency and validity of your models	• Upgrade costs of the tool
• Synchronization of models with delivered code	• Ongoing usage/maintenance fees
• Support for different views and/or potential solutions to a problem	• Time lost waiting for the tool to do its job
• Generation of documentation	• Time lost over-using the tool (for example, making your diagrams look pretty, extraneous information, and so on)
	• Migration costs to port models to another tool
	• Increased effort to synchronize models with other artifacts, such as source code
	• CASE tools often promote syntax over communication between developers (in other words, your model looks good but doesn't necessarily work)
	• Generated code often too simplistic, or cluttered with extraneous information required by the tool
	• Poor user interfaces often hamper the modeling effort
	• Inadequate integration with other tools reduces productivity and/or requires integration work
	• Internal toolsmithing to integrate with other tools, often not budgeted but necessary

that you should know why you are creating an artifact. Knowing the purpose for an artifact indicates the extent of the work that you need to perform to complete your model. You stop as soon as your model fulfills its purpose. In turn, you will have insight into what you require of your tools. By knowing your actual requirements, you can then determine whether a given tool will actually provide the most value for your situation. In my experience, a gut-feeling approach to choosing your tools is often the most effective approach, albeit one that senior management may not trust you to take. The principle *Know Your Tools* tells you that you should know the features of the tools that you are using. The practice *Use the Simplest Tools* tells you to select the simplest tool (even if it's a CASE tool) that will do the job.

Overcoming CASE Tool Misconceptions

There are several common misconceptions regarding CASE tools that need to be addressed:

CASE Tool Misconception #1: Agile modelers don't use CASE tools. Agile modelers follow the practice *Use the Simplest Tools*, and if the simplest tool for the job is a CASE tool, then that's what they'll use.

CASE Tool Misconception #2: UML requires CASE. A lot of developers associate the Unified Modeling Language (UML) with CASE tools, yet nothing could be further from the truth. Throughout this book, even in this chapter, you've seen many hand-drawn UML diagrams.

CASE Tool Misconception #3: You start modeling with CASE tools. As you saw in the section, "The Evolution of a Model," you typically want to start with simple tools and only migrate to CASE tool usage when it makes sense to do so. Yes, CASE tools can be very useful if they generate code for you, or if they can reverse-engineer an understandable model from existing code, but at first you are better advised to work with simple, flexible tools.

CASE Tool Misconception #4: The CASE tool is the master. No matter how good your CASE tool, fundamentally only the source code is in sync with the source code (Beck 2000). Agile modelers realize that as soon as you generate code from a model, or write code based on a model, the code is now the primary artifact and not the model. You may choose to reverse-engineer your code at some point to update your model, following the practice *Update Only When It Hurts*.

Generated Source Code

Figure 10.3 includes a step for generating source code from a CASE tool model and a step for reverse-engineering models from existing code. These steps can be very effective, or a complete disaster, depending on the CASE tool. With respect to code-related features, here is what agile modelers will look for in CASE tools:

Conformance to your coding standards. You must expect to edit the source code that your tools generate for you. If the code generated varies dramatically from your own code, then it is harder to work with and reduces the benefit of generating the code to begin with. Therefore, you need to either choose tools that you can configure to conform to your coding conventions or rework your coding conventions to conform to the tool (putting you at the mercy of the whims of the vendor).

Support for customization. CASE tools should provide the ability to enable you to define what type of code you want generated. Do you want scaffolding code, such as getter and setter operations, generated for you? Do you want code generated that is required by the frameworks that you are using, such as remote interfaces for Enterprise JavaBeans (EJBs)? Do you want code generated for an n-tier environment using a browser-based user interface or for a fat-client architecture that uses a graphical UI?

Minimal intrusion. Some tools are intrusive, putting identifiers into your source code comments such as unique IDs or proprietary marks to indicate which code was generated. Some tools are even more intrusive and limit your changes to certain parts of the generated source code, often indicating these sections with comments. These "intrusions" are typically put in place for the convenience of the tool vendor, making it easier to reverse-engineer their own code. The intrusions are not there for your convenience and they are not needed. As CASE tools mature, and the vendor understands reverse-engineering more thoroughly, the intrusions are slowly dropped over time.

Support for flexible reverse-engineering. Developers typically work on a small portion of a system at a time, and they may only be concentrating on one aspect of that portion at any given time. To support this process effectively, you need to be able to reverse engineer only a portion of the system at a time, perhaps ten C++ classes out of the three hundred that comprise your system, and only generate the types of diagrams that you need right now, perhaps a single UML class diagram to start.

Ease of use. If a tool is difficult to use, it is difficult to learn, increasing its costs to you and thereby decreasing the value of the tool.

Multi-language support. Many systems are developed using several languages; for example, a web-based system may include HTML, JavaScript, Perl, Java, and proprietary database code. Ideally a CASE tool should support the languages that you intend to work with.

Here are strategies to help you remain agile using CASE tools with code generation capabilities:

Recognize that code generation doesn't automatically imply agility. A tool that generates poor quality code, or even the wrong code, isn't going to be of much help to you. Don't get fooled by slick marketing material. Work with a CASE tool, and determine if it meets your specific needs.

You need to understand what is generated. Hunt and Thomas (2000) warn against "evil wizards," code generators that produce code that you do not understand. Although generating very complex code automatically sounds good on the surface because then you don't need to pay for people with the necessary expertise, what happens when you need to modify the generated source code to meet your exact circumstances or to fulfill a new requirement? An implication of the principle *Embrace Change* is to not put yourself into a position that makes it very difficult to change.

Iterate, iterate, iterate. You should reverse-engineer your code back into your model(s) on a regular basis to reduce the overhead. Reverse-engineering a few small changes made by a couple of developers is easier than reverse-engineering several weeks of changes from an entire team. When you reverse-engineer code, you often find that you need to reposition graphical items because they've changed size and that the tool has difficulty mapping the new version of the code to the existing model.

Generated Documentation

If the primary reason why you're using a CASE tool is to generate documentation, then you clearly aren't taking an AM approach to development. The principle *Software Is Your Primary Goal* indicates that the production of software, not documentation, should be your focus. Choose tools that are easy to work with and that generate high-quality source code for you over tools with nifty documentation-generation features. The documentation generated by most CASE tools is comprehensive, catering to the "telephone book" school of thinking as opposed to the agile documentation (Chapter 14) school of thinking. Yes, the principle *Enabling the Next Effort Is Your Secondary Goal* tells you that documentation is still an important consideration; it's just not your primary one. Yes, many teams need to provide documentation to external groups, but as you saw in Chapter 8, there are significantly better ways to communicate with others than documentation. In short, generate documentation with CASE tools sparingly because these features make it easy for you to do the wrong thing.

Use the Media

Agile modelers use tools to their full advantage to utilize the media of the tools. For example, they will take advantage of:

Color. Coad, Lefebvre, and DeLuca (1999) describe in detail how to use color effectively in your UML class diagrams, using different colors to indicate different types of classes. You can use different colors of marker in whiteboard sketches to indicate different issues. For example: you may decide to use red on a deployment diagram to indicate things you're not sure of, blue on a data model to indicate lookup tables, and blue on data flow diagrams to indicate items that are currently out of scope for your project.

Size. You can use different-size sticky notes to indicate different types of items on essential UI prototypes, as you saw in Figure 10.6 where large sticky notes indicate data entry fields.

Flexible drawing tools. Tools such as Microsoft Visio (www.microsoft.com) are popular because they enable you to draw a wide range of diagrams and to mix and match symbols. Because of Visio's flexibility, you can easily draw very sophisticated free-form diagrams. Free-form diagrams are particularly useful for architecture diagrams and diagrams that are presented to project stakeholders who require more intuitive graphics than what is typically promoted by notations such as the UML.

Three-dimensional (3D) mock-ups. In some situations, you discover that you need to gain a perspective on an issue that only 3D mock-ups can provide. For example, with SWA Online, you need to worry about shipping products. When someone has ordered several items, the way that the items are packed can affect your cost (you want to use the smallest boxes possible) and the shipping costs charged to your customer (the smaller the package, the lower the cost). Another example would be the development of an air traffic control system. Not only do you need to worry about the design of the software, but also the placement of the furniture and the design of the room are considerations because air traffic controllers need to physically see the airplanes as well as their computer screens.

TIP **Don't Get Too Retentive**

People make mistakes. They pick up the blue marker and start drawing with it instead of the black marker. They use a 2" by 2" sticky note instead of the 2" by 4" one. They use Microsoft Visio to create a diagram instead of your corporate standard Microsoft PowerPoint. Or perhaps, you forgot to pick up a pack of blue index cards as well as white and yellow ones. Your models don't need to be perfect; they just need to be good enough. Remember, *Content is More Important Than Representation.*

The Effect of Tools on Models

> **When all you have is a hammer, everything looks like a nail.**
>
> **–Unknown**

Do the modeling tools you use have an effect on your work? My experience is that they do. You need to recognize that this is a serious problem. First, if your tools don't fully support your chosen notation(s), then you may not create the same models that you would if you had a more fully functional tool. Second, when a tool makes it easy to go in one direction over another, you won't get the same model. If your tool makes it easy to apply common design patterns, you are much more likely to do so than with a tool that doesn't, conflicting with the practice *Apply Patterns Gently*. Third, the level of model support will affect the quality and types of models that you create. For example: you are likely to get a different answer using a tool that supports the UML, user interface development, and database modeling than with a tool that just supports the UML. A tool's supported notations emphasize certain ways of looking at problems. They reflect a specific modeling methodology such as ICONIX (Rosenberg and Scott 1999) or Catalysis (D'Souza and Wills 1999), which in turn affects the way you will structure your models. Fourth, you are likely to get a different model when using simple tools than when using more complex ones—your project stakeholders are more likely to actively participate with your modeling efforts when you're using simple tools, giving you a better understanding of what they need. Also, simple tools are far more flexible and don't suffer from the modeling limitations (such as only supporting a defined notation) of most CASE tools.

Having said this, people are very likely to have a greater effect on the quality of your models than tools will. Agile modelers with good people skills are likely to gain a better understanding of requirements than those without. An agile modeler that understands and can apply a wide range of techniques, such as those described in Appendix A, will likely be more effective than one that has fewer modeling techniques in their intellectual toolkit because they will be far more effective at the practice *Apply The Right Artifact(s)*.

Using the Simplest Tools In Practice

The practice *Use The Simplest Tools* advises you to use the modeling tool best suited for the job, one that provides the best value for your investment in learning and working with it, with a preference for simple tools such as index cards and whiteboard sketches. More complicated tools, such as word processors, drawing tools, and even full-fledged CASE tools, are viable options for agile modelers to work with. Let the principles *Know Your Tools* and *Maximize Stakeholder Investment* guide your tool selection efforts. Agile modelers prefer the simplest tools that get the job done and choose wisely.

11

Agile Work Areas

The physical environment in which you work has a significant impact on how effective you are as an agile modeler. Remember the parable: A horseshoe was lost for want of a nail, a horse was lost for want of a shoe, a knight was lost for want of a horse, an army was lost for lack of a knight, and a kingdom was lost for lack of an army. Does it make sense that your organization be lost for lack of a whiteboard marker? I hope not. Yet I have been in organizations where people had to carry their own markers with them. If they left markers behind in a meeting room, they would soon be gone. For some reason, this organization purposely maintained a chronic shortage of whiteboard markers—one of the most effective tools that people can use to enhance communication (see Chapter 8, "Communication"). Aaarrrggghhh!!! For agile modelers to be effective they need access to the appropriate resources, and they need a work area that enables Agile Modeling practices.

Agile Modeling Room

What qualities make agile-modeling areas effective? In my experience the following factors, presented in priority order, are critical for creating an effective work area:

You need dedicated space. The most effective teams have their own working areas. Yes, space is at a premium in many organizations, but if senior management wants your team to succeed, they have to provide the resources that you need. You should not have to wait to find an available meeting room to get some modeling done. You should not have to worry about somebody erasing your whiteboards or throwing your index cards in the trash. I've worked in companies with a severe shortage of space. We had to wait for days to find meeting rooms. Progress ground to a halt.

Significant whiteboard space. As far as I'm concerned, you can never have too much whiteboard space. Luckily whiteboards are incredibly inexpensive. My preference is whiteboards floor to ceiling, wherever empty wall exists, even on support pillars if they're more than a foot (30 cm) wide. Developers should have their own private whiteboard space so that they can sketch diagrams on them on their own, with their development pair (many projects teams, particularly XP teams, follow a pair programming approach), or with several coworkers. Don't have this whiteboard space? Talk to your facilities people, the folks responsible for the physical premises within your organization. Tell them that whiteboards are a priority for your team. Not allowed to have whiteboards? Have senior management pull some strings for you, or simply install the whiteboards yourself and ask for forgiveness later. Do you know you can purchase whiteboard wallpaper? I've used it and it works. If you can't find whiteboard wallpaper, you next option is to purchase 8x4 sheets of whiteboard. Using either technology you can easily cover a large room in a couple of hours.

Digital camera. Digital cameras can be used to take snapshots of your modeling artifacts. Use digital cameras to take pictures of critical diagrams to display them on internal project web sites, to capture images of paper-based models such as essential UI prototypes or CRC models, to capture a snapshot of a diagram describing an alternative approach you've decided against but may want to revisit in the future, or simply to capture a permanent copy of a diagram for version control. Digital cameras are inexpensive and easy to use. I suggest purchasing a high-resolution camera, one that will capture the minute details, because the price difference isn't that great. Digital cameras often pay for themselves quickly. The alternative is for one of your highly paid developers to transcribe the models that you want to capture onto paper. Digital cameras are also a good substitute for the printing whiteboards that were popular in the early 1990s—digital cameras are more flexible, far more portable, and less expensive.

Modeling supplies. The practice *Use the Simplest Tools* suggests that working with the simplest tool will get the job done. Therefore, you need access to those tools. You need ready access to whiteboard markers, sticky notes (have different colors and different sizes), index cards (you may also want different colors and sizes as well), writing paper, flip-charts, tape, stick pins, string, and whatever other modeling supplies that your team requires.

A bookshelf or storage cabinet. You need somewhere to store your modeling supplies and reference books.

Large table. Some techniques, such as CRC modeling, require a large table to work on. Other times you need a table to place your notebooks on, or more importantly, somewhere to put food when you have lunch delivered.

Computer. Having a computer in your modeling area can often prove advantageous, particularly if you need to research information on the Internet during a modeling session (something I would rather have someone do offline after a modeling session) or simply to access previous models that have been placed under version control. You may even want to have a CASE tool installed on this computer so you can capture your work in your chosen tools. However, never forget that complicated tools introduce a barrier to communication and may actually be counterproductive for the team as a whole. See Chapter 8 for a detailed discussion of communication. If you are going to have a computer in your working area, then make sure you get a good one because you don't want a group of people waiting on a machine.

Chairs. Although stand-up working sessions are incredibly productive—people focus on getting the work done and appear to be more willing to contribute—the reality is that people want to be able to sit down occasionally. I believe in having a few chairs in a working area. It's interesting that it's called a working area and not a sitting area, so that if some people want to sit down, they can. Sitting is particularly important at the beginning of a project because your modeling sessions are likely to be longer, as described in Chapter 13, "Agile Modeling Sessions," and your team will be more likely to sit. During the construction phase of your project, modeling sessions have a tendency to be much shorter, often between ten and twenty minutes long. In this case, a stand-up session is much more palatable.

Wall space to attach paper. It's good to have some nonwhiteboard wall space. You'll have somewhere to attach paper artifacts. If possible have corkboard installed, or worst case simply have a few sections of plain wall space.

Projector. If you are going to have a computer in your working area, you should also consider having a projector to attach it to so you can display images on the wall. Displaying images promotes communication because everyone can see the information. However, teams make the common mistake of trying to capture information in a CASE tool during a modeling session. They have a "CASE jockey" who works the tool as everyone models, often projecting onto a whiteboard where others will draw over the image. Unfortunately, this approach is incredibly unproductive because everyone on the team ends up waiting for the CASE jockey to capture the information. A better approach would be to use the more flexible tools, such as the whiteboards, to work together. Later use the less flexible tool, the CASE tool, to capture the results. To support the whiteboard modeling effort you may choose to have the CASE jockey display existing models, the difference would be that you don't try to update the models as you move forward.

Reference books. When you are modeling, you often need to access common reference information, such as the UML notation for a specific concept or the definition of a design pattern. In Table 11.1, I provide a short list of books that I have found useful during modeling sessions. In fact, I typically ask my clients to order at least one copy of each book for the team and suggest that developers have their own copies to mark up as they please.

Table 11.1 Suggested Modeling Reference Books

TITLE	USAGE
The Object Primer, Second Edition Edition: The Application Developer's Guide to Object Orientation. (Ambler 2001a)	Reference book for a wide range of techniques, including the UML diagrams.
UML Distilled, Second Edition: Applying the Standard Object Modeling Language (Fowler and Scott 1999)	Good reference manual for UML.
Analysis Patterns: Reusable Object Models (Fowler 1997)	Defines solutions to common problems found in business applications.
Design Patterns: Elements of Reusable Object-Oriented Software (Gamma, Helm, Johnson, and Vlissides 1995)	Defines solutions to common object-oriented design problems.
A Systems of Patterns: Pattern-Oriented Software Architecture (Buschmann, Meunier, Rohnert, Sommerlad, and Stal 1996)	Defines solutions to common object-oriented architecture and design problems.

Food. Having food available in your working area is often appreciated by all and will help to build camaraderie. A varied selection is a good idea. Not everyone has the same tastes or eating habits. I personally gravitate toward hard candies; they're small and store well. Also include fresh fruit.

Toys. Having something to play with in your hands can help you get "unstuck" when you're working. Many teams enforce politeness rules by allowing people to throw a foam ball at someone who is being rude or inconsiderate.

TIP **Access to Resources Gauge Management Support**
My experience is that management's willingness to give you the tools that you need to do your job is a critical indicator of their actual support for your team. Everything presented in the Agile Modeling Room section is perfectly reasonable and frankly not very expensive. Yes, sometimes you have a space crunch, and you do not have enough room for your team to have their own work area. I can't help but think that your organization should consider addressing its physical facilities problems before it tackles a new software project. Can't get any whiteboard markers because the allocated budget for the year has already been spent? Consider firing the accountant for being pennywise and pound-foolish. The bottom line is that you're not asking for much. If senior management can't provide them, chances are pretty good that

they really don't believe in your project, an issue that you desperately need to address as soon as you can.

TIP   Consider Digital Photo Software
With the increased use of digital cameras to capture whiteboard images, we're starting to see software that cleans up your pictures and potentially even captures textual information contained in them. A quick search on the web is definitely warranted.

Effective Work Areas

There is more to your work area than just the space(s) used for modeling. You need space that supports the rest of the project lifecycle. In addition to modeling, you need space to program and test your system, implying the need for workstations for developers. The underlying process, such as XP or the Unified Process, that you use with AM (see Chapter 1) should provide advice regarding work areas that are conducive to that process. For example, on an XP project, your working area must include workstations for pairs of developers, whereas a UP project team may decide that everyone will work in his or her own private cubicle or office. It is important to understand that you will very likely need to combine the advice presented by these processes with the advice I provide in this chapter to design your overall work area. Team size will also affect the configuration of your work area—larger teams may want several working areas with a shared common space.

Making This Work in the Real World

Very few organizations have more space than they need. It is very easy to explain that a development team needs a dedicated workspace; it is a very different thing to obtain and keep that workspace. It is very easy to explain that people should work together in a common area, but the reality is that people need their privacy sometimes. It is very easy for XP to insist that people work together at shared desks; it's very hard to do so in organizations where your importance is indicated by the size of your desk* or office. I have applied the following techniques at various organizations over the years to set up effective work areas:

Communicate the importance of having an effective workspace to senior management. This issue is one that is worth spending political capital on because your team cannot be effective without an environment conducive to the

---

*I once worked at a company where you instantly knew how high up the corporate hierarchy was by the configuration of their desk—people from level 1 to level 7 had desk configuration A, from 8 through 12 desk configuration B, and so on. You knew someone was truly important, very likely a senior vice president, when they had their own unique desk (typically large and made of expensive hard wood).

work they are trying to accomplish. It may mean that other people are moved to another area within your organization; it may mean that you need to do some redecorating (perhaps removing existing cubicles to clear an area); or it may mean that you obtain new office space completely. Do it. The cost is minimal compared to the increase in productivity that will result.

Communicate the importance of having an effective workspace to the team. Everyone who is actively participating on the project, including both developers and project stakeholders, should understand why their workspace has been configured in this "new" way. They might not be familiar with shared workspaces or the required etiquette for such environments, and they very likely are not aware of why the new workspace is critical to the success of your effort. Talk with them about it.

Get rid of the headphones. For a work area to be effective, it should enable communication within your team. But if everyone is wearing headphones so they can listen to their favorite music, then they clearly aren't communicating well.

Allow people to keep their former offices. If some people are concerned that they're going to lose their "good desk/office/..." if they join your project, consider allowing them to keep them. Insist that they work in the team work area during regular hours, but allow them to keep their personal workspace so they can maintain their corporate image. Yes, this is a little dysfunctional, but you need to make concessions like these when you are introducing new techniques like AM.

Provide private areas. To enable people to make private phone calls, have private conversations with another team member, or simply to get away from it all for a few minutes, many project teams need access to small meeting rooms. I've worked on some projects where a room was dedicated to the team although it is far more common for meeting rooms to be a shared resource within the entire organization.

I cannot overstress the importance of having adequate resources—note the use of the word "adequate" instead of "extravagant." Always remember to apply the principle, *Maximize Stakeholder Investment* and ask for resources that you need and can justify.

Agile Modeling Teams

There is no "I" in "agile."

The bottom line is that Agile Modeling AM is a collection of synergistic practices that are supported and enhanced by a defined set of practices and values—without people willing to follow those practices, people with the right attitude who are willing to work and learn together, AM will be for naught. For AM to be successful within your organization, development teams must include both developers and the project stakeholders who ideally will actively work side-by-side with the developers. To build an effective development team you need to:

- Recruit a few good developers
- Recognize that there is no "I" in agile
- Require that everyone actively participates
- Model in teams

Recruit a Few Good Developers

The first step for building an effective team is to recruit the right people for that team. Cockburn (2001b) points out that while many methodologies define the roles that developers may take on a software project and the types of tasks people in those roles perform, what they often don't do is define the type of people who are best suited for those roles. For someone to be effective in a role, they should be a reasonably good fit for it—they may not have all the requisite skills, but they should be able to grow into them. In my experience, an effective agile modeler exhibits most of the following traits:

Team player. First and foremost, agile modelers actively seek to work with others because they recognize that they don't have all the answers and that they desperately need several points of view to be effective. Software development is a lot like swimming, it's dangerous to do it alone. To paraphrase a common refrain about teamwork, there is no "I" in agile.

Communicative. Agile modelers have good communication skills. They can present their ideas. They listen to others. They actively seek feedback. They can write reasonably well when needed.

Practical. Agile modelers should be practical. They should be able to focus on fulfilling the needs of their users and to not add unnecessary bells and whistles (something often referred to as gold plating) to their models. They should be satisfied with producing the simplest possible solution that gets the job done.

Inquisitive. Agile modelers enjoy exploring the problem domain as well as the solution space.

Skeptical. Agile modelers do not take things at face value but instead ask further questions, exploring an issue until they understand it sufficiently. They don't assume that a product or technique works according to its marketing literature; instead, they try it out for themselves.

Realistic. Agile modelers should be humble enough to know that they don't have all the answers, and sufficiently cautious to recognize that they should prove their models with code sooner rather than later.

Courageous. Agile modelers are willing to propose an idea, to model it, and then to try to prove it with code. If it doesn't work, they try to rework their approach or even discard it as appropriate. It takes courage to offer your ideas to your peers and then to try to validate them.

Experimental. Agile modelers should be willing to try new approaches, such as applying a new (or old) modeling technique. They should also be open to agile software development techniques in general and be willing to go against the grain of conventional wisdom when needed in order to validate ideas such as reducing the amount of documentation on a project.

Disciplined. It's very easy to say to yourself "adding this extra feature isn't going to hurt anything" or "I know better than my project stakeholders" and then act inappropriately. It takes discipline to stay on the agile path.

What happens if you don't exhibit all of these traits, yet still want to become an agile modeler? Don't worry. You can grow into the role with a little effort. Believe me, I'm not practical or realistic 100 percent of the time, and often I can become very uncommunicative. Nobody is going to exhibit all of these traits all the time. Instead, people will exhibit these traits to some extent. Everyone is different, and these differences bring strength to agile development teams. To some people, being inquisitive comes naturally. Other people need to consciously work on it. We're only human.

Generalists or Specialists?

Specialists are not to be trusted. Specialists are masters of exclusion, experts in the narrow.

Emperor Leto II, from *God Emperor of Dune* by Frank Herbert

When recruiting members for your team, you need to address the ratio of generalists to specialists that you wish to include. You need to consider the nature of modern software development. The lifecycle of the Enterprise Unified Process (EUP) (Ambler, 2001b) is depicted in Figure 12.1. The process workflows listed along the left-hand side hint at the potential complexity of software development—you may need to business model, gather requirements, analyze and design your system, and so on. This is clearly just the tip of the iceberg. The phases, Inception through to Production, listed across the diagram, are indicative of a changing focus throughout your project that requires different skills at various times. Software development is clearly very complex and an effort that requires significant skill and experience. It is important to understand that this complexity is inherent in software development in general, not just in the EUP—project teams taking an extreme Programming (XP) (Beck 2000) approach to development, a DSDM (Stapleton 1997) approach, or a SCRUM (Beedle and Schwaber 2001) approach also need to deal with these complexities. Although their lifecycles may not depict it as explicitly as the EUP's, XP's lifecycle is explored in detail in Part Three of

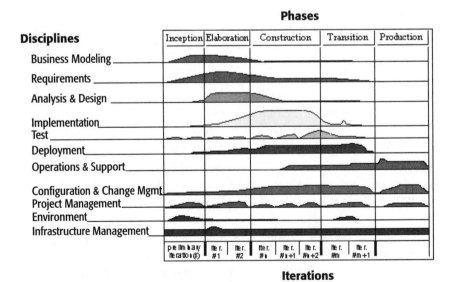

Figure 12.1   The lifecycle for the Enterprise Unified Process (EUP).

this book. Project teams following these methods still perform configuration management activities, management activities, and so on (albeit in different manners).

To address the complexity of software development, the first reaction of many organizations is to build a team of specialists. The general idea is that specialists are very proficient at a specific task and are therefore more efficient. To become efficient at software development, all you need to do is put together a team of specialists who work on their part of the project and hand-off their work to other specialists who evolve it from there. This is effectively the "assembly-line" school of thought, which works very well if you are mass producing cars, but in my experience does not work very well when you are attempting to hand-craft software. Furthermore, this approach is geared towards larger teams—if there are X distinct tasks required to develop software, then you need at least X specialists following this approach. How big is X? 20? 50? 100? Depends on how finely you define the specialties, doesn't it? If you are of the single artifact developer mindset, then just to handle modeling alone you may need over twenty specialists. There are that many artifacts listed in Appendix A, "Modeling Techniques," of this book. If you are of the single role developer mindset, then you have eleven roles on an EUP project just to cover the workflows. Specialists often have difficulties working with others. Either they lack the humility to recognize that people with different specialties than their own have something of value to add, or they are so narrowly focused that they don't realize that what they are doing is causing someone else later on to do significant rework (or perhaps the work that they are doing is simply being ignored). Another problem with specialists is their skills may not be very good at all, even in their own specialty. The high rate of technical change within the IT industry provides an environment where developers can work with a new technology for several months, become reasonably familiar with it, and claim to be an expert because few others are available with the same level of experience. Clearly there is a problem with building a team from people who are only specialists.

WARNING **Many Developers Specialize to Their Detriment**
Because of this inherent complexity of software development, a common trap is for developers to fall into the *Single Artifact Developer* anti-pattern (Ambler 2001a) where someone defines himself as a person that works on one type of artifact (for example: code, a use case model, or a data model) or into the *Single Role Developer* anti-pattern where someone defines herself as a person that performs one kind of task (for example: modeling, testing, or coding). In other words, the person is specializing in a specific role, a tendency that is often encouraged within large organizations following prescriptive processes (if they're following any process at all). The problem is that developers who fall into this trap are too narrowly focused to be productive on an agile software development project, although if they are willing to expand their horizons this issue can be overcome.

How about building a team of only generalists? Everyone would have a fairly good understanding of how to develop software, but unfortunately they wouldn't have the detailed knowledge required to get the job done. Your project will need people intimately familiar with the techniques and technology that you are using. If you're working with Enterprise JavaBeans (EJB), then you want developers with expertise in Java programming and in EJB development. A team working with Oracle on the backend will also want someone with Oracle database administration experience, and a team developing software for a brokerage will want people that understand the nuances of stock and bond trading.

In my experience, neither extreme works well. Instead, what you want is something in the middle. One approach is to build a team with some people who are generalists and some who are specialists; the generalists provide the glue within the team and focus on the bigger picture whereas the specialists focus on the detailed complexities of your project. This approach works well because the strengths of the generalists balance the weaknesses of specialists and vice versa, and it is often quite useful for a generalist to pair with a specialist because of this balance. A better approach would be to build a team comprised of people who are generalists with one or two specialties. For example: I would claim that I am a generalist because I have a pretty good handle on how it all fits together, yet I have specialties in business application software modeling, object persistence, and Java programming. One of my current co-workers is a generalist with specialties in modeling, EJB development, and testing, whereas another is a generalist with specialties in telecommunications networking and Java programming. The advantage of building teams from generalists that have one or more specialties is that they quickly find common ground with their co-workers, they're all generalists after all, and they have the necessary background to appreciate the importance of other specialties. The main disadvantage is that these people are often at senior level. A person easily needs ten to twenty years to gain sufficient experience to become a generalist, and thus generalists are difficult to obtain. You're very lucky if people such as this form a portion of your team.

> **TIP** **Novices Specialize at First**
> People who are new to development are typically overwhelmed by the vast range of knowledge that they need to gain. That's only natural. Most people will start out by focusing on one or two aspects of development, perhaps programming in Java or gathering user requirements, and then they use that experience as a base and branch out from there. They'll slowly build up their skillset with experience, perhaps gaining a specialty or two in the process and a better understanding of how it all fits together.

Recognize That There Is No "I" in Agile

In effective teams, everyone on the team realizes that they are supposed to be working together as a team. You saw in Chapter 1, "Introduction," that the first value of the Agile Alliance (2001a) is to prefer "individuals and interactions to processes and tools" and the third of four values is to prefer "customer collaboration to contract negotiation." The Agile Alliance also defined a collection of principles (Agile Alliance 2001b) for agile software development, including "business people and developers must work together daily throughout the project." These values and principles clearly indicate a preference toward teamwork within agile environments, toward people working together toward a common goal. This preference rings true with my own experiences as a software developer. The quality of my work is dramatically improved when I am working with one or more other people. My philosophy is that development is a lot like swimming. It is very dangerous to swim alone. That belief is reflected in the practice *Model with Others*.

Several years ago, I worked on a billing system and supporting customer service application for a large telecommunications firm. Part of that effort was the design of the user interface (UI) that the customer service representatives would work with. Because I had worked on a similar system previously for another client and because I have some experience at UI design, I jumped right into the creation of a prototype. The prototype was based on the requirements for the new billing system. We had invested significant time developing detailed use cases that had been reviewed and signed off by a committee representing our users (this wasn't an agile project). I thought I had a very good idea of what needed to be developed. Without any help from the project user representatives, most of them were attending a use case training course that week (long after they had learned about use cases from the developers, but that's another story about corporate dysfunction) and weren't readily available to me, I started prototyping. We were deploying to the Win32 platform, so I created a graphical user interface (GUI) that complied with the Microsoft UI design guidelines (Microsoft Corporation, 1995) and fulfilled the user requirements for the system. Or so I thought. I had modeled, on my own, close to 20 screens, many of which you could navigate between. In parallel, I had created a user interface flow diagram on the whiteboard in my cubicle, so I had the UI prototype to the point where it seemed to make sense. The UI prototype was amazing, at least in my mind, and I had clearly saved the project a significant amount of time by nailing down this critical part of the design. Then reality got in my way. When the user representatives returned, I was eager to show them what I had done so that we could declare victory and move on with the project; at the time I had not yet internalized AM's value of *Humility*. I was shocked to find that the prototype was completely unacceptable to them. Although we were deploying to a Win32 environment, we needed to follow the corporate design guidelines that mandated a monochrome text-based UI, not a color GUI, a constraint that hadn't been reflected in the requirements I was working from because it was assumed that everyone knew this, even though up until that point it was news to the developers. There were also very specific ways that certain information had to be displayed so that our system would look and feel like other customer service applications that our users currently worked with, yet another new constraint. Although the user interface flow diagram proved of some value, the vast majority of my effort had to be scrapped. I continued the UI prototyping effort from scratch, working closely with several of the user representatives who knew the existing system, or sometimes portions thereof, and who could provide guidance on how to design the user interface. When I had worked alone, I had fallen into the trap of not obtaining input from others. I was not following AM's principle of *Rapid Feedback*, and thus started to go in the wrong direction without knowing it. When I obtained feedback I then realized my mistake, a mistake that was obvious to my project stakeholders but not to my fellow developers. I got back on track by effectively following the practices *Active Stakeholder Participation* and *Model with Others*—several heads were clearly better than one.

Effective teamwork and effective communication (covered in Chapter 8, "Communication") are enablers of agility. Teamwork requires trust, something that must be built over time as you work with people and get to know them. Agile modelers actively seek out input and help from others; they are also happy to provide input and help to their fellow teammates, including both developers and project stakeholders, as required. AM's values of *Humility* and *Feedback* are critical factors promoting effective teamwork and communication. There is no "I" in team, and my experience is that there is no "I" in agile either.

Require that Everyone Actively Participates

I only have one rule: Everyone fights and nobody quits or I'll shoot you myself.

Sergeant Rasczak, From the movie, *Starship Troopers*

I couldn't have said it better myself. Software development works best when everyone works together. They are prepared to help their fellow teammates, and they are willing to take on a wide variety of tasks. When someone doesn't actively participate, when they sit in a modeling session as a passive observer or they don't help someone when asked, they not only reduce the overall productivity of your team but they also force someone else to do the work that they could have performed. People who are not actively participating are dead weight and are slowing down your project—either motivate them to join the effort or invite them to leave, either way you're better off.

There is always a lot of work to go around. There isn't any valid reason for someone to not be productive. Luckily, as you saw in Chapter 7, "Order from Chaos: How the AM Practices Fit Together," AM includes several practices that promote active participation. First, *Active Stakeholder Participation* insists that project stakeholders are expected to be actively involved in the software development effort, adding a valuable resource to your overall project efforts. Second, the practice *Collective Ownership* reduces barriers to participation by allowing everyone to work on anything that they need to—artifacts are owned by the team, not by the individuals that created them. Third, the practice *Model with Others* makes it difficult for people to hide because it motivates you to seek out help when you are modeling.

Model in Teams

Why is it important to build an effective team? Because modeling is best done by groups of people, not individuals. The practice *Model with Others* indicates that you should work together in teams when you are modeling. What it doesn't tell you is how to do so effectively. How big should the team be? Who should be on it? How do you ensure that a modeling session is effective?

There are several common styles of modeling teams:

Development pair. Many agile software development teams adopt the practice of having developers work together in pairs; in fact, pair programming is an explicit practice of XP (Beck 2000), and this includes modeling in pairs as well. It is quite common for you and your development pair, I prefer to avoid the term programming pair because you do far more than program, to discuss an idea or approach by working on a model together—perhaps creating a sketch on a whiteboard or writing a few CRC cards. Part Three of this book describes modeling on XP teams in detail.

Small impromptu/ad-hoc team. An impromptu/ad-hoc modeling team is one that is put together quickly, often in a matter of seconds, to address a specific issue. Once the team has addressed the issue, it just as quickly disbands. Agile developers will often form small ad-hoc modeling teams, often composed of two or three people, when they realize that they need help with what they are working on—perhaps they need more information about the business domain from a project stakeholder or need technical help from another developer. It's very easy to put together an ad-hoc modeling team when the entire team is co-located—when you know who is the best person to work with, you can simply walk over to them and ask for help and when you don't know who can help, you simply shout out something like "does anyone know anything about XYZ?" and hopefully someone does. When your team isn't co-located, it becomes much harder to put together an ad-hoc modeling team—it takes longer to identify who can help you, it becomes harder to work with them because you need to either communicate with them at a distance via a technology such as email or phone (see Chapter 8 for a discussion of communication strategies), or you need to wait until you can get together physically.

Designated team. Sometimes you will have designated teams of people who are specifically brought together to model. At the beginning of a project you may decide to have a requirements modeling session in which you bring together a group of users whose goal is to help you to identify initial requirements for your system and to identify your project's scope. People are designated to this team, the team fulfills its task, and the team disbands. Yes, some of the users may become involved with the project on a full time basis in the role of "customer" or "user representative," but that is a different issue. It is common to have a designated architecture team for a project, often comprised of all the developers on small project teams or a subset of developers on large project teams.

TIP Give Pair Development a Chance
Although pair development appears less productive on the surface because two people appear to be doing the job of one, the reality is that this approach is actually quite effective. Studies (Williams et. al. 2000) have shown that pair development results in greater consistency, efficiency, quality, and job satisfaction among developers. In my own anecdotal experience, pair development works—I have found that when you honestly try it for a month,

although many people will be skeptical at first (good for them!), after this time period, the vast majority of people will be exceptionally reluctant to go back to their old "single developer" ways.

WARNING **Members of Designated Modeling Teams Do More Than Model** Earlier, I argued that the most effective people on a development team are those that are able and willing to take on a variety of tasks, one of which is hopefully modeling. You may be a member of the designated architecture team, but that doesn't mean that architectural modeling is the only thing that you do. Ideally, you will also roll up your sleeves and write some code. The danger is that many developers prefer to focus on a single specialty and will use the fact that they are on a designated modeling team to justify taking just one role, such as architect or business analyst, on your team. The problem is that these people become out of touch with what the rest of the team is doing. They are not actively involved and likely not very interested in other aspects of the project, increasing the chance of "office politics" within your team due to lack of shared vision.

In my experience, small teams, either development pairs or small ad-hoc teams, perform the vast majority of modeling on agile software development projects. When you step back and think about it, this makes a lot of sense—when you follow the highly iterative and incremental approach favored by agile software development teams, you find that ad-hoc modeling efforts fit in very well. Furthermore, many agile developers, particularly those on XP teams, frequently choose to work in pairs because they find pair modeling to be very effective. Important work still occurs in designated modeling teams, often at the beginning of a project to gather initial requirements or to perform initial architecture or design modeling.

Making This Work in the Real World

Whenever I suggest the ideas presented in this chapter to my clients, the response always seems to be along the lines of "Yes, this all sounds good but we can't do that here because . . ." Sigh. Everyone seems to be convinced that their situation is different, and it is in some respects, but the reality is that the important things really are the same. People are people are people. Individuals have strengths and weaknesses; they have their own unique skill sets, their own priorities, and their own base of experience. There will always be interpersonal conflicts; there will always be new friendships formed and existing relationships to build upon. You can always build an effective team if you choose to do so, and you can always find an excuse for not doing so. In my experience, organizations that choose to be successful at team building often:

Communicate the importance of active stakeholder participation. I cannot stress this enough—project stakeholders must recognize that their active involvement with your project is critical to its success, and developers must understand that they need to work closely with their stakeholders.

Communicate the value of teamwork. The bottom line is that you're in this together, so work together effectively.

Ask people to try a new approach. Some people will always find an excuse for why a new approach, such as co-locating developers and project stakeholders, won't work. They'll often be unwilling to accept your arguments for the new approach, having made up their minds that it isn't going to work. When this is the case, I will ask them to give the new approach a fair shake, often asking them to honestly try it for a specified period of time (often a month or two) with the promise that at the end of the period we'll get back together to discuss the issue.

Rethink the composition of your team. If some people are unwilling to work in the manner that I've described in this chapter, one option that's open to you is to replace them with someone else. Some people simply don't have the skills, or the desire, to be part of a team—they work alone and are willing to live with the career-related consequences of that decision.

Stress the importance of learning new skills. It's very difficult to truly become a generalist with several specialties, requiring years of hard work to gain the necessary experience. If you haven't yet made this investment in your career, does that mean you can be involved with an agile modeling project? Of course you can. You don't need to know everything about software development, but you should be willing to learn new skills when the opportunity presents itself.

Building an effective team is a difficult task, one that is critical to the success of your project. The first step is to start with good raw material by recruiting good developers, people who may not have all the skills that they will need but at least are willing to learn them. The next step is to nurture the right attitude within the team—they need to work together to succeed. Everyone should actively participate in the development of your system and when modeling to work together in teams along the lines of the AM practice *Model with Others*. It takes time to build and nurture an agile modeling team, but doing so is one of the best investments your organization can make.

Agile Modeling Sessions

A modeling session is an activity where several people focus on the development of one or more models. Modeling sessions are an important part of any software development effort because they provide an opportunity for people to collaborate together in order to communicate their needs, to come to a better understanding, and ideally to work toward a solution. Traditionally the effectiveness of modeling sessions seems to range widely, from being very productive to virtually useless. In my experience, to be effective at Agile Modeling you will need to rethink your approach to modeling sessions, focusing on what works and excluding what doesn't. You need to consider the following issues:

- Duration
- Types of modeling sessions
- Participants in modeling sessions
- The formality of modeling sessions

Modeling Session Duration

Many organizations need to rethink the time that they invest in individual modeling sessions. The duration of effective modeling sessions often ranges from several minutes to several days, with the majority of the sessions lasting between ten and thirty minutes. Why such a wide range? To answer this question, you need to first consider when modeling sessions occur—modeling occurs throughout your entire development efforts. You need to understand that your focus changes throughout the project lifecycle. At the beginning of the lifecycle, you are typically more concerned with understanding "the big picture;" in the middle of the lifecycle, you are more concerned with building specific parts of your system; and at the end of the lifecycle, your focus is on transitioning your system into production. This change in focus will motivate different styles of modeling sessions, including different durations, throughout your effort.

You are likely to hold long modeling sessions at the beginning of the project lifecycle. During this phase of your project, there is a great need to define the scope for the project, to set the initial requirements, and to identify a candidate architecture based on those requirements. To reach these goals, you often find that you need to hold initial modeling sessions that may take several hours or even several days because you have a lot of ground to cover at the start of your project. In my experience, modeling sessions longer than two or three days put your project at risk—the longer you go without feedback, the greater the chance that what you are modeling does not reflect the requirements or the architecture. AM's principle of *Rapid Feedback* implores you to reduce the time between modeling something and verifying your model, either by reviewing it with someone else or by following the practice *Prove It with Code*. Another issue with long modeling sessions is that fatigue begins to set in among participants; modeling can be a mentally draining activity, reducing the quality of their work. Furthermore, the need of participants to return to their regular jobs makes it difficult for many participants to invest more than a couple of days at a time.

Sometimes there is significant pressure to have longer modeling sessions. Many people will argue that you want to get requirements identification over with as soon as possible. However, AM's principle *Embrace Change* tells you that this is a naïve goal at best because your stakeholders' understanding of what they need will evolve as the system does. Another common argument for longer sessions is that key personnel are only going to be available once, so you'd better take advantage of them while you can. Common justifications for this include that some people must travel great distances to attend your modeling sessions or they are too busy to take time away from their regular jobs to attend a series of sessions. The travel issue can be dealt with by applying alternative means of communication, covered in Chapter 8, such as videoconferencing and email. The argument that someone is too busy to participate is a red herring—it's far easier to schedule time for several small sessions than one large one. People will also argue that it's a lot of work to organize modeling sessions; therefore, it's better to have a few large ones than a lot of smaller ones. My advice is to loosen up a bit, make them less formal and therefore easier to organize.

You are likely to hold short modeling sessions, typically 10 to 20 minutes in length, during construction. At this point in time, your focus is implementing specific requirements, ideally "small requirement chunks." What are examples of small requirement chunks? On an XP project (Beck 2000) you would implement a user story, on a Feature-Driven Development (FDD) project (Coad, Lefebvre, and DeLuca 1999) you'd implement a feature, and on a Rational Unified Process (RUP) project (Kruchten 2000) you'd implement a portion of a use case. You'll be working very iteratively at this point, working with your project stakeholder to explore the pertinent requirements, perhaps creating an essential UI model or discussing the logic of a business rule, then moving forward to discuss a potential solution for that requirement. Often you will create a whiteboard sketch to facilitate the discussion and then move on to code and test the solution. Agile developers iterate quickly between these steps, modeling requirements with their project stakeholder(s) for a few minutes and then modeling the potential solution for a few minutes (ideally in a small group of two or three developers following the practice *Model with Others*). When you work on small requirement chunks and proceed iteratively, you quickly discover that short modeling sessions are sufficient.

How do you keep a modeling session short? First, prefer stand-up modeling sessions around a whiteboard or table because most people are only willing to stand up for short periods of time. Second, make it a habit to hold short modeling sessions, therefore when the sessions go longer people will start to feel uneasy about it. Third, keep the modeling session focused on a single topic. This is one of the advantages of working on a single, small requirement chunk at a time. Fourth, as the principle *Model with a Purpose* advises, stop modeling once you've fulfilled your goal.

Types of Modeling Sessions

Part of being effective at AM is rethinking the type of modeling sessions that you hold. A common problem that I see again and again is something that I call "single artifact modeling sessions." The problem is so common in fact that I've been tempted to write it up as a process antipattern (Brown, McCormick, and Thomas 2000). Common examples of single artifact modeling sessions, when you take them at face value, include use-case modeling sessions, data modeling sessions, and even class modeling sessions. The problem is that the modeling effort is too narrowly focused, although each one of those artifacts is important in its own right, they simply aren't robust enough to be effective. I've seen use-case modeling sessions that produced bloated use cases because the team started to record business rules, technical requirements, and even information about domain entities in their use cases because they didn't consider working on other artifacts. I've seen data modeling sessions that resulted in what appeared to be a great data model, at least at first, but that eventually proved to need significant refactoring—the data modelers focused only on data-related issues and didn't consider critical behaviors because "that was something the application programmers would worry about." Similarly, I've seen class modeling sessions produce models that resulted in horrendous performance because the object modelers chose to ignore database issues. Their object-oriented analysis and design (OOA&D) methodology was based strictly on the UML, the industry standard, and because UML still doesn't include a data model, they ignored these critical design issues. Besides, they felt the data administrators would deal with the critical design issues.

Why do single artifact modeling sessions occur? Many times they are driven by people who exhibit the *Single Artifact Developer* antipattern (Ambler 2001c). These are developers who focus on a single artifact such as use cases, data models, or class models. When this is your focus, naturally having modeling sessions that focus on the creation of that single artifact makes sense to you. This perception clearly goes against the tenets of AM, which explain that you need *Multiple Models* in your intellectual toolbox, that you should *Create Several Models In Parallel*.

A better approach is to hold what I call phase modeling sessions, a modeling session where your focus is on creating models pertinent to the major phases of traditional development, such as requirements, analysis, architecture, and design. In requirements modeling sessions, your focus would be on defining what your project stakeholders want your system to do. Analysis modeling sessions focus on fleshing out the requirements, architecture modeling sessions focus on identifying a high-level strategy for how your system will be built, and design modeling sessions focus on identifying a detailed strategy for building a portion of your system. In each of these modeling sessions, your team works on several models at once, as appropriate to the phase. For example: in a design modeling session, you may work on UML class diagrams, UML state charts, and physical data models. Note that teams following the RUP may want to consider these workflow-modeling sessions to stay consistent with RUP terminology.

The best approach is simply to hold agile modeling sessions. Agile software development is highly iterative, particularly on a day-to-day basis, where it is quite common to identify a requirement, analyze it, and propose a potential design strategy within minutes if not seconds. In my experience, that is the way that people actually work, including both developers and stakeholders. For example: when a stakeholder tells me that they need to maintain the surface address for their customers, I quickly start thinking about changing the design of the customer editing screen, adding a new class called SurfaceAddress that the Customer class will interact with, and then making changes to my database on the back end to support this new requirement. Within seconds, I go from thinking about requirements, through analysis, and then to design. From the project stakeholder side of things, I have often run across stakeholders who not only had a requirement but also had a strategy for fulfilling that requirement. Power users who work with both the system and who create ad-hoc reports from the database commonly have ideas about how things should be built. In this case, the power user is jumping from requirements straight to design. Yes, it's not the role of your stakeholders to determine how a system should be built; that's a responsibility for developers (see Chapter 9). Therefore, you have an issue to deal with in this situation. If this is the way that people actually work, they quickly iterate between phases, then doesn't it make sense for your software process to reflect this fact? This is where agile modeling sessions come in. In an agile modeling session, you apply the practices of AM, and, in particular, you *Create Several Models In Parallel*, you *Apply The Right Artifact(s)* as needed, and you *Iterate to Another Artifact* as needed. An agile modeling session is one where you model requirements when you need to, where you model your design when you need to, and so on. Yes, you still want to consider requirements issues, analysis issues, and so on when you are modeling, but now you will be iterating back and forth between them.

My advice is to never have single artifact modeling sessions, even if your intention is in fact to work on several artifacts at once. This can be hard in some organizations, particularly those that have been following traditional approaches in the past and therefore may be predisposed to highly-specialized efforts such as data modeling sessions or organizations that have bought into the "use-case driven" marketing rhetoric that dominates object-oriented development methods right now. Phase modeling sessions are often advisable at the beginning of a project when fundamental issues such as the scope of the effort and what your architecture should be are yet to be determined. Phase modeling sessions are also appropriate when you are first adopting agile software development practices and your organization is still struggling with the inherent cultural changes required to do so—phase modeling sessions may be a palatable baby step away from single artifact modeling sessions. Agile modeling sessions are common for short modeling sessions during construction as well as for teams experienced in agile software development when they hold longer modeling sessions that are common at the beginning of a project.

Participants in Modeling Sessions

Who should you include in a modeling session for it to be effective? There are two categories of roles in modeling sessions: active participants and supporting participants. The active participant category contains three basic roles: Project stakeholders who provide information about the business and help prioritize requirements; analysts who specialize in working directly with project stakeholders to potentially gather/ elicit information from them, document that information, and validate that information; and developers who work on the models. Active participants are first-class modeling citizens; they do the "real work" of modeling and are critical to the success of your project.

> **TIP** **There Are Advantages and Disadvantages to Including Analysts**
> You need to be careful with how you involve analysts, sometimes known as business analysts or requirements analysts, on your project. Although they specialize in working with project stakeholders, clearly a very good thing, and can often prove adept acting as a bridge between project stakeholders and hard-core developers whose communication skills may be lacking, they can also act as a barrier to project productivity. When a business analyst is involved on a project many developers will choose to use them as a crutch, to let the analyst focus on working with stakeholders and thereby freeing themselves up to focus on the technology. This isn't very good. You really want developers to interact closely with project stakeholders and apply their technical skills to build the appropriate software. In AM, there are two primary ways that analysts can be effective. First, in situations where the developers are co-located with project stakeholders, the analysts can help build initial rapport between stakeholders and developers and mentor the developers in communication and modeling skills. At the same time, the developers should mentor the analysts in the technology, remember the principle *Everyone Can Learn from Everyone Else*, to make them more effective. In this situation, your goal should be for your business analysts to take on full development roles, they should no longer specialize, as quickly as possible. Second, when your team does not have ready access to project stakeholders, clearly a serious problem that threatens your likelihood of success, they can gather information from project stakeholders for the developers and present that information in a format that the developers need. However, you are introducing an opportunity for information to be

distorted and misinterpreted by not having direct communication. Think back to the "telephone game" that you used to play as a child where one child whispered a message to another, who then whispered that message to another, and so on until the message got back to the original child. The more people in between the transmitter and the receiver, the greater the distortion.

The supporting participant category encapsulates three roles: facilitator, scribe, and observer. Many modeling sessions work perfectly well without anyone in these roles, particularly small sessions between developers who are modeling to understand a portion of the design of the system that they are working on. However, larger modeling sessions, particularly ones early in the project, will often have people who fulfill these roles. Let's explore them in detail:

Facilitator. A facilitator is someone who is responsible for planning, running, and managing modeling sessions. As a result, facilitators have good meeting skills, they understand the modeling process, and they ask valid, intelligent questions to elicit information from the active participants. The role of facilitator is often taken up by the coach, an XP role, or project team lead. This is usually a senior person that the developers and stakeholders trust and respect and who has good communication and modeling skills. Large organizations may have professional meeting facilitators on staff that they typically use for more formal modeling sessions. The advantage of professional meeting facilitators is that they are very thorough and good at their jobs. The major disadvantage is that they are often better suited for prescriptive processes and may need some coaching in agility. Although smaller and informal modeling sessions may not have a designated person whose only role is to facilitate, there still needs to be someone(s) responsible for ensuring that the modeling session is run effectively.

Scribe. A scribe is a person responsible for recording information during a modeling session. As a result, scribes need good listening skills, good oral communication skills (they will often need to ask questions to determine exactly what the active participants mean), and they have an ear for business logic and technical details. There are two schools of thought regarding whom to put in the scribe role: a professional scribe, often a technical writer, or a developer. I prefer putting a developer in that role, both to help grow them as communicators as well as to ensure that they are actually picking up what is being discussed. To hear a user tell you what they actually want and how they actually work with your software can be a good lesson in humility, as opposed to the really neat features that you mistakenly believe they can't wait to receive. To be fair, and to ensure that everyone on your team has the opportunity to improve his or her skill set, you should make this role a rotating one that an individual fills occasionally. Finally, if you're going to have scribes in your modeling sessions, you may decide to simply record all information in the models that you are creating. Then, you are best to have two or even three people scribing—you can't write as fast as several people can talk, and because each person has their own unique background, they will pick up (as well as miss) different types of information.

Observer. Traditionally, an observer is someone who is not there to participate in a modeling session but instead is supposed to sit back and watch what occurs so that they can learn the process. Perhaps they are a facilitator in training or they are involved with an upcoming project that will take the same approach that your team is following. Someone who sits there and does nothing? That doesn't sound right. A more agile approach is to put "observers" to work, as active participants if they have domain knowledge or modeling skills or worst case as scribes. The goal of an observer is to learn the process, and the best way to learn things is through hands-on experience. By having them involved with the modeling session not only do you increase the number of people actually adding value in your modeling session, you also improve their learning experience. Two birds, one stone.

How many people should be involved with a modeling session? Just barely enough. Every single person should have a valid reason for being there, not just a political reason such as "Sally Jones insists that someone from her group attends." If Sally Jones provides someone, then they should come to the modeling session prepared to work and be willing to follow through on any action items that they are assigned during the modeling session, such as obtaining more information or being involved in a follow up effort. There is often significant political pressure for too many people to be involved in a modeling session, particularly at the start of a project, pressure that is hard to counteract. I will very often hold a large requirements gathering session at the beginning of a project that has far too many people, twenty or thirty people in these meetings are common although sometimes you can have several hundred people in some situations, just to let everyone know that their voices are being heard as well as to help identify the handful of project stakeholders that can actually contribute something of value. I'll also do the same thing when it comes to architecture, involving a wide range of technical people throughout the organization. But there are diminishing rates of return once you've reached groups of seven or eight people—there is less of a chance that a new person will bring new information to the group, assuming you're picking participants in an intelligent manner, and there is less opportunity for an individual to actively participate because you are dividing the amount of "air time" between a greater number of people. Finally, the more people you have in a modeling session the more formal it needs to become to manage the effort.

The Formality of Modeling Sessions

First and foremost, just because a modeling session is formal it doesn't mean that it is necessarily less agile. Yes, formality has a bad reputation among many developers, but that doesn't mean that a formal session cannot be an effective one. At one end of the spectrum, you have very formal modeling sessions such as Joint Application Development (JAD) sessions (Wood and Silver 1995). Traditionally, a JAD is a facilitated and highly structured meeting that has specific roles (facilitator, participant, scribe, and observer), defined rules of behavior including when to speak, and suggestions for room organization (typically a U-shaped table). Before a JAD session, you commonly distribute a well-defined agenda and an information package that everyone is expected to read. Official meeting minutes are written and distributed after a JAD, including a list of action items assigned during the JAD that the facilitator must ensure are actually performed. At the other end of the spectrum are impromptu/ad hoc "stand-up" modeling sessions where the impetus for having them is often the realization that you need some help. People are quickly gathered, hopefully the "right" people are readily available, you work together standing around a whiteboard, and once you're done you quickly disband.

The formality of modeling sessions can be anywhere in between these two extremes, and, in fact, modern application of the JAD approach is often less formal. Table 13.1 suggests when each style may be applicable. Because your immediate needs often include applicability factors from each type of formality, you need to decide how formal to make your session. For example: how formal would you want to make a ten-person, half-day modeling session where all ten people work at the same physical location and can be scheduled within a two-day notice? How about a five-person, two-day modeling session where two people need to fly in from another location? The answer is the same for both situations: just formal enough. The greater the formality, the more work you need to do to hold the modeling session, and according to the principle *Maximize Stakeholder Investment*, any work that you do should have positive value for your project. Distribute an agenda if it will help people to prepare properly for the session; don't forget that your agenda could be as simple as an email. Distribute meeting minutes if appropriate; the minutes could be as simple as an email listing point-form action items assigned to individuals and a URL pointing to a web page of digital

Table 13.1   When Each Formality Style Is Applicable

MODELING SESSION STYLE	APPLICABILITY
Formal (for example, traditional JAD)	• Large groups (greater than eight participants) • Long modeling sessions (greater than one day is typical) • Participants from different geographical areas • Participants from different organizations or organizational areas • Qualified facilitator available • Project has ability to tolerate increased time required of formal modeling sessions • Regulatory requirement to hold formal modeling sessions (try to negotiate this requirement away)
Informal (for example, ad hoc)	• Smaller, co-located groups • People are readily available, willing, and able to participate • Shorter modeling sessions (less than one hour is typical) • Time-to-market a critical factor for your project

pictures of the diagrams that you created during the modeling sessions. AM's practice *Create Simple Content* applies to management artifacts as well as models.

TIP Formal Sessions Can Still Be Agile
There is nothing wrong with formality as long as it is applied in the appropriate situations. In the end, it boils down to using the right tool for the job, and every so often a formal modeling session is the best approach. Having said that, it has been several years since I've been involved in one.

How to Make This Work in the Real World

There are two common challenges for organizations to overcome with respect to modeling sessions:

1. **No modeling sessions at all.** Some organizations do not hold modeling sessions as a regular part of their software development efforts—either they have no one on staff with modeling skills, the developers don't want to model, the project stakeholders are unwilling to invest the time to be involved with modeling efforts, or the organization simply has never tackled a software development project before. When this is the case, the first step is to identify the root cause and address it appropriately. If there is no one on staff with adequate modeling skills, your staff needs training and mentoring, often from consultants or contractors, and perhaps you need to hire someone with those skills. If either the developers or project stakeholders are unwilling to be involved with modeling sessions, education is clearly warranted.

2. **Ineffective modeling sessions.** A far more common problem occurs when organizations hold too many modeling sessions, hold them for too long, invite too many people to them, or require excessive formality. These organizations must first recognize that they have a problem and that there are viable alternatives to their current approach. The next step is to identify the problem areas and deal with them appropriately following the advice presented in this chapter. Very often this will become a political issue, one that weak managers will avoid dealing with. In my mind, you need to make a decision: are you taking an agile approach to development or not? If you choose to be agile, you need to be prepared to step on a few toes—many of the people outside of your team think and work in non-agile ways that conflict with your goals and approaches. In Chapter 29, I describe techniques for overcoming common adversities that you will face when you introduce AM into your organization. One of the most important strategies available to you is to remain resolute about being agile.

The advice presented in this chapter is simply common sense. It isn't impossible to adopt these techniques. Thousands of project teams manage to hold effective modeling sessions every day. You merely need to choose to be one of them.

Agile Documentation

. . . anyone who leaves behind him a written manual, and likewise anyone who receives it, in the belief that such writing will be clear and certain, must be exceedingly simple-minded . . .

—Plato

When I initially started work on Agile Modeling, I wanted to focus solely on principles and practices for effective modeling, but I quickly discovered that this scope was not sufficient. I also needed to consider how to be effective at the creation and maintenance of documentation. Some agile models will "evolve" into official system documentation, although the vast majority will not, and therefore it is relevant to discuss how to be agile doing so.

Let's start with understanding the relationships between models, documents, source code, and documentation, something depicted in Figure 14.1. From AM's point of view, a document is any artifact external to source code whose purpose is to convey information in a persistent manner. This is different from the concept of a model, which is an abstraction that describes one or more aspects of a problem or a potential solution addressing a problem. Some models will become documents, or be included as a part of them, although many more will simply be discarded once they have fulfilled their purpose. Some models will be used to drive the development of source code, although some models may simply be used to drive the development of other models. Source code is a sequence of instructions, including the comments describing those instructions, for a computer system. Although source code is clearly an abstraction, albeit a detailed one, within the scope of AM it will not be considered a model because I want to distinguish between the two concepts. Furthermore, for the sake of discussion, the term documentation includes both documents and comments in source code.

In this chapter I address the following topics:

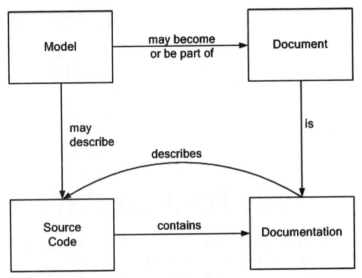

Figure 14.1   The relationship between models, documents, documentation, and source code.

- Why do people document?
- When does a model become a document?
- What are the trade-offs associated with documentation?
- What does it mean to travel light?
- When is a document agile?
- What type of documents do you need?
- Effective hand-offs
- Strategies for increasing the agility of documentation

Why Do People Document?

Agile developers recognize that documentation is an intrinsic part of any system, the creation and maintenance of which is a "necessary evil" to some and an enjoyable task for others, an aspect of software development that can be made agile when you choose to do so. There are four valid reasons to create documentation:

1. **Your project stakeholders require it.** The creation of documentation is fundamentally a business decision, not a technical one. You are investing the resources of your project stakeholders in the development of the documentation; therefore, they should have the final say on whether their money is to be spent that way. If your project stakeholders request a document from you, perhaps at your suggestion, and understand the trade-offs involved (more on this later), then you must create the document. It is important to note that eXtreme Programming (XP) is very explicit about documentation being a business decision (Jeffries 2001b) but that

the Unified Process (UP) does not appear to share this philosophy, a concept that UP teams need to adopt to apply AM effectively.

You should create documentation only when your project stakeholders ask you to? Preposterous you say! Well, in my experience, this isn't preposterous. Your project stakeholders include a wide variety of people, including all of the clients of your system, and therefore they should have a reasonably good idea of what they want. Maintenance developers, or someone representing them if they are not in place yet, will request system overview documentation. Users and their management will likely request user documentation. Operations staff will request operations documentation. Yes, you will need to work closely with them to determine what they actually need. Someone is going to have to decide to pay for the development and subsequent maintenance of the documentation, and you may even need to explain the implications of what is being requested, but this is doable.

2. **To define a contract model.** Contract models define how your system and an external system interact with one another. Some interactions are bi-directional, whereas others are uni-directional, making the interaction(s) explicitly to everyone involved. Contract models are often required when an external group controls an information resource that your system requires, such as a database, legacy application, or information service. The AM practice *Formalize Contract Models* states that a contract model is something that both parties should mutually agree to, document, and change over time if required. It is important to understand that your project stakeholder should still verify the development of a contract model—it is their money that you are spending, and they can choose to be at risk and not have the contract model in place.

3. **To support communication with an external group.** It isn't always possible to co-locate a development team and it isn't always possible to have project stakeholders (or at least the ones you need at the time) available at all times. When you need to work with an external group of people, you need to find ways to communicate with them, and shared documentation is often part of the solution in combination with occasional face-to-face discussions, teleconferencing, email, and collaborative tools. To use documentation as your primary means of communication is a mistake because it's far too easy to misunderstand something that has been written, but it is a good supporting mechanism. A good way to think of documentation in this situation is that it is your option of last resort. Note that this in effect is an extension of the practice *Model to Communicate* into the realm of documentation.

4. **To think something through.** Many people will write documentation either to verify for themselves some group work they had just been involved with or simply to increase their own understanding. This in effect is an extension of the practice *Model to Understand* into the realm of documentation.* The act of

---

*Although I have cheated a bit here and applied the practices *Model to Communicate* and *Model to Understand* to the creation of documentation I want to emphatically point out where AM is concerned the concepts of "model" and "document" are orthogonal. I apologize if this is a bit frustrating, but unfortunately the world is a fuzzy place. Embrace fuzziness!

writing, of putting your ideas down on paper, can help you to solidify them and discover problems with your thinking. What appears clear and straightforward in your mind can often prove to be very complicated once you attempt to describe it in detail, and you can often benefit from writing it down first. For this reason, I suggest that people write comments before they write their code (Ambler 2001a), a strategy that I have been following for years.

This likely differs from what you are used to doing, which makes sense because I'm talking about how to become more agile in your approach to documentation. Why is this different, and why is it more agile? In my experience, developers in non-agile environments are often forced to create documentation for less-than-ideal reasons, often based on political reasons and sometimes due to sheer ignorance, and therefore may not have been allowed to be as effective as they possibly can. Questionable reasons for creating documentation, and how to combat them, include:

The requester wants to be seen to be in control (although isn't actually doing anything of value). People will request documents, such as specifications and detailed architecture documents, that they can sign off on and say, "Yes, go ahead and build us one of these." Whenever I find myself in this situation, I ask the individual(s) requesting the documents if they also want to be seen as responsible for the project's failure because the development team was too busy writing documentation and not building software. I'll then suggest that instead of requesting documentation they should instead request access to the software itself, even if it is just an internal release of the software, so they can provide constructive feedback about it. They can still be seen to be an active participant in the project and can do so in a productive manner.

The requester wants to justify their existence. This typically occurs when someone who is "dead wood" is desperate to be seen doing something. This is an insidious problem because the requester often has what appears on the surface to be a good reason for requesting the documentation, it's something they've been doing for years, and management often believes it's necessary. To address this problem, ask the requester what they intend to with the document, why they need it, why creating that documentation for them is more important than other work that my team needs to do, and so on to try to determine the actual value of what they're doing. These are valid questions to ask, albeit uncomfortable ones for someone that doesn't add much value to the development effort.

The requester doesn't know any better. Many people have been working in organizations that have been following non-agile processes for years, processes that were likely documentation-centric, processes that produced a lot of documents for review throughout the process and finally software at the end of it. This is what they're used to so they are simply asking you for something they've received in the past. The idea that you can produce software early in the project, that it's your primary goal, is new and often radical to many people.

Your process says to create the document. Although this isn't a problem with agile software processes, it definitely can be one with prescriptive software processes. The most common reasons for this problem include people wanting to justify their existence, people not understanding the software development process or at least the implications of what they are requesting, and situations where the primary goal is to bill for hours as opposed to develop software effectively. Once again, the best strategy to address this problem is to explore whether the creation of the document actually provides value to your efforts.

Someone wants reassurance that everything is okay. Your project stakeholders are investing significant resources in your project team, they're taking a risk on you, and they want to know that their investment is being well spent. To get this reassurance, they'll ask you for documentation, status reports or overview documents perhaps, not understanding that you need to take time away from your true goal of developing software and not realizing that a better request would be to see the software itself (as indicated earlier, they don't know any better). You need to recognize when your project stakeholders are looking for reassurance, something common at the beginning of a project if they don't trust your team yet, and find an alternative way to provide that assurance (perhaps by showing them working software).

You're specifying work for another group. Although I identified this situation in Chapter 1 as one where AM likely isn't appropriate, the situation is still a common one for justifying the creation of significant amounts of documentation. Documentation is one way to communicate, but it isn't the best way (see Chapter 8). Try to find alternative approaches, such as occasional meetings with the other group or use of collaborative tools, to reduce your reliance on documentation.

Your development contracts are routinely subject to re-competition. This problem is endemic in firms that work for government agencies, although businesses will often threaten their contractors with putting a project up for bid again if they don't perform. So what? If your primary goal is to develop software, then focus on doing so and you're much more likely to perform adequately enough to keep the contract. The direct client in this situation is often operating under the misguided belief that if you don't perform they can take the documentation that you produce and provide it to the next contractor who will start from there. This borders on delusional in my opinion. If you're doing such a bad job that you lose the contract chances are good that you've also done a bad job of the documentation and therefore the next contractor will need to rework it. Even if you've done a perfect job of the documentation, yet still lose the contract, the next contractor will likely have people with different skills and enough time will have passed that they will need to revisit the requirements anyway. No matter how you look at it, the next contractor is unlikely to take advantage of the documentation you produce.

When Does a Model Become Permanent?

On the surface, the lifecycle of an agile model is fairly straightforward. Figure 14.2 depicts a high-level UML statechart for models. Models will start out as an idea such as

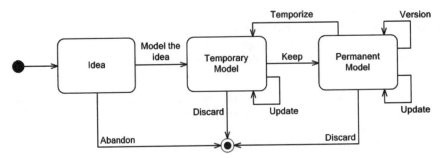

Figure 14.2   A UML statechart that depicts the lifecycle of an agile model.

"we need to understand how we're going to build this," "how do the users want this to work," or "we need to show what we're going to deliver" that you either choose to model or to abandon. (For the sake of our discussion, any activity you choose to perform instead of modeling counts as abandonment.) The model starts out being temporary, one that you intend to discard once it has fulfilled its immediate purpose, the typical fate of the vast majority of models created by agile developers. These models are often hand-drawn sketches resulting from the practice *Model to Understand*, although many of the models created as the result of *Model to Communicate* are also discarded once the idea has been communicated to your intended audience. You'll naturally update temporary models as needed, often creating them, working on them, and then discarding them over a short period of time: many agile models are created by two or three people in a couple of minutes to facilitate their discussion, whereas other agile models are created in modeling sessions of several people over a period of several hours. The interesting transition depicted in Figure 14.2 occurs when you decide to keep a temporary model, to make it permanent, to make it one of your project team's official documents. A temporary model becomes a "keeper" when it meets all of the following criteria:

- There is a clear and valuable reason to make it permanent.
- There is an audience for which the model provides value.
- Your project stakeholders are willing to invest in having it evolved into documentation.

NOTE **Models Aren't Necessarily Documents**
An implication of Figure 14.2 is that models are not always documents; many models are temporary in nature. Furthermore, documents aren't always models. For example: I would not consider a user manual to be a model. This is important because many people believe otherwise. When they hear the word "model" they automatically translate it to "document" and all the negative connotations (although rarely the positive ones) that word implies. Repeat after me—Models are not necessarily documents, models are not necessarily documents, models are not necessarily documents. I like to say that the concepts of "model" and "document" are orthogonal because you can clearly

have one without the other. In my experience, acceptance of this idea is an important step toward becoming more agile.

Points #1 and #2 are driven by the principle *Model with a Purpose*: you should not only have a valid reason for creating the model in the first place, but your documents should also have a definite purpose. You should know whom you are creating the documentation for—perhaps a subgroup of your development team, your users, or the team(s) that will maintain and operate your system once you've released it—and what they need from that documentation. The fundamental idea is that the creation and maintenance of a document is a burden on your development team, and if you want to increase someone's burden you should be able to justify why. It's as simple as that. Documentation is a burden, and when people recognize this simple fact they put themselves in a significantly better position to consider it appropriately. The burden of documentation is often underestimated, not only does it sap resources (and hence budget) from your project team but it also saps morale because few developers enjoy writing documentation and particularly resent writing needless documentation. Yes, effective documentation can provide significant benefits to your project team and project stakeholders, and as the principle *Maximize Stakeholder Investment* tells you, the benefits should outweigh the increased burden on your team. It's important to note that sometimes the benefits are received by someone else other than the people experiencing the costs. For example: your development team is impacted by the costs of creating system documentation that your maintenance developers benefit from. The implication is that when you are considering the costs and benefits of documentation you need to look at the entire picture, the trade-offs of which are described in the *What Are the Trade-offs Associated with Documentation?* section. Point #3 is also driven by the principle *Maximize Stakeholder Investment* and the concept that because it is the resources of your project stakeholders that are being invested that they should be the one to direct how those resources are invested, for better or worse.

As you can see in Figure 14.2, you can rethink your decision about making a model permanent, often because you realize that the benefit provided by the model is far less than the burden of maintaining it. When this happens, the model is either discarded outright or, more commonly, the owners of that model simply stop keeping it up to date and it starts to "gather dust." Sometimes these models are revived months or years later by the development team, the maintenance team, or the "redevelopment team" if the system is being rewritten. These stagnant models are often reviewed, recognized as being significantly out of date, and either then discarded or used as a template from which to create a new version of the model. Ideally, this new version is leaner than the original model, because if the original model didn't provide positive value to your effort then an updated version of it following the same approach likely won't provide value either. Techniques for doing so are discussed in the Section *Strategies for Increasing The Agility of Documentation*.

NOTE **Temporary Models Can Be Long Lived**
Just because a model is temporary doesn't mean that you discard it immediately. Temporary models, all models in fact, should be discarded once they are no longer needed. Many models, particularly sketches, are discarded

almost immediately—you draw them on a whiteboard and then erase them. Other models may exist for a much longer period, often evolving throughout that period. For example, development teams commonly draw one or more system architecture diagrams on a shared whiteboard and leave the drawings there for weeks, evolving the diagram(s) over time as they explore how they are going to build the system.

There are two basic reasons why many models are temporary. First, if a model serves its purpose and no longer adds value, then it should be discarded so that it's not getting in your way. Remember, travel light. Second, many models are superceded by other artifacts such as other models, source code, or test cases. When this happens, you do not need the first model anymore so why keep it around? You may decide to keep the first model, however, if it's not being truly superceded by the new artifact(s). For example, although a UML Class Diagram may be replaced by Java source code, you may decide to keep that diagram because it provides an overview of your code. In this case, the class diagram hasn't truly been superceded.

What Are the Trade-Offs Associated with Documentation?

Agile developers recognize that effective documentation is a balancing act, the goal being to have just enough documentation at just the right time for just the right audience. To accomplish this you must address the following issues:

Software development versus documentation development. This is the fundamental issue that you need to grapple with—any time spent creating documentation is time spent not developing new functionality for your users. At one end of the spectrum are projects where no documentation is written at all, whereas at the other end no software is written at all; neither extreme is likely to be appropriate for your situation. Remember that your primary goal is to produce software—you want to support your users' business activities, you want to generate revenue for your organization, you want to receive feedback on your work, you want to prove to your users that you can produce—but that you need to counteract this with your secondary goal, which is to enable the next effort.

Software developers have the knowledge; technical writers have the skill. Like it or not, few technical people have good writing skills, if only for the simple reason that they haven't taken the time to gain them. The best person suited to write documentation is the one that knows the topic being written about, in this case the developers of the system. Many teams will simply hand off a system, or portion thereof, to a technical writer and ask them to "figure it out." This has the advantage of minimizing the effort on the part of the developer but increases the effort required by the technical writer and increases the chance that they'll get it wrong. A better approach is for the developer to write the initial version of documentation and then hand it off to a technical writer for clean up. This is likely more effective, the developer does a "knowledge dump" and the technical writer refactors the material to present it effectively, but has the disadvantage that the developer may not know how to get started or even what to write about. A third approach, the best one in my opinion, is to have the technical writer and developer work together* to write the documentation, learning from each other as they do so.

What is required during development is often different than what is required after development. You have different needs during development than you do post-development—for the sake of discussion, post-development activities include the period where you are transitioning a release into production, and when the release is in production, the Transition and Production phases of the Enterprise Unified Process (Ambler and Constantine 2002). During development you're exploring both the problem and solution spaces, trying to understand what you need to build and how things work together. During post-development you want to understand what was built, why it was built that way, and how to operate it. Furthermore, during development you are much more willing to tolerate rough drafts, sketches, and greater inconsistency—it's your own work after all—whereas during post-development, you typically want more formal documentation. Finally, during development you likely want less documentation, you prefer to travel light, than you do during post-development.

Willingness to write documentation versus willingness to read it. How many times have you been asked a question by someone that was clearly documented in a manual that they have at their desk? Happens all the time. The abbreviation "RTFM," read the !@#$%^& manual, is a common response in email. The implication is that you can write documentation but it doesn't mean that people are going to read it—if this is the case, why are you writing so much?

Do you document as you work or when you are finished? One extreme is to write all of your documentation in parallel with developing software. You capture relevant information as you progress, but as your software evolves you will also need to rework your documentation. This not only slows your development efforts down, but it also results in wasted effort—documentation that you wrote yesterday will need to be rewritten or discarded today. You are no longer traveling light. When your requirements have not yet stabilized, and you are taking an iterative approach to development, excessive documentation can become very expensive to maintain because you are constantly updating it to reflect changes. The other extreme is to wait until you are finished and then write the documentation. The primary advantage being that you are writing about a known and stable thing (the release of the software that you just built). There are clearly several disadvantages to this approach. You have likely forgotten some of the reasons behind the decisions that you made, you may not have the right people anymore to write the documentation, you may not have funding to do the work, or the will to write the documentation may no longer

---

*I'm reticent to introduce the term "pair documentation," similar conceptually to XP's pair programming practice, but if anyone wants to take it and run with it then be my guest.

exist. An effective middle ground is to take notes of important decisions that you make, often something you can do in your source code, and to retain copies of the critical diagrams and models that you create during development. In other words, travel as light as you possibly can but no lighter.

Internal versus external documentation. Do you place all of your documentation in your code, do you write "self-documenting" code for that matter, or do you place all of your documentation in external artifacts? Once again, you need to find an effective middle ground. When your audience is developers, the best place to put the majority of the documentation is in the source code. Yes, you will likely also need a system overview document for this group, but the reality is that these people aren't going to trust, let alone read, documentation outside of the code—and if they're really smart, they won't trust the documentation in the code either. However, the audience for documentation is much wider than just developers. You will likely need to write documentation for people that won't have access to the source code or at least don't have the ability to understand it, such as users, senior management, and operations staff. These audiences will require external documentation written to meet their exact needs.

Project-level versus enterprise-level documentation. Not all of the documentation that you will write will be specifically for your project team or for the team(s) taking over your system. Some of it may need to be made available at an enterprise level. AM's practice *Reuse Existing Resources* advises you to take advantage of existing artifacts, including but not limited to system documentation and models within your organization. This may include existing definitions of business rules, existing interfaces to legacy systems and their documentation (effectively existing contract models), a corporate metadata repository describing the data resources throughout your company, or an enterprise business model. Where did these resources come from? The source information came from other project teams such as yours and is likely administered by a corporate team of specialists. Yes, this is clearly a situation that is likely to promote needless bureaucracy but it is still possible to be agile— the centralized administration teams need to find a way to work with yours effectively. During development, they should provide the resources such as existing models and metadata that you need and act as consultants when you need help understanding and working with those resources. Post-development they should help you capture relevant information to feed back into the shared enterprise resources, for example, part of the process of transitioning your system into production may be to ensure that updates to your corporate business rules and metadata repositories are made. Centralized administration teams need to be customer focused to be truly agile, they must provide real business value for their efforts, and actively strive to understand how and why the resources that they manage are used by their customers.

Quantity versus quality. The basic trade-off is the "security" of having the document against your trust in its accuracy. What would you rather have, a 2000-page system document that is likely to have a significant number of errors in it but a lot of details or a 20-page, high-level overview? The large document would very likely have most of the information that you need to maintain and enhance your system, but would you trust the information contained in it? The short document likely wouldn't contain the detailed information you need, but it would provide a map from where you could dive into the source code, or other documents, for details. You'd be more likely to trust this document because it's shorter, worst case you could easily update or simply rewrite it if you found it to be grossly inaccurate, and it deals with high-level concepts such as your system architecture that will change more slowly than the detailed minutiae contained in the larger document. I am not saying that a larger document is automatically of lower quality than a shorter one, but I am saying that it is likely to be perceived as such until proven otherwise.

What Does It Mean to Travel Light?

One of the greatest misunderstandings people have about the concept of traveling light is that it means you don't create any documentation. The reality is that nothing could be further from the truth. What traveling light does mean, at least in the context of AM, is that you create just enough models and just enough documentation to get by. On extremely rare occasions, that may mean you create no models whatsoever, perhaps on a very small project, or even no documentation. But for the vast majority of projects, you need to create some models and some documents.

How can you ensure that you're traveling light? A good rule of thumb is that you shouldn't create a model or document until you actually need it—creating either too early puts you at risk of wasting your time working on something you don't actually need yet. I once worked on a commercial software system—one that organizations can either buy and install out of the box or, more typically, purchase and then modify it to meet their exact needs. One day our sales person got a new lead on a company that wanted our system, but this company was in a new domain that we didn't have experience in yet. We figured we were going to get this sale, and we eventually did get it, so before we even met with the client, myself and a couple of others started modeling the expected changes that we thought we would need to make. After several days of modeling sessions, we came to the conclusion that the changes were going to be easy, our system was amazing after all, and we would have no problem supporting this new client. Then we talked to them. Of the seventy or so new requirements we had identified we had gotten about half of them right, not bad considering we didn't know what we were talking about, but we had missed several hundred others. Naturally, our models based on our faulty requirements were of little value and we had to discard them and start fresh, something that was made a little harder because we needed to shift our mindset away from our original approach. Even worse, we went into the first meeting with a cocky attitude because we thought we knew it all, an attitude that would have lost us the customer if it wasn't for the fancy maneuvering of our sales person. The bottom line is that we didn't need the model at the time we created it. Instead we should have waited to create the model after talking to our client and after securing the sale.

As another example, the RUP (Kruchten 2000) suggests that you create a Software Architecture Description (SAD) document to define your architecture. Yes, defining your system's architecture is a very good thing to do, but do you need to create a document early in the project? Sometimes yes, sometimes no. A couple of years ago I worked on a mission-critical system where we developed our architecture model on a common whiteboard as a collection of free-form diagrams, effectively following the practice *Display Models Publicly*. Because the process told us to create a SAD we did so, even though most of the developers were working from the whiteboard sketches. Because the RUP product (Rational Corporation 2001) provides a good Microsoft Word template for a SAD we used it as the basis from which to work. A few of the developers printed out diagrams from the SAD document (we had transcribed our sketches into Microsoft Visio) to tack to their cubicle walls because they couldn't easily see the diagrams from where they sat. Every time the whiteboard sketches changed sufficiently we would have to update the electronic versions of the diagrams plus corresponding sections in the SAD document. The advantage of having the SAD document was that it provided a description of what we were building, a document that we distributed to management and made available to anyone within the organization that was interested. The disadvantage, from what I could tell, was that nobody was using the SAD document effectively. I'm not sure the managers ever looked at it, and if they did it was a cursory inspection at best because we never received any feedback from them. The developers who needed copies of the diagrams could have taken a digital snapshot of the sketches and either created a shared architecture web page or printed them out. This would have also been a SAD document, albeit in a different form, according to the principle *Content is More Important Than Representation* because it still would have described our architecture (which is the fundamental purpose of a SAD document). By the same reasoning, our whiteboard sketches were also a SAD document, although one that wasn't permanent and one that was fixed in a permanent location. In my opinion we had made three fundamental mistakes and thus were traveling heavier than we needed to: we chose the wrong format for the documentation, we documented too early, and we created too much documentation. The added overhead of maintaining the SAD as a Word document slowed us down because we had that information in several locations—on the whiteboard that we were actually working from, in the Word document (which was almost superfluous), and in our code. Furthermore, we could have been developing software instead of documentation, and worse yet the update effort took up a large portion of the time of one of our senior developers so he couldn't help to mentor and coach the junior developers. Granted, it was useful to have this document at the end of the project as one of our deliverables to the maintenance team, but we certainly didn't need it during development and it clearly did the project team more harm than it did good.

Traveling light requires you to think about what you are doing. At the beginning of your project, ask yourself what you think you're going to need based on the nature of your project. Development of an air traffic control system will likely require greater documentation than development of a Web site made from static HTML pages. As the project progresses you'll find that your initial estimate of your documentation needs changes with experience, perhaps you'll need more or less. Highsmith (2000) likes to use the analogy of hiking—packing too light or too heavy can lead to disaster. At worst it kills you and at best it forces you to turn back and rethink your strategy. Imagine crossing a desert with insufficient water; you're traveling too light. Or you're trying to cross the same desert with a 100-pound pack strapped to your back; now you're traveling too heavy. Now imagine building a mission-critical e-commerce application without providing any documentation describing how to operate it. Your project effectively fails because you've traveled too light. Now imagine building the same system with thousands of pages of documentation that you must update and validate every time you change the system. You fail again because you're traveling so heavy that you cannot respond quickly to changes in the marketplace. Traveling light means just enough models and documentation; too little or too much puts you at risk.

When Is a Document Agile?

Agile documents are good enough in the eyes of the beholder.

Regardless of what some people will tell you, documentation can in fact be quite effective. When is a document agile? When it meets the following criteria:

Agile documents maximize stakeholder investment. The benefit provided by an agile document is greater than the investment in its creation and maintenance, and ideally the investment made in that documentation was the best option available for those resources. In other words documentation must at least provide positive value and ideally provides the best value possible. For example: if the creation of a user document provides a 50 percent payback on investment, but providing a training course to your users provides 100 percent payback, then you're better off choosing the training because it's a better investment.

Agile documents are "lean and mean." An agile document contains just enough information to fulfill its purpose. In other words, it is as simple as it can possibly be. For example: portions of an agile document could be written in point form instead of prose—you're still capturing the critical information without investing time to make it look pretty, which is in accordance to the principle *Content is More Important Than Representation*. Agile documents will often provide references to other sources of information. For example, a contract model describing the interface to an external system could indicate that the SOAP 1.1 protocol is being used and provide a reference to the XML DTD and schema definition that define the XML documents transmitted between systems. When writing an agile document remember the principle *Assume Simplicity*, that the simplest documentation will be sufficient, and follow the practice *Create Simple Content* whenever possible. One way to keep agile documents lean and mean is to follow pragmatic programming's (Hunt and Thomas 2000) DRY (don't repeat yourself) principle. Also, don't forget to work with your document's audience—what is lean and mean for you may be completely insufficient for them.

Agile documents fulfill a purpose. Agile documents are cohesive; they fulfill a single defined purpose. If you do not know why you are creating the document, or if the purpose for creating the document is questionable (see earlier), then you should stop and rethink what you are doing.

Agile documents describe information that is less likely to change. The greater the chance that information will change, the less value there is in investing significant time writing external documentation about it—the information may change before you're finished writing and it will be difficult to maintain over time. For example: your system architecture, once it has stabilized, will change slowly over time, so it's a good candidate for external documentation.

Agile documents describe "good things to know." Agile documents capture critical information, information that is not readily obvious such as design rationale, requirements, usage procedures, or operational procedures. Agile documents do not capture obvious information. For example, documentation indicating that the F_NAME column of the CUSTOMER table captures the first name of a customer really doesn't provide a lot of value to me. Documentation indicating that the customer table does not include data for customers residing in Canada's Yukon Territory because that data is stored in an ASCII flat file on another system due to regulatory reasons is likely good information to know.

Agile documents have a specific customer and facilitate the work efforts of that customer. System documentation is typically written for maintenance developers, providing an overview of the system's architecture and potentially summarizing critical requirements and design decisions. User documentation often includes tutorials for using a system written in a language that your users understand, whereas operations documentation describes how to run your system and is written in language that operations staff can understand. Different customers, different types of documents, and very likely different writing styles must be accomodated. You must work closely with the customer, or potential customer, for your documentation if you want to create something that will actually meet their needs. For example, I would be reticent to write the system documentation for the maintenance developers without involving some of them in the effort. Yes, sometimes you can't get these folks involved (you may have none on staff at the moment) or you may not be able to identify who within your maintenance organization will be the eventual "owners" of your system. When you don't have the customers involved, you're at risk of creating too much documentation or unnecessary documentation and hence becoming less agile. You will often discover that when you involve the customers they often have a very good idea of what they actually need and can often provide examples of what works well for them and what doesn't.

Agile documents are sufficiently accurate, consistent, and detailed. Have you ever learned how to use new software by using a book describing a previous version of that software? Did you succeed? Likely. Was it a perfect situation? Likely not. Did it cover all the new features of the software? Of course not, but it still got you up and running with the software package. Were you willing to spend your own money, perhaps on the order of $30, to purchase the latest version of the book you needed? Likely not, because it wasn't worth it to you. Agile documents do not need to be perfect, they just need to be good enough.

Agile documents are sufficiently indexed. Documentation isn't effective if you cannot easily find the information contained in it. Would you purchase a reference manual without an index or table of contents? Your indexing scheme should reflect the needs of a document's audience. Luckily, word processors include features to easily create tables of contents, indexes, and even lists of figures and tables.

> **WARNING** **Sometimes Documentation Needs to Be Perfect**
> **You need to take the advice that agile documents need to be just good enough with a grain of salt. If you are writing the operations manuals for a software system for a nuclear power plant, then I highly suggest you get it right! However, few systems are truly that critical, so investing the effort required to get their documentation perfect isn't appropriate. You need to make a judgment call when it comes to writing documentation. The key issue is to identify how much ambiguity the customers of the document can accept and yet still be effective.**

What Types of Documents Should We Create?

You will need to create documentation on your project; this is true even of the most "extreme" XP projects, let alone RUP projects. But what types of documentation will you *potentially* need to create? Table 14.1 lists some of the most common documents that you may decide to create as part of your development effort, documents that you will deliver as part of your overall system. Table 14.1. does not include management artifacts, such as project schedules, software deliverables (for example: source code and test suites), or interim work products (for example: temporary models).

> **NOTE** **Sometimes Non-Agility Enables Agility**
> **Agile software development is new to many organizations, and, as a result, there is significant fear and uncertainty concerning its viability. Although it's frustrating at times, this is actually a good thing because it means that people care. Because of this fear you may be required by your project stakeholders to create extraneous documentation to help put them at ease, something that is particularly true of senior management who have likely been burned in the past by other new techniques and technologies. Often the creation of a single document, perhaps an executive overview, will give your project stakeholders enough of a "warm and fuzzy feeling" about your project to allow you to work in the manner of your choice (for example: in an agile way).**

When Should You Update Documentation?

In this respect documents are just like models. My recommendation is to follow the practice *Update Only When It Hurts*. Agile documents, like agile models, are just good enough. Many times a document can be out of date and it doesn't matter very much.

Table 14.1 Potential Documents Created By Your Development Team

DOCUMENT	AUDIENCE	DESCRIPTION	ADVICE
Contract models	Other Teams	A document describing the technical interface to a system or portion of a system.	• Contact models may already be in place for existing systems.
Design decisions	Developers, Maintenance Developers, Project Managers	A summary of critical decisions pertaining to design and architecture that the team made throughout development	• Focus on decisions that are not obvious had other reasonable alternatives, or ones where you explored what initially looked like a reasonable alternative that in the end proved insufficient for your needs. • The goal of this effort is to avoid needless refactoring at some point in the future or rehashing a previously made decision. • Design decisions are often documented throughout other artifacts, such as system overviews and source code, although you may choose to have a separate document when appropriate to the situation.
Executive overview	Senior Management, User Management, Project Management	A definition of the vision for the system and a summary of the current cost estimates, predicted benefits, risks, staffing estimates, and scheduled milestones.	• This document is typically used to gain funding and support for your project and to provide status updates to important project stakeholders who may not be actively involved with your project on a day-to-day basis. • Have the courage to make this publicly available to everyone that should have access to it, even when it contains bad news, according to the principle *Open and Honest Communication*.

Table 14.1 continued

DOCUMENT	AUDIENCE	DESCRIPTION	ADVICE
Operations documentation	Operations Staff	This documentation typically includes an indication of the dependencies that your system is involved with; the nature of its interaction with other systems, databases, and files; references to backup procedures; a list of contact points for your system and how to reach them; a summary of the availability/reliability requirements for your system; an indication of the expected load profile of your system; and troubleshooting guidelines.	• Your operations department often has a standard format for this type of documentation or at least may have good examples from other systems that they can provide you to base your document(s) on.
Project overview	Developers, Managers, Maintenance Developers, Operations Staff	A summary of critical information, such as the vision for the system, primary user contacts, technologies and tools used to build the system, and the critical operating processes (some applicable to development, some applicable to production, such as how to back up data storage). Also provides references to critical project artifacts such as the source code (the project name in the source code control system is often sufficient), where the permanent models pertaining to the system (if any) are, and where other documents (if any) are.	• I typically create and maintain this document during development. • Keep it short and to the point. I don't ever remember one getting beyond ten printed pages. • This document serves as a starting point for anyone new to the team, including maintenance developers, because it answers fundamental questions that they are likely to have. • Whenever you first share this document with anyone, ask him or her to keep track of major issues that they were not able to easily resolve using this document, or any misinformation they discover, to provide insight into potential updates for the document.

continues

Table 14.1 continued

DOCUMENT	AUDIENCE	DESCRIPTION	ADVICE
Requirements document	Developers, Maintenance Developers , Users, User Managers	This document defines what the system will do, summarizing or composed of requirements artifacts such as business rule definitions, use cases, user stories, or essential user interface prototypes (to name a few).	• XP projects typically favor low-tech requirements, artifacts such as user stories, and CRC cards. • RUP projects tend toward more formal requirements, artifacts, and documentation.
Support documentation	Support Staff	This documentation includes training materials specific to support staff; all user documentation to use as a reference when solving problems; a trouble-shooting guide; escalation procedures for handling difficult problems; and a list of contact points within the maintenance team.	• You will find that your support department often has a standard escalation procedure in place; therefore, you will not need to write one. And like the operations department, the support department may have standard templates or examples that you can work from.

Table 14.1 continued

DOCUMENT	AUDIENCE	DESCRIPTION	ADVICE
System documentation	Maintenance Developers, Developers	The purpose of this document is to provide an overview of the system and to help people understand the system. Common information in this document includes an overview of the technical architecture, the business architecture, and the high-level requirements for the system. Detailed architecture and design models, or references to them, may also be included where appropriate.	• System documentation helps to reduce perceived risk on the project by providing "truck insurance," the assurance that if the development team leaves, or gets hit by a truck*, critical information about the project is left behind. Unfortunately, this is typically false insurance–if you lose someone, then no matter how good the documentation is, you have a serious problem on your hands because new people still need to be identified, assigned to your system, and need to learn the system. You're much better off increasing your project's "truck number," the minimum number of people that if you lost them would put your project at risk, by supporting knowledge sharing practices, such as *Active Stakeholder Participation, Collective Ownership,* and *Model with Others*.
User documentation	Users, User Managers	Your users may require a reference manual, a usage guide, a support guide, and even training materials. It's important that you distinguish between these different types of documents because the way that each one is used varies: one is for quick lookups, one is for discovering about how to work with the system, one is for how to obtain additional help, and one is for training.	• I typically base my usage guide and training materials on the use cases for the system–the use cases describe how the actors work with the system; therefore, they should be a good foundation on which to base both of these documents. • User documentation should be considered part of the user interface for your system and therefore should undergo usability testing.

*I was once on a project where the project manager, lead developer, and architect (myself) were in a car that was hit head-on by a transport truck. We all walked away from it, but that would have been a serious blow to the project if we hadn't–not to mention our families!

For example: at the time of this writing, I am working with the early release of the JDK v1.3.1, yet I regularly use reference manuals for JDK 1.2.x—it's not a perfect situation, but I get by without too much grief because the manuals I'm using are still good enough. Would the manuals for Java v1.0.x be sufficient? Likely not, because there has been a significant change since that release and my productivity loss would be much greater than the cost of new manuals.

In addition to the fundamental requirement of your project stakeholders authorizing the investment of resources required to do the work, you should use the following heuristics for deciding when to update documentation:

- Update contract models and re-release them ideally before, and minimally parallel to, releasing the item(s) that the model describes.

- Documentation that is intended as part of the system, such as operations and user manuals, should be updated and released before or with the system itself.

- The customer of the documentation is being inordinately harmed, including a significant loss of productivity, because the documentation is not updated (for example: it hurts).

Yes, it can be frustrating having models and documents that aren't completely accurate or that aren't perfectly consistent with one another. This frustration is offset by the productivity increase inherent in traveling light, in not needing to continually keep documentation and models up to date and consistent with one another. Do you want to write software or write documentation?

Effective Documentation Handoffs

A documentation handoff occurs when one group or person provides documentation to another group or person. Agile developers desperately try to avoid documentation handoffs because they are not a very good way for people to communicate. Unfortunately documentation hand-offs are a reality in some situations—often your development team is so large it cannot be co-located, perhaps a subsystem is being created by another company (implying the need for a contract model), perhaps important project stakeholders are not readily available to your team, or perhaps regulations within your industry or organization require the production of certain documents. The following strategies can help to increase the effectiveness of documentation handoffs:

Avoid documentation handoffs. As you migrate to an agile software development process you will constantly run into people who are not as agile, and who see nothing wrong with documentation handoffs. Point out that there are better ways to communicate—face-to-face conversations, video conferencing, telephone conferencing—that you should consider before writing documentation, and whenever possible try to find a better way that fulfills your needs.

Support handoffs with other means of communication. If you can't avoid providing documentation to someone else, you should at least strive to support the handoff with face-to-face communication or other approaches. This may enable you to write less documentation, therefore allowing you to focus on other activities and will help you to avoid some of the common disadvantages of documentation, such as misunderstanding the material.

Avoid documentation handoffs. Chances are good that the people you are interacting with don't like writing and receiving documentation either—at least it doesn't hurt to ask.

Write agile documentation. See the section *Strategies for Increasing the Agility of Documentation*.

Avoid documentation handoffs. I can't stress this enough.

Strategies for Increasing the Agility of Documentation

If you can't avoid writing a document, how can you at least write it in an agile manner? The following strategies should help:

Focus on the customer(s). Identify who the potential customer(s) for your documentation are and what they believe they require, and then negotiate with them the minimal subset that they actually need. To discover what they believe they require, ask them what they do, how they do it, and how they want to work with the system documentation that you are to produce. By understanding the needs of your customers you will be able to deliver succinct and sufficient documentation and deliver it where they will actually need it and find it—it doesn't matter how well written a document is if nobody knows that it exists.

Keep it just simple enough, but not too simple. Follow the principle *Use the Simplest Tools* and the practices *Create Simple Content* and *Depict Models Simply* when creating documentation. The best documentation is the simplest that gets the job done. Don't create a fifty-page document when a five-page one will do. Don't create a five-page document when five bullet points will do. Don't create an elaborate and intricately detailed diagram when a sketch will do. Don't repeat information found elsewhere when a reference will do. Write in point form. Document only enough to provide a useful context. Start with a document that's minimal enough for the needs of its customers then augment it as needed. To determine what is truly the minimum amount of documentation required by my customers I will actively explore how they intend to use the documentation and why they are using it that way.

The customer determines sufficiency. Years ago, I worked for a large Canadian financial institution. One of their policies was that you couldn't transition a system to someone else until they were willing to accept it. They would inspect your code and supporting artifacts, and if they felt the artifacts weren't up to par, then you needed to improve it and try again. Sometimes you would work on improving the artifacts together, and sometimes not. This practice provided a fair and effective quality gate between developers and the customers of our work. As writer of the documentation your job is to ensure that the documentation has true meaning and provides value; your customer's role is to validate that you have done so.

Document with a purpose. You should only create a document if it fulfills a clear, important, and immediate goal of your overall project efforts. Don't forget that this purpose may be short term or long term, it may directly support software development efforts, or it may not.

Prefer other forms of communication to documentation. Highsmith (2000) believes that the issue is one of understanding, not of documentation; therefore, you should not overrate the value of documentation. Your goal is to ensure that maintenance developers understand how the system works so they can evolve it over time, not to produce a mound of documentation that they may or may not use. Your goal is to ensure that your users work with your system effectively, not that they have a pretty help system available to them. Your goal is to enable your support and operations staff, not bury them with paper. Documentation supports knowledge transfer, but it is only one of several options available to you, and it often isn't the best option, as discussed in Chapter 8. Conversations with project stakeholders, having them actively involved with development, and being available to work through any issues with them often go much further than the best documentation. Documentation becomes a better option for you the greater the distance, either physical or temporal, between the individuals who are communicating.

Put the documentation in the most appropriate place. Where will somebody likely want a piece of documentation? Is that design decision best documented in the code, added as a note on a diagram, or best placed in an external document? The answer to this question should be driven by the needs of the customer of that information; where are they most likely to need that information? The answer is also driven by your desire to follow the principle *Quality Work*—you should record the information where it enhances your work the most. You should also consider issues such as indexing, linking, and accessibility when writing documentation because you don't always know who will eventually become its customer.

Wait for what you are documenting to stabilize. Delay the creation of all documents as late as possible, creating them just before you need them. For example: system overviews are best written toward the end of the development of a release because you know what you've actually built.

Display models publicly. When models are displayed publicly—on a whiteboard, corkboard, or internal Web site—you are promoting transfer of information and thus communication through the application of what Cockburn (2002) refers to as an "information radiator." The greater the communication on your project, the less need for detailed documentation because people already know what you're doing. Having said that, don't forget to indicate the status of your models so that people can put them in context—you'll treat a model that is still a draft much different than one that has been baselined for your current release of software.

Start with models you actually keep current. If you've chosen to keep your UML deployment diagram, your user interface flow diagram, and your physical data diagram up to date throughout development then that is a good sign that these are valuable models that you should base your documentation around. Models that weren't kept up to date likely weren't because there was little sense in doing so, so not only are they out of date, they aren't of value anyway.

Require people to justify documentation requests. Does the person know what they're asking for and why they need it, or are they asking for it because they've been told to ask for it? Are users asking for documentation because they were burned in the past by developers, or their colleagues were burned in the past, and now they ask for everything in the hopes they'll get something? Does the requester understand the trade-offs that are being made, that documentation comes at a cost? See the section *What Are the Tradeoffs Associated with Documentation?*. In my experience, when you explore the documentation issue with your project stakeholders, you quickly discover they're asking for it because they don't trust you, they often don't understand the implications of what they're asking for, and they often don't know that there is an alternative (for example: less documentation). Really good questions to ask are what they intend to use the documentation for and how they actually use the documentation. When you ask those questions you often discover that they don't use all the documentation, that they instead just want it there as a security blanket more than anything else. There are much better ways to address fear than writing documentation. You should also consider explaining the AM principle *Maximize Stakeholder Investment* to them because everyone should be able to show that what they are doing provides the best value possible to your organization.

Write the fewest documents with least overlap. One way to achieve this is to build larger documents from smaller ones. For example: I once worked on a project where all documentation was written as HTML pages, with each page focusing on a single topic. One page described the user interface architecture for our system, a page that included a user interface flow diagram and appropriate text describing it. The table of contents pages for the system documentation and the support guide both linked to this UI architecture page. This information was defined in one place and one place only, so there was no opportunity for overlap.

Get someone with writing experience. Technical writers bring a lot to the table when it comes time to writing documentation because they know how to organize and present information effectively. Don't have access to a technical writer? Consider reading and following the advice presented in *UnTechnical Writing* (Bremer 1999) or taking a night-school course in writing fundamentals. Also try writing documentation with a partner, just as there is significant value in pair programming (www.pairprogramming.com), there is similar value in "pair documenting." You may also consider purchasing text-to-speech software that allows you to listen to what you've written, a great way to discover poorly written passages.

Table 14.2   Critical Points Regarding Agile Documentation

1.	The fundamental issue is effective communication, not documentation.
2.	Documentation should be "lean and mean."
3.	Travel as light as you possibly can.
4.	Documentation should be just good enough.
5.	Models are not necessarily documents, and documents are not necessarily models.
6.	Documentation is as much a part of the system as the source code.
7.	Your team's primary goal is to develop software; its secondary goal is to enable your next effort.
8.	The benefit of having documentation must be greater than the cost of creating and maintaining it.
9.	Never trust the documentation.
10.	Each system has its own unique documentation needs; one size does not fit all.
11.	Ask whether you NEED the documentation, and why you believe you NEED the documentation, not whether you want it.
12.	The investment in system documentation is a business decision, not a technical one.
13.	Create documentation only when you need it—Don't create documentation for the sake of documentation.
14.	Update documentation only when it hurts.
15.	The customer, not the developer, determines whether documentation is sufficient.

Make it easy to remember the fundamentals. Table 14.2 summarizes the critical points made in this chapter. Consider photocopying and publicly posting the copy where you and your coworkers will see it so as to act as a reminder of how to take an agile approach to documentation.

How Does This Work?

Your project team should ruthlessly focus on creating documentation that provides maximum value to its customers. You should create documentation only when it is the best option available to you; when you have better options, you should naturally choose one of them instead. The simplest documentation that gets the job done is your goal. Like an agile model an agile document just needs to be good enough for its intended audience. How does this work? How could it not work? Although agile software development process, such as AM value working software has over-comprehensive documentation that doesn't mean that you will not develop any documentation; you should just develop documentation that makes sense. Just as knee-jerk documentation is wrong, knee-jerk non-documentation is just as wrong. Think first, then act.

The desire to get models perfect is one of the reasons why people fall into the "analysis paralysis" trap—they're too afraid to move on from modeling because they want to get it right first. I also suspect this is why people invest a lot of time in documentation and maintenance of their models—when something changes they rush back and update that issue throughout the myriad of artifacts they've been maintaining. This is a comfortable feeling for them because they believe they're accomplishing useful work—unfortunately, from the point of view of Agile Modeling nothing could be further from the truth. The true goal of software developers is to develop software that meets the needs of their users. How relevant is maintaining mounds of documentation to achieving that goal? Not very. Yes, you need some documentation but not a lot. What I'm getting at is an aspect of eXtreme Programming's (XP) practice of traveling light. You want to maintain a minimal amount of artifacts that is appropriate for your situation—for an XP project that minimal amount of artifacts could be source code and your test cases, whereas on a Rational Unified Process (RUP) project it would include these things as well as other artifacts such as requirements and architecture models. At the same time, you want to invest the bare minimum effort in the artifacts that you do maintain. Doing more work than you need to doesn't make sense, and that means you will update your artifacts within the tolerances of your project.

CHAPTER 15

The UML and Beyond

The UML is not even remotely complete.

The Unified Modeling Language (UML) (Object Management Group 2001) defines the industry standard notation, and semantics for properly applying that notation, for software models of systems built using object-oriented (OO) or component-based technology. The artifacts of the UML, described in Appendix A, "Modeling Techniques," are: Activity diagram, Class diagram, Collaboration diagram, Component diagram, Deployment diagram, Sequence diagram, State Chart diagram, and the Use Case diagram. In fact, finding modeling books or tools that do not use the UML is difficult these days. The UML provides a common and consistent notation with which to describe OO and component software systems, decreasing the learning curve for developers because they only need to learn the one modeling language (in theory at least). The UML is clearly a step in the right direction, if only for the reason that we are no longer fighting the "notation wars" of the mid-1990s, but it isn't perfect.

The goal of this chapter is to help you see through the marketing hype and misconceptions surrounding the UML—to be an effective modeler you must have a firm understanding of the realities of the UML. In this chapter I argue that:

■ The UML is not sufficient for the development of business software.

■ The UML is more complex than what most developers need.

■ The UML is not a methodology or process.

■ The vision of Executable UML is ahead of its time.

The UML Is Not Sufficient

AM's *Multiple Models* principle tells you that you need to have many modeling techniques in your intellectual toolkit if you want to be effective as a developer. Appendix A of this book presents an overview of many common modeling artifacts, including but not limited to those of the Unified Modeling Language (UML), and as you can see, there is a wide selection of models available to you. Each model has its strengths and weaknesses; therefore, no single model is sufficient for all of your software development needs. Although the UML is in fact quite robust, the reality is that it isn't sufficient for your modeling needs. For example, when I design the user interface of an application, I generally like to create a user interface flow diagram (see Figure 15.1). This diagram enables my team to explore how users will interact with the system from a birds-eye view, and thus ask very important usability questions long before we've built the user interface. Unfortunately, the UML currently doesn't include such a diagram, and it may never include one. So if you limit your modeling repertoire to the artifacts defined by the UML, you forgo the potential productivity enhancements of

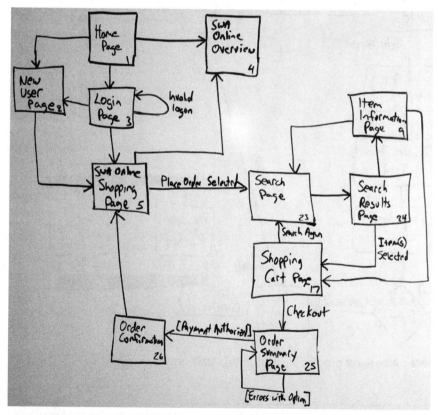

Figure 15.1   A diagram that represents navigational flow within a user interface.

this technique. Similarly, it is quite common for business application developers to create data models representing the physical design of their database, yet the UML does not yet have this sort of model either—luckily, work is being done to add a data model to the UML (Naiburg and Maksimchuk 2001).*

Although the UML defines an important collection of models, I highly suggest adopting them in accordance with the practice *Apply Modeling Standards*. The reality is that the UML has narrowed the range of discussion within the modeling community. Yes, sometimes it is possible to use UML diagrams in situations for which they really weren't intended. For example, using UML Activity diagrams to model business processes is quite common (see Figure 15.2). However, this often proves less than ideal. For example, in UML Activity diagrams you cannot depict a storage location for information, such as the in box on someone's desk or a relational database, information that is often critical to know when you are exploring the current physical business process—yes, you could add a process bubble entitled "Put Order in Box" but it does

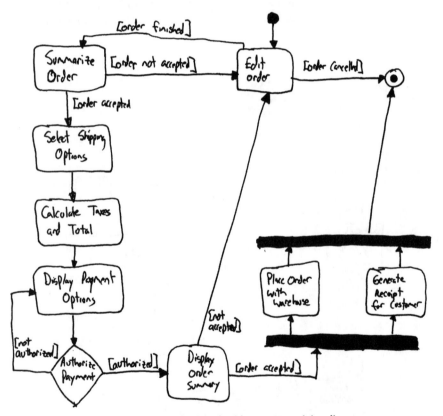

Figure 15.2 A business process depicted with a UML activity diagram.

---

*I do not expect the notation presented in this book to be adopted by the Object Management Group (OMG). However, I do see this book as an important step towards a data modeling profile for the UML. Regardless, this book is still a good read.

not have the same visual impact that you would achieve with a data store symbol entitled "In Box" had you instead used a data flow diagram (DFD) to model the process.
There are many situations where a UML Activity diagram is your best modeling
option; unfortunately, modeling an existing physical business process isn't one of
them. Agile modelers follow the practice *Apply the Right Artifact(s)* and choose to follow the best technique for the situation; in this case, creating a DFD is a better option
than a UML Activity diagram.

In my opinion, the UML is not sufficient for the needs of business application development, although it is an important part of the overall picture. Even the Rational Unified Process (RUP) (Rational Corporation 2001), which comes from the same
organization that first proposed the UML, explicitly includes non-UML artifacts such
as business rules, data models, and user interface flow diagrams. Why is it important
to recognize that the UML isn't complete? First, it puts you in a better position to evaluate development tools. Tool support for the UML is important but not sufficient—the
tool(s) also need to support other modeling artifacts that your project requires. Second,
it puts you in a position to better evaluate developers (including consultants and contractors). An interesting question to ask in a job interview is "what's missing from the
UML?"—someone with actual experience developing real-world systems will easily
answer this question; someone with book knowledge will think it's a trick question.

The UML Is Too Complex

When you examine the artifacts that have been defined for the UML, you quickly see
that the notation and semantics for that notation is far more than you likely need. A
common refrain within the object community is that 80 percent of your object modeling
needs can be satisfied with 20 percent of the notation, an "objectification" of Pareto's
law I suppose, that the UML has far too much in it. The UML is huge. It's intimidating
to someone who is new to object-oriented development. The UML is strange: On the
one hand, it has too little in it, and, on the other hand, it has too much in it.

The UML Is Not a Methodology or Process

A common misunderstanding about the UML is that it is a process, yet nothing could
be further from the truth. The UML defines notation for a collection of diagrams and the
semantics (rules) for applying that notation. That's it. It does not define when to create
each diagram nor does it even define how to create each diagram, it merely defines
what the diagrams are. I believe that there are several reasons for this confusion:

- People haven't taken time to learn about the UML.
- Confusion with the Unified Process (UP). The UML and the UP originated
  within the same organization, Rational Corporation, and have similar names.
  The UP is in fact a process, one that I describe in Part 4 of this book, and many
  developers have a problem distinguishing between the two.

■ Historical precedent. Previous modeling languages, such as data modeling notations or process modeling notations, were in fact associated with methodologies. In fact, the notations that formed the foundation of the UML—Object Modeling Technique (OMT) notation (Rumbaugh et. al. 1991), Booch notation (Booch 1994), and the Objectory notation (Jacobson et. al. 1992)—were all associated with methodologies themselves. Many developers naturally associate a modeling language with a methodology, but with the UML this simply isn't the case.

Forget about Executable UML (for Now)

Ever wish you could draw a few diagrams, press a button, and have a working software system that meets your needs? Sound like magic? Perhaps, but that's a major part of the Executable UML vision. The basic idea is that you will use a CASE tool to develop detailed UML diagrams and then supplement them by specifications written in a formal language, presumably the OMG's Object Constraint Language (OCL) (Warmer and Kleppe 1999). The basic idea behind executable UML is that systems can be modeled at a higher level of abstraction than source code, simulated to support validation of your efforts, and then translated into efficient code. This higher level of abstraction should help to avoid premature design, enable you to change your system as your requirements evolve, and delay implementation decisions until the last minute. In my opinion, this sounds great in theory, but unfortunately there are several problems to making this work in practice:

The UML isn't sufficient. The UML is clearly not sufficient for business application development, as I argued earlier, so trying to generate a system only from UML models at the present moment simply won't suffice.

Integrating a collection of tools to support executable UML is currently difficult. Let's assume that one or more tool vendors decide to implement the executable UML vision and fill in the gaping holes inherent in the UML. How would they make it work? Ideally, some companies would focus strictly on building a good modeling tool and others focus on taking the output from those tools to produce a working executable on a given platform. Some vendors would produce plugins for J2EE environments, others for .NET environments, and others yet for mainframe environments. To support this, we would need a common standard for sharing information between tools. The OMG's XML Metadata Interchange (XMI) standard comes to mind, although because XMI is based on the OMG's UML and Common Warehouse Metamodel (CWM) on its own, it isn't yet sufficient for fully specifying software from end-to-end. Although the CWM provides insight for specifying persistence-related information, we still need to specify other aspects of a system, such as its user interface. Because there isn't a complete standard in place, the various vendors will add to their own unique extensions making multi-vendor tool integration difficult.

A single vendor approach will likely prove too narrow. Another approach would be for a tool vendor to support both modeling and code generation features in their tool, something perfectly reasonable in theory. But, because of the wide range of platforms, and the range of design options within those platforms, the tool vendors will need to focus on a single niche. Perhaps one vendor will specialize in generating J2EE development supporting Java Server Pages (JSPs), servlets, Enterprise JavaBeans (EJBs), and relational databases. Perhaps another will specialize in generating Java-based fat-client applications, whereas another generates a Win32 fat client application. The implication is that organizations that develop for several platforms will need several major development tools, tools that must be purchased and supported often at great expense. Furthermore, the wide range of required functionality of such a tool makes it difficult for vendors to specialize and focus on a single aspect of the xUML vision, likely resulting in slower improvement in the overall development environment.

I have no doubt that we will begin to see some interesting tools* emerge over the next few years based on the executable UML vision, but I suspect that this vision will fall just as short as other similar visions have done in the past . . . we will always need programmers. Would such a tool be agile? Potentially. If it is possible to build a tool that is easy to use, that generates software that is sufficient for your environment, and that provides better value for your investment (in accordance with the principle *Maximize Stakeholder Investment*) than do other approaches to development, then I would have to say yes. Do I expect to see any tool that meets these requirements anytime soon? No. Perhaps my experiences in the 1980s when CASE tool vendors bombarded the IT industry with similar promises has made me a little jaded, but my expectation is that the complexity of software development and the pace of technological change will outstrip the ability of tool vendors to generate reasonably efficient source code to meet my current needs. In other words, I fully expect the cobbler's children to go without shoes, or in this case for developers to go without "ultimate tools," for quite some time. In Chapter 10, "Using the Simplest Tools Possible?," I explore effective and realistic tool usage in greater detail.

Making the UML Work in Practice

The following strategies should help you to make the UML work for you in practice:

Use the UML as your modeling core. For object-oriented and component-based development, you should use the UML as a base collection of modeling techniques that is then supplemented with other techniques to meet your project's unique needs. Furthermore, I wouldn't replace the UML with other artifacts. Although I am convinced that my own notation for class modeling (Ambler 1995) is superior to that of the UML's, the reality is that my notation isn't in common

---

*Some interesting tools exist that support the concept of executable models, but they need to extend the UML to do so.

use and therefore, if you use it, you would make your diagrams difficult for others to understand and thus reduce communication on your project team.

Adopt a critical subset of the notation. If you only need 20 percent of the UML notation to do 80 percent of your modeling work, then start with that critical 20 percent. Good starting points are Martin Fowler and Kendall Scott's (1999) *UML Distilled 2/e* or my own *The Object Primer 2/e* (2001a).

Educate all developers in the UML.

Beware of UML hype. An unfortunate side effect of the popularity of the UML is that it has become a marketing buzzword for tool vendors, consultants, and even methodologists. It's nice that a consultant is a UML expert, but what you really need is a development expert. Whenever a new technology, such as XML or .NET, or a new technique, such as XP, is released, members of the UML community jump on the bandwagon and write books titled "[Buzzword] and UML" or "UML for [Buzzword]." Instead of asking the question, "How do we apply the UML with buzzword?" they would be better off asking, "How do we model a buzzword-based application?" in my opinion.

The diagrams defined by the UML are important tools for an agile modeler to have in their intellectual toolkit. In this chapter, I explored several issues pertaining to effective adoption of the UML, and hopefully cleared up any misconceptions that you may have regarding the UML.

PART

Three

Agile Modeling
and eXtreme
Programming (XP)

In this part, I describe how to use AM and XP together. This section includes the following chapters:

- **Chapter 16: Setting the Record Straight.** This chapter explores the concept and nature of modeling on an XP project, showing once and for all that modeling is an important aspect of XP.

- **Chapter 17: Agile Modeling and eXtreme Programming.** This chapter describes the conceptual fit between XP and AM and shows how XP's practices of refactoring and test-first design can be used to enhance your agile modeling efforts.

- **Chapter 18: Agile Modeling Throughout the XP Lifecycle.** This chapter overviews the XP project lifecycle and shows where AM techniques can be applied to improve your effectiveness.

- **Chapter 19: Modeling During the XP Exploration Phase.** This chapter describes how AM practices can enhance the identification of the initial requirements for an XP project and in the development of a candidate architecture for the SWA Online case study.

- **Chapter 20: Modeling During an XP Iteration: Searching for Items.** This chapter describes in detail how the practices of AM are applied during the implementation of a search page for the SWA Online case study.

- **Chapter 21: Modeling During an XP Iteration: Totaling an Order.** This chapter explores how an XP team might model the totaling of an order for the SWA Online case study.

CHAPTER 16

Setting the Record Straight

*In the time it would take you to code one design,
you can compare and contrast three designs using pictures.*

–Kent Beck, in *Extreme Programming Explained*

Agile Modeling (AM) is a chaordic, practices-based software process whose scope is to describe how to model and document in an effective and agile manner. In Chapter 1, "Introduction," I stated that one of the goals of AM is to address the issue of how to apply modeling techniques on software projects taking an agile approach such as eXtreme Programming (XP) (Beck 2000). Because the scope of XP is much greater than that of AM and XP covers the full development lifecycle, XP is a candidate "base process" into which the techniques of AM may be tailored. Furthermore, although XP clearly includes modeling as part of its process, it is not as explicit about how to do so as many developers would prefer; hence an opportunity for AM. Luckily, XP, like AM, is also an agile practices-based methodology, which makes the conceptual fit between the two methods much easier than between AM and a prescriptive process such as the Unified Process (Kruchten 2000; Ambler 2001b), the topic of Part Four of this book.

People seem to have several common misconceptions regarding modeling on an XP project. The three most common misconceptions are that you don't model at all, that you don't document at all, or that, if you do model, your only options are the modeling artifacts of the UML. I'll address these misconceptions in turn in this chapter, but first, I want to explore why they occur so that you can recognize other misconceptions when they arise. From what I can gather based on the conversations on the AM mailing list, www.agilemodeling.com/feedback.htm, the source of these misconceptions is often the result of one or more of the following:

Second-hand knowledge of XP. The Internet is a major source of information for many developers, in particular newsgroups and emails from colleagues. As people learn a new technique, they often join a newsgroup or mailing list, such as extremeprogramming at Yahoo groups (groups.yahoo.com), and start monitoring the group or list. Someone will post something, which may not be accurate, and many people will accept it as official, particularly when they haven't had an opportunity yet to try it out for themselves. Don't believe everything that you hear.

Questionable sources of information regarding XP. Determining the quality of published material, be it electronic or printed form, is often hard. Sometimes honest mistakes are made (that's happened to me more than once), and sometimes people publish misleading information on purpose. When you're just learning a new subject, you often cannot distinguish between high-quality sources of information and questionable ones. If you base your understanding on questionable sources, getting the wrong idea about XP is very easy. Visit the Agile Modeling Resources page, www.agilemodeling.com/resources.htm, for an up-to-date list of what I believe to be good sources of information regarding XP and other agile software processes.

Difficulty seeing beyond their current environment. Many developers find themselves in less-than-ideal environments. XP requires you to adopt practices that are often foreign to your current environment; pair programming and test-first development are new to most organizations, and sometimes these practices simply aren't feasible to adopt. If you cannot adopt the practice of pair programming, then XP isn't going to work for you. But instead of proclaiming that XP doesn't work in their environment, many people will instead proclaim that XP doesn't work at all. The reality is that XP does in fact work in the right situations; your situation just may not be one of the right ones.

Too much focus on the word "extreme." XP's name is both one of its greatest strengths and one of its greatest weaknesses. Because of the name, when some people hear XP's advice to travel light and to reduce the amount of documentation that you create and maintain, they translate it to "create no documentation at all." That's extreme, right? Or they'll hear XP's advice to use simple modeling techniques, such as user stories and CRC cards, and somehow translate that advice to "you don't model at all." That's extreme, right? Sigh.

In this chapter, I will set the record straight regarding the three most common issues that concern modeling and XP:

1. Modeling is a part of XP.
2. Documentation happens.
3. XP and the UML?

Modeling Is a Part of XP

User stories are a fundamental aspect of XP, as are Class Responsibility Collaborator (CRC) cards. User stories provide a high-level overview of the requirements for a system; they are reminders to have a conversation with your project stakeholders regarding their requirements; they are used as a primary input into estimating and scheduling, and they drive the identification of development tasks and acceptance test cases. CRC cards are used to explore structure, perhaps for conceptual modeling to understand the problem domain or for design to work through the structure of your software. User stories and CRC cards are both models (see Appendix A, "Modeling Techniques"); therefore, modeling is clearly a part of XP. XP developers will also create sketches, often on a whiteboard or a piece of paper, whenever user stories and CRC cards aren't the best option. In *Extreme Programming Explained* (Beck 2000), the first book written about XP, Kent Beck includes hand-drawn sketches of class diagrams and other free-form diagrams. The bottom line is that modeling is a fundamental aspect of XP.

Documentation Happens

Documentation is also an important part of XP. Ron Jeffries (2001b) offers the following advice:

> "Outside your extreme programming project, you will probably need documentation; by all means, write it. Inside your project, there is so much verbal communication that you may need very little else. *Trust yourselves to know the difference.*"

There are several interesting implications of that statement. First and foremost, the XP community recognizes that documentation should be produced for people external to your team, people that AM would term project stakeholders. Second, the statement points out that verbal communication between team members reduces the need for documentation within the team. A reduced need for documentation is the result of project team members being co-located, making communication easier, and aspects of XP, such as *Pair Programming* and *Collective Ownership,* that promote communication between developers. Chapter 14, "Agile Documentation," argued that documentation is only one form of communication, one that is typically the least effective, that more effective techniques, such as face-to-face communication can easily replace. Third, the statement recognizes that sometimes you do, in fact, need internal documentation for your team. This is consistent with the advice presented in *Extreme Programming Installed* (Jeffries, Anderson, and Hendrickson 2001) where the authors point out that information resulting from conversations with your project stakeholders regarding user stories are captured as additional documentation attached to the card. I discuss this in detail in Chapter 18, "Agile Modeling Throughout the XP Lifecycle." Fourth, the statement suggests that XP team members should know when documentation is required and be allowed to act accordingly. Fifth, the statement implies that you should trust the team and give them control over their own destiny. Trust can be difficult in many organizations. If the team is untrustworthy, then you have a serious problem that needs to be dealt with, regardless of whether they are following XP. Or if they are trustworthy, but your organizational culture doesn't allow you to act based on that trust, then once again you have a serious problem to deal with. You may believe that there isn't enough documentation when you are an outsider to an XP team and when you haven't been actively involved in the conversations and interactions that have replaced the need for documentation. When this is the case, instead of forcing the team to write documentation, invest the time to determine if they need the documentation that you believe is missing—suggest the documentation to the team, and if there is an actual need for it, then they'll create it. As Ron Jeffries likes to say, "It's called Extreme Programming not stupid programming" (Jeffries 2001e). Finally, the most important implication for XP teams is that if you need documentation, then write it.

The need for documentation on an XP project is reduced by several of its practices. First, because of test-first development and a focus on acceptance testing, there is always a working test suite that shows that your system works and fulfills the requirements implemented to that point. For the developers, these tests act as significant documentation because they show how the code actually works. When you think about it, tests make a lot of sense. When you are learning something new, do you prefer to read a bunch of documentation or do you look for source code samples? Many developers prefer to start at source code samples, and the test suite provides these samples. Second, XP's focus on simplicity and the practice of refactoring result in very clean and clear code. If the code is already easy to understand, why invest a lot of time writing documentation to help you to understand it? This applies to both internal and external documentation—why add comments to code that is already clear and unambiguous? If the code isn't clear, then refactor it to improve its quality, or, as a last resort, write documentation. Even though some development environments make it easy to include documentation in your code, Java's Javadoc utility is such an example; you only want to invest in documentation when it makes sense to do so and not just because it is easy.

What confuses many people regarding XP and documentation is that XP doesn't specify potential documents to create during development. This is unlike the Unified Process (Kruchten 2000; Ambler 2001b), which suggests a slew of potential project artifacts. Instead, the suggestion is to work together with your project stakeholders in an environment of rapid feedback and trust them to determine the things that they need, not just documents but any type of project enhancements (Jeffries 2001b). Once again, you need to have the courage to trust the people involved with the project. In Chapter 14, I discuss a collection of documents that you may choose to create, and I provide advice for when to consider creating the documents.

One of the greatest misunderstandings people have about XP regards the concept of traveling light—many people believe that it means you don't create any documentation, but nothing could be further from the truth. Traveling light actually means that you create just enough models and documentation; too little or too much puts you at risk. As I suggest in Chapter 14, a good rule of thumb to ensure that you're traveling light is that you shouldn't create a model or document until you actually need it—creating either too early puts you at risk of wasting your time working on something you don't actually need yet.

Documentation on an XP project is a business decision, not a technical one. This is consistent with AM's philosophy regarding documentation, discussed in Chapter 14. Jeffries (2001b) says it best:

"If there is a need for a document, the customer should request the document in the same way that she would request a feature: with a story card. The team will estimate the cost of the document, and the customer may schedule it in any iteration she wishes."

XP and the UML?

Because XP has reached buzzword status within the IT community, whatever that means, many people are now asking two typical questions: "Can you use buzzword1 with buzzword2?" and if yes then, "How do you use buzzword1 and buzzword2?" together. Hence, we're starting to see people asking about using XP with web services, CORBA, EJB,* .NET, Linux, open source software (OSS), and of course the UML. I want to explore the relationship between XP and UML, so let's ask the two typical questions:

1. **Can you use UML with XP?** Yes. You can apply the artifacts of the UML— activity diagrams, class diagrams, collaboration diagrams, component diagrams, deployment diagrams, sequence diagrams, statechart diagrams, and use case diagrams—when you are taking an XP approach to development.

2. **How do you use UML with XP?** Minimally, you should apply AM's practice of *Apply the Right Artifact(s)* and use UML artifacts on your XP project only where appropriate. Ideally, you should apply all of the principles and practices of AM when doing so.

Wait a minute. One of AM's principles is *Multiple Models*, which tells you that you need to have modeling skills pertaining to a wide variety of artifacts within your intellectual toolkit. Yes, the artifacts of the UML are a good start but unfortunately not enough: As I argue in Chapter 15, "The UML and Beyond," the UML is not sufficient for the real-world needs of business application developers, although luckily, as Appendix A, "Modeling Techniques," shows, we have far more than the artifacts of the UML at our disposal. Seems to me that we have a problem here. If the UML is not sufficient for the development of business applications, and if you are trying to develop such an application following the XP methodology, then perhaps "How do you use UML with XP?" is the wrong question to be asking. One of the problems with the buzzword approach to software development is that when you limit your vocabulary to buzzwords, you correspondingly limit your solution space to whatever can be described by those buzzwords. Therefore, I believe that two more questions need to be added to the buzzword approach: "Is using buzzword1 with buzzword2 the right question to be asking?" and, if not, "What is the right question?" When you ask these questions about XP and UML, you quickly realize that the right question to be asking is more along the lines of "How do you model effectively on an XP project?" This is a question addressed by AM, and in particular this chapter.

---

*I actually discuss how to adopt XP practices, as well as AM principles and practices for that matter, within an EJB project in the book *Mastering EJB 2/e* (Roman, Ambler, and Jewell 2002).

TIP **Not All UML Artifacts Are Appropriate**
User stories (Beck 2000) are an important part of XP—user stories form the foundation of the requirements for your system; they are a primary input into your project planning efforts (referred to as The Release Game); they are the primary artifact used to define what your team will be working on in a given construction iteration; and they are used to drive the development of your acceptance test cases. The UML does not include user stories but instead describes an artifact called a Use Case Diagram that depicts the interrelationships between actors that interact with the system and use cases that describe usage-based requirements for your system. As I show in Appendix A, use cases and user stories are alternatives to each other. Although clearly different artifacts, they are both used to describe usage-based requirements. So when you are using one, you very likely won't be using another. The implication is that because user stories are an integral part of XP you clearly will not want to apply use cases on your project, hence you will not need to create UML use case diagrams. Once again, remember to follow the AM practice *Apply the Right Artifact(s)*.

Another interesting buzzword combination to consider is how do you use the Model Driven Architecture (MDA) (Object Management Group 2001b) approach with XP? The MDA is part of the Object Management Group's (OMG) vision to support interoperability with specifications, defining the relationships among OMG standards (such as the UML and CORBA) and how they can be used together in a coordinated manner. The MDA defines an approach to system specification that distinguishes between platform independent models (PIMs) that specify the system in a manner that abstracts away technical details and models that are in turn realized by platform specific models (PSMs) that take into account technical considerations. The MDA also distinguishes between formal models and informal models. Formal models are based on a language, such as the UML, that has a well-defined syntax and semantics and possibly a defined way to show the validity of its constructs, such as rules of analysis, inference, or proof. Informal models, as you would expect, do not have a sufficient definition behind them. The MDA requires the use of formal models and not informal ones because of its focus on specifying the interoperability between systems. Basically, the MDA defines a set of guidelines for structuring system specifications expressed as formal models.

Now to my question: "Can XP and the MDA be used together?" Following the strict definition of the MDA, the answer would have to be no. Models such as Class Responsibility Collaborator (CRC) cards (Cunningham and Beck 1989; Wilkinson 1995) and user stories (Beck 2000) are an integral part of the XP development process and because they are not formally defined, that academically disallows the use of MDA and XP. Practically, however, the answer may in fact be yes. The MDA is being used by CASE tool companies as a conceptual framework from which they are borrowing ideas. Frankly the idea of having platform independent and platform specific models has been around for decades, and conceivably it will be common to see MDA-compliant tools just as we see UML-compliant tools today. Just like UML-compliancy is in the eye of the beholder, every CASE tool has its idiosyncratic implementation of the UML. We will also see the same thing with the MDA. Because an XP team is free to adopt any tool that it wishes, granted that it should be a tool that improves the productivity of the people using it, an XP team could in fact work with an MDA-compliant tool if the situation warrants it. Of course, that MDA-compliant tool would need to automate user stories and CRC cards in such a way as to not lose the benefits that these artifacts currently provide, many of which are derived from the fact that these artifacts are created using simple tools such as index cards. This leads me to suspect that in practice the answer will likely still prove to be no.

And the Verdict Is?

Modeling and documentation are important aspects of XP, just like they are important aspects of any other software development methodology. However, XP explicitly advises you to minimize the effort that you invest in these activities to be just enough. Luckily, the focus of AM is to make you as effective as possible when you are modeling and documenting. In the next chapter, I explore the fit between the two methodologies.

CHAPTER 17

Agile Modeling and eXtreme Programming

Routine is not organization, any more than paralysis is order.

—Sir Arthur Helps

In Chapter 1, "Introduction," I stated that Agile Modeling (AM) should be tailored into an existing full lifecycle methodology in order to improve its approach to modeling. Because modeling is clearly a part of eXtreme Programming (XP) (Beck 2000), see Chapter 16, the potential exists for AM to add value to an XP project. Assuming, of course, that it is possible to tailor AM into XP and that you can do so without detracting from what currently exists within XP. In particular, XP's practices of refactoring and test-first development clearly do a very good job of filling in for two critical goals—promoting clean design and thinking through your design before writing code—that are typically associated with traditional modeling processes. In my experience, both refactoring and test-first development are complementary to AM and arguably enablers of several AM practices. In this chapter, I explore the following issues:

- The potential fit between AM and XP
- Refactoring and AM
- Test-First Development and AM
- Which AM practices should you adopt?

The Potential Fit between AM and XP

A critical issue that must be addressed is how well AM fits in with XP. Table 17.1 lists the practices of AM and either maps them to existing principles or practices of XP or discusses the potential fit of the AM practice when it is not explicitly a part of XP. Because XP was used as a foundation for AM, see Chapter 1, many AM practices map straight to XP. However, because AM's focus is on modeling, several practices are clearly new, hence the potential for AM to bring value to an XP project.

The fact that AM's practices are complementary to XP isn't sufficient; there should also be a philosophical alignment between the two methodologies as well. I believe that there is. First, AM has adopted the four values of XP—*Courage, Simplicity, Communication*, and *Feedback*—and added a fifth one, *Humility*, one that is clearly compatible with XP. Second, the principles of AM are closely aligned with those of XP. Nine of eighteen are adopted directly from XP, and the remaining ones—*Software Is Your Primary Goal, Enabling the Next Effort is Your Secondary Goal, Model with a Purpose, Multiple Models, Content is More Important Than Representation, Everyone Can Learn From Everyone Else, Know Your Models, Know Your Tools*, and *Maximize Stakeholder Investment*—are clearly compatible with XP's philosophies. The three modeling-specific principles may cause a hard-core XP developer to pause for a moment, but on reflection should not prove arguable. *Model with a Purpose* advises that you shouldn't work on a model without good cause, *Multiple Models* says that you have a wide range of techniques available that you may choose to apply (including but not limited to CRC cards, user stories, and the diagrams of the UML), and *Know Your Models* suggests that you need to know what you're doing to be effective.

Refactoring and AM

Refactoring (Fowler 1999) is a technique to restructure code in a disciplined way, a technique that is a fundamental practice of XP. The basic idea is that you make small changes to your code, called refactorings, to support new requirements and to keep your design as simple as possible. An important aspect of refactoring is that each change that you make to your code leaves it semantically the same as before you made the change. For example: if you change the name of an operation, then all the source code that invokes the operation will still invoke it by using the same name. The advantage of refactoring is that it enables programmers to safely and easily evolve their code to fulfill new requirements or to improve its quality.

Is refactoring compatible with AM? Yes. Refactoring is a coding technique, and because AM does not address programming-related issues there is no technical overlap between the two. What about a conceptual overlap? AM addresses design modeling and refactoring addresses design improvement of source code. This begs the question, "What do you do when you have an existing design model and you refactor your code?" Although it's an interesting question, the real issue is that you have two artifacts, a design model and source code, that describe the design of your system. The source code has changed; now you need to decide whether or not you wish to update the model. The way that you originally arrived at the model is irrelevant to this issue; you could have arrived

Table 17.1   Applicability of AM Practices on an XP Project

AM PRACTICE	FIT WITH XP
Active Stakeholder Participation	This practice is simply a new take on XP's *On-Site Customer* practice. AM uses the term project stakeholder in place of customer and focuses on the concept of their active participation, hence *Active Stakeholder Participation* and not *On-Site Stakeholder*.
Apply Modeling Standards	This is the AM version of XP's *Coding Standards* practice.
Apply Patterns Gently	This practice reflects the YAGNI principle to the effective application of patterns within your system, in conformance to XP's practice of *Simple Design*.
Apply the Right Artifact(s)	This practice is not explicitly described by XP principles and practices, although it is aligned with the XP philosophies of "if you need it do it" and using the most appropriate tool or technique for the job at hand.
Collective Ownership	AM has adopted XP's *Collective Ownership* practice.
Consider Testability	This is a reflection of XP's *Testing* practice with respect to modeling—when you are modeling something, perhaps with CRC cards or sketches, you should keep in the back of your mind what test cases you'll need to support the ideas captured in your models. See Chapter 10 for a detailed discussion of AM and testing.
Create Several Models in Parallel	This is a modeling-specific practice. XP developers can clearly work on several models—such as CRC cards, acceptance test cases, and sketches—if they choose to do so.
Create Simple Content	This is complementary to XP's *Simple Design* practice that advises you to keep your models as simple as possible.
Depict Models Simply	This is complementary to XP's *Simple Design* practice that suggests that your models do not need to be fancy to be effective, perfect examples of which are CRC cards and user stories.
Discard Temporary Models	This practice reflects XP's *Travel Light* principle, which AM has adopted, explicitly advising you to dispose of models that you no longer need.
Display Models Publicly	This practice reflects XP's (and AM's) value of *Communication*, its principle of *Open and Honest Communication* (adopted by AM), and reflects its practice of *Collective Ownership*.

Table 17.1   continued

AM PRACTICE	FIT WITH XP
Formalize Contract Models	This practice is not currently reflected within XP, though perhaps it can be found in its "if you need to then do it" philosophy. This practice was included in AM to provide guidance for how to deal with the very common situation of integrating with other systems.
Iterate to Another Artifact	This practice explicitly states, in a general form, the practice of XP developers to iterate between working on various artifacts such as source code, CRC cards, and tests.
Model in Small Increments	This practice supports XP's iterative and increment approach to development. Both XP and AM prefer an emergent approach to development and not a big design up front (BDUF) approach.
Model to Communicate	This practice is modeling-specific, describing one reason why you would want to model, a practice that reflects XP's and AM's principle of *Open and Honest Communication*.
Model to Understand	This practice is modeling-specific, describing the primary reason why you would want to model. This practice is consistent with XP's existing use of CRC cards to explore design issues and is effectively a generalization of the concept.
Model With Others	This is the AM version of XP's *Pair Programming* practice.
Prove It With Code	This is the AM version of XP's *Concrete Experiments* principle. In fact, it was originally called *Concrete Experiments,* although it was renamed when it evolved into a practice.
Reuse Existing Resources	This concept is not explicitly included in XP, although it clearly isn't excluded either. XP developers are practical; if there is something available that can be appropriately reused, then they will likely choose to do so.
Update Only When It Hurts	This practice reflects AM and XP's *Travel Light* principle, advising that you should update an artifact only when you desperately need to.
Use the Simplest Tools	This practice reflects AM and XP's *Assume Simplicity* principle and is consistent with XP's preference for low-tech tools such as index cards for modeling.

there because you took an AM approach to develop it, you could have taken a BDUF approach, or you could have adopted an existing model and are coding to it (for example: several organizations have developed persistence frameworks based on the design that I present at www.ambysoft.com/persistenceLayer.html). The issue is irrelevant to the type of design model, be it a UML class diagram, CRC cards, a physical data model, or a procedural structure chart. The good news is that AM provides advice for how to deal with such a situation. In particular, the practice *Discard Temporary Models* suggests that you should consider whether you really need the design model; if not, get rid of it. The practice *Update Only When It Hurts* suggests that having artifacts, such as the design model and the code, out of sync is often unreasonable.

How do you apply AM and refactoring together? Apply AM practices as appropriate when you are modeling, use those models as input into your programming efforts, and refactor your code as you normally would have. If you discover that you need to attempt a major refactoring, get the team together to discuss it, modeling whenever appropriate, then approach the major refactoring as you would have in the past: as a collection of small refactorings.

Modeling tools that reverse-engineer your code can prove valuable when you are refactoring code, particularly when you are unfamiliar with that code. Many developers think visually; they grasp information communicated by pictures more readily than they do information communicated textually. So CASE tools that quickly import a bit of code and create diagrams from them can be very useful. It's quite common for CASE tools to import object-oriented source code, perhaps written in Java or C++, and generate UML class diagrams that show the static structure of the code and UML sequence diagrams that depict its dynamic nature. These diagrams can be used to quickly understand the existing code, which is the first step in refactoring it.

Test-First Development and AM

Test-first development is a development practice in which you work in very short cycles: you consider a test, write the test and business code for it, get it to work, then continue. These tests are collected into a development integration testing suite that must be successfully run whenever code is submitted to your shared repository. This practice is integral to XP.

Is test-first development compatible with AM? Yes. Like refactoring, test-first development is more of a coding practice, so there is little opportunity for technical overlap. However, there is room for conceptual overlap because test-first development clearly delves into the realm of detailed design since it provides developers with an opportunity to think through their code before they write it (as well as important feedback regarding their code). If you've chosen to do a little modeling before writing your code, perhaps to think through an issue larger than a single test case, then that's okay. In fact, it may even make your test-first development efforts easier, particularly if you have adopted AM's *Consider Testability* practice.

Following a test-first approach agile developers quickly discover whether their ideas actually work or not—the tests will either validate their models or not—providing rapid feedback regarding the ideas captured within the models.

How do you apply AM within a test-first development environment? As with refactoring, simply apply AM practices as appropriate when you are modeling, use those models as input into your programming efforts, and iterate between modeling, testing, and programming as needed.

Which AM Practices Should You Adopt?

Only adopt the practices that add value to what your team is trying to accomplish. Ideally that will be at least the core practices of AM, therefore it would be fair to claim that you are in fact "doing AM," as I indicate in Chapter 5, and perhaps you can even adopt the supplementary practices, as well. You should note that your goal isn't simply to be able to say that you're agile modeling, your goal is also to improve your productivity as software developers.

The possibility clearly exists to use AM and XP together. You have seen that there is a conceptual fit between AM and XP and that XP's practices of refactoring and test-first design complement AM. What remains to be seen is how the practices of AM can be used to enhance XP projects. This is the primary issue addressed by the next four chapters.

CHAPTER 18

Agile Modeling Throughout the XP Lifecycle

Though this be madness, yet there is method in it.

—William Shakespeare

To explain how the practices of Agile Modeling are applied on an eXtreme Programming (XP) (Beck 2000) project, I will work through a portion of the SWA Online case study (see Chapter 1, "Introduction") and show how modeling is used throughout the XP lifecycle. XP has a project lifecycle? Yes. Figure 18.1 depicts a high-level view of the XP project lifecycle modified from (Wells 2001) to indicate a mapping of Beck's project phases (the Death phase, not shown, would follow maintenance).

First and foremost, don't get hung up on the term "phase." Although the term phase may bring connotations of waterfall development, the fact is that phases can occur iteratively, something that is apparent in Figure 18.1 by the fact that it is possible to move back and forth between the Planning, Iterate to Release, and Productionizing phases. Phases aren't necessarily long—the Planning phase may only take several hours, for example. Furthermore, XP teams typically don't think of themselves as working in phases, they just think of themselves as working. Also, it's quite common to be working in multiple phases at once; in fact, the Productionizing phase is often subsumed into the Iterate to Release phase. In short, the concept of phases within XP is weak at best and for the most part isn't given much thought by XPers. The important thing about the concept of phases is that it communicates the idea that the "flavor" of your effort changes throughout an XP project. Furthermore, phases do provide a handy way to organize the rest of this chapter, so let's address the development effort one phase at a time.

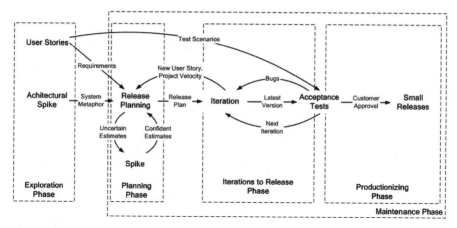

Figure 18.1   The XP project lifecycle.

Exploration Phase

The first phase that an XP project experiences is the Exploration phase (Beck 2000), which includes the development of the architectural spike and the development of the initial user stories. From a requirements point of view, Beck suggests that you require enough material in the user stories to make a first good release and so that the developers are sufficiently confident that they can't estimate any better without actually implementing the system. Every project has a scope, something that is typically based on a collection of initial requirements for your system. Although the XP lifecycle presented in Figure 18.1 does not explicitly include a specific scope definition task, it implies one with user stories being an input into release planning. User stories are a primary driver of the XP methodology—they provide high-level requirements for your system and are the critical input into your planning process. The implication is that you need a collection of user stories, anywhere from a handful to several dozen, to get your XP project started.

However, there's a potential problem. When a project begins, a software approach may not have been chosen for it. This decision is often made once the scope of the effort is understood and people have been identified to work on the project because, as Cockburn (2002) suggests, you want to choose the process that best aligns with the nature of your project, team, and organizational culture. The implication is that if the decision hasn't yet been made to take an XP approach then the people performing the IRUF effort may choose to create something other than user stories—shall statements, features, and use cases are common options. If this is your situation, you will need to convert these artifacts into user stories, working with your customers as needed (to remain consistent with the terminology commonly in use by XP teams, I will use XP's term customer, instead of AM's term project stakeholder). Luckily, shall statements and features are very similar to user stories so that should be straightforward for you if this is your situation. And because use cases typically have greater scope than user stories, the easiest approach is to simply declare them to be user stories and then go about splitting them as you normally would to reduce them to a manageable size. Chapter 19, "Modeling During the XP Exploration Phase," describes an example of modeling during the XP Exploration phase.

Planning Phase

Following the Exploration phase is the Planning phase (Beck 2000), the purpose of which is for you and your customers to agree on a date by which the smallest, most valuable set of user stories will be implemented. When you are release planning, you will brainstorm the tasks for a given user story (Wake 2002), writing a task card for each task, providing you with enough insight about the user story to accurately estimate the effort required to implement it. A task card, see Figure 18.2 for examples, typically lists a text description of what you need to do to accomplish the task. Sometimes a task card may be described using a model instead of text. For example, Newkirk and Martin (2001) provide an example of a task that was described as a sketch of an HTML page similar to the one presented in Figure 18.3 (their Figure 6.2). The team may have simply sketched this figure on a whiteboard or used a combination of sticky notes and flip chart paper to create an essential user interface prototype at first. Once they were happy with what they had, they quickly transcribed it onto an index card. Both a whiteboard and sticky notes are far more flexible than pen and paper, so they are a better option for you when initially thinking through the design of a user interface component such as this one. You want to transcribe your sketch onto a card to have a record of your design to base your coding efforts on during the next iteration (see the following table), and cards are the preferred medium of choice to do so—distributed teams might choose to record tasks electronically, perhaps in a

Submit Search to DB	Build Search Result Page
• Parse the criteria customer defined from the search page. • Convert wild cards (*, _) to SQL equivalents. • Build SQL SELECT statement based on search criteria, ordering by the item number. • Invoke statement in DB.	• If a database or network error is detected, build a standard error page indicating the problem. Otherwise: • At the top of the page indicate the number of items in the result set. • If no items resulted from the search, display the text message "No items found based on your criteria." Otherwise: • List the resulting databases rows on the page, listing the item number, item name, unit price, and a link that leads to detailed information for the specific item.

Figure 18.2   Example task cards pertaining to searching for items.

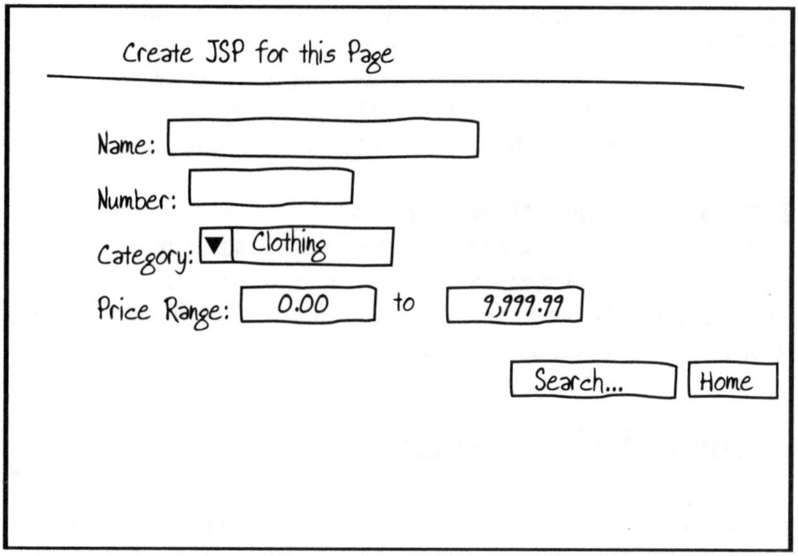

Create JSP for this Page

Name:

Number:

Category: ▼ Clothing

Price Range: 0.00 to 9,999.99

Search...   Home

Figure 18.3 A hand-drawn sketch representing what needs to be built for the item search page.

Wiki (Leuf and Cunningham 2001) or other collaborative environment. In this case, a sketch of the screen is a more effective description of the task than free-form text.

Modeling is clearly a potential activity during this phase. For example: Figure 18.4 depicts a sketch representing the logic of a task—the team chose to create this sketch

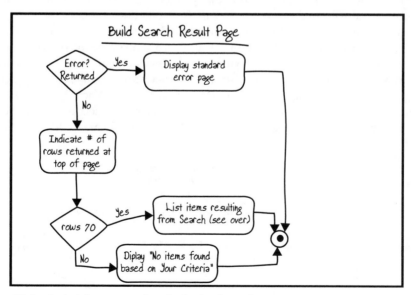

Figure 18.4 A sketch representing the logic of a task.

instead of writing text for it because they were more comfortable with a quick diagram. This is perfectly fine. The AM principle *Model with a Purpose* advises that you should know your audience and create models that reflect their needs (in this case, your team itself is the audience of the task cards), and the AM practice *Apply The Right Artifact(s)* advises you to create the best type of model suited for the task at hand.

> **TIP** **XP Teams Keep Their Models in a Box**
> **XP teams prefer simple tools, and one of their favorites is index cards. They use index cards for user stories, for tasks (see Figures 18.2, 18.3, and 18.4 for examples), and for Class-Responsibility Collaborator (CRC) models. What's the best way to store a collection of index cards? In an index-card box.**

Iterations to Release Phase

The Iterations to Release Phase (Beck 2000) encompasses the primary effort of an XP project, more typically referred to as construction iterations or simply iterations, as this is where your major development efforts, including modeling, programming, testing, and integration, occur. Figure 18.5 (Wells 2000) depicts the lifecycle for an iteration. Iteration planning is the same type of effort as release planning, described in the preceding section, the only difference being that the focus is on the user stories assigned to the current iteration. When you are working on iteration N you will find that new user stories, ones that have not been estimated, have been added in; therefore, you need to go through the effort of identifying tasks so you may accurately estimate each user story. After estimating the new stories, and perhaps revisiting the other stories just to be on the safe side, you may find that you have too many or too few stories for the iteration and will need to move stories to/from other iterations.

From the point of view of modeling, the interesting aspect of an iteration is shown in the development aspect of Figure 18.5. Figure 18.6 shows a detailed lifecycle (Wells 2000). A lot of the modeling that occurs during development happens in stand-up meetings where the team gathers to discuss what they are currently working on, often asking for advice regarding how to approach a specific issue. When this happens, discussing the issue around a whiteboard, drawing sketches as needed to enhance the communication effort, is quite common. Stand up meetings are called exactly that

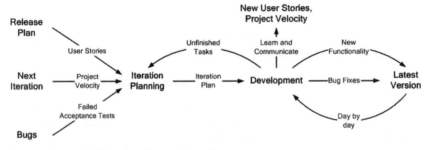

Figure 18.5 The lifecycle of an XP iteration.

Figure 18.6   The lifecycle of XP development.

because everyone stands up when attending them, which tends to make them brief (Beck and Fowler 2001). Figure 18.6 hints at the idea that after the stand-up meeting the team breaks up into pairs to work on their parts of the system.

An alternative view is presented in Figure 18.7, which depicts a typical XP developer's day (Wake 2002). It explicitly shows that people pair up after the stand-up meeting, often starting with a quick design session as required to formulate an initial design strategy for what they are working on. A fundamental aspect of XP is that people work together in pairs, following a practice called Pair Programming, which would have been more appropriately called Pair Development, which is defined as a

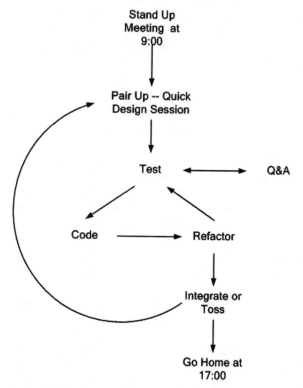

Figure 18.7   A typical XP developer's day.

dialog between two people trying to simultaneously program (and analyze and design and test) and understand how to program better (Beck 2000). XP developers will hold a quick design session, what AM calls an ad hoc or impromptu modeling session (see Chapter 13, "Agile Modeling Sessions"), whenever they are not sure how to proceed with programming (Jeffries, Anderson, and Hendrickson 2001). The basic idea is that you get a few people together to work through the issue, in other words follow AM's *Model to Understand* practice, to spend a few minutes discussing ideas and modeling as necessary. You will naturally want to follow the practice *Apply The Right Artifact(s)* and work on the type of models that are appropriate for the issue you are discussing. For example: CRC cards are a good option if you are exploring the structure of your code, and an essential user interface prototype may be just the thing if you are exploring the design of your user interface. You'll sometimes find that a design issue will require several models, perhaps you need to create both a CRC model and an essential UI prototype to fully explore the problem, and you will therefore want to follow the practices *Create Several Models in Parallel* and *Iterate to Another Artifact*. These modeling sessions are typically very short, hence the name quick design session, lasting anywhere from ten to thirty minutes. To gain feedback regarding your design, you want to quickly get back to coding, following the practice *Prove It with Code*, to determine if your approach works or not. If it works, then that's great; if it doesn't, then go back to the whiteboard for another quick design session.

Chapter 20, "Modeling During an XP Iteration: Searching for Items," works through an example of modeling during an iteration by examining how to approach the implementation of searching for an item as part of implementing the system for the SWA Online case study. Chapter 21, "Modeling During an XP Iteration: Totaling an Order," works through a different example—how to model the taxation, discounting, and totaling of an online order—in a similar manner.

Productionizing

XP's Productionizing phase (Beck 2000) focuses on certifying that the software is ready to go into production, perhaps by what I call "testing in the large" techniques (Ambler 1999; Ambler and Constantine 2002), such as system testing, load testing, and installation testing to name a few. During this phase, you will slow down the rate at which you evolve the software; evolution doesn't stop, but the risk of whether something should go into the next release becomes important. Note that on many projects this phase is little different than a typical construction iteration. The major difference is that you release your system into your production environment instead of into your development sandbox.

How does AM apply in this phase? In two ways. First, you may find that you need to model as part of your rework efforts resulting from newly discovered defects. Second, this point in your project is a good time to consider cleaning up your documentation. Although the XP philosophy is to write clear, understandable code and to include effective comments in the code as necessary, the reality is that you still need supporting documentation. Remember that you have a wide range of project stakeholders, including users, senior management, operations staff, and support staff. These people do not have access to the code, nor would many of them understand it even if they did, so they will require other forms of documentation (see Chapter 14, "Agile Documentation," for a discussion of agile documentation). This documentation should be at the request of project stakeholders. As the AM principle *Maximize Stakeholder Investment* points out, their resources are being invested in the documentation; therefore, they have the final word on what should be done. I prefer to write documentation such as this late in the project lifecycle because what you are writing about, the system, has become relatively stable for the current release; therefore the documentation you write will be stable too. You may also need to produce the following:

System documentation. For developers, including maintenance professionals, this is the most important type of documentation. The purpose of this document is to provide an overview of the system and to help people understand the system. Common information in this document includes overviews of the technical architecture and the business architecture, the high-level requirements for the system, a summary of critical design decisions, architecture-level diagrams, and important design models (if any).

Operations documentation. This documentation typically includes an indication of the dependencies that your system is involved with; the nature of its interaction with other systems, databases, and files; references to backup procedures; a list of contact points for your system and how to reach them; a summary of the availability/reliability requirements for your system; an indication of the expected load profile of your system; and troubleshooting guidelines.

Support documentation. This documentation includes training materials specific to support staff; all user documentation to use as a reference when solving problems; a trouble-shooting guide; escalation procedures for handling difficult problems; and a list of contact points within the maintenance team.

User documentation. Your users may require a reference manual, a usage guide, a support guide, and even training materials. You need to distinguish between these different types of documents because the way that each one is used varies: one document is for quick lookups, another is for discovering how to work with the system, another is for how to obtain additional help, and the other document is for training.

Maintenance

The XP Maintenance phase (Beck 2000) is actually the normal state of XP projects because you keep evolving them over time. This phase encompasses the Planning, Iterations to Release, and Productionizing phases for releases 2 through N of your system. By implication, this phase also includes production-oriented activities, such as the operation and support of your system. Systems built taking an XP approach are put into production just like systems built using any other approach, even though production issues are outside of the scope of both AM and XP. However, it is important to recognize that your team needs to take production-related issues into account, which is why AM explicitly includes operations and support staff as potential project stakeholders. Remember, there is little value in building a system if you can't deploy it and then keep it in production.

How Do You Make This Work?

How should you approach modeling during development on an XP project? Beck (2000) suggests that you should apply the XP practice of *Small Initial Investment* and draw a few pictures at a time. He states that the XP strategy is that anyone can design with pictures all they want, but as soon as a question is raised that can be answered with code then the designers must turn to code for the answer. In other words, you should then seek *Rapid Feedback* to discover whether your pictures are on target by following the AM practice *Prove It with Code*.

When should you consider modeling during development on an XP project? Whenever creating a model is more effective than writing code. In other words, follow the AM principle *Maximize Stakeholder Investment* and the AM practice *Apply The Right Artifact(s)*.

How should you model? Follow AM's practice *Use the Simplest Tools* and prefer tools such as index cards, whiteboards, and sticky notes instead of more complicated CASE tools. Simple tools tend to promote interaction and communication, two factors that are critical to your success. Although XP favors the use of index cards to record user stories, CRC models, and story tasks, there is nothing wrong with using a CASE tool as long as its use provides positive value to your effort. Chapter 10, "Using the Simplest Tools Possible?" explores modeling tool usage in greater detail.

How should you document? XP teams prefer to write clean, easy-to-understand source code—their philosophy is that only the source code is in sync with the source code. However, remember that AM's principle *Model with a Purpose* states that you should understand the needs of a model/document's audience. If the audience for documentation is your system's users or your senior management, then clean source code isn't going to do it. Instead, you will need to develop external documentation for this audience. Your stakeholders should request this documentation; understand the costs involved, one of which is the fact that any time you spend writing documentation isn't spent writing software; and be willing to accept those costs.

XP developers need to recognize that you can model on an XP project and that modeling is in fact a part of XP already with its existing application of user stories and CRC cards. More importantly, XP developers must abandon any preconceived notions that they may have about modeling—that big modeling up front (BMUF) is the only approach to modeling, that models are permanent documents that must always be updated, that you need to use complex CASE tools to model, and that the UML defines the only models available to you—and approach modeling from a new perspective. One such perspective was presented in this chapter: that you can tailor Agile Modeling into a software process based on eXtreme Programming and remain effective as software developers. The next three chapters present examples of doing exactly this.

CHAPTER 19

Modeling During the XP Exploration Phase

The difficult we do at once; the impossible takes a bit longer.

—American Seabees

The first phase that an XP project experiences is the Exploration phase (Beck 2000), which encompasses the development of the initial user stories and the development of the architectural spike. Every project needs to start somewhere, even XP projects. This chapter explores how to apply Agile Modeling's practices throughout this phase of an XP project and discusses the following topics:

- Initial requirements up front (IRUF)
- Metaphors, architectures, and spikes
- Setting the foundation for your project

Initial Requirements Up Front (IRUF)

From a requirements point of view, Beck suggests that you require enough material in the user stories to make a first good release and to make the developers confident that they can't estimate any better without actually implementing the system. Every project has a scope, something that is typically based on a collection of initial requirements for your system. Although the XP lifecycle presented in Chapter 18, "Agile Modeling Throughout the XP Lifecycle," does not explicitly include a specific scope definition task, it implies one with user stories being an input into release planning. User stories are a primary driver of the XP methodology—they provide (very) high-level requirements for your system and are the critical input into your planning process. Therefore, you need a collection of user stories, anywhere from a handful to several dozen, to get your XP project started.

However, there's a potential problem. When a project begins, a software approach may not have been chosen for it. This decision is often made once the scope of the effort is understood and people have been identified to work on the project because as Cockburn (2002) suggests, you want to choose the process that best aligns with the nature of your project, team, and organizational culture. If the decision hasn't yet been made to take an XP approach, then the people performing the IRUF effort may choose to create something other than user stories—shall statements, features, and use-cases are common options. If this is your situation, you will need to convert these artifacts into user stories, working with your customers as needed. (To remain consistent with the terminology commonly in use by XP teams, I will use XP's term customer, instead of Agile Modeling (AM)'s term project stakeholder.) Luckily, shall statements and features are very similar to user stories, so they should be straightforward for you if this is your situation. Because use-cases typically have greater scope than user stories, you can simply declare them to be user stories and then go about splitting them as you normally would to reduce them to a manageable size.

For example, assume that your initial requirements up front (IRUF) modeling efforts resulted in the use-case diagram of Figure 19.1 and a corresponding collection of use-cases, and you have subsequently decided to take an XP approach to develop-

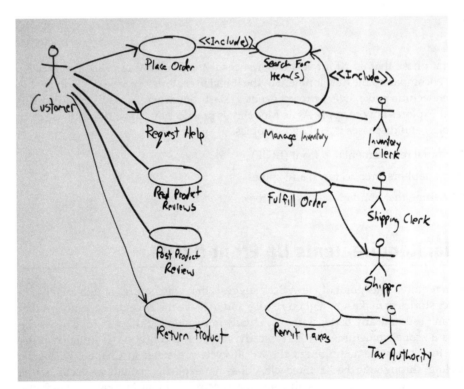

Figure 19.1   A high-level use-case diagram for SWA Online.

ment. You need to translate these use-cases into a collection of user stories, both of these artifacts are described in detail in Appendix A, "Modeling Techniques," several of which are presented in Figure 19.3. The Place Order use-case has been "converted" into a collection of eleven user stories whereas the Search For Item(s) use-case became a single user story because it was relatively simple. Luckily, the team that had identified the initial requirements had written up a reasonably good description for the Place Order use-case (see Figure 19.2). So all we needed to do was work through the description and introduce user stories as appropriate, writing each user story on an individual index card. Why index cards? Index cards are easy to work with, both when we are writing them and when we are using them to plan our project—several people can work on them simultaneously as a team by moving them around on a table or tacking them to a bulletin board. As part of our release planning effort, we may discover that we need to split some of these proposed user stories further, but for now they should prove sufficient.

1. The use-case begins when a customer chooses to place an order.

2. The customer searches for items via the use-case Search for Item(s).

3. The customer adds an order item to their order.

4. The customer indicates the number of a given item they wish to order.

5. The system calculates the subtotal for the item by multiplying the unit price by the number ordered.

6. The customer repeats steps 2 through 5 as necessary to build their order.

7. The customer finishes adding items to their order.

8. The customer provides their ship to and bill to information, including their name, phone number, and surface address.

9. The system calculates the subtotal for the entire order by adding the subtotals of the individual line items.

10. The system calculates the taxes applicable for the order according to the business rule Calculate Taxes for an Order.

11. The system calculates applicable discounts for the order according to the business rule Calculate Discounts for an Order.

12. The system displays the applicable taxes and discounts.

13. The system calculates the grand total for the order by adding the applicable taxes to the order subtotal and subtracting the discounts.

14. The system displays a summary of the order.

15. The customer verifies that the order is what they want.

16. The system schedules the order for fulfillment (see the use-case Fulfill Order).

17. The system produces a receipt for the customer that summarizes the order.

Figure 19.2   The basic course of action for placing an order.

The customer can add an item to an existing order.

The customer can remove an item from an existing order.

For each individual order item, the system displays the name of the item, the item ID code from the catalog, the unit price, the number of items the customer has ordered, and the subtotal before taxes and discounts.

Customers can search for inventory item(s).

The customer can indicate their shipping address for an order.

The customer can indicate their billing address for an order, which may or may not be the same as their shipping address.

The system calculates and displays a subtotal before taxes, discounts, and shipping and handling for an order.

The system calculates and displays a grand total for an order.

The system calculates and displays applicable taxes, discounts, and shipping and handling charges for an order.

The system allows a customer to look over an order to verify it before scheduling it for fulfillment.

The system generates an email summary of an order and sends it to the customer when the order is scheduled for fulfillment.

The system allows a customer to update an order before scheduling it for fulfillment.

Figure 19.3   User stories for the Place Order and Search For Item(s) use-cases.

The user stories presented in Figure 19.3 may be sufficient for now because they provide enough insight for us to begin development. Yes, as the project progresses we would need to identify user stories for other aspects of the system, particularly order fulfillment and inventory management, but placing orders is clearly our number one priority for SWA Online, so these are the user stories that we can start with. Remember, we develop software incrementally, not as one "big bang," so it's valid to work this way. Having said that, we could also work through all of the use-cases indicated in Figure 19.1 and identify a large collection of user stories to be used as input into the Release Planning phase. We could also do something in between these two extremes and flesh out the high priority use-cases at first, likely choosing to explore the Manage Inventory and Fulfill Order use-cases in addition to Place Order and Search for Inventory Items, and leave the rest for later. Which approach should we take? The approach that requires the identification of the least number of user stories that gets our project stakeholders to the point where they are confident that we understand the system's scope enough to move forward into development of the first release.

TIP   **You May Not Get Technical Requirements At First**

In XP, as in AM, your customers (project stakeholders) are the primary source of requirements. Sometimes they won't define user stories pertaining to technical issues, such as performance and system availability (Wake 2002). Yes, you have the option to suggest these requirements to them, but your customers have the final say on what becomes a user story and what doesn't. Later in the lifecycle, they may realize that these requirements are in fact important to them; therefore, you may need to refactor your system to handle those requirements. Last minute changes happen; there is nothing wrong with it.

Metaphors, Architectures, and Spikes

The second aspect of the Exploration phase focuses on your system architecture. Architecture within an XP project is less formal than in traditional methodologies, with a preference for keeping your system flexible—XP recommends that you embrace change, as does AM, whereas architecture-driven approaches advise you to build the skeleton of the system first because some things are difficult to change (Wake 2002). The XP approach is to identify a metaphor that describes how you intend to build your system. The metaphor acts as a conceptual framework, identifying key objects and providing insight into their interfaces. The metaphor is defined during an architectural spike early in the project, during the first iteration or during a pre-iteration that is sometimes referred to as a zero-feature release (ZFR) (Wake 2002). Beck (2000) suggests that you choose user stories for the first iteration so you will be forced to "create the whole system, even if it is in skeletal form." Do you identify the system metaphor during a pre-iteration/architectural spike or during the first iteration? It doesn't really matter as long as you identify the system metaphor at the beginning of your project.

Just because XP focuses on a system metaphor, that doesn't imply that you won't have an architecture, nor does it imply that you're not going to have any architectural diagrams. For example, Newkirk and Martin (2001) created a high-level diagram (their Figure 4.1) that overviews their architecture to enable them to better understand what they were building. A similar whiteboard sketch is presented in Figure 19.4 for SWA Online. Notice how the diagram combines UML use-case diagram notation for actors, the stick figures, and free-form diagramming—the AM principle *Content Is More Important Than Representation* advises that modeling your ideas properly is more important than using sanctioned diagramming notation or making your diagrams look pretty. This diagram also shows an application of the AM principles of *Depict Models Simply* and *Create Simple Content*: It is just good enough to indicate our proposed technical architecture and no more.

The development team would draw the diagram of Figure 19.4, following the AM practice *Model with Others* and standing up around a white board. The diagram is based on the user stories of Figure 19.3 and the use-case diagram and corresponding use-cases depicted in Figure 19.1. The team isn't going to ignore the material captured by the use-case diagram and use-cases just because they're not official XP artifacts, whatever that means; instead they would follow the AM practice *Reuse Existing Resources* and take advantage of the use-case diagram and use-cases. You can see that our candidate architecture seems to handle both order placement and order fulfillment activities. The team has also indicated two aspects of the architecture that it feels are uncertain—it believes it can place a shipment pickup request using XML to shippers

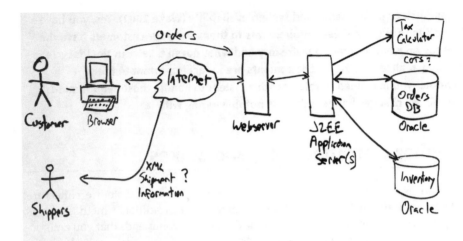

Figure 19.4 An architectural overview for SWA Online.

and calculate applicable taxes through a commercial off-the-shelf (COTS) system—by labeling them with question marks (Ambler 2001a, Ambler 2002). At some point, they will need to do spikes for these aspects of the system to determine if they are feasible and potentially include these tasks as part of their initial architecture spike (just enough code to show that this candidate architecture will work).

TIP **Modeling, Not Models, Is the Important Thing**
When applying AM's practices on an XP project, remember that a primary value of XP, as of AM, is communication. The value isn't in the models that you create, it is in the modeling effort itself that a model has helped you understand what your stakeholders want, or how you intend to fulfill their needs, or that a model has helped you communicate that what you are doing is important. Although we may choose to follow AM's *Display Models Publicly* practice and leave Figure 19.4 on the whiteboard for awhile, the figure doesn't really provide a lot of value to our team anymore, except perhaps to indicate that we still have two outstanding issues to address. Because the team was involved in creating the figure and because they are now developing based on the technical vision captured in the diagram, they know the technical architecture and likely will not need to look at the diagram again. Other people may learn about your architecture, perhaps through osmotic communication (Cockburn 2002) described in Chapter 8, "Communication," as they walk by the figure, and perhaps you'll choose to show the diagram to your project stakeholders to help you explain your approach (a good example of applying AM's *Model to Communicate* practice).

Although Figure 19.4 provides some insight into your technical architecture, the figure really doesn't provide much insight into your system metaphor. For SWA Online, traditionally a grocery store metaphor would be a likely candidate. An order is just like a shopping cart. Customers browse through your online store placing items into their carts, they pull items that they don't want out of their carts, and eventually they take their carts to the checkout where taxes, fees, discounts, and their order total are calculated. Then the selected items would be placed in boxes and shipped, similar to the way that bag-boys in grocery stores put purchased items in bags and give them to the customer. The development team would have discussed this metaphor in parallel to sketching the overview diagram, perhaps drawing a free-form sketch such as the one presented in Figure 19.5 on another section of whiteboard, just as AM's *Create Several Models in Parallel* practice suggests. This sketch would likely be erased once the team had agreed on the metaphor—the team followed the AM practice *Model to Understand,* and now the practice *Discard Temporary Models* would apply. The sketch in Figure 19.5 is of course optional; some people like to draw when they speak, whereas others don't—do whatever works best for you.

> **TIP** **Don't Focus on Common Infrastructure Early In the Project**
> A fundamental philosophy of XP is to not overbuild your system, only build what you need today and have the courage to trust that you can build what you need tomorrow at that point. Many non-XP teams start a project by working on common infrastructure, perhaps building a persistence layer (Ambler 2001d) or a messaging framework upon which they intend to build the rest of the system. Although this is very interesting work, it doesn't provide the functionality that your project stakeholders actually need. If you need these common facilities, that will become apparent over time, and you will slowly build them as needed and refactor your code to use them. This is what emergent design is all about. Why do XP teams prefer this approach? Because of their belief in YAGNI (You Aren't Gonna Need It)—they don't want to invest any time building software unless they know they need it right now. If you know you aren't going to be building common infrastructure right away, then you also don't need to model

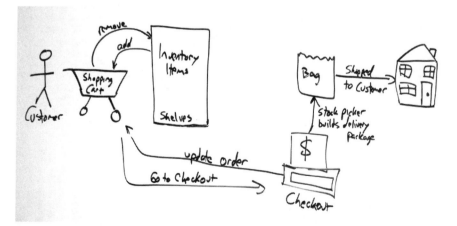

Figure 19.5   A sketch drawn while identifying a metaphor for the system.

it right now either. Your architectural modeling efforts early in the project should be focused on the simplest solution possible that meets the high-level requirements that have been identified for you. Building infrastructure early gives you a false sense of security because you have running code and can show progress even though no actual progress towards fulfilling the needs of project stakeholders has been achieved (Newkirk and Martin 2001).

Setting the Foundation for Your Project

Your initial collection of user stories and architecture spike forms the foundation for the rest of your project. During construction iterations, you will implement the user stories, reworking them to reflect your improved understanding of what you are building as your project progresses, evolving your system over time. Your system metaphor will help to guide your development efforts and your system architecture will emerge as a result. The next two chapters describe modeling efforts during a construction iteration.

CHAPTER 20

Modeling During an XP Iteration: Searching for Items

We're extreme, not stupid.

—Ron Jeffries

The Iterations to Release Phase (Beck 2000), more typically referred to as construction iterations or simply iterations, encompasses the primary effort of an eXtreme Programming (XP) project because this is where your major development efforts including modeling, programming, testing, and integration occur. Figure 20.1 (Wells 2000) depicts the lifecycle for an iteration. Iteration planning is the same type of effort as release planning, described in Chapter 18, "Agile Modeling Throughout the XP Lifecycle." The only difference is that the focus is on the user stories assigned to the current iteration. When you are working on iteration N, you will find that new user stories, ones that have not been estimated, have been added in. Therefore, you need to go through the effort of identifying tasks so that you may accurately estimate each user

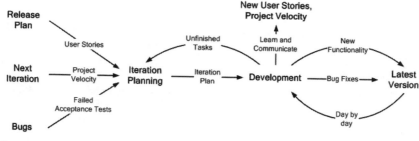

Figure 20.1 The lifecycle of an XP iteration.

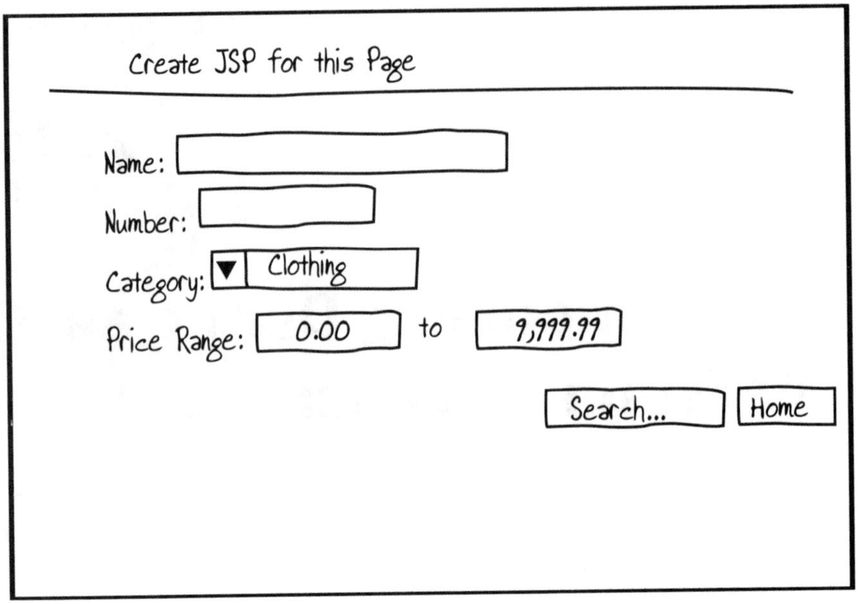

Figure 20.2 A hand-drawn sketch representing what needs to be built for the item search page.

story. After estimating the new stories, and perhaps revisiting the other stories just to be on the safe side, you may find that you have too many or too few stories for the iteration, and you will need to move stories to/from other iterations.

The Task

To gain insight into how Agile Modeling's (AM) practices can be applied to an XP project, let's work through a quick example. Figure 20.2 presents a task card containing a sketch of an HTML page for searching for items and Figure 20.3 depicts the task card submitting searches to the database, both of which were first presented in Chapter 18. Let's assume that we've done the work to build the HTML page, and we are at the point

Submit Search to DB
- Parse the criteria customer defined from the search page.
- Convert wild cards (*, _) to SQL equivalents.
- Build an SQL SELECT statement based on search criteria, ordering by the item number.
- Invoke statement in DB.

Figure 20.3 The task card for searching the database.

where we need to implement the code to implement the actual search. Let's also assume that we've already built similar things in the past—we need to pull information out of an HTML response, replace any wild cards within the criteria with SQL equivalents (for example, replace * with %), build a string representing a SQL statement, and submit the string to our database—therefore, we don't need to spike anything.

> **TIP** **Spike Unfamiliar Tasks**
>
> **If you have never implemented an aspect of a task before, perhaps you are updating information in a legacy database and this is the first time that you've run across this feature before, then you should experiment a bit to learn how to go about implementing the feature. This experimenting is called a spike solution (Jeffries, Anderson, and Hendrickson 2001), and the goal is to do just enough work to drive through the problem in one blow. In the case of the legacy database update, you may write just enough code to update a single record or perhaps even just a single column within a record in the database. When you are working on a spike solution, you often hold a quick design session to address that aspect of the task and then jump right into development. Naturally, before spiking something you should ask your teammates if they have performed a similar task before, and if so, then ask them to help.**

What modeling would we consider doing? Pulling information out of the HTML response is fairly easy to code and so is replacing wild cards within the text. We may even want to consider refactoring (Fowler 1999) our existing code, if we haven't already done so, to include classes or components that implement the two common services. Building a SQL statement is also straightforward. You simply write code to concatenate strings together, although building an SQL statement does hint at something we may want to model: our database design.

Modeling the Physical Database Schema

To build an appropriate SQL statement, we need to know the layout of the database, including the names of tables and columns and the type of the column. Knowing what indices exist for the tables we are accessing and any relevant stored procedures for searching those tables provides some insight into potential performance and implementation issues that we want to consider. Many development teams will create and maintain a physical data model that depicts some or all of this information. Very good data-modeling tools exist that will not only generate the DDL (data definition language) that you need to create the tables in your database and triggers on those tables but that will also reverse-engineer existing legacy schemas so you can understand legacy data schemas that you may need to access.

As the project progresses, our team has chosen to maintain and update a physical data model, automatically generating the database code that we require, to reflect new requirements. In the case of this task, we would want to ensure that the database

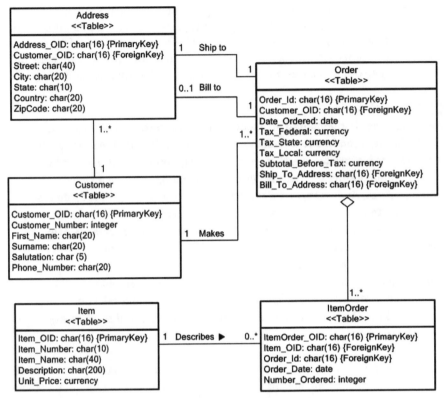

Figure 20.4 A simple data model for SWA Online.

This figure applies a UML-based data modeling notation that I first introduced in *The Object Primer 2/e* (Ambler, 2001a) and later evolved for *Mastering EJB 2/e* (Roman, Ambler, Jewell, & Marinescu, 2002).

includes columns that store the name of an item, the item number, the item category (for example: clothing, electronic goods), and the price as Figure 20.3 implies. Luckily, the current data model, depicted in Figure 20.4, for the work we have already done indicates that most of this information exists in the database. There are two potential problems:

1. **The primary key of the Item table is not the item number.** The Item_Number column is not the primary key, but instead the Item_OID column is. The Item_OID is a persistent object identifier (Ambler 2001e), something that data professionals often refer to as a surrogate key. According to the task card, we must order the results by order number, something that is easy to achieve with SQL's "ORDER BY" clause, albeit something that may have slow performance because the primary key isn't the same column we are sorting on. If we find that we have performance problems, we may want to use our CASE tool to add and generate a secondary index based on Item_Number.

2. **The item category does not exist.** Although the HTML page enables users to pick the category from a drop-down list box, see Figure 20.5, we discover that

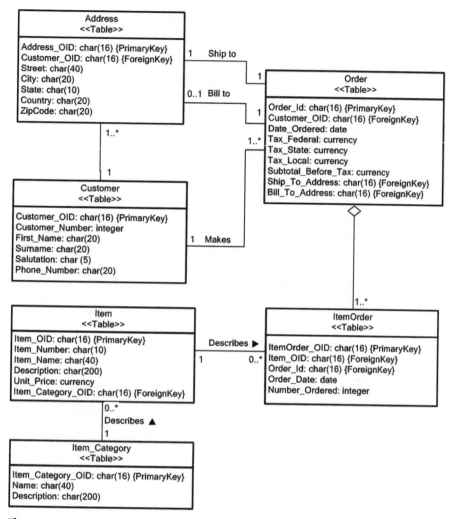

Figure 20.5   The updated data model.

the list of categories has been coded into the source code that generates the HTML. Although this worked well at the time, it isn't sufficient for our needs now. First, we would modify the data model to add the Item_Category lookup table. To maintain the relationship between items and categories, we would also add the Item_Category_OID column to the Item table. Second, we would formulate and then write test code to validate that these new features within the database work. Third, we would generate the DDL code to modify the database schema and then run the code against the database. (Naturally we would have first backed up the database before making any changes.) Fourth, we would need to write code to populate data into this new schema, first to load the information describing the categories into the new table and to update the Item_Category_OID column in the Item table to an appropriate default value to maintain referential integrity within our database. Fifth, we would want to refactor the code that generates the HTML screen to read data from the Item_Category table instead of having the categories hard coded. Finally, we would need to run our integration test suite against the entire code base to ensure that our changes haven't broken another part of the system. We would have to fix any problems that we find. Likely problem areas would include any code that accesses the Item table and that may now be broken because the Item table schema has changed. We may have some refactoring to do.

How does everyone stay up to speed regarding the current data schema? First, during the stand-up meetings each day (see Chapter 18) anyone who has made a change to the database schema the previous day should say so. Second, the data model is a good candidate for printing and putting up on the wall, following the practice *Display Models Publicly*. This way when you're having quick design sessions and you need to consider a database change you have the schema in front of you, and, if you like, you can even hand-draw changes as you talk about them. Note that you don't need to print out your diagram every time you make a tiny change; let AM's practice *Update Only When it Hurts* guide you with this. (Most people can live with a diagram that has a few hand-drawings on it.) If you do make it a habit to print your diagrams, I highly suggest investing in a plotter—taping printer-size pages together quickly becomes tedious.

Observations

I have a few important observations to make regarding the implementation of this task:

The modeling effort was brief. We didn't need to do a lot of modeling to implement this task. In fact, all we had to do was make a few simple changes to our existing physical data model from which we generated the code we needed to change the schema of our database.

Modeling saved us time. This approach was far more effective than simply writing the DDL code. Not only did our tool generate the simple code required to add the new column and table but it also generated the database triggers required to maintain referential integrity within the database. A trigger is an operation that is automatically invoked as the result changes to data within a database. The required triggers include a delete trigger on the Item_Category table that will prevent a deletion from occurring if a record exists in the Item table that references the given category; an insert trigger on the Item table checks to see whether the category exists that the new item references; and an update trigger on the Item table does the same. Yes, this code is straightforward and easy to write, but it's a lot easier to generate. Also, the physical data model depicts our database schema in an easy to understand manner, critical information required by any developer writing code that needs to work with the database.

We modeled first. We modeled right away, setting the foundation for the rest of our effort. The simple change to the database set in motion several refactorings to the Item class due to the addition of the insert and update triggers on the Item table within the database—the code that inserted and updated Item objects into the database now had to detect the error codes generated by the triggers and act accordingly.

TIP Everyone Doesn't Need Training on All Your Development Tools

The idea of using a CASE tool on an XP project to maintain your DB schema brings up an interesting issue—do you train everyone on how to use the CASE tool? On the SWA Online team, we have one person, Brendan, who is working on his certification as an Oracle DBA and is very eager to do any database-related work. He has been working with the tool for several years now. We also have Marion, someone who has been developing for years and who has significant database and data modeling experience, who also has worked with the tool. Other developers on the project—Henri, Ed, Marc, and Tyler—have all paired with Brendan and Marion from time to time to work on the data aspects of the project, but they have minimal experience with the tool. Should you train the others on the tool? Right now your project team is working smoothly, you have two people intimately familiar with the tool and four that could use it if they needed to. If anyone wanted to learn more about the tool, they would be more than welcome to pair up with Brendan or Marion whenever a database-related task came up. If they wanted formal training, in fact, I would consider giving it to them at the time. Would I send everyone to go on the training course? Likely not. Because it wouldn't provide a lot of value to do so.

CHAPTER 21

Modeling During an XP Iteration: Totaling an Order

Use your own best judgment at all times.

–Nordstrom Corporate Policy Manual

Developers on an XP (Beck 2000) project will model as part of their construction efforts. In Chapter 20, "Modeling During an XP Iteration: Searching for Items," we explored how to apply AM principles and practices when developing the functionality for searching for order items within the SWA Online system. Now let's consider a different example. Tasks are different from one another, and you will find that you will use different modeling techniques to address each one.

The Task

Figure 21.1 depicts two user stories that describe the totaling of an order, indicating that the system calculates applicable taxes, discounts, and shipping and handling charges for an order. Working through XP's Planning Game practice, you decide to

The system calculates and displays a subtotal before taxes, discounts, and shipping and handling for an order.	The system calculates and displays a grand total for an order.

Figure 21.1 User stories for displaying summary information for an order.

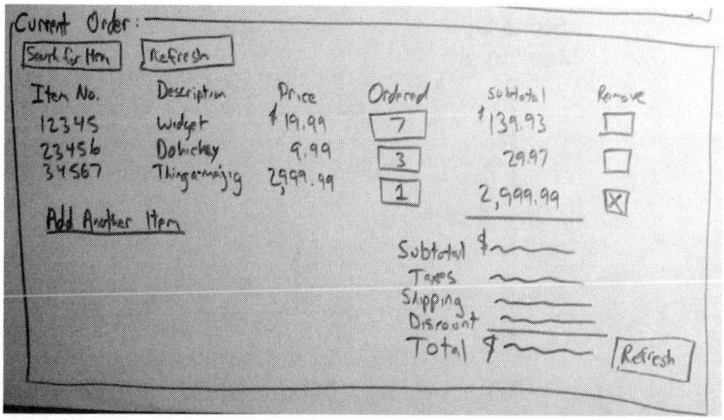

Figure 21.2   A whiteboard sketch of depicting the total portion of an order.

create a quick user interface prototype for this portion of an order, depicted in Figure 21.2, to explore what you need to build—you follow the practice *Model to Understand*. You quickly realize that the first user story is quite large, and you decide to split it into four separate stories, which you see in Figure 21.3: one for the subtotal, one for taxes, one for discounts, and one for shipping and handling charges. You discuss these new user stories as a team and provide estimates for each one that you present to your customer, whom you ask to prioritize the user stories. She decides to make the discount user story low priority, so you put it at the bottom of your stack of story cards. She makes the other stories high priority, and you assign them to this iteration.

The user stories pertaining to subtotaling the order and producing the final total are clearly easy to implement; they're simple addition. But the other two stories are clearly more complicated. Because this is SWA Enterprise's first foray into selling directly to consumers, it has never had to deal with complex taxation or shipping issues before. What do you do?

Requirements Modeling to the Rescue

First, recognize that you need to identify requirements for these two user stories. Consult your source, your on-site customer. You ask Wendy, your customer, to help

The system calculates and displays a subtotal for an order.	The system calculates and displays applicable discounts for an order.
The system calculates and displays shipping and handling charges for an order.	The system calculates and displays taxes for an order.

Figure 21.3   Reworked user stories for displaying summary information for an order.

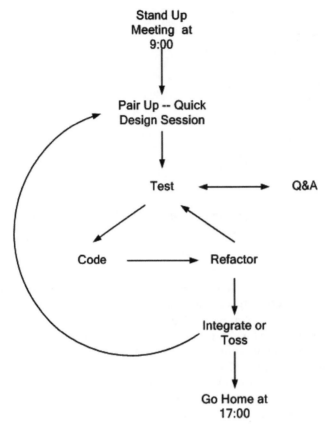

Figure 21.4 A typical XP developer's day.

explain these user stories to you—an example of Q and A from Figure 21.4, which you first saw in Chapter 18, "Agile Modeling Throughout the XP Lifecycle." During Q and A, the customer is available to provide immediate answers, often to make decisions regarding how something should work or to provide information to the developers. Luckily, Wendy has previously worked in your existing shipping department so she has some idea how shipping and handling charges may work; however, she does not have any knowledge of tax rules. She tells you that, for now, assume a flat shipping and handling charge of $5 and that your state tax of 6.5 percent is the only applicable tax and it should be applied to all products that SWA Online will carry. She agrees to add the appropriate acceptance tests for these two decisions to the test suite that she has been evolving throughout the project. She also tells you that she will look into both issues for you and get back to you in the next day or so.

TIP **In XP, Acceptance Tests Are XP Requirements Artifacts**
Often the customer will be asked to write an acceptance test answering the question or sometimes to write a new story (Wake 2002). Acceptance tests are

> **an interesting aspect of XP—instead of writing a detailed requirements document and then developing based on its contents, XP teams build up a collection of acceptance tests with their project stakeholders and ensure that their system fulfills those acceptance tests. This leads many XP developers to claim that acceptance tests are requirements, and you know what, they're right.**

You now have a place to start because your customer has made a decision. Yes, the details are likely to change when more information is available, but you'll deal with the changes when you know about them. After all, you're part of an XP team, so you embrace change. As Figure 21.4 indicates, you get into a Test-Code-Refactor cycle and start coding. With XP, you start with a test so that you know when you are done. You design and implement just enough to get that test running, and whenever you see a chance, you simplify the design through refactoring.

Help from an Outside Expert

Later that day, Wendy drops by your desk as you and your pair are programming. She tells you that she has left a voice mail with someone in accounting who should be able to explain the relevant tax rules to you. She has also been in contact with a friend of hers, Jake Blues, who works at Fly-By-Nite Shipping, the courier whom SWA Enterprises intends to use for the first release of the system. Jake is available tomorrow morning at 9 a.m. for a half-hour conference call that Wendy wants the two of you to attend. You also take the opportunity to show the work that you have completed on the user story, showing that a line has been added to the order summary indicating the shipping and handling charges and the new total for the order (the original subtotal plus the new charges). She doesn't like the way it looks on the screen (you got the alignment wrong), and you promise to correct the problem.

The next morning you, your current pair, and Wendy get together in a meeting room and call Jake. The three of you agree to take notes to ensure that you record the information from Jake. Jake informs you that Fly-By-Night negotiates shipping rates with its clients and provides an electronic spreadsheet for each quarter; he emailed a sample to Wendy earlier that morning. There are two basic reasons why a new spreadsheet is produced quarterly—the overall rates may change based on changing costs for the shipping company, fuel being the main factor, and the amount of business that you do with them may change (the more you ship, the lower your rates). The spreadsheet is generated by Fly-By-Night's accounting department and is provided to their customers no less than two weeks in advance of any rate changes. Within the spreadsheet, the rates vary by the weight of the package being shipped, the size of the box, and the distance the package is going. Weight is measured in ranges—for example < 6 oz., 6 to 12 oz., and so on—as is the size of the box. Distance, on the other hand, is measured in zones. Jake asks you for your fax number so he can send you a map indicating the zones. The zones are fairly straightforward, working outwards from their major distribution center in rough circles. An entire state is either in a zone or it is out of it, and this zone system has been in place for almost ten years without changing for seven years now. He provides you with a few more details and offers to be available by phone and email if you have any more questions.

A Quick Design Session

After the phone call, the three of you walk back to your work area and decide to have a quick design session to understand your approach to implement the calculation of shipping and handling charges. Wendy points out that not only do you need to charge the right amount for Fly-By-Night's fees, you also need to cover your own internal fees. Wendy remembers that the accounting department feels that $0.50 a shipment was a fair price, but she would need to verify that with them. More importantly, you need to understand how to calculate the shipper's portion of the fees. The three of you start by working through some CRC cards, presented in Figure 21.5, to identify the potential classes and responsibilities that you believe you need. In parallel, you also sketch on the whiteboard a UML Sequence diagram, presented in Figure 21.6, which shows the interaction between the classes to support this functionality. Both CRC cards and UML Sequence diagrams are described in detail in Appendix A, "Modeling Techniques." You work back and forth between the two models for about ten minutes

Shipping Cost Calculator	
Knows SWA costs	Shipping Cost Matrix
Calculate shipping cost for an order	State
Determine box size for an order	
Determine weight for an order	
Determine zone for an order	

State	
Knows delivery zone the state is in	

Order Item	
Knows number of items ordered	Item
Knows item	

Shipping Cost Matrix	
Knows applicability dates	
Knows box size ranges	
Knows weight ranges	
Knows delivery zones	
Knows shipment cost for a given box size and weight range within a delivery zone	

Order	
Knows ship-to address	Shipping Cost Calculator
Knows order items	Order Item
Calculate shipping and handling costs	

Item	
Knows weight	
Knows width	
Knows height	
Knows breadth	

Figure 21.5   CRC cards relevant to calculating shipping costs.

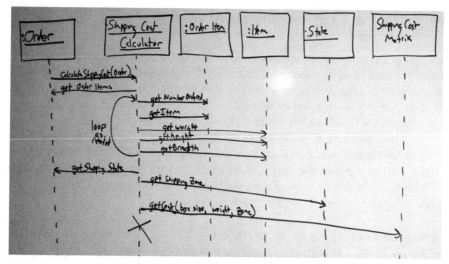

Figure 21.6   A sequence diagram for calculating shipping costs.

until you think you have a good strategy for implementing the calculation. Now you're ready to start coding. As you work on these models, you also discuss how you will need to test this functionality, information that Wendy records on index cards, one for each acceptance test.

The CRC cards and the UML sequence diagram aren't perfectly consistent with one another. That's ok. In general, agile models don't need to be in sync with one another; they just need to be good enough, and these two models are. When you discover that two artifacts are out of sync, you should follow the practice *Update Only When it Hurts* and fix them only if it provides positive value to your project.

During this process you followed the AM practices:

- *Apply the Right Artifact(s)* when you chose to work with CRC cards to identify the static structure of your software and sequence diagram to explore the dynamic nature of the interactions between those classes. Yes, you could have sketched a UML class diagram instead of creating CRC cards, but as you learned in Chapter 10, "Using the Simplest Tools Possible?" the cards are easier to work with and are more inclusive.

- *Create Several Models in Parallel* when you chose to work on both the models at once.

- *Iterate to Another Artifact* when you chose to work back and forth between models.

- *Consider Testability* when you identify acceptance tests while working on the sequence diagram and CRC cards.

- *Discard Temporary Models* once you are finished coding the information captured by your models. They likely won't provide any more value to you, so you might as well erase the diagram from the whiteboard and throw away the cards.

Formalizing a Contract Model

You're just about to start coding when Wendy points out that you're not done yet. You need to introduce a new user story for accepting the spreadsheet from Fly-By-Night Shipping and getting the new figures into the system. She indicates that this is a high priority item that will likely need to be included in the next iteration. You realize that your team may want to follow the practice *Formalize Contract Models* and put together a short document describing this interface to the shipping company. The document would likely include a paragraph or two describing the process of receiving the spreadsheet, an example of the spreadsheet itself, and a description of the import process (either automatic or manual, depending on your solution). This document would become part of your overall system documentation.

> **TIP You Can Use Patterns on an XP Project**
>
> **Does the application of patterns go against XP's practice of Simple Design? Depends on how you use them. Joshua Kerievsky (2001) says it best: "Start simple, think about patterns but keep them on the back burner, make small refactorings, and move these refactorings towards a pattern (or patterns) only when there is a genuine need for them." In other words, follow AM's practice *Apply Patterns Gently*.**

What about Changes in the Future?

Later that day, Wendy hears back from the accountant she contacted regarding the tax rules. It appears that if you ship a product to someone within this state, then a state tax of 6.5 percent applies for all products; otherwise, no sales taxes are collected. He also indicated that individual states are in the process of considering laws that require the collection of taxes for online sales where the shipping address is in their state, and he feels that it is very likely that some states will pass these laws within the year. He also indicated that the Federal Government is considering a value added tax (VAT) of 3 percent on online sales, although it is unlikely that this will come about any time soon. Finally, he pointed out that most foreign countries have duties and sales taxes that would be applicable once SWA Online went international.

This information has made Wendy a little nervous. What would happen if the tax rules changed suddenly? You reply that the project team would act accordingly at that time. She asks whether or not you need a big design session to ensure that your system can handle these changes. You reply that you don't want to overbuild your system to implement functionality that you may not ever need, and you certainly wouldn't want to have to maintain that additional code over time either. But she's still worried; she wants to make sure that the team understands that the way you handle taxes will need to change over time. So you suggest a compromise—instead of overbuilding your software, why don't you simply record these potential requirements and describe them to the rest of the team at tomorrow's stand-up meeting? Wendy accepts this idea, it's

Change Case: Individual States Introduce Online Sales Tax

Likelihood: Very likely within 6 to 12 months

Potential Impact:

- We'll need to collect taxes according to each individual state.
- We will need to remit taxes and transaction information as appropriate to each state.

Change Case: Federal Government Introduces Online Sales Tax

Likelihood: Unlikely within the next two years

Potential Impact:

- We'll need to collect federal sales taxes accordingly.
- We will also need to remit taxes and transaction information as appropriate to the government.

Change Case: Foreign Countries Levy Duties and Taxes on Shipments

Likelihood: Certain once we go international

Potential Impact:

- Minimal if we use a shipper that handles this for us.
- Otherwise, we will need to calculate and remit taxes and duties to each country accordingly.

Figure 21.7   Recording the potential requirements regarding tax rules as change cases.

worked well in the past, and you quickly write up some index cards as depicted in Figure 21.7.

Both AM and XP exhort you to embrace change; yet in practice, embracing change can be particularly difficult. At first, deciding to go at risk and trusting that you can solve tomorrow's problem tomorrow, and therefore you don't need to overbuild your system today, is difficult. This philosophy is often very difficult for your project stakeholders to accept, particularly when they've been involved with failed software developments before or when their career success is tied into your project. Platitudes to embrace change likely will not be sufficient without proof that you can, in fact, solve tomorrow's problem tomorrow. You will need to find a compromise position, and change cases are one such technique for doing so. By creating change cases, you show your project stakeholders that you recognize the associated risks of the potential changes, and you ease their concerns. Change cases will help to increase their trust in your team, hopefully to the point where they are comfortable with the concept of embracing change—without this trust, your team will have a serious problem moving forward because you will not have sufficient stakeholder support. When creating change cases, you may also gain important insights concerning current design decisions, although that doesn't give you license to overbuild your software based on these insights.

Observations

Once again, modeling activities proved effective for our XP development efforts. The quick sketch of the total section of an order helped to put our effort into perspective. Our quick design session where we explored the calculation of shipping and handling charges proved beneficial. A little bit of modeling helped us to identify an approach to design that seemed very straightforward.

Most of the models described in this chapter were created using simple tools. We used a whiteboard to sketch a UML sequence diagram and a user interface prototype. We used index cards for user stories, CRC cards, and change cases. The only exception was the contract model describing the interface that we have with our shipping company, a model that would likely be best developed with a word processor.

Although we needed to gather requirements concerning the calculation of taxes, we didn't need to model anything. Gathering requirements was simple enough that we went straight into construction. Yes, we did in fact have a user story pertaining to taxes, arguably a very high-level requirement, but that clearly isn't anywhere close to a traditional requirements model. The acceptance tests that our customer developed to validate our work are much closer to documented requirements, they describe functionality that our system must implement, so that's the closest thing to documented requirements that we have for taxes. This worked perfectly well because the acceptance tests met the needs of our customer by focusing on producing the functionality that they required—remember the principle, *Software Is Your Primary Goal.*

In Part Three of this book, you have seen that modeling is an important aspect of XP and that modeling has always been so regardless of what some of XP's detractors may tell you. You've also seen that the principles and practices of AM and XP fit well together, which is to be expected considering AM has adopted many aspects of XP, and that AM can be used to enhance your XP development efforts. In Part Four, we similarly explore the fit between AM and the UP.

How to Make This Work in the Real World

Modeling is clearly a part of XP, but it is a very small part when compared to other activities such as programming or testing. This works because of many of the primary benefits of modeling—such as supporting communication and exploring pertinent issues—are achieved through other means. There are several interesting impications for using AM with XP:

- AM should be used in small doses to enhance XP.
- Keep it simple—although many modling techniques are described in Appendix A, XP teams may only need to apply one or two of them.
- XP practitioners need to recognize that modeling does not have to be the dysfunctional, paper-intensive burden they fear it to be.
- AM might be what makes XP palatable within organizations that are leery of "vanilla XP."

Agile Modeling and the Unified Process

In this part I describe how to use Agile Modeling and the Unified Process (Jacobson, Booch, and Rumbaugh 1999; Kruchten 2000; Ambler 2001b) together. This section includes the following chapters:

- **Chapter 22: Agile Modeling and the Unified Process.** This chapter overviews how modeling occurs on an UP project, and explores the fit between AM and the UP.

- **Chapter 23: Agile Modeling Throughout the Unified Process Lifecycle.** This chapter explores the disciplines of the UP in greater detail.

- **Chapter 24: Agile Business Modeling.** This chapter describes how to apply AM principles and practices for business modeling activities on an UP/AM project.

- **Chapter 25: Agile Requirements.** This chapter describes how to apply AM principles and practices for requirements activities on an UP/AM project.

- **Chapter 26: Agile Analysis and Design.** This chapter describes how to apply AM principles and practices for analysis and design activities on an UP/AM project.

- **Chapter 27: Agile Infrastructure Management.** This chapter describes how to apply AM principles and practices for the modeling portions of the Infrastructure Management discipline, including suggestions for scaling AM to larger projects.

- **Chapter 28: Adopting AM on an UP Project.** This chapter presents strategies for overcoming common impediments that you may experience while adopting AM on UP projects.

CHAPTER 22

Agile Modeling and the Unified Process

As we've discussed throughout this book, AM is a chaordic, practices-based software process whose scope is to describe how to model and document in an effective and agile manner. The practices of AM should be used, ideally in whole, to enhance other, more complete software processes such as eXtreme Programming (XP) (Beck 2000), the Rational Unified Process (RUP) (Rational Corporation 2001), and the Enterprise Unified Process (EUP) (Ambler 2001b) to name a few. These processes cover a wider scope than AM. In the case of XP and the RUP, this is true for the development process and with the EUP, the full software process including both development and production. Although these processes all include modeling and documentation activities in one form or the other, there is definitely room for improvement. In the case of XP the modeling processes should be better defined, as we discussed in Part Three. In the case of both the RUP and the EUP, the modeling processes could definitely stand to be made more agile.

In this chapter I explore in detail how AM can be used in conjunction with the various instantiations of the Unified Process (UP), including but not limited to the RUP and the EUP. To understand an UP/AM approach to development, we need to cover:

■ How modeling works in the Unified Process

■ How good is the fit between AM and UP?

■ Choose to be agile

How Modeling Works in the Unified Process

All efforts, including modeling, are organized into disciplines (formerly called work-flows) in the UP and are performed in an iterative and incremental manner. The lifecycle of the EUP is presented in Figure 22.1, a superset of the current lifecycle for the RUP. I like to say that the UP is serial in the large, iterative in the small, and delivers incremental releases over time. The five phases of the EUP clearly occur in a serial manner over time. During the Inception phase your focus is on project initiation activities. Once your initial scope is understood your major focus becomes requirements analysis and architecture evolution during the Elaboration phase. During the Construction phase, your focus shifts to building your system. In the Transition phase, you move to deliver your software, and finally you operate and support your software in the Production phase. However, on a day-to-day basis you work in an iterative manner, perhaps doing some modeling, some implementation, some testing, and some management activities.

In the RUP there are three disciplines* that encompass modeling activities for a single project: Business Modeling, Requirements, and Analysis and Design. EUP adds a fourth discipline, Infrastructure Management, that includes enterprise-wide requirements and architecture modeling activities. All four disciplines are described in Table 22.1. Chapter

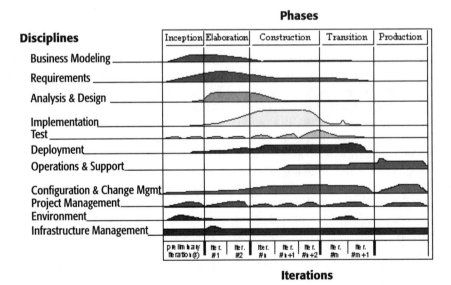

Figure 22.1 The lifecycle for the Enterprise Unified Process (EUP).

---

*The Implementation discipline is arguably a fourth one because it includes an activity called "Structure The Implementation Model" which is essentially a second look at the design model to organize it in such a way as to avoid integration and build problems.

Table 22.1   The Modeling Disciplines of the Unified Process

WORKFLOW	PURPOSE
Business Modeling	The purpose of this discipline is to model the business context, the scope, of your system.
Requirements	The purpose of this discipline is to engineer the requirements for your project, including the identification, modeling, and documentation of those requirements. The main deliverable of this discipline is the Software Requirements Specification (SRS), also referred to as the Requirements Model, which encompasses the captured requirements.
Analysis and Design	The purpose of this discipline is to evolve a robust architecture for your system based on your requirements, to transform the requirements into a design, and to ensure that implementation environment issues are reflected in your design.
Infrastructure Management (EUP only)	This discipline encompasses activities that are outside of the scope of a single project, including: • Enterprise requirements modeling, the act of creating and evolving models that reflect the high-level requirements of your organization. • Enterprise architectural modeling, the act of creating and evolving models that depict the business and technical infrastructure of your organization.

23, "Agile Modeling Throughout the Unified Process," explores the disciplines of the UP, and how AM principles and practices can enhance them, in greater detail.

How Good Is the Fit?

Now that we understand the basics of how modeling in the UP works, we can examine how well AM fits in with it. Luckily many of AM's principles and practices are arguably a part of the UP already, although perhaps not as explicitly as I would like. Table 22.2 examines how well each individual AM practice is currently implemented in the UP, if at all, and discusses how to adopt the practice within the scope of the UP. My experience is that it is relatively straightforward for UP teams to adopt AM practices if they choose to do so. This is because the UP is very flexible. One of its underlying principles is that you should tailor it to meet your unique needs, making it easy to merge AM practices into the UP.

Table 22.2 The Fit between UP and AM

PRACTICE	FIT
Active Stakeholder Participation	AM has a wide definition for project stakeholders, including users, management, operations staff, and support staff to name a few. This definition is compatible with the UP. The UP clearly includes project stakeholders, such as users and customers, throughout most of its disciplines. To be successful, UP project teams should allow project stakeholders to take on modeling roles such as Business Process Designer and Requirements Specifier as appropriate; there is nothing in the UP that prevents this. The more active project stakeholders are, the less of a need there will be for reviews, management presentations, and other overhead activities that reduce your team's development velocity.
Apply Modeling Standards	The application of modeling standards, in particular the diagrams of the UML, is a significant part of the UP. Furthermore, the RUP product (Rational Corporation 2001) includes guidelines for the creation of many modeling artifacts, guidelines that your teams should consider adopting and following as appropriate, and explicitly suggests that you tailor the guidelines that they provide for your exact needs. To remain agile, however, UP teams must recognize that you often need to bend the guidelines and standards. In other words, don't let them become a straight jacket.
Apply Patterns Gently	UP teams are free to apply modeling patterns. The RUP product describes many common modeling patterns as part of their efforts for a variety of modeling disciplines. This practice enhances the UP with its advice to ease into the application of a pattern. The UP does not make this concept as explicit as it could.
Apply The Right Artifact(s)	One of the strengths of the UP is that it provides some advice for when to create each type of model. Recent incarnations of the RUP product include significant advice for non-UML artifacts such as data models and user interface storyboards (UI flow diagrams).
Collective Ownership	AM's concept of collective ownership can be used to enhance the efforts on UP projects, assuming that the team culture supports the concept of open and honest communication. The UP supports collective ownership with its strong focus on configuration management issues (it has a discipline dedicated to this task), although its change management processes may potentially get in your way if developers and project stakeholders are unable to distinguish when to formalize change control and when not to. To be fair, this is a problem regardless of when you apply AM on an UP project, or on any type of project for that matter. UP teams should turn the configuration management dial up a few notches and allow anyone on the project to access and work on any artifact that they wish, including models and documents.
Consider Testability	The UP includes a Test discipline in its lifecycle, making testing an explicit issue that everyone should keep in mind as they work. The UP also includes many opportunities to review modeling artifacts, if you choose to follow this form of validation. To fully adopt this practice the consideration "Is it testable" should be included in all modeling activities.

Table 22.2   continued

PRACTICE	FIT
Create Several Models in Parallel	The UP clearly includes this concept. One only has to look at the activity diagrams that depict each discipline to see that several artifacts are potentially worked on in parallel. However, this concept could be communicated better because the near-serial flow in the activity diagrams presented for each major modeling activity doesn't communicate this concept well. There is a larger issue as well when you consider the lifecycle as a whole. Because the UP has organized its modeling efforts into separate disciplines, for very good reasons, it isn't as apparent that not only can you work on several business modeling artifacts in parallel but you can also work on requirements-oriented artifacts, analysis-oriented artifacts, architecture artifacts, and design artifacts too. UP teams can turn the dial up a few notches by reading between the lines of the discipline activity diagrams and the UP lifecycle diagram and choosing to perform activities from several disciplines simultaneously when it makes sense to do so.
Create Simple Content	This practice is a choice made by the modeler(s), albeit one that must be implicitly supported by the rest of the development team. UP teams will need to adopt modeling guidelines that allow models that are just good enough and the customers of those models (including programmers, project stakeholders, and reviewers) must also be willing to accept simple models. This is a cultural issue, one that is often difficult for many organizations to adopt.
Depict Models Simply	See *Create Simple Content.*
Discard Temporary Models	Modelers on UP teams are free to discard anything that they wish. As with the Simplicity practices your organization's culture must accept the concept of traveling light, of developing and maintaining just enough models and documents, and no more.
Display Models Publicly	UP teams are free to follow this practice. UP teams can turn the communication dial up a notch by following the principle *Open and Honest Communication* by making all artifacts available to everyone as well as to publicly display the critical models used by the project team.
Formalize Contract Models	The UP includes the concept of integrating with external systems. These systems are typically identified on use case models and the RUP suggests introducing "boundary classes" to implement the interface to these systems. At the time of this writing the RUP appears weak with respect to activities such as legacy system analysis and enterprise application integration (EAI). The explicit adoption of this practice clearly strengthens the UP's integration activities and fits in well with it's concepts of use case realizations—the interaction between systems can be specified with one or more use cases and then the corresponding use case realization becomes the formalized contract model.

continues

Table 22.2 The Fit between UP and AM (continued)

PRACTICE	FIT
Iterate To Another Artifact	This practice can be easily adopted by UP teams. As mentioned previously, the unfortunate depiction of UP modeling activities as quasi-serial processes and the division of modeling activities into separate disciplines can hinder the iterative mindset required of agile modelers.
Model in Small Increments	This practice is clearly an aspect of the UP. The UP's support for iterations implies that you can incrementally develop your model throughout the project. UP teams can easily turn the iterative and incremental dial up a few notches by preferring smaller, simpler models that quickly lead to implementation and testing.
Model to Communicate	The UP implicitly includes this practice. UP teams can turn the communication dial up a few notches by following the principle *Model With a Purpose* by knowing who their audience for the model is and what they require of that model.
Model to Understand	See *Model to Communicate*.
Model With Others	The UP implicitly includes this practice. Every modeling discipline clearly includes several roles; each role is filled by one or more people. UP teams can turn the communication dial up a few notches by adopting tools that support team modeling, such as whiteboards and collaborative modeling tools (see Chapter 8) over single-user modeling tools.
Prove it With Code	The UP explicitly includes this practice. At the end of each "iteration, except perhaps for the ones during the Inception phase (Ambler and Constantine 2000a), the UP specifically states that you should have a working prototype. Furthermore, the UP insists that you have a working end-to-end prototype at the end of the Elaboration phase (Ambler and Constantine 2000b) that proves your architecture.
Reuse Existing Resources	Reuse is an implicit part of the UP, and reuse management is an explicit part of the EUP. UP teams can turn the reuse dial up a few notches by actively preferring to reuse existing resources instead of building them from scratch, including but not limited to existing models, existing components, open source software (OSS), and existing tools.
Update Only When It Hurts	In theory this can be an easy concept for UP teams to adopt as it dramatically reduces the effort expended to keep your artifacts up to date. However, in practice many organizations prove to have a problem with this concept, particularly if they have a strong "traceability" culture. Traceability is the ability to relate aspects of project artifacts to one another, the support for which is a strong feature of the UP because it's an important aspect of its Configuration and Change Management discipline. Furthermore, the RUP product includes tool mentors for working with Rational RequisitePro (hyperlink "http://www.rational .com"), a requirements traceability tool, making it appear easy to

Table 22.2 continued

PRACTICE	FIT
	maintain a traceability matrix between artifacts. My experience is that organizations with traceability cultures will often choose to update artifacts regularly, even if it isn't yet painful to have the artifacts out of date, and update the traceability matrix that relates everything to one another. To turn their productivity dial up several notches UP teams should choose to travel light, to loosen up a bit and allow project artifacts to get out of sync with one another. Maintain a traceability matrix between artifacts only when there is a clear benefit to do so AND their project stakeholders understand the issues involved as well as authorize the effort. A traceability matrix is effectively a document and is therefore a business decision made by project stakeholders.
Use the Simplest Tools	The RUP product includes tool mentors that make it easier for teams to work with tools sold by Rational Corporation. However, the reality is that UP teams are welcome to use any development tool that they want and Rational tools compete on their merits just like the products of any other company. UP teams can turn their productivity dial up several notches by expanding their horizons to include simple tools such as whiteboards, index cards, and sticky notes in addition to CASE tools.

Choose To Be Agile

In this chapter you've seen that modeling is an important part of the Unified Process, the RUP instantiation of it includes three disciplines: Business Modeling, Requirements, and Analysis and Design. EUP adds a fourth discipline, Infrastructure Management that includes significant modeling efforts. You've also seen that the potential exists to take an UP/AM approach to development, if you choose to do so. The next chapter explores how AM can be used to enhance the UP disciplines and Chapters 23 through 27 work through examples of taking an UP/AM approach to the SWA Online case study. Chapter 28 explores specific issues that pertain to adopting AM on a UP project. The greatest issue that UP teams face with respect to AM is the need to take an agile approach to development, which is possible for an UP project team to do, but in practice proves to be a difficult path to take. Choosing to succeed is often the most difficult decision to make.

CHAPTER 23

Agile Modeling throughout the Unified Process Lifecycle

What can be more palpably absurd than the prospect held out of locomotives traveling twice as fast as stagecoaches?

— The Quarterly Review, England, in 1825

To understand how to apply the principles and practices of Agile Modeling on a Unified Process (Jacobson, Booch, and Rumbaugh 1999) project, we must explore how modeling fits into the UP project lifecycle. To do this, we will examine the UP from the point of view of the enhanced lifecycle of the Enterprise Unified Process (EUP) (Ambler, 2001b), as it is currently the most comprehensive lifecycle available for the UP. As you see in Figure 23.1, the EUP extends the original UP lifecycle with a new phase, Production, and two new disciplines: Infrastructure Management and Operations and Support. To understand how to model on an UP/AM project, let's first examine the modeling disciplines and then focus on the non-modeling disciplines.

The Modeling Disciplines

This section explores the four modeling disciplines in greater detail, with a particular emphasis on the types of modeling artifacts that you may wish to create. AM's modeling practices are clearly applicable to these four disciplines. The fit between AM's practices and the UP was explored in Chapter 22, "Agile Modeling and the Unified Process." Chapters 24 through 27 explore the application of AM practices within each UP modeling discipline by working through a portion of the SWA Online case study. The four modeling disciplines are:

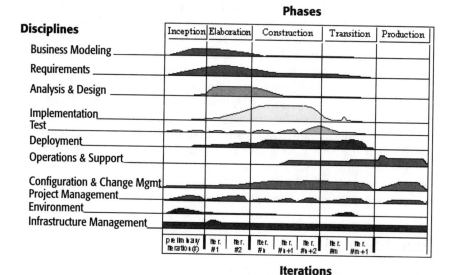

Figure 23.1   The lifecycle for the Enterprise Unified Process (EUP).

1. Business Modeling

2. Requirements

3. Analysis and Design

4. Infrastructure Management

The Business Modeling Discipline

The purpose of the Business Modeling discipline is to explore the business environment in which your system will operate. Most of your business modeling activity occurs during the UP's Inception and Elaboration phases, although you will find that you need to perform some business modeling efforts during the Construction phase and sometimes even during the Transition and Production phases. Your goals are:

■ To understand the target organization(s) where your system will be deployed

■ To understand the issues that the target organization(s) need to have addressed by your system

■ To ensure that your development team and project stakeholders have a common understanding of the target organization(s)

■ To derive system requirements for the target organization(s) (Rational Corporation 2001)

In many ways the Business Modeling discipline is simply traditional systems analysis (Gane and Sarson 1979; Yourdon 1989) with a "use case twist."

Table 23.1 lists potential UP deliverables for the Business Modeling discipline, the modeling artifacts that you should consider creating (described in Appendix A, "Modeling Techniques"), and how each deliverable is potentially used by your project team. You will want to follow the practice *Apply the Right Artifact(s)* and create only the ones that your situation warrants. You also want to remember to *Travel Light* and keep only those artifacts that provide positive value to your project. Table 23.1 also distinguishes between a RUP version and a more agile (AM) version of a domain model. Whichever version you choose depends on how far you want to take your domain modeling efforts.

Chapter 24, "Agile Business Modeling," works through the Business Modeling discipline for a portion of the SWA Online case study, applying AM practices wherever appropriate. The AM practice with the biggest impact on this discipline, and the Requirements discipline, is *Active Stakeholder Participation*. The UP has always promoted working closely with your users and AM makes this practice even more explicit.

The Requirements Discipline

The purpose of the Requirements discipline is to engineer the requirements for your project. This includes identifying with project stakeholders (and maintaining an agreement regarding the requirements) what your system should do, providing developers with a better understanding of the requirements, delimiting the system, providing a basis for estimating, and defining a user interface for your system (Rational Corporation 2001). As you see in Figure 23.1, most requirements modeling activities occur during the Inception and Elaboration phases, although you will still identify and explore requirements during the other phases as well (particularly during Construction).

Table 23.2 lists the potential modeling artifacts that you may decide to create as part of your Requirements discipline efforts. As with Table 23.1, the candidate artifacts are described in Appendix A. Note that the table uses AM terms in the Candidate Artifacts column instead of RUP terms. Use case story boards are listed twice: an AM version that uses non-UML artifacts and a RUP version that constrains itself to UML artifacts.

The artifacts that you worked on as part of your Business Modeling efforts often evolve into requirements versions of them, following your version-control strategy (see the Change and Configuration Management discipline section later in this chapter) as appropriate. Because of the similarity of these two disciplines, the Business Modeling discipline focuses on understanding the business and identifying high-level requirements. The Requirements discipline focuses on detailed requirements. Agile modelers don't bother to differentiate between the two types of artifacts. For example, instead of having a Supplementary Business Specification and a Supplementary Specification, they'll simply have a Supplementary Specification (if they have one at all). Chapter 25, "Agile Requirements," works through the Requirements discipline for the SWA Online case study.

The Analysis and Design Discipline

The purpose of the Analysis and Design discipline is to evolve a robust architecture for your system, to produce a detailed design for your system based on its requirements, and to adapt your design to reflect the realities of your implementation environment

Table 23.1   Potential Modeling Artifacts for Business Modeling

UP DELIVERABLE	CANDIDATE ARTIFACTS	USAGE
Business Architecture Document	• Organization Chart • Technical Requirement • Constraint Definition	Overviews your current business environment and potentially proposes a re-engineered view of that environment. It describes the structure and culture of your organization, proposed changes to your organization, and strategies for achieving those changes. The document indicates technical requirements and constraints that pertain to system size, performance, and quality attributes. It also contains a subset of your context model, the architecturally significant use cases or business processes that offer important capabilities within your business and which cover critical aspects of your organization.
Business Glossary	• Glossary	Defines common vocabulary used in other artifacts.
Business Object Model (AM)	• CRC Model • UML Class Diagram	Describes your business environment. Because much of the suggested effort for creating business object models (Rational Corporation 2001) is often considered high-level analysis activities (Ambler 2001a)—in particular the creation of Activity, Collaboration, Sequence, and State chart diagrams—a simpler approach is often taken which focuses just on domain modeling via creation of a CRC model or a UML Class diagram.
Business Object Model (RUP)	• UML Activity Diagram • UML Class Diagram • UML Collaboration Diagram • UML Sequence Diagram • UML State Chart Diagram	Domain information, such as the definition of business entities and their relationships, is described using UML Class diagrams. The dynamic interactions between those entities can be modeled using UML Collaboration diagrams or UML Sequence diagrams, and the dynamic nature of the entities themselves with UML State chart diagrams. UML Activity diagrams are used to describe business processes.

continues

Table 23.1 Potential Modeling Artifacts for Business Modeling (continued)

UP DELIVERABLE	CANDIDATE ARTIFACTS	USAGE
Business Rules	• Business Rule	Identifies the critical business rules pertinent to your system.
Business Use Case Model	• UML Use Case Diagram • Essential Use Cases	Describes the intended functions of the business, ideally in a technology-independent manner. An important part of the model is business use case specifications, technology-independent use cases, which this book refers to as essential use cases.
Supplementary Business Specification	• Change Cases • Constraint Definition Feature • Technical Requirement	Presents any necessary definitions of the business not included in the context model or the domain model. It may contain behavioral and usability requirements, documented using features or constraints, as well as reliability, performance, and scalability issues documented as constraints or technical requirements.

Table 23.2 Potential Modeling Artifacts for Requirements

UP DELIVERABLE	CANDIDATE ARTIFACTS	USAGE
Context Model	• Data Flow Diagram (DFD) • UML Use Case Diagram	Describes the current business, often at the scope of the proposed system. As you will see in Chapter 25, a DFD is often preferable to the suggested application of a UML Use Case diagram (Rational Corporation 2001).
Glossary	• Glossary	Defines the common business and technical vocabulary used in other artifacts.
Supplementary Specification	• Change Cases • Constraint Definition • Feature • Technical Requirement • Business Rules	Records any necessary requirements not included in the Use Case model. It may contain business rules, behavioral and usability requirements, documented using features or constraints, as well as reliability, performance, and scalability issues documented as constraints or technical requirements.
Use Case Model	• UML Use Case Diagram • System Use Cases	Serves as the primary requirements artifact in the UP. Your Use Case model is typically comprised of a UML Use Case diagram, Use Case specifications, and definitions of the actors.
Use Case Story Board (AM)	• User Interface Flow Diagram • Robustness Diagram	Shows how a use case is supported by your system's user interface. The robustness diagram is used to explore the use case and to identify the various controller, boundary, and entity classes. The User Interface flow diagram is used to provide a birds-eye view of the user interface for the single use case. (Sometimes User Interface flow diagrams are created to overview the entire user interface for a system.) Note that it is common to use one diagram but not the other when story boarding.

continues

Table 23.2 Potential Modeling Artifacts for Requirements (continued)

UP DELIVERABLE	CANDIDATE ARTIFACTS	USAGE
Use Case Story Board (RUP)	• Feature or Constraint • UML Class Diagram • UML Sequence Diagrams or • UML Collaboration Diagrams • Usage Scenario	Uses features or constraints to describe usability requirements, typically as free-form text that pertains to your user interface. UML Sequence diagrams, although UML Collaboration diagrams, are often drawn to identify the classes (including boundary/interface classes, entity classes, and controller classes) required to support the use case. A UML Class diagram is typically used to explore the structure of the identified classes. Usage scenarios may be written to describe user interactions with the system.
User Interface Prototype	• User Interface Prototype or Essential User Interface Prototype	This is a "traditional" mockup of your system's user interface, perhaps using a UI prototyping tool or an implementation language such as Visual Basic or Java. Agile modelers will often use essential user interface prototypes to explore requirements and user interface prototypes for analysis and design purposes with the project stakeholders.

(Rational Corporation 2001). With respect to models, the primary input into this discipline is your requirements artifacts, although your business models provide important context as well. As you can imagine, feedback from implementers and testers is clearly important to your design effort, indicating the benefit of adopting AM's *Rapid Feedback* principle as well as AM's *Prove it With Code* practice. As you see in Figure 23.1, the majority of your analysis and design modeling efforts occur during the Elaboration and Construction phases.

Table 23.3 lists the potential modeling artifacts that you may choose to create as part of your analysis and design efforts. Two versions of use case realizations are indicated, one suggested by the RUP and an agile one that agile modelers are more likely to consider. An important note about use case realizations is that they describe the realization of a use case AND related requirements artifacts, such as business rules and constraints, and not just use cases as the name implies. Chapter 26, "Agile Analysis and Design," works through the Analysis and Design discipline for the SWA Online case study.

> **TIP** **Modeling in the Unified Process Is Challenging**
>
> **Modeling within the Unified Process appears to suffer from several problems. First, it's overly complex. To be fair, it needs to be complex to handle a wide range of applications and the folks at Rational are very clear that you need to tailor the process to your environment (for example, cut out what you don't need). Second, the disciplines need to be reworked. Requirements are identified as part of Business Modeling and Requirements. Third, some of the artifacts need to be rethought. As Tables 23.1, 23.2, and 23.3 all indicate, there is clearly opportunity to simplify major UP artifacts. A common theme is the creation of artifacts that use simple tools, described in Chapter 10, "Using the Simplest Tools Possible," instead of artifacts that lend themselves to automated CASE tools such as Rational Rose.**

The Infrastructure Management Discipline

The Infrastructure Management discipline focuses on the activities required to develop, evolve, and support your organization's infrastructure artifacts, such as your organization/enterprise-wide models, your software processes, standards, guidelines, and your reusable artifacts. Your software portfolio management efforts are also performed in this discipline. In short, infrastructure management is a cross-project effort, a concept that is not yet covered by the RUP (Kruchten 2000). Table 23.4 lists the modeling artifacts promoted by the EUP, including organization-wide modeling standards. On the surface, the Infrastructure Management discipline seems to go against the grain of AM, and if you implement this in a non-agile manner, it in fact could easily do so, but as Chapter 27, "Agile Infrastructure Management," discusses, it is possible to take an agile approach to the Infrastructure Management discipline.

Table 23.3 Potential Modeling Artifacts for Analysis and Design

UP DELIVERABLE	CANDIDATE ARTIFACTS	USAGE
Analysis Model	• UML Class Diagram • Use Case Realizations (see below)	Describes the analysis of your requirements model, serving as a conceptual overview of the system. This is often a temporary model, one that is either discarded or evolved into your design model. Agile modelers typically evolve (portions of) their Business Object Model, if they created one, into an Analysis Model.
Data Model	• Data Model	Describes the logical (optional) and the physical representation of persistent data in the system, including any behavior defined in the database.
Deployment Model	• UML Deployment Model	Depicts the hardware nodes, the software components distributed to those nodes, and middleware that connects the nodes of your system. This is often a critical architectural model for your system.
Design Model	• UML Class Diagram • Use Case Realizations (see below)	A collection of models that describe the realization of use cases and serves as an abstraction of your source code.
Use Case Realization (AM)	• UML Sequence Diagrams • Robustness Diagram • CRC Model	Used to analyze a use case, tying the requirements described within the use case to the analysis model and/or design model. Agile modelers will often create UML Sequence diagrams for complex portions of logic within the use case (better yet they'll rework the logic). CRC cards are a good option for exploring the structure of the classes to support the use case instead of a UML Class diagram as RUP suggests. Another option is to create a Robustness Diagram for the use case to identify potential classes (see Chapter 26).
Use Case Realization (RUP)	• Usage Scenario • UML Sequence Diagrams or UML Collaboration Diagrams	Usage scenarios describe, in text, flows of logic through the use cases. Each flow of logic may then be explored via an interaction diagram, typically either a UML Sequence diagram or a UML Collaboration diagram. Sequence diagrams are the most common approach as they are well suited for exploring sequential business logic (hence the name).

Table 23.4 Potential Modeling Artifacts for Infrastructure Management

EUP DELIVERABLE	CANDIDATE ARTIFACTS	USAGE
Enterprise Requirements Model	• Use Case Diagram • Essential Use Case • Business Rule • Constraint • Technical Requirement	Reflects the high-level requirements of your organization (Jacobson, Griss, Jonsson 1997). A high-level Use Case diagram is often the primary artifact, supported by essential/business use cases that are technology-independent (and thus long lived), referencing other requirements artifacts such as business rule and constraint definitions. Your project's requirements model should reflect, in great detail, a small portion of this overall model.
Domain Architecture Model	• UML Component Diagram or Data Model	Depicts the high-level business structure of your systems. In a component/object environment, a UML Component diagram is often used that depicts the large-scale, reusable domain components that are evolved over time by your project teams. Individual components are in turn described by UML Component diagrams or UML Class diagrams (if modeled at all). In a data-oriented environment, an enterprise data model is best suited for this, ideally one that shows high-level data subject areas. Subject areas in turn are described by other data models showing greater detail.
Technical Architecture Model	• Network Diagram	Depicts the high-level technical infrastructure that supports your business. Network diagrams are often used to depict your hardware/network environment, although free-form diagrams are also common.
Modeling Standards	N/A	Agile modelers follow the practice of *Reuse Existing Resources* and will adopt, and modify if appropriate, existing standards and guidelines applicable to the *Apply Modeling Standards* practice.

Non-Modeling Disciplines

There is far more to the UP than its modeling disciplines. Modeling is an important part of the UP and because the modeling disciplines affect other disciplines, and vice versa, we need to examine how the principles and practices of AM can potentially affect these other disciplines. The non-modeling disciplines that we must examine are:

- Implementation
- Test
- Project Management
- Configuration and Change Management
- Environment
- Deployment
- Operations and Support

The Implementation Discipline

The purpose of the Implementation discipline is to write and initially test your software and to integrate the results of individual developers into an executable system. Your design model(s) are the primary driver of these efforts. When taking a UP/AM approach to development, the principle *Software Is Your Primary Goal* will be a primary motivator for you to focus on this discipline, and the practice *Prove It With Code* will drive you in this direction as well. Implementers, including both application programmers and database administrators (DBAs), will provide feedback regarding your design model, feedback that you should act on. Ideally, the implementers and the modelers are the same people, something that is easily supported by the UP as people are able to take on several roles in a project.

The Test Discipline

The purpose of the Test discipline is to verify and validate the quality and correctness of your system. This includes both software testing activities such as unit testing and integration testing as well as user-based testing activities such as usability testing and user-acceptance testing. An important goal of this discipline is to ensure that defects are identified and addressed appropriately before your system is deployed. Your requirements and design models are critical inputs to your testing efforts. While modeling, agile modelers follow the practice *Consider Testability* to ensure that their work is not only testable but easy to test. Because agile modelers value simplicity, they follow the practices *Depict Models Simply* and *Create Simple Content*, resulting in models that are easy to understand by their audience, and in the case of this discipline, the audience for some models includes people responsible for testing the system.

The Project Management Discipline

The purpose of the Project Management discipline is to guide an UP/AM project, including activities that pertain to scheduling, risk management, staffing, and the monitoring of your project. On an UP project, regardless of whether you have tailored it with the principles and practices of AM, you work in an incremental and iterative manner. Your project efforts are organized into iterations, indicated along the bottom of Figure 23.1. Your project schedule is driven by use cases, which are written either as part of your Business Modeling or Requirements discipline efforts. The use cases, or portions thereof, are assigned to each iteration to define what is to be built during that iteration. As your project progresses you will gain a better understanding of your requirements, and your ability to implement those requirements, and therefore will need to rework your schedule to reflect this (remember AM's principle *Embrace Change*). The point to be made is that your modeling efforts are affected by your project management efforts; you will want to focus on (albeit not solely) the use cases for your current iteration to ensure that you stay on schedule, and that your project management efforts are affected by your modeling efforts. To do this, you update your schedule to reflect the current state of your models.

The Project Management discipline is potentially affected by several of AM's principles. First, the principle of *Open and Honest Communication* implies that project managers should be forthcoming both with their team and with their project stakeholders, even when it isn't convenient to do so. Second, the principles *Software Is Your Primary Goal*, *Enabling the Next Effort is Your Secondary Goal*, and *Travel Light* provide clear guidance as to how to prioritize your efforts. Project teams who take an UP/AM approach are software-centric, not documentation-centric. These principles affect the artifacts that you create during development, the manner in which you create them, and what you finally deliver to your project stakeholders.

The Configuration and Change Management Discipline

The purpose of the Configuration and Change Management discipline is to ensure the successful evolution of your system, to control changes to and maintain the integrity of your system's artifacts. Taking an UP/AM approach to development you will find that this discipline involves less work. First, you have fewer artifacts to manage because you travel light and *Use the Simplest Tools*, you often find that you don't want to keep many of your models and therefore *Discard Temporary Models* whenever possible. Second, you will change the modeling artifacts that you do decide to keep less often than you did in the past because you follow the practice *Update Only When It Hurts*.

Although this discipline becomes easier, it also becomes more important because you are also following AM's practice of *Collective Ownership*. Everyone must have access to your configuration control system, must understand your process, and must follow it accordingly. Furthermore, in situations where your system must integrate with another one, something that is quite common in practice, AM implores you to *Formalize Contract Models* that describe this integration. These contract models should be put under configuration management control, emphasizing the importance of this discipline.

WARNING **Think Very Carefully Before Investing in a Requirements Traceability Matrix**

Traceability is the ability to relate aspects of a project's artifacts to one another. A requirements traceability matrix is the artifact that is often created to record these relations. It starts with your individual requirements and traces them through any analysis models, architecture models, design models, source code, or test cases that you maintain. My experience is that organizations with traceability cultures will often choose to update artifacts regularly, ignoring the practice *Update Only When it Hurts*, so as to achieve consistency between the artifacts (including the matrix) that they maintain. This is not traveling light. The benefits of having such a matrix is that it makes it easier to perform an impact analysis that pertains to a changed requirement because you know what aspects of your system will potentially be affected by the change. However, if you have one or more people familiar with the system, which you want to have anyway, and if you want to be effective at enhancing the system, then it is much easier and cheaper to simply ask them to estimate the change. Traceability matrices are highly overrated because the costs to maintain such matrices, even if you have specific tools to do so, typically far outweigh the benefits. Make your project stakeholders aware of the real costs and benefits and let them decide. After all, a traceability matrix is a document and is therefore a business decision to be made by them.

The Environment Discipline

The purpose of the Environment discipline is to configure the processes, tools, standards, and guidelines used by your project team. Your agile modeling efforts are both supported by and affect this discipline. The AM practice *Apply Modeling Standards* depends on having access to modeling standards and guidelines, and one aspect of this discipline is to identify and modify applicable standards and guidelines for your team. AM's principle *Local Adaptation* is supported by this discipline because tailoring your software process to meet the needs of the team and of individuals is an aspect of your Environment efforts. AM's practice *Use the Simplest Tools* affects this discipline because it simplifies the tool configuration process. There's not much configuration work required to work with index cards, whiteboards, and sticky notes.

The Deployment Discipline

The purpose of the Deployment discipline is to ensure the successful deployment of your system. Your efforts in this discipline are most affected by how well you thought through the deployment itself, something that is supported by your deployment modeling efforts as part of the Analysis and Design discipline. AM's principle *Work With People's Instincts* can improve your deployment efforts. If one of your co-workers or project stakeholders thinks that a portion of your deployment strategy isn't going to work, then you should reconsider it.

The Operations and Support Discipline

The purpose of the Operations and Support discipline is to perform the activities required to successfully operate and support your software. This discipline makes it explicit within your project lifecycle that operations and support efforts are significant considerations within your organization, the implication being that operations staff and support staff are important project stakeholders. This realization affects how your team supports and promotes the AM practice *Active Stakeholder Participation*—some of the active participants should represent this contingent.

How Do You Make This Work?

First and foremost, for AM to work effectively with the UP you need to instantiate the UP in an agile manner because AM works best when tailored into an agile process, a concept that is discussed in more detail in Part 5. It is possible to instantiate the UP in a manner that it is reasonably agile, although it's also possible to instantiate it in such a way that it is an unbearable anchor around the necks of developers. To succeed when taking an UP/AM approach, you need to choose to be agile.

Second, you need to focus on producing quality software, not on producing documentation. This is related to my first point: that you need to be agile. Many organizations that adopt the RUP product (Rational Corporation 2001) like it because it's complex, it describes a wide range of development roles, it's robust, and it describes how to create a wide range of artifacts. The problem is that, in their exuberance, some development teams forget that their primary goal is to develop software that meets the needs of their project stakeholders and instead get lost wandering through the documentation wilderness. Documentation is fine in adequate doses, but as Chapter 14, "Agile Documentation," argues, too much documentation puts your project at risk. The RUP product is a great resource when used appropriately, but you shouldn't necessarily create a supplementary business specification just because it tells you how to do so. Agile modelers travel light and create only the artifacts that they need to fulfill their goals and no more. Project teams that take an UP/AM approach will pare their efforts down to the bare minimum.

Third, recognize that you have a choice of artifacts available to you. Although the RUP suggests specific types of models, you'll see in the following chapters that you can easily substitute other artifacts, particularly those built using simple tools, and still achieve your goal of understanding or communicating an issue. For example, a CRC model can often suffice in place of a UML Class diagram, or an essential user interface prototype built from sticky notes and flipchart paper instead of something built using a prototyping tool. Appendix A includes descriptions of several modeling artifacts that you may decide to substitute in place of more complex and less inclusive techniques suggested by the RUP or even the EUP.

CHAPTER 24

Agile Business Modeling

One of the greatest pains to human nature is the pain of a new idea.

–Walter Bagehot

You learned in Chapter 23, "Agile Modeling throughout the Unified Process Lifecycle," that the purpose of the Business Modeling discipline is to explore the business environment in which your system operates. In this chapter we'll work through a portion of the SWA Online case study, described in Chapter 1, "Introduction", to explore how Agile Modeling's principles and practices can be applied to improve your business modeling efforts in a Unified Process environment.

How will you perform business modeling on an UP/AM project? First, at the beginning of your project hold an initial modeling session with your project stakeholders, to both explore the initial requirements for your system as well as to build a common business vision with your project stakeholders. Chapter 13, "Agile Modeling Sessions," provides advice for taking an agile approach to organizing, holding, and then following up on such a modeling session. Depending on the level of detail that we decide to go to with our modeling efforts, and on the amount of time that we decide to invest in this initial modeling session, we are likely to include Requirements discipline (Chapter 25, "Agile Requirements") activities and perhaps even Analysis and Design discipline (Chapter 26, "Agile Analysis and Design") activities. Don't worry, it's very unlikely that the "process police" will arrest you for doing so. Second, we need to be prepared to perform follow-up modeling sessions if we are unable to come to a common vision in our first session. Third, once we agree to a common vision it is likely that any future business modeling efforts will simply occur during short, ad hoc modeling sessions instead of larger, formal sessions.

We would work on the following artifacts as part of our Business Modeling discipline efforts if we chose to take the UP/AM approach to developing the SWA Online project:

- A business/essential use case model
- A simple business object model
- An agile supplemental business specification
- A business vision

A Business/Essential Use Case Model

Understanding the high-level requirements for your system, particularly early in a project when you are trying to identify the scope of your effort, is important. The RUP (Rational Corporation 2001) suggests that you create a business use case model, including a use case diagram as well as supporting documentation, to explore the high-level requirements for your system. Figure 24.1 depicts a digital picture of a whiteboard sketch of the high-level use case diagram that we created during this session. Other information was also gathered, in particular important business rules, constraints, and technical requirements that we parked in our business supplementary specification described later in this chapter. The goal of our initial modeling session was to understand the high-level requirements, not just to identify high-level use cases, so we followed the practice *Create Several Models In Parallel* and worked on several artifacts during the session.

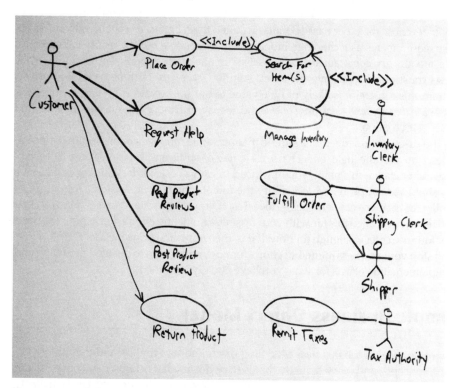

Figure 24.1   A high-level use case diagram for SWA Online.

An interesting thing happened during our modeling session when we applied the <<include>> stereotype on the diagram. As you can see the Search for Item(s) use case is included by both the Place Order and the Manage Inventory use cases. This was confusing at first for several of our project stakeholders, so we needed to mentor them a bit in the technique. At the beginning of the modeling session we spent a few minutes describing the concept of use case modeling to provide everyone with a basic understanding of the technique. Doing this provides several benefits:

- It improves communication because everyone can understand the diagrams created.

- It helps to build rapport with our project stakeholders because it puts everyone in a position of learning new skills; we're learning about the business and they're learning about software development.

- As our project stakeholders gain modeling skills it increases their ability to actively participate on the project.

When you look at Figure 24.1 you quickly gain an understanding for what we're trying to accomplish with the SWA Online system, although not how we intend to accomplish it. The model is arguably an essential use case diagram (Constantine & Lockwood 1999; Ambler 2001a), what the RUP would call a business use case diagram, because it shows a technology independent view of the system. You can implement a fully manual system or a fully automated system based on this diagram. Yes, the use case "Post Product Review" could be better renamed "Write Product Review" to make it more general, but our project stakeholders chose the other name because it suited them better. You should always strive to make requirements as technology independent as possible but the reality is that many systems are already constrained to a subset of architectural options. For example, SWA Online is constrained to an Internet-based solution, so investing time trying to abstract away from this constraint is likely of little value to our immediate efforts. Remember the principle *Maximize Stakeholder Investment* and focus your modeling efforts on tasks that provide positive value.

The use cases are described in a simple manner; agile modelers often find that a point-form description of the logic for each use case may be sufficient. You don't need to specify the system in detail at this point; you only need to gain a basic understanding of what the system should accomplish and to identify the initial scope for the system. A point-form description of each use case and actor does this. If your project stakeholders allow it, you may not even need to go this far with your business modeling efforts. Perhaps identifying three or four use cases is enough for now. If it is, then apply the principle *Model With A Purpose* and stop your business modeling efforts for now, moving on to detailed modeling and even implementation efforts for what you have already identified.

A Simple Business Object Model

An important goal of the Business Modeling discipline is to understand the underlying business concepts, and one way to do that is to perform what is known as conceptual or domain modeling. The RUP suggests that you create a collection of UML artifacts, described in Chapter 23, but for many projects (including SWA Online) this is typically overkill. For SWA Online a better approach is to create a simple business object model that focuses solely on the structure of business concepts and identifies major business entities and the relationships between them. Structured methodologies typically suggest the use of logical data models (LDMs) for this purpose, something that you should consider if you're building a system using structured or procedural technologies. Traditional object-oriented development methodologies typically suggest creating a class diagram.

Agile modelers, on the other hand, follow the practice *Use The Simplest Tools* and *Apply The Right Artifact(s)*, and often choose simpler techniques such as CRC cards for conceptual modeling. CRC cards are easy to learn to use (you can teach people to use them in less than 10 minutes) and therefore are more inclusive than other conceptual modeling techniques. You can and should use CRC cards to explore requirements with your project stakeholders.

Figure 24.2 shows two CRC cards that are part of a conceptual model for SWA Online. Across the top of the card is listed the name of the class, the left-hand side lists the responsibilities of the class (the things that it knows, data, and the things that it does, behaviors), and the right-hand side lists the classes that it needs to collaborate with to fulfill its responsibilities. The collaborators indicate the existence of a relationship between classes. For example, we know that customers have a relationship with orders because the Customer card lists Order as one of its collaborators. We don't know the exact details of this relationship, something we want to explore later, but for now this is sufficient to gain an understanding of the business domain that our system operates in. In addition to customer and order, our CRC model will likely include cards named Order Item, Tax, Shipping and Handling Charge, Inventory Item, Shipment, and Warehouse (among others) that capture important domain concepts.

> **TIP You Don't Need to Create Every Artifact**
>
> A common misconception regarding the UP is that you need to create every single artifact that it suggests. This isn't the case—something that both the RUP (Kruchten 2000; Rational Corporation 2001) and the EUP (Ambler 2001b) are very clear about. Follow the principle *Local Adaptation* and tailor the UP to your exact needs. If creating an artifact, or a portion thereof, will provide value to your project then create it, otherwise don't.

An Agile Supplementary Business Specification

With an UP/AM approach your Supplementary Business Specification (SBS) artifact collects the business modeling requirements that don't seem to fit well anywhere else. When agile modelers explore high-level requirements, as we did in our initial requirements modeling session with our project stakeholders, they will often identify related business rules, constraints, technical requirements, and even potential future requirements for a system. Agile modelers prefer to "park" these requirements—often writing them on flipchart paper, index cards, or a whiteboard. They capture just enough information so that you know what the requirement is when you want to explore it in

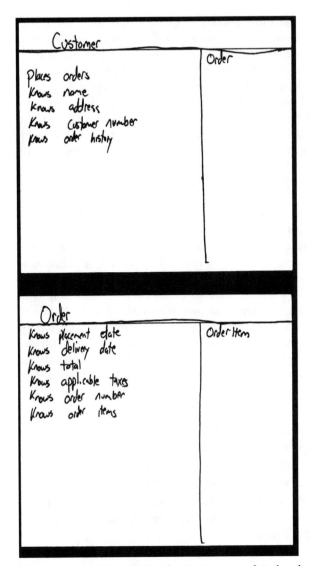

Figure 24.2   CRC cards for the Customer and Order classes.

greater detail later during construction. Your goal is to capture just enough information to understand the requirement, so that it can be estimated and scheduled into a future iteration. For now this information would form your SBS.

Assuming that your project stakeholders are comfortable with the idea of you traveling this light then you have nothing more to do than gather up your paper and cards and perhaps take digital photos of information captured on your whiteboard—exactly the tools we used in our initial requirements modeling session. If this isn't the case you need to consider transcribing this information into a more complicated tool such a word processor or CASE tool. Chapter 10, "Using the Simplest Tools Possible?" discusses the concept of using the simplest tools and Chapter 14, "Agile Documentation," discusses how to write agile documentation. UP/AM teams can greatly benefit from the advice presented in both chapters. For SWA Online we were able to convince our project stakeholders to allow us to keep most of our information recorded in our simple tools, although they insisted on a document that contained one-line descriptions, sometimes just a name, for each business rule, constraint, technical requirement, and potential future requirement.

Potential future requirement? An important part of your scoping effort is to identify both what is currently in scope and what is currently out of scope, and by identifying a requirement as a change case you are explicitly stating that it is out of scope for your current project efforts. During both your Business Modeling and Requirements discipline efforts your team will often identify requirements for future releases of your system as well as *potential* requirements that you may need to implement at some point. You don't want to lose this information, although at the same time you don't want to invest too much time exploring it nor do you want to invest any time overbuilding your software. However, there is some value to your architectural efforts—potential requirements may provide insights into the merits of one architectural alternative over another.

Change cases, described in Appendix A, are a simple technique for documenting potential requirements. Figure 24.3 depicts two change cases for SWA Online, each of which we captured on single index cards as we modeled with our project stakeholders. Change cases describe requirements you may, or may not, need to support in the future but you definitely do not need to support today. Change cases are often the result of brainstorming with your project stakeholders, where questions such as, "How can the business change?" "What legislation can change?" "What is your competition doing?"

```
Change: Expansion into North America
Likelihood: Very Likely
Timeframe: 12-18 Months
Impact:
     Must support shipments to customers in Canada and Mexico.
     Relationships with new shippers may be needed.
     Relevant taxes and duties need to be calculated.
     Product set sold within those markets likely to be different due
     to legal issues and local preferences.
     Support for multi-lingual site (English and French are official
     languages of Canada, Spanish of Mexico)
-----------------------------------------------------------------
Change: Sale of Virtual Products (online music, video, books, ...)
Likelihood: Very likely
Timeframe: 6-12 months
Impact:
     Must be able to bypass physical shipping process.
     We may need to support digital licenses for some products.
     There may be limits (period of availability, number of copies) on
     sales of individual items.
```

Figure 24.3 Two change cases for SWA Online.

and "Who else might use the system and how?" are explored. On the technical side, developers will often ask fundamental questions such as, "What technology can change?" and "What systems will we need to interact with?" that will lead to the identification of change cases. Change cases should be realistic, for example "We enter the insurance business" for a bank or "We need to support the latest technology in our system" are reasonable change cases but "Our sales staff is abducted by UFOs" isn't. Furthermore, change cases typically describe requirements that are reasonably divergent from what you are currently working on, requirements that would potentially cause major rework to fulfill. By identifying change cases you are now in a position to intelligently choose between what would otherwise appear to be equal architectural or design decisions. You should only bring relevant change cases into the decision making process when your current requirements are not sufficient to help you to choose between alternatives. Another advantage is that you can now explain to your project stakeholders why you chose one approach over another, as I like to say you have a story to tell. However, I cannot stress enough that change cases should not be used as excuses to gold plate your system. Stay agile and don't overbuild your system.

So what do you do when you think you have a change case that you truly believe needs to be implemented now? Simple. Discuss it with your project stakeholders. Ask them if the change case is an immediate requirement, and if so act accordingly. If it isn't an immediate requirement then accept the fact and move on. Never forget that it is the project stakeholder's responsibility to prioritize requirements, not yours.

Would there be harm in modeling for the future? This is a slippery slope because I suspect that if you model it then you are much more likely to build it. It would require great discipline not to overbuild, I believe, because once you've got it captured as a collection of bubbles and lines it will be far too easy to convince yourself that there's no harm in overbuilding just this once. Having said that there's nothing wrong with drawing a few throw-away sketches as you discuss a change case; just don't over model any models you intend to keep.

TIP **Iterate between Disciplines**
Although this chapter focuses on the Business Modeling discipline, the reality is that you iterate between each discipline rapidly. You may do a little business modeling, a little requirements modeling, some analysis, then some more requirements modeling, then some analysis quickly followed by design and so on. Agile modelers typically do not bother to distinguish between the different "flavors" of modeling, they just model appropriately as the situation calls for.

A Business Vision

An important reason we decided to hold our initial requirements modeling session with our project stakeholders was to identify a common business vision within the group. However, it's easy to say that you need to reach a common consensus between project stakeholders but much more difficult to achieve it in practice. Individual project stakeholders have different backgrounds, different priorities, and different preferences. To build a consensus everyone needs to recognize this, communicate what they need from the system, listen to what others have to say, and be prepared to negotiate. Whenever I'm working with a group that has a problem coming to consensus we'll write down everyone's issues on a whiteboard where everyone in the room can see and discuss them. This visually depicts the extent of the group's differences and provides a focus for their discussion. Sometimes we'll remove an issue from the board, or better yet simply cross it out because we often want to record scoping decisions after the issue's originator recognized that it wasn't required or at least wasn't important as other issues. I also like to draw lines between contradictory issues so as to highlight the need to discuss them, often using a specific color marker for just that purpose.

The RUP (Rational Corporation 2001) suggests that you create a business vision document to record the results of your visioning efforts. Agile modelers recognize that communication, not documentation, is your true goal. You want to come to a consensus regarding the business vision. In practice vision documents can be very dangerous things. In a situation where there is actual consensus regarding the vision then the effort you invest documenting that vision is a make-work effort and you'd be much better investing your time working on software to show your stakeholders what you're accomplishing, just as the principle *Software is Your Primary Goal* implores. In situations where there isn't consensus, a vision document can be used to cover up this problem. Once it's on paper someone can easily hold up the document and trumpet the idea that a common vision has been reached when that isn't actually the case—a recipe for disaster later in the project. Instead of investing time documenting a false vision, you would be much better served working with your project stakeholders to explore their needs further.

How to Make This Work in Practice

Business Modeling appears to be the least-understood discipline within the UP. I suspect that this is the result of the overlap between it and the Requirements discipline. In many ways the Business Modeling discipline's artifacts are simply high-level starts at the Requirements discipline's artifacts, as you shall soon see. This is perfectly fine, but it does seem confusing for many developers. Don't let this ambiguity worry you. With respect to this discipline agile modelers will focus on understanding the business environment and identify the initial scope of their system, at least at a high-level, and work closely with their project stakeholders to do so.

Agile Requirements

Meetings are indispensable when you don't want to do anything.

—John Kenneth Galbraith

You learned in Chapter 23, "Agile Modeling throughout the Unified Process Lifecycle," that the purpose of the Requirements discipline is to engineer the requirements for your project. This includes identifying with project stakeholders what your system should do, providing developers with a better understanding of the requirements, delimiting the system, providing a basis for estimating, and defining a user interface for your system (Rational Corporation 2001). In this chapter we'll work through a portion of the SWA Online case study, described in Chapter 1, "Introduction," to explore how Agile Modeling's principles and practices can be applied to improve your requirements efforts in a UP environment.

How will you perform requirements modeling on an UP/AM project? As we discussed in Chapter 24, "Agile Business Modeling," we would likely start by holding one or more formal modeling sessions at the beginning of our project, during the Inception phase, to identify the initial requirements for the system and to come to a common vision for the system. During these sessions we would also want to identify the scope of the system, or at least the scope of the release that we are currently working on. Once we've achieved these goals the rest of our requirements modeling efforts are likely to occur in short, informal ad hoc modeling sessions (described in Chapter 13, "Agile Modeling Sessions"). Because we've tailored AM into the UP we will need to have ready access to project stakeholders to help identify and prioritize requirements for us, enabling our team to follow the practice *Active Stakeholder Participation*. The requirements artifacts that you create form what the RUP (Rational Corporation 2001) calls the Software Requirements Specification (SRS), formerly known as the Requirements Model in previous versions of the RUP.

Taking an UP/AM approach to developing the SWA Online system we would work on the following artifacts as part of our Requirements discipline efforts:

- The context model
- Use case model
- Use case story board
- Supplementary specification

The Context Model

Although our business use case model, described in Chapter 24, can be used to provide a good overview of our system, it doesn't put the system into context. A use case model is useful at describing what a system does but not so good at showing the system within its external environment. The combination of what the system should accomplish as well as an indication of the context of the system defines the scope for your efforts. The RUP (Kruchten 2000; Rational Corporation 2001) suggests that scope information be documented in the vision document for your system if you choose to create such an artifact (remember that agile modelers choose to *travel light*). Your scope definition may be a single statement, in the case of SWA Online it would be something as simple as "To sell our products to customers via the Internet," or a statement with greater detail such as "To sell physical, but not virtual, products to existing or new customers in the Continental United States."

> **TIP** **Consider Your Enterprise Requirements Model**
> **Your organization may have a high-level requirements model that describes your enterprise, an artifact of the Infrastructure Management discipline (see Chapter 27, "Agile Infrastructure Management"). If this is the case an agile modeler will follow the practice *Reuse Existing Artifacts* and use this model as input into their requirements efforts. Enterprise requirements models can help to provide context for your system. After all, the goal of your project is to support a subset of your organization's overall requirements.**

A more detailed approach is to develop a context model that shows how your system fits into its overall environment. Context models are often depicted using a use case diagram, as you see in Figure 25.1, or as a dataflow diagram (DFD) as in Figure 25.2 (this style of diagram is often called a "level-0" DFD). It is important to understand the scope of your system so as to limit your development efforts. The first statement was too vague; it could be taken to mean that you are selling to international customers, a significantly greater effort than selling only within the USA, as well as selling virtual products such as online music which would require the addition of an online delivery system as well as a physical one. You may find that your scope changes over time, a decision made by your project stakeholders, so be prepared to embrace change.

So which is the best artifact to describe the scope of your system? A statement, a DFD, or a use case diagram? Depends on your situation. Statements are straightforward but

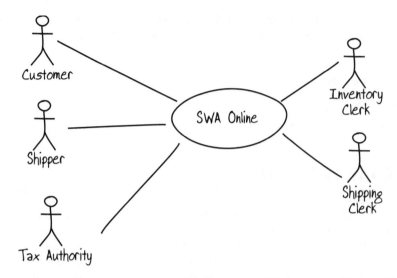

Figure 25.1 A business use case diagram used to model the context of SWA Online.

often not as communicative as a diagram. The DFD of Figure 25.2 shows the system in the center of the diagram and its relationships with other external entities—organizations, people, or other systems—that are outside the scope of your control yet still interact with your system. A major advantage of this approach is that it depicts in reasonable detail the major flow of information between your system and the outside world. The use case diagram of Figure 25.1 takes a different tack, depicting the system in the center once again and the actors (organizations, people) that interact with your system. The main advantage of this approach is that it depicts both the external and internal actors that interact with your system, as opposed to the DFD that just depicts the external ones.

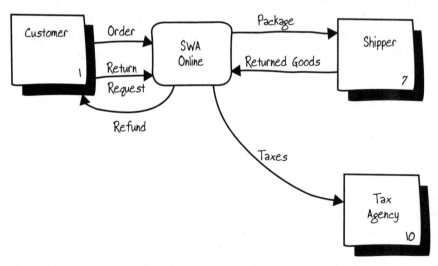

Figure 25.2 A data flow diagram (DFD) used to model the context of SWA Online.

The main disadvantage is that it does not indicate any detail regarding the interactions between the system and the actors.

Which diagram should you create? Both have their advantages and disadvantages, so perhaps you should consider creating both? No! That isn't very agile. A better approach is to create one diagram, breaking the rules a bit and combining the best of both diagrams into one as you see in Figure 25.3. Notice how internal entities are indicated with an "I" in the top corner of the two entities, my own style, and how numeric identifiers with the entities are dropped. ID numbers are difficult to maintain manually and it's easier to have a rule that entity names are unique to enable them to be identifiers if needed. The figure could just as easily have used a use case diagram notation, although had it shown data flow I would have broken a serious use case modeling rule. Luckily our project stakeholders like DFDs so the notation used in Figure 25.3 works. Remember that the principle *Model With a Purpose* recommends that you know your audience, enabling you to pick the artifacts best suited to them.

> **TIP** **Don't Be Afraid to Break the Rules**
> Although general practice is to not include internal entities on a level-0 DFD, the idea is that you introduce internal entities when you start digging into the details. We chose to do so anyway in Figure 25.2 because it enabled us to avoid drawing a second diagram. The important thing to notice is that the world hasn't come to an end and the modeling police haven't charged us with software process malpractice. Yes, we have arguably gone against the practice *Apply Modeling Standards*, but in doing so we have reduced both development and maintenance costs.

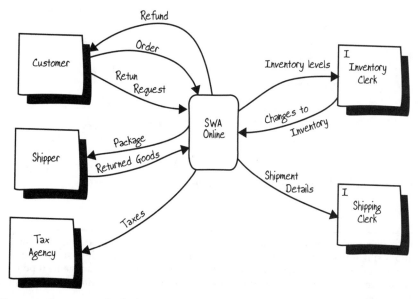

Figure 25.3   A DFD including internal entities to model the context of SWA Online.

Use Case Model

So how would we approach detailed requirements modeling for SWA Online? First, let's assume that the project has progressed to the point where we are now in the Construction phase, and that our original use case diagram presented in Figure 25.4 is still the most current version. The two of us are working together as a pair and our team will be implementing the order definition and placement portions of the basic course of action for the "Place Order" use case in this iteration. We won't be implementing search functionality, any sort of error or exception handling, tax calculations, or discount calculations right now as that work has been scheduled to a future iteration.* The basic course of action of a use case is often called the "happy path" because that is the logic path where everything works. The alternative courses of action describe logic paths

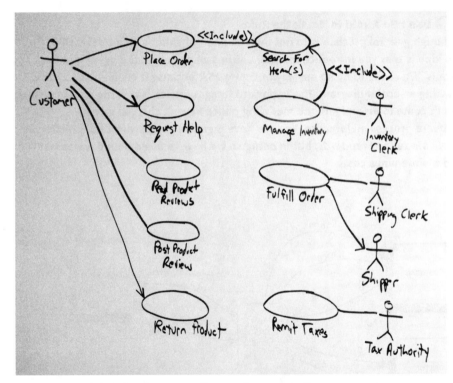

Figure 25.4 A high-level use case diagram for SWA Online.

---

*This example reveals a common problem with use cases—they are often too coarse-grained to schedule into a single iteration. You are often motivated to either schedule a single use case across multiple iterations, something that is uncomfortable from a project management point of view, or refactor your use case into a collection of smaller ones which is often uncomfortable from a modeling point of view.

where things don't work well. In the case of placing an order this would include being out of stock of an item that the customer has requested. However, our goal this iteration is to focus simply on a portion of the happy path for now. The other requirements will be worked on either by other subteams or perhaps by us at a later date.

We decide to flesh out the logic for the basic course of action, which is presented in Figure 25.5, and in parallel work on essential UI prototypes relevant to this use case, one of which is presented in Figure 25.6. We work on these two artifacts in parallel because they each approach the problem from a different direction, the use case describes what the customer does to place an order and the essential UI prototype specifies what the user interface of SWA Online must include to support this behavior. Notice how the use case invokes the "Search for Item(s)" use case on line two, consistent with the application of the <<include>> stereotype in Figure 25.4. Even though this functionality is invoked in the part of the use case that we're currently focused on

1. The use case begins when a customer chooses to place an order.

2. The customer searches for items via the use case "Search for Item(s)"

3. The customer selects and adds an order item to their order.

4. The customer indicates the number of a given item they wish to order.

5. The system calculates the subtotal for the item by multiplying the unit price by the number ordered.

6. The customer repeats steps 2 through 5 as necessary to build their order.

7. The customer finishes adding items to their order.

8. The customer provides their ship to and bill to information, including their name, phone number, and surface address.

9. The system calculates the subtotal for the entire order by adding the subtotals of the individual line items.

10. The system calculates the taxes applicable for the order according to the business rule *Calculate Taxes for an Order.*

11. The system calculates applicable discounts for the order according to the business rule *Calculate Discounts for an Order.*

12. The system displays the applicable taxes and discounts.

13. The system calculates the grand total for the order by adding the applicable taxes to the order subtotal and subtracting the discounts.

14. The system displays a summary of the order.

15. The customer verifies that the order is what they want.

16. The system schedules the order for fulfillment (see the use case Fulfill Order).

17. The system produces a receipt for the customer summarizing the order.

Figure 25.5 The basic course of action for placing an order.

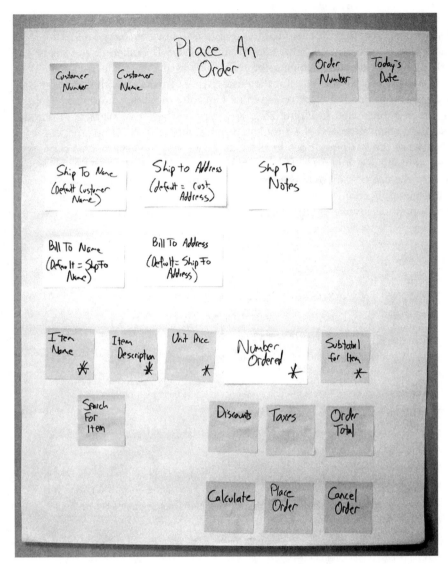

Figure 25.6 An essential UI prototype depicting the requirements for a screen/page.

we won't be implementing that functionality yet because it's not in scope. Instead we'll stub out what we need, perhaps going straight to a results page listing the theoretical results of our search. Later on in the project the searching functionality will be added as appropriate, just not now (remember, we're working incrementally). Also notice how the use case doesn't take into consideration any sort of technology issues yet, issues that we may decide to add in later on during analysis (Chapter 11, "Agile Work Areas") or design (Chapter 12, "Agile Modeling Teams"). Right now we just want to understand the basic process of placing an order; we can worry about implementation details later (potentially in a few minutes from now). The use case describes logic that we won't be implementing this iteration, such as the calculation of taxes and discounts, functionality that we'll need to stub out when we're coding.

Although we know that we'll be implementing the UI in a browser, we still choose to work with sticky notes and flipchart paper instead of an HTML editor, because the paper is more flexible and flexibility is what we need right now. As we initially explore the requirements we will add UI elements, moving them around very quickly and we want to use a tool that supports this effort. Later on, once the requirements for the page(s) have stabilized we'll switch over to an HTML editor because we'll want to make our UI more concrete for our project stakeholders to evaluate. For now we keep it simple.

We are following several of AM's practices during this effort. We are clearly following the practice *Create Several Models in Parallel* because we are working on a use case and essential UI prototype, and *Model With Others* because the team is currently comprised of the two of us and as least one project stakeholder that is providing requirements. We are also following the practice *Depict Models Simply*. I would argue that Figure 25.6 depicts a simple requirements model of the order placement page. I would also argue that Figure 25.5 is a good example of an application of the practice *Create Simple Content* because it provides just enough details to describe the business logic of the use case. We are also following Apply *The Right Artifact(s)*—business rules are being captured outside of the use case, although you could argue that the logic for calculating the grand total of an order is a simple business rule, in a separate business rules artifact (for now you would want to create placeholders for *Calculate Taxes for an Order* and *Calculate Discounts for an Order*, either sections in a word processing document or as individual index cards). Furthermore, user interface requirements are being captured in a separate artifact, the essential UI prototype, and if we felt the need "data requirements" could be captured in a conceptual model (see Chapter 24). We also followed the practice *Iterate To Another Artifact*, moving back and forth between working on the use case and the essential UI prototype—as we added features to the UI prototype we realized we were missing logic in the use case and vice versa. Finally, we applied the practice *Use The Simplest Tools*—the UI prototyping was done using paper and the use case logic was written on a whiteboard.

A common problem that developers following the UP seem to run into is how to write use cases effectively. A common problem is to include everything but the kitchen sink in a use case—people will mistakenly document business rules, constraints, data requirements, and even user interface requirements in use cases. Agile modelers, on the other hand, will follow the practices *Apply The Right Artifact(s)*, *Create Several Models in Parallel*, and *Iterate to Another Artifact* when they are modeling. The end result is that they will not try to put everything in their use cases, but instead use each type of artifact for what it is good for. For example, in Figure 25.5 you see that step 10 invokes the Calculate Taxes For An Order business rule described later in Figure 25.5. Instead of embedding the business rule in the use case, something we could have easily done, we instead defined the business rule as a first-class entity on its own and simply referenced it from the use case. This approach makes sense because it keeps our artifacts simple and easy to understand. This approach also makes it easy to reference the business rule from other artifacts, perhaps our source code that implements this functionality. Furthermore, even if we don't know the exact details of how to calculate taxes right now the undocumented business rule provides a placeholder reminding us to look into it. We can still proceed with working on the rest of the use case, modeling it further (see Chapter 26, "Agile Analysis and

Design") and hopefully getting into implementation quickly (remember the practice *Prove It With Code*).

> **TIP Consider Transcribing Your Use Case Diagram into an Electronic Tool**
> On an UP project use case diagrams are primary artifacts, being the centerpiece of your requirements efforts. Figure 25.4 did not change from our initial business modeling efforts (Chapter 24). In fact it's the same diagram. The reality is that our use case diagram will very likely need to be updated over time. In future iterations it is likely that we'll introduce new use cases, we'll split existing use cases up when we realize that alternative courses have become more complex than we originally thought, and we may even assign existing use cases to future releases. If you decide to maintain any requirements artifacts over time this is the one that you are likely keep. My suggestion would be to keep this diagram on a whiteboard for as long as you can. I've seen diagrams such as this survive (evolving along the way) right through to the deployment of a nine-month project, so it is possible to do without a "pretty picture" created using a drawing or CASE tool. When there becomes a clear need to migrate your diagram into such a tool then do so, but until then Travel Light and leave it on your whiteboard. It's amazing how little documentation you truly need when you choose to do without it.

Assuming that we were satisfied with our modeling efforts, more than likely an effort that took between thirty and sixty minutes, we would either continue on through analysis (Chapter 11) and design (Chapter 13) and finally into implementation or we would first invest a few minutes to update the project team's object model with what we have just learned. I prefer to keep object models as simple as possible, using CRC cards to do so as you saw in Chapter 24, because they are easy to work with and very accessible to project stakeholders. Not only can they be used to show the major entities within your domain but their responsibilities as well, including both data and behavior.

Use Case Story Board

A use case story board shows how a use case is supported by the user interface for your system. This is arguably an analysis or even a design activity because with a use case story board you are exploring how you are going to implement the requirements described by the use case. Agile modelers don't worry about distinctions such as this, we're more concerned with *Applying The Right Artifact(s)* to get the job done—there isn't a practice called "Place Modeling Activities In The Right Category" within AM. If the UP wants to categorize use case story boarding, and related user interface prototyping activities, as requirement modeling tasks then so be it.

A very effective artifact for use case story boarding, and for analyzing the logic of your use cases is general, are robustness diagrams (Rosenberg and Scott 1999). Robustness diagrams depict the major objects—classified into boundary/interface objects, entity objects, or control/process objects—that participate in fulfilling an actor's interaction with a system as defined by a usage scenario. Boundary/interface objects represent user interface elements such as screens, reports, HTML pages, or emails that actors interact with such as the search page and shopping cart page. Entity objects are objects that are typically found in your domain model, such as Order and Item. Control/process objects serve as the glue between boundary/interface objects and entity objects, implementing the logic required to manage the various objects and their interactions. Figure 25.7 shows a whiteboard sketch. Once again we've followed the practice *Use The Simplest Tool*, representing the logic contained in the Place Order use case of Figure 25.5. The boundary/interface objects are depicted as circles with a "T" stuck into their side, control/process objects have an arrowhead on the top, and entity objects have an underline.

By drawing this robustness diagram we quickly gain a sense for the work that we need to do to implement this use case—as you can see we need to create six major user interface items, very likely HTML pages seeing as we're deploying to the Internet. We also have seven process classes to build and four entity classes. Yes, this is a high-level view of what we need to do, and once we get into detailed design and implementation we will discover that there is more to it than this, but for now this is a good start.

Is Figure 25.7 sufficient for our need, which was to explore the user interface to support this use case? This is a question that agile modelers constantly ask themselves—the principle *Model With A Purpose* tells us to stop modeling once the purpose has been fulfilled. Although we have identified the boundary/interface classes that we need we don't know what each one should accomplish, hence we may decide to create essential user interface prototypes such as the one presented earlier in Figure 25.6 and perhaps even a traditional user interface prototype. We also don't yet have a handle on the relationships between the various boundary/interface classes, something that a user interface flow diagram is good at. Also, as part of our analysis and design activities we may decide to develop UML sequence diagrams to explore how to implement this use case (something we do in Chapter 26).

User interface (UI) flow diagrams can be used to explore the relationships between major user interface elements, such as HTML pages in the case of SWA Online. Taking an UP/AM approach to modeling the scope of a UI flow diagram will either be a single use case or the entire system. In this case we've decided to create one for the entire system, depicted in Figure 25.8, because the user interface for this release SWA Online system is quite small. If we expected the system to have a large number of pages, 15 isn't too bad but fifty is definitely pushing it, then we would likely want to avoid a single "all-encompassing" diagram. Figure 25.8 enables our team to explore how customers will interact with SWA Online from a birds-eye view, and thus ask very important usability questions long before we've built the user interface. Does it make sense to be able to go from one page to another? Should a customer be able to go directly from the order confirmation page to the item information page? By looking at our user interface from this new perspective we are able to ask new questions of our project stakeholders, perhaps triggering them to identify new requirements that will help to improve our system in the process.

The scope of Figure 25.8 is several use cases, making it a diagram that we would evolve over time. In fact our team initially reserved a section of our white board space so we evolve this diagram over time; luckily we used whiteboard wallpaper to cover

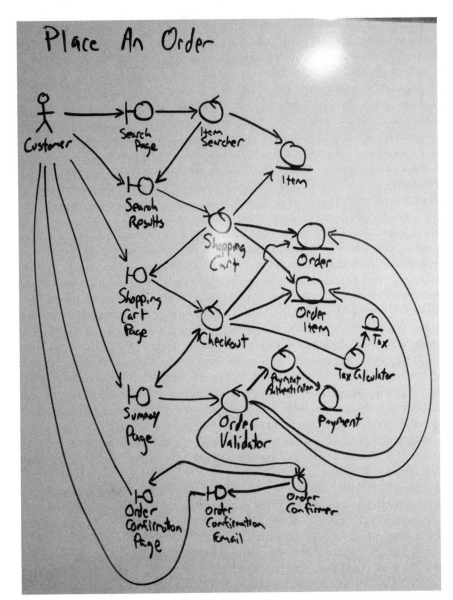

Figure 25.7   A robustness diagram for the Place Order use case.

most of our walls so we have a lot of working space. By taking this approach we didn't need to transcribe the diagram into a more sophisticated tool, such as Microsoft Visio, instead we just updated it as required. Eventually we'll decide to either erase the diagram, following the practice *Discard Temporary Models*, take a digital photo of it if the diagram is still of value to us but we need the whiteboard space, or perhaps we'll transcribe it into an electronic tool if that makes sense at the time.

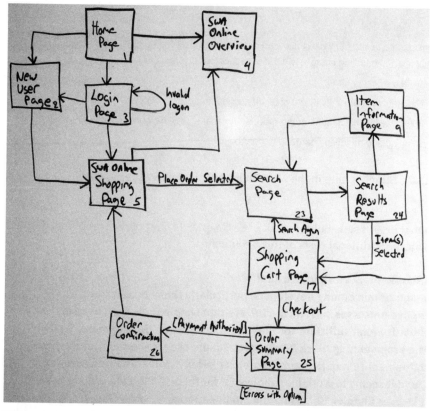

Figure 25.8   A diagram representing navigational flow within a user interface.

Supplementary Specification

A supplementary specification is where the vast majority of your systems requirements are documented. It supplements your use case by including business rule definitions, constraints, technical requirements, and any other non-use case requirement pertinent to your system. Because most of the contents of a supplementary specification are text based you are likely to choose to use a word processor. However, if there isn't a clear need to create and maintain your supplementary specification as an official document then you may wish to reconsider this approach. Agile modelers choose to follow the principle *Travel Light* and will therefore question the existence of any document. For example, Figure 25.9 depicts two business rules that have been recorded on index cards instead of in a word processor. We've followed the practice *Use The Simplest Tools*, something that agile modelers always do. When we discussed the merits of maintaining a supplementary specification as a word processing document, as well as the inherent costs, and compared them with doing the same thing with index cards we decided to proceed with the index cards. The creation of documentation is a

Maximum Order Total

The maximum amount that we will allow an order to reach is $10,000 USD before taxes and any shipping and handling charges. This is to reduce our exposure to the risk of fraud.

Calculate Taxes For An Order

1. The state tax (currently 6.5%) shall be applied on all products sold by SWA Online.

2. Taxes shall be calculated on the order subtotal after any discounts have been applied.

3. Shipping and handling charges are not taxed.

Figure 25.9   Business rules in the SWA Online supplementary specification.

decision that project stakeholders make, see Chapter 14, and our stakeholders decided not to incur the additional costs of this document.

TIP Simple Tools Work in the Real World

A common refrain among developers, particularly those familiar with prescriptive processes such as the UP, are that simple tools such as cards and whiteboards aren't sufficient for real-world application development. Really? eXtreme Programming (Beck 2000) practitioners use simple tools all the time. In fact, their entire requirements model is typically stored as a box of index cards, and it seems to work incredibly well for them. CASE tools clearly have their place, as Chapter 10, "Using the Simplest Tools Possible?" argues, but so do simple tools.

When agile modelers work on the various aspects of a supplementary specification, such as an individual business rule, the principle *Maximize Stakeholder Investment* guides us to record just enough information to understand what is required. For example, the business rules shown in Figure 25.9 are rather sparse—they include a name for the business rule and a prose description and that's it. Other information that we could have recorded but chose not to was the source of the business rule (for example Sally Jones), the date and time that the rule was recorded, a record of the rule being reviewed, or a unique identifier for the rule. We have no intention to act on any of this information so we've decided not to record it. Yes, we may regret this decision later, but we'll definitely regret investing the additional time recording this information when we didn't need to. Agile modelers have the courage to trust that they can deal with any problems that arise when they actually do.

The constraints depicted in Figure 25.10 and the business rules in Figure 25.9 are good examples of the results of two of AM's simplicity practices:

Depict Models Simply. We could have used a more complex language, such as OCL (Warmer and Kleppe 1999), to write the requirements. However, we used simple prose instead because this approach was faster and far more readable by our project stakeholders (who wrote many of the requirements themselves).

Shipper

SWA Online will use our existing shipping company, Fly-By-Night Shipping, for the first release.

Database

SWA Online will use Oracle 11i to persist data as SWA Enterprises already has a corporate license agreement with Oracle Corporation.

Figure 25.10   Two constraints for SWA Online.

Create Simple Content. Each requirement is cohesive. It describes one concept and one concept only. For example, we could have chosen to write a single requirement to describe every single technical environment constraint imposed upon the team instead of one that focused only on the database. This requirement would have specified the database, middleware, application server, and so on that we needed to use.

TIP **There's Nothing Wrong with Technical Constraints**

Why are our project stakeholders specifying technology decisions for us? Isn't that "illegal" in the software development world? No. AM includes both senior management and operations staff as project stakeholders, and a myriad of other roles within your organization, and very often these two groups of people will define constraints that you need to conform to. This includes constraints that specify technical choices such as your database. Agile modelers will of course explore these constraints to ensure that they're realistic—if the manager of operations suggests Oracle because you already have a corporate license, that's a good reason; if a senior manager suggests Oracle simply on the basis of a magazine article they read, then you should thank them for the suggestion.

How to Make This Work in Practice

The Requirements discipline can be daunting at first, and the myriad documents and models suggested by the RUP (Rational Corporation 2001) can lead project teams to become very documentation centric. This does not need to be the case, as I've shown in this chapter. To take an agile approach to this discipline you need to:

1. **Focus on software, not documentation.** When you tailor AM into the UP you must remember that your primary goal is to develop software, not documentation. Question every single artifact that your instantiation of the UP recommends, and create it only if it is absolutely essential to your effort.

2. **Keep it simple.** Create the most minimalist version of each artifact that you can. You saw that the business rule definitions of Figure 25.9 were just enough to document the idea, nothing more and nothing less.

3. **Proceed iteratively.** On an UP/AM project you do not take a big-modeling-up-front (BMUF) approach and create a comprehensive, all-encompassing software requirements specification (SRS). You will start by identifying a high-level model at first; a model with enough information to guide your development efforts but one that isn't highly detailed. Agile modelers gather the details as the work proceeds, returning to requirements modeling efforts as required, and assigning new work to future iterations (or releases) as appropriate. For example, as you start to implement the order placement functionality you will realize that you don't quite understand the exact details of how it should work; perhaps there are limits on how many items of a given type you may order. If this is the case you have new functionality that must be estimated, prioritized, and assigned to a future iteration. Perhaps your logic is out of order—maybe the customer should provide their billing and shipping information first. Perhaps there should be a way for customers to define a profile so as to define billing and shipping information once, implying another new requirement that must be dealt with in a future iteration.

4. **Keep it simple.** You can use simple tools. For example, our supplementary specification was a box of index cards, not a word processing document, and it seemed to work fine. A great benefit of the RUP product is that it provides templates for key artifacts; however, that's also a significant problem because it makes it easy to become documentation centric and to not travel light.

5. **Work as a team.** Agile modelers work closely with developers; they are often actively involved with implementation themselves, as well as testers. By collaborating closely with the other people involved in your project you improve communication and thereby reduce the need for documentation, which in Chapter 8, "Communication," you learned to be a very poor communication vehicle. If your testers are actively involved in developing the requirements they don't need extensive documentation to formulate acceptance tests because they know the requirements. In fact, in Part Three of this book you learned that on XP projects that project stakeholders are responsible for writing user acceptance tests (potentially with the aid of test professionals) and they don't need extensive documentation to do so. If it's possible for XP surely it must be possible for UP.

CHAPTER 26

Agile Analysis and Design

There is no such thing as rule-governed creativity.

–Emperor Leto II

in *God Emperor of Dune* by Frank Herbert

The purpose of the Analysis and Design discipline is to evolve a robust architecture for your system, to produce a detailed design for your system based on its requirements, and to adapt your design to reflect the realities of your implementation environment (Rational Corporation 2001). The primary inputs into this discipline are your requirements artifacts (see Chapter 25, "Agile Requirements") and, less so, your business models (see Chapter 24, "Agile Business Modeling"). In this chapter we will explore how to take an agile approach to this discipline of the Unified Process (UP) (Jacobson, Booch, and Rumbaugh 1999), applying the principles and practices of Agile Modeling (AM) to do so.

How will you perform analysis and design modeling on a UP/AM project? During the Inception phase most of your effort will focus on analysis of your business and requirements models, although you will still be doing design work as needed. During the Elaboration phase you will focus mostly on architecture, although analysis will also be important and design work will become more prevalent as you prove your architecture. During the Construction phase your focus will be on analysis and design activities. Your architecture should have been baselined and proven before leaving the Elaboration phase, although changes can occur later in the lifecycle if appropriate—agile modelers follow the principle Embrace Change so accept the fact that they may need to change their architectural approach if it proves insufficient as their understanding of the requirements evolves. During the Transition phase your modeling efforts will focus on rework resulting from defects discovered by system and user testing efforts.

It is important to understand that your approach to scheduling on a UP project is use case driven, requirements driven is arguably a better term, with specific requirements (often centered around use cases) being assigned to each iteration. The basic idea is that you will evolve your system, and any associated artifacts that you choose to maintain, throughout each iteration. You will analyze the requirements assigned to the iteration, possibly creating use case realizations for each use case and its associated supplementary requirements. If you're taking an object-oriented (OO) approach to development, the assumption of this chapter, you'll create models that lend themselves to OO development such as UML class diagrams and UML state charts. If you're taking a structured/procedural approach to development you would similarly create artifacts that lend themselves to that paradigm, such as structure charts. If your system is working with data, and most do, then you'll also need to evolve a data model over time.*

To explore the Analysis and Design discipline on a UP/AM project we will consider the following issues with respect to developing the SWA Online system:

- Rethinking analysis and design models in the UP
- Architectural modeling
- Creating use case realizations
- Time to update our use case?
- Time to use a CASE tool?
- Design class modeling
- Data modeling
- Embracing change
- How does this work in practice?

Rethinking Analysis and Design Models in the UP

In Chapter 23, "Agile Modeling throughout the Unified Process Lifecycle," you learned that in the UP an Analysis Model describes your analysis of your requirements model, serving as a conceptual overview of the system. This is often a temporary model, one that is either discarded or evolved into your design model. You also learned that a UP Design Model is a collection of models describing the realization of use cases and serving as an abstraction of your source code. My experience is that some UP project teams can become very non-agile with respect to these two models,

---

*Many applications must work with legacy data and therefore don't have the opportunity to evolve their data schema, at least not much. In these cases you'll want to follow the practice *Formalize Contract Models* and gain access to a physical data model of the legacy database. Hopefully one already exists, otherwise you will need to develop one for yourself.

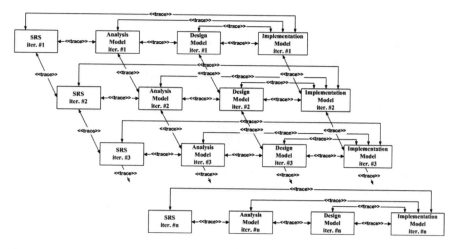

Figure 26.1   Traceability between the major artifacts of the Unified Process.

particularly when they start trying to baseline versions of their models and to maintain some semblance of traceability between them.

Figure 26.1 explores the concept of traceability between the major artifact sets within the UP—the System Requirements Specification (SRS), the Analysis Model, the Design Model, and the Implementation Model. It does not consider other artifact sets such as the Business Model and the Test Model, nor does it present sub-artifacts such as use cases and classes that potentially exist within the major models because the diagram is sufficiently complex as it is. Following an iterative and incremental approach to development, which is exactly the approach that an UP/AM project team takes, traceability between artifacts becomes very interesting. The diagram depicts the basic concept that the design model for iteration *n* is developed based on both the analysis model of iteration *n* and the existing design model from iteration *n-1*, therefore to maintain full traceability you need to trace it back to both of these models. To do this you would need to have the relevant artifacts baselined, something you may be doing already as part of the Configuration and Change Management (C&CM) discipline, and maintain a traceability matrix between the previous version of a model, in this case design model *n-1*, and the current version of any input artifacts, in this case analysis model *n*. You naturally also need to maintain the traceability matrix between artifacts within each major model as well, and you would need to consider baselining the matrix itself at the end of each iteration so as to maintain full traceability throughout your project.

Yikes! Teams that take this approach clearly are not traveling light. Even if they only choose to maintain a traceability matrix that is current for the current iteration, evolving it along with their other project artifacts and not worrying about traceability from one version to the next clearly have a lot of work to do, work that is taking away from their software development efforts.

What would an agile modeler do? First, they realize that the concepts of an analysis model and a design model are perfectly fine. They just don't get hung up on them.

Second, they realize that they don't really have an analysis model and a design model per se, they just have modeling artifacts that they may or may not wish to maintain over time—"analysis model" and "design model" are simply categories into which their artifacts are organized. In other words they follow the practice *Apply The Right Artifact(s)* and don't worry all that much about academic categorizations of their work. Third, they don't go overboard on traceability. They realize that a traceability matrix, regardless of the tool used to create and maintain it, is simply a document and like every other document the decision to create and maintain it is the domain of their project stakeholders. Therefore they discuss the concept with their project stakeholders, presenting both the advantages (easier change management) and disadvantages (increased documentation burden on the team) and let them decide whether they wish to pay for this effort, which is in accordance to the principle *Maximize Stakeholder Investment*.

Architectural Modeling

UP development teams will typically perform initial architectural modeling during the UP Inception phase and during the Elaboration phase focus their Analysis and Design discipline efforts on architecture. During this phase an architectural prototype is developed as part of the Implementation discipline to show that the architecture does in fact work—you follow the practice *Prove It With Code*. The primary architectural artifact in the UP is called a System Architecture Document (SAD), a document that summarizes your system architecture. Taking a UP/AM approach, agile modelers will create a SAD if it provides value to their project and when their project stakeholders are willing to invest in its creation and maintenance, just as they would any other document. If your team does create a SAD, it typically contains:

■ A summary of the architecturally significant requirements (if they're documented elsewhere you would simply reference the requirements to remain agile).

■ Overview diagrams representing the critical views of your system (see below).

■ Documentation describing the diagrams as appropriate.

Agile modelers will typically create one or more overview diagrams, also called navigation diagrams, which present an overview of the "landscape" of their system. Just like a road map depicts the organization of a town, your overview diagram(s) depict(s) the organization of your system. Overview diagrams are the instantiation of your system's architectural views. Kruchten (1995) describes a "4+1 view" of architecture, which the RUP adopted initially and later expanded upon. The five views are:

1. **Logical view.** This view models the functional features that your system provides to its end users.

2. **Process view.** This view models how your system fulfills non-functional requirements, such as performance, system availability, concurrency and

distribution, system integrity, and fault-tolerance. It also specifies which thread of control executes each operation of each class identified in the logical view.

3. **Development view.** This view models the organization of the actual software modules (components, subsystems), often organized in layers, which can be developed by one or more developers.

4. **Physical view.** This view models how your system will be deployed, often including sub-views for your development, testing, and production environments.

5. **Scenario (use case) view.** This view models a subset of architecturally significant use cases or usage scenarios that show how elements of the first four views fit together.

Agile modelers realize the concept of various architectural views is important, it's an implication of the principle *Multiple Models*, but that no one set of views is right for every project. Instead, agile modelers will follow the practice *Apply the Right Artifact(s)* and let the nature of the project define the types of models they create. The type of overview diagram(s) that you create depends on the nature of the system that you are building. For example, a team building a complex business application using J2EE-based technology will likely find that a UML component diagram and a UML deployment diagram are appropriate for use as architectural overview diagrams. However, a team building a corporate data warehouse will likely gravitate toward a data model and UML deployment diagram on which to base their architecture. Different projects, different architectural views, hence different types of overview diagram(s). You need to be flexible in your approach because one size does not fit all.

How should we model the architecture for SWA Online? We start by gathering the entire development team for an initial modeling session. This ensures that we hear a wide range of opinions as well as build consensus regarding our architectural approach. Not only do we want an architecture that works, we want one that everyone believes in. Although we could have decided to leave it in the hands of a single person, perhaps someone who has built this sort of system before, we instead chose to follow the practice *Model With Others* and play it safe—remember, software development is a lot like swimming, it's dangerous to do it alone. We also decide to keep this modeling session short, although we are prepared to go over time if necessary, and schedule it for two hours. The principle *Rapid Feedback* prompts us to model a little bit and then seek to validate our models, likely by creating an architectural prototype via the practice *Prove It With Code*. A less-than-agile approach would be to model for several days or even weeks, the idea being to specify the architecture in great detail to ensure that we have it right. However, the longer we go without concrete feedback the likelier the chance that we've gotten it wrong. We're far better off thinking through the big issues now and then immediately start into prototyping the "skeleton" (Jacobson, Booch, and Rumbaugh 1999) of our application to verify that our approach works, or in the worst case to identify areas where we need to rethink things. The bottom line is that everything works on a whiteboard sketch. It isn't until you try things in practice that you discover what actually works.

During our modeling session we focus on two diagrams, the UML deployment model of Figure 26.2 and the UML component model of Figure 26.3, both of which we

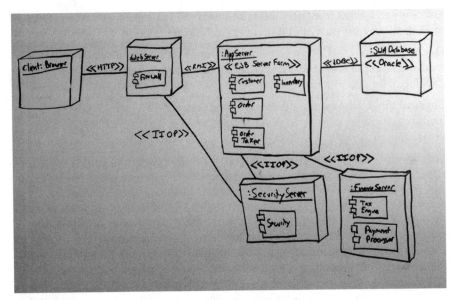

Figure 26.2 A UML deployment diagram for SWA Online.

drew on the whiteboard following the practice *Create Several Models in Parallel*. The deployment model helped us to explore the proposed configuration of our system and the component model enabled us to explore potential business components and their

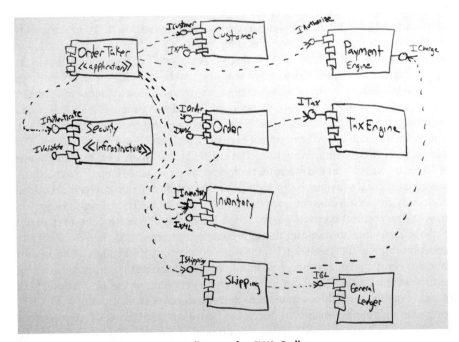

Figure 26.3 A UML component diagram for SWA Online.

interrelationships. The two diagrams are clearly related. The deployment diagram shows how some software components are deployed, which was the motivator to work on both of them at once.

Are these two diagrams sufficient? At the beginning of the project, yes they are, so as the principle *Model With A Purpose* implores we should stop working on them because they fulfill their purpose. Based on the information contained in Figure 26.2 we can now proceed with setting up a development environment, during which we'll quickly discover whether or not our approach is feasible. We will likely find that we've missed something, or that something doesn't quite work as we expected, but that's okay. In fact, this is good stuff to discover as early as possible. Figure 26.3 provides us with guidance as to how we might decide to organize our business code, although during the modeling session one developer points out that he doesn't understand how we'll build a large-scale business component using EJB technology (our chosen technology platform). A discussion quickly ensues and one developer steps up to the whiteboard and presents an approach that he has seen work before in the past, the diagram for which is shown in Figure 26.4. He explains that a component's interface is defined by one or more session beans and that his past experiences have led him to not provide direct access to EJB entity beans. A session bean will either interact with EJB entity beans, other EJB session beans, normal Java objects, or the database(s) on the back end. The arrows on the diagram indicate the type of object that can invoke operations on other objects, for example following this approach EJB entity beans are not allowed to invoke operations on session beans but they are allowed to interact with other entity beans. The team discusses the advantages and disadvantages of this approach for a few minutes and decides to adopt these design guidelines for now. As agile modelers they choose to follow the practice *Apply Modeling Standards*, although reserve the right to change the guidelines if their architectural prototyping efforts show that this approach won't work well for the project.

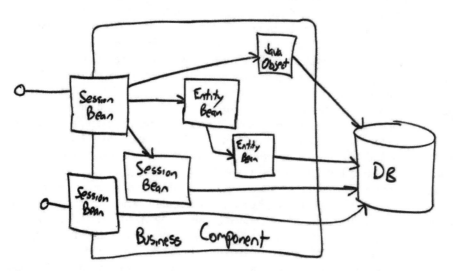

Figure 26.4 A free-form sketch describing a strategy for implementing a business component.

TIP **You Can Travel Light Architecturally**
**When most or all of your communication is face-to-face you will find that
overview diagrams, even ones that are hand drawn, are often sufficient to
describe your architecture. SADly many UP development teams mistakenly
invest time developing a comprehensive SAD when they don't need to—pun
intended.**

During our architecture modeling session we invited two of our key project stakeholders to the modeling session. We have nothing to hide from them because we sub-
scribe to the principle of *Open and Honest Communication*. This decision was very
fortunate because we had several questions regarding the requirements that became
apparent as we discussed architectural options, so we benefited from the practice
Active Stakeholder Participation because we had our questions answered on the spot.
Yes, it can be embarrassing when project stakeholders discover that the developers
don't know everything, for example during our initial architecture session it became
apparent that several developers needed to receive training on EJB and Oracle databases, two of the main technologies chosen for this project. This was something that
the development team realized but that our project stakeholders might not have, but
it's not a big deal. They would have found out eventually, they'll be paying the training bill after all, and it shows that we're only human.

When we created these two overview diagrams, a critical concern of our modeling
efforts was the principle *Assume Simplicity*. The practice *Create Simple Content* indicates
that we wanted to identify the simplest architectural approach(es) possible. The more
complicated our architecture, the greater the chance that it won't be understood by
individual developers and the greater the opportunity for error and breakdown. The
principle *Work With People's Instincts* guided our efforts when trying to identify the
simplest approach—our implementation efforts will quickly reveal what is simple and
what isn't, right now the best we can do is make an educated guess. Furthermore, we
wanted our diagrams to contain the right level of information, showing how various
aspects of our system work together but not the details (future design sessions can
address the details), following the practice *Depict Models Simply*. We followed the practice *Use the Simplest Tools* to do the job—whiteboard sketches were all we needed to
model the critical aspects of our architecture.

You should recognize that your architectural models will reveal your system's
dependencies on other systems or their dependencies on yours. For example, your system may interact with a credit-card processing service via the Internet, access data
from a legacy relational database, or produce an XML data structure for another internal application. Network diagrams and UML deployment diagrams are very useful
for identifying these dependencies, as are process-oriented models such as workflow
diagrams, UML activity diagrams, and data-flow diagrams. The implication is that
these dependencies indicate the potential need to follow the practice *Formalize Contract
Models* between your team and the owner(s) of the systems that yours share dependencies with. Ideally many of these models will already be in place; the credit card
processor likely has a strictly defined protocol that you must follow and the legacy
database likely has a physical data model defined for it, although new functionality
such as the XML data structure will require adequate definition. Sometimes you will

need to perform an analysis of the existing interface to a legacy system if accurate documentation is not in place, and other times you will need to design a new interface. In both cases a corresponding contract model will need to be developed, either by your team, the other team(s), or co-jointly as appropriate.

Creating Use Case Realizations

A use case realization is an artificial artifact in the sense that it is effectively a collection of one or more models that describes the implementation of a single use case. You create a use case realization by analyzing a use case and tying the information described within the use case to your analysis and/or design. Although the RUP (Rational Corporation 2001) associates use case realizations with system use cases, when you stop and think about it system use cases can be thought of as the realization of business/ essential use cases. Having said that, our focus will be on realizing system use cases.

The RUP suggests that you explore flows of logic through the use cases, often referred to as usage scenarios, via interaction diagrams—either UML sequence diagrams or UML collaboration diagrams. Sequence diagrams are the most common approach as they are well suited for exploring sequential business logic (hence the name) such as that described by usage scenarios. As you develop each interaction diagram you identify collaborations between objects, which translate to operations implemented by classes, and identify relationships between the classes. When one object collaborates with another there is an implied relationship between the corresponding classes, either an implicit one or an explicit one. The UML recognizes several types of relationships between classes, including association, aggregation, composition, inheritance, and dependency. The implication is that as you develop your interaction diagrams you are identifying important aspects of the static structure of your software, information that is typically captured by a UML class diagram in the RUP. If you are sketching the interaction diagrams by hand you might choose to work on the class diagram at the same time, or if you are working with a sophisticated UML-based CASE tool then it is likely that it is automatically doing this work for you. Either way you are effectively following the AM practice *Create Several Models In Parallel*.

The RUP approach to use case realizations isn't the only one available to you. Agile modelers will often create UML sequence diagrams for complex portions of logic within a use case, or better yet they'll rework the logic, but will often opt for CRC cards instead of a UML class diagram because they'll follow the practice *Use The Simplest Tools* and will choose index cards over white boards or CASE tools for this effort. Agile modelers that aren't comfortable with UML sequence diagrams will often opt to create a Robustness Diagram first to identify potential classes and often follow with sequence diagrams (Rosenberg and Scott 1999). It is important to recognize that you often have a choice, that you should follow the principle of *Local Adaptation* and tailor your approach to reflect the skills, experiences, and preferences of your team.

TIP **There's No One "Official" Way**
To explore the logic of a use case, some people will choose to create the
robustness diagrams, whereas many will go straight to sequence diagrams.

Some people prefer CRC cards to explore the static structure of software and others prefer UML class diagrams. You'll even vary yourself—one day you'll take one approach and the next day another.

Figure 26.6, which you saw in Chapter 25, shows a whiteboard sketch of a robustness diagram representing the logic contained in the Place Order use case of Figure 26.5. It depicts many of the high-level classes that we will likely need to create to implement the functionality described by the use case. With these classes identified it is much easier for us to create a UML sequence diagram, depicted in Figure 26.7, for this use case. In parallel we also developed the analysis-level class diagram of Figure 26.8, also a whiteboard sketch. We chose to create a class diagram instead of CRC cards in this case, taking an approach in between the two suggested approaches described earlier. (Normally I would use CRC cards, but in the next section I want to discuss issues associated with transcribing a whiteboard sketch to a CASE tool model so chose to show a UML class diagram instead.)

1. The use case begins when a customer chooses to place an order.

2. The customer searches for items via the use case "Search for Item(s)"

3. The customer adds an order item to their order.

4. The customer indicates the number of a given item they wish to order.

5. The system calculates the subtotal for the item by multiplying the unit price by the number ordered.

6. The customer repeats steps 2 through 5 as necessary to build their order.

7. The customer finishes adding items to their order.

8. The customer provides their ship to and bill to information, including their name, phone number, and surface address.

9. The system calculates the subtotal for the entire order by adding the subtotals of the individual line items.

10. The system calculates the taxes applicable for the order according to the business rule *Calculate Taxes for an Order.*

11. The system calculates applicable discounts for the order according to the business rule *Calculate Discounts for an Order.*

12. The system displays the applicable taxes and discounts.

13. The system calculates the grand total for the order by adding the applicable taxes to the order subtotal and subtracting the discounts.

14. The system displays a summary of the order.

15. The customer verifies that the order is what they want.

16. The system schedules the order for fulfillment (see the use case Fulfill Order).

17. The system produces a receipt for the customer summarizing the order.

Figure 26.5   The basic course of action for placing an order.

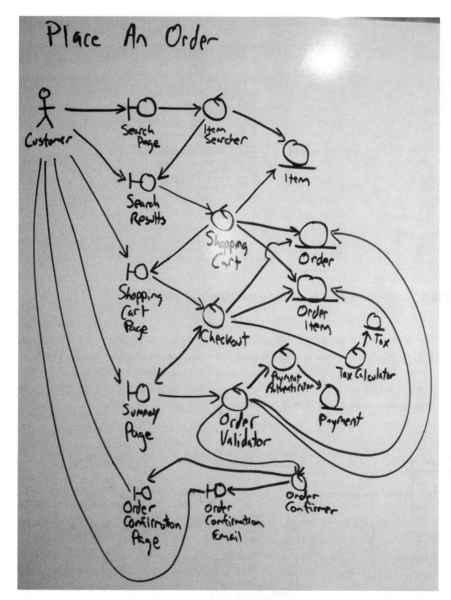

Figure 26.6   A robustness diagram for the Place Order use case.

Take a close look at the robustness diagram and the use case—they're not consistent. When we drew the robustness diagram we realized that we had forgotten to include steps to collect payment for the order. We quickly called over Wendy, our on-site project stakeholder who acts as our primary source of requirements, and verified that we do in fact need to charge for the things we sell. Yes, even though this is an obvious requirement that we really don't need to verify with our users, a fundamental concept of AM is that our project stakeholders are the only valid source of requirements, so we

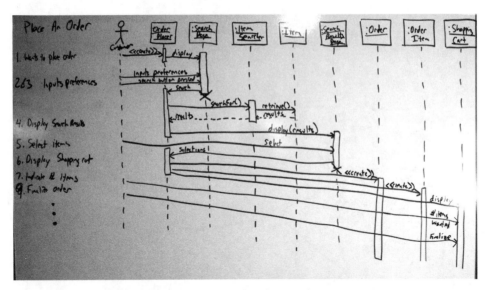

Figure 26.7   A UML sequence diagram for the Place Order use case.

have gotten in the habit of suggesting new requirements to Wendy no matter how obvious we feel the requirements are. Although we were working on an activity of the Analysis and Design discipline, in this case we quickly backtracked to the Requirements discipline to work on our use case. This happens a lot—UP/AM teams will commonly iterate back and forth between the various UP disciplines.

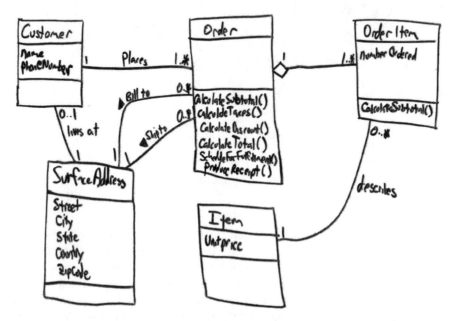

Figure 26.8   An analysis-level UML class diagram based on the Place Order use case.

Time to Update Our Use Case?

Should we update the use case logic? We're clearly missing an important requirement, collecting payments for orders. Furthermore, Figure 26.5 is still a business/essential use case because it doesn't reflect technology/implementation decisions yet. It would be reasonable to rework the use case to better describe what we're working on. We first baseline the original version of the use case via our chosen configuration management process, a procedure described by the Configuration and Change Management discipline. We have decided to maintain our use cases as official documentation; project stakeholders are interested enough in having a reasonable definition of the requirements to invest in the creation and maintenance of the use case diagram and use cases. The use case is also inconsistent with the user interface prototype for placing orders, depicted in Figure 26.9, indicating that we also need to calculate shipping and handling charges. This prototype was created in parallel to our efforts by other developers on our team, based on our essential UI prototype that we had created earlier and on

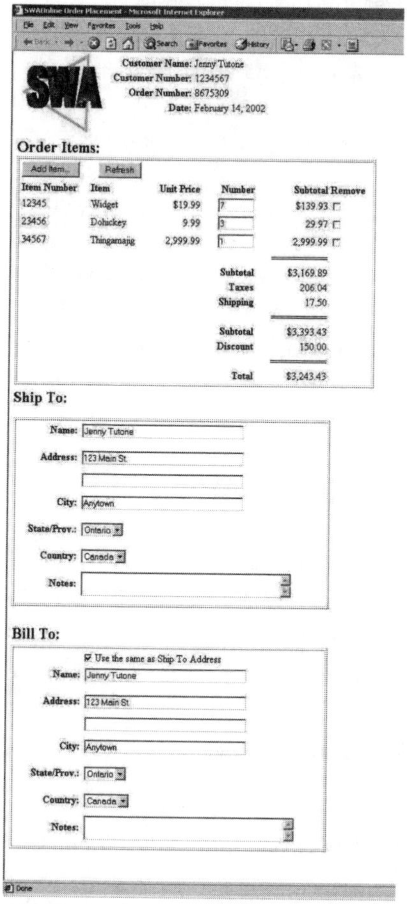

Figure 26.9   An HTML-based user interface prototype for placing orders.

1. The use case begins when a customer chooses to place an order.

2. The system displays the Shopping Cart Page for placing an order.

3. The customer searches for items via the use case "Search for Item(s)"

4. The customer adds an order item to their order. [Alternative Course: The Customer Removes an Order Item]

5. The customer indicates the number of a given item they wish to order.

6. The customer chooses to refresh the page.

7. The system calculates the subtotal for the item by multiplying the unit price by the number ordered.

8. The system redisplays the Shopping Cart Page.

9. The customer repeats steps 3 through 8 as necessary to build their order.

10. The customer finishes adding items to their order.

11. The customer provides their ship to and bill to information, including their name, phone number, and surface address.

12. The customer chooses to checkout. [Alternative Course: The Customer Chooses to Continue Shopping.]

13. The system calculates the subtotal for the entire order by adding the subtotals of the individual order items.

14. The system calculates the taxes applicable for the order according to the business rule *Calculate Taxes for an Order.*

15. The system calculates applicable discounts for the order according to the business rule *Calculate Discounts for an Order.*

16. The system calculates the shipping and handling charges for the order according to the business rule *Calculate Shipping and Handling Charges.*

17. The system calculates the grand total for the order by adding the applicable taxes to the order subtotal and subtracting the discounts.

18. The system displays the Summary page.

19. The customer verifies that the order is what they want.

20. The customer indicates how they wish to pay for the order. [Alternative Course: The Customer Chooses to Continue Shopping.]

21. The system confirms the payment. [Alternative Course: Payment Isn't Confirmed]

22. The system schedules the order for fulfillment (see the use case Fulfill Order).

23. The system displays the Order Confirmation Page.

24. The system generates and sends an order confirmation email to the customer.

Figure 26.10   The updated basic course of action for placing an order.

additional input from Wendy. It is clear that the practice *Update Only When It Hurts* is applicable in this case.

Figure 26.10 depicts the updated use case. Notice how it now references aspects of the user interface, indicating the HTML pages that customers use to place orders—as a result the use case is no longer technology independent. Had we chosen to implement this system using graphical user interface (GUI) technology such as Visual Basic or Java Swing the use case would very likely be worded differently to reflect the different way of working with that style of UI. Notice however that we're not bringing design-level considerations into the use case, for example we don't indicate that the OrderValidator class validates an order even though this is depicted in Figure 26.6. Also notice the addition of references to alternative courses, flows of logic for when things don't go perfectly, something that commonly occurs when evolving a business/essential use case into a system use case. We've also tightened up the language of the use case. For example, the original version used the terms "order item" and "line item" whereas the new one just uses "order item." This wasn't a big deal, but Wendy indicated that the proper term is order item so we made this minor change to avoid any confusion.

As we rewrite the use case we notice that there's a problem with the user interface prototype—there's no way for the customer to indicate that they wish to checkout. We realize that we need another button labeled "Checkout" that invokes the order confirmation process that is indicated in Figure 26.6. The practice *Create Several Models in Parallel* has served us well in this instance, enabling us to find an error in our work early on while it is still easy to fix.

There also isn't any sort of indication of the user's email address, which we need to send an order confirmation. This suggests two possibilities—instead of using a customer number to identify customers, as Figure 26.9 indicates, perhaps we should consider using email addresses instead. Email addresses uniquely identify a customer and they're something that the person is likely to remember. We suggest this idea to Wendy, our on-site project stakeholder, and she says that she likes it but will need to sleep on it before making a decision.

TIP **Expect to Find Problems with Your Requirements**
It is quite common to find problems in use case logic while you are creating use case realizations. One of the values of the practice Create Several Models in Parallel is that you often find such errors because you approach the same problem from different directions. Agile modelers view this as a form of model testing because you are validating the content of one model with that of another. Yes, you may still get it wrong in both models but as you have seen in this example it is possible to catch problems with your work.

Should we update Figure 26.6 since it is also out of sync? The diagram doesn't include the concept of calculating shipping and handling charges. In this case the answer is likely no. We aren't going to keep the robustness diagram much longer. In fact, we'll erase it once we've finished our design class modeling (see the next section) based on the information that it contains. We could decide to update the diagram with two extra bubbles, one for a controller/process class ShippingChargeCalculator and another for a ShippingCharge entity class, but it's fresh on our minds so we instead decide to put this information straight into our design class model. The robustness diagram has served its purpose so we follow the practice *Discard Temporary Models* and erase it from the whiteboard.

Time to Use a CASE Tool?

The Figures 26.6, 26.7, and 26.8 lead to an interesting issue—each of them provides a different view of the same information, with enough similarities between them to suggest the use of a CASE tool instead of whiteboard sketches. Agile modelers will often consider using CASE tools to create design-level diagrams, particularly when a CASE tool exists that is easy to work with and will also generate quality source code for the environment that they are working in. Luckily several CASE tools exist that support J2EE, the platform that SWA Online is being developed on, so this is an option.

> **TIP** **Sometimes a CASE Tool Is Simplest**
> The practice *Use The Simplest Tools* guides us to pick the simplest tool that will do the job. When the job is writing source code a CASE tool that generates quality code is simpler than using a programming tool that forces us to write that same code by hand.

We discuss our modeling experiences to date and decide that having the class diagram in a CASE tool makes a lot of sense because we can generate Java source code from it. Sequence diagrams are also likely candidates to be captured in the CASE tool because the tool will evolve our classes, and hence our class diagrams, to reflect the information captured in the sequence diagrams. However, we don't intend to keep the sequence diagrams as part of our official documentation so we decide to leave it up to the individual modelers—if they don't want to use the CASE tool for sequence diagrams that's fine, but they do need to use it to capture structural information about our software. We decide to continue drawing robustness diagrams by hand, we've found that they're useful as temporary analysis artifacts but not something that we want to maintain over time.

To ensure that we are effective using the CASE tool the team decides to reverse engineer our code regularly, as suggested in Chapter 10, "Using the Simplest Tools Possible?" to keep the class diagram in sync with our code. This decision in effect makes our CASE tool a primary development tool, not just a modeling tool. As an aside, a common trend for CASE tool vendors that support code generation is to also support integration of their tools with popular IDEs for that language.

Design Class Modeling

We realize that we've been investing a fair bit of time modeling, and very little coding, and that begins to worry us. The longer we go without feedback the greater the risk that what we're modeling isn't going to work well. Agile modelers believe in the principle *Rapid Feedback* and thus prefer to follow the practice *Prove It With Code*—they model a little, code a little, test a little, and then iterate. Thinking about it, we realize that our modeling efforts have had too great of a scope. By focusing on a fairly large use case, Place Order, we've bitten off a little more than we would normally prefer to chew. For example our robustness diagram indicates the need for eighteen different classes, and this is at an analysis level. At design these could easily become forty or fifty classes. A broad approach can work well at first when we're defining initial requirements, but when we get into detailed design we are much better off focusing on a small subset at a time. Therefore, we decide to shift gears a bit and focus our initial efforts on working with orders; the functionality concerning customers, payments, and addresses can be tackled later.

We begin to transcribe the analysis class diagram of Figure 26.11 into our CASE tool. Although it is a reasonably good analysis-level diagram it doesn't reflect our architectural approach based on domain components. Figure 26.3 indicates that we believe that we need an order component and Figure 26.4 indicates that we should introduce one or more EJB session beans to implement its public interface (the functionality that the component provides to external components and applications). Figure 26.11 depicts our design translation of the information captured by the analysis diagram to reflect our component strategy.

We introduced a session bean called OrderComponent to implement the public interface of the component, effectively implementing the Façade design pattern (Gamma, Helm, Johnson, and Vlissides 1995). This pattern advises you to introduce a class that routes method invocations to other classes that you do not want the outside world to access, reducing coupling within the overall system. As agile modelers we normally follow the practice *Apply Patterns Gently* and ease into the application of a pattern, although in this case Façade is a very simple one so we effectively eased completely into it right at the start.

Agile modelers prefer to follow the practice *Apply Modeling Standards*, which should include conventions for naming model elements such as classes. Because this component-based approach is a fundamental aspect of our architecture we would want to put a naming convention in place for these façade classes. We ask around and discover that we're the first to implement a domain component, in this case the Order component, so nobody else has considered a naming convention yet. Nobody has a problem with the convention of BusinessNameComponent, resulting in names such as OrderComponent and CustomerComponent. We also considered BusinessNameFacade as a convention but our fellow teammates preferred the first approach.

It isn't clear from our class diagram how the logic of operation of OrderComponent works. We can make an intelligent guess based on the names but that's about it. UML

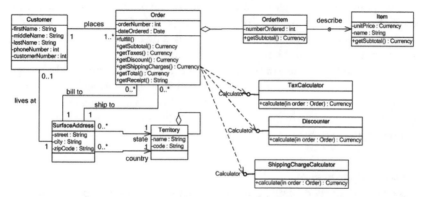

Figure 26.11 A design-level UML class diagram based on the Place Order use case.

class diagrams are very good at modeling the static structure of object-oriented software, or the depiction of classes and relationships between them, but not very good at modeling the dynamic nature, or the depiction of objects collaborating with one another to fulfill responsibilities. At some point we'll need to follow the practice *Apply The Right Artifact(s)* and explore the implementation of each of these operations. Likely candidates for doing so are source code, UML sequence diagrams, and UML collaboration diagrams. The choice of which artifact you'll use will depend on the complexity of each operation, the greater the complexity the more likely it is that you'll want to model before coding it, and your familiarity with each type of model.

OrderComponent has a dependency with Item because it interacts with instances of Item to search for them, invoking its EJB finder operations as appropriate. Finder operations? What finder operations? The finder operations are not shown in Figure 26.11 for two reasons:

1. **The CASE tool generates finders.** Because there is a standard way within EJB for implementing finder operations, they are something that our CASE tool can easily generate so we don't need to explicitly indicate them at first. It is quite common for tools to not show the code that they generate because you quickly get used to having it done for you so there's not reason to clutter your diagrams with this "common" information—agile modelers choose to *Depict Models Simply*. In addition to EJB finder operations, the CASE tool also generates remote interfaces, getter operations that provide access individual data attributes, setter operations that update individual data attributes, and the scaffolding code required to maintain associations between objects (Ambler 2001a).

2. **Finders are easy to code.** We've coded several finder operations in the past, and doing so again will be easy. Including the finder operations on our model won't be of much value. It's much easier to let the CASE tool generate what it cases, then update the code as we see fit, and then reverse-engineer our changes back into our model as Chapter 10 suggests.

Is the class diagram of Figure 26.11 good enough? That depends on why we're creating the model in the first place, as the principle *Model With A Purpose* implores. In this case our goal is to model enough so we can start coding. Having said that, it appears that we may have gone too far with our modeling efforts—we could have started by modeling the OrderComponent and Item classes and started coding based on that, focusing on the functionality to search for items (see Chapter 20, "Modeling During an XP Iteration: Searching for Items," for a discussion of doing exactly this on an XP project). Once that functionality was in place we could have returned to our class model and modeled the concept of an Order and OrderItem, programming and testing that functionality. Then we could have added the TaxCalculator, Discounter, and ShippingChargeCalculator one at a time. The approach that we've taken so far is much closer to a "big design up front" (BDUF) approach than we'd normally prefer, whereas the other approach that I just described is more in line with the practice *Model In Small Increments*.

TIP **Take Baby Steps at First**
This chapter has purposely deviated a bit from the more extreme approach to modeling described in Part Three of this book. I did this because I wanted to

show that there is a range of opportunity for applying the principles and practices of AM on software projects—you can take the highly iterative and programming-intensive approach typical of XP projects or the still iterative but more modeling-intensive approach described here. Many modelers who are familiar with a big modeling up front (BMUF) style of working will find the approach described in this chapter radical enough. As they become more comfortable with agile development they may decide to become more extreme over time.

Data Modeling

We decide to focus on implementing OrderComponent and Item at first. We use our CASE tool to generate the source code for us and we use that as our starting point. For now our goal is to implement and test the functionality for searching for items, the first step of which is to implement the finder method of the item class. This operation has to:

1. **Take a collection of parameters that represent the search criteria.** To do this we need to identify the parameters to the operation, something that we've already done with our UI prototyping work of Figure 26.12. From this sketch we know that the potential search criteria is currently the name of the item, the item number, the category that the item is in, a minimum price, and a maximum price. A customer may decide to specify one or more of these criteria.

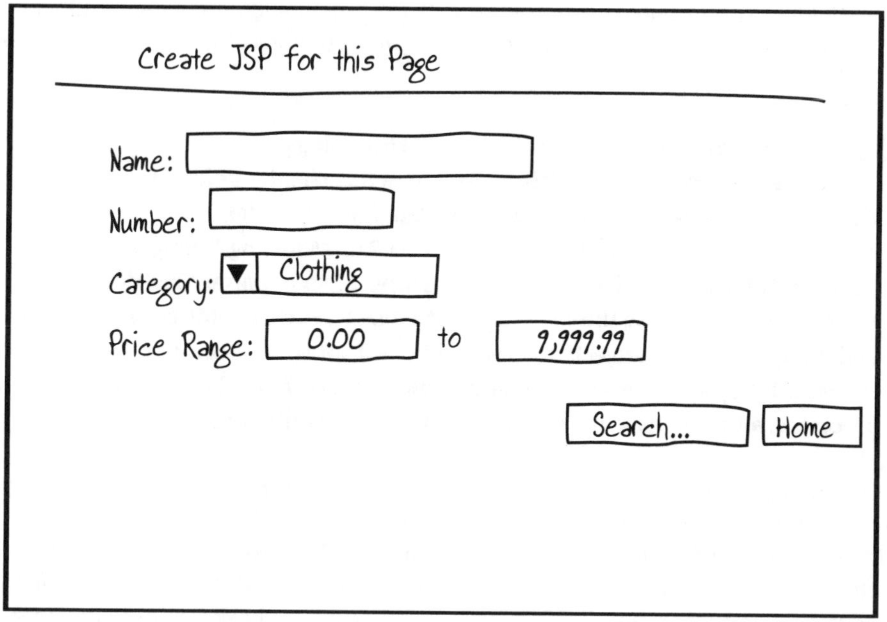

Figure 26.12 A hand-drawn sketch that represents what needs to be built for the item search page.

2. **Parse the criteria.** Parsing the search criteria is also easy, the only challenging part is to convert wildcard characters such as "*" to the SQL equivalents of "%", something we can do with a single-purpose class.

3. **Formulate a SQL SELECT statement representing the search criteria.** Because (for now) we've decided to take a bean managed persistence (BMP) approach instead of a container-managed persistence (CMP) approach, we need to write SQL code to interact with the database (Roman, Ambler, Jewell, and Marinescu 2002). To do this we need to map the individual search criteria attributes to columns within the database. The implication is that we need to know what the existing database schema is and update it if need be. We're implementing this system using a relational database to store our data, the schemas of which are typically modeled using physical data models. Figure 26.13 depicts our existing data model, using an unofficial UML-like notation (Ambler 2001a), which other members on our team have created using a data modeling CASE tool. Like our OO CASE tool that we're using to model our UML class diagram this tool generates, and reverse engineers, source code specific to our database including data definition language (DDL) to create the schema as well as triggers necessary to maintain referential integrity within the DB. As you can see the columns do in fact exist in the database already.

4. **Return the results of the search.** The response from the database, which may be an exception that needs to be handled, must be dealt with appropriately. Figure 26.11 indicates that the findItems() operation of OrderComponent returns an XML document, therefore we need to write the code to package the response in that format. To do this we decide to introduce two operations to Item, one to build an appropriate error message XML document and another to build an XML document containing one or more representations of items that match the criteria.

TIP **Many Artifacts Aren't Specific to a Methodology**

You've seen several of the models presented in this chapter before. For example, Figure 26.12 was used in Chapter 20 to explain how to model during an XP iteration and Figure 26.13 was used in Chapter 21, "Modeling During an XP Iteration: Totaling an Order," for the same purpose. An important insight is to recognize that you'll use the same types of artifacts, such as UML class diagrams and change cases, on projects following different software processes. Another insight is that you may even arrive at the same answer following different processes, although how you get to that answer may differ dramatically.

We implement the find functionality and begin testing it, only to discover that the response time is extremely variable. The problem is that it's possible to define very wide-ranging searches, for example if someone merely presses the search button the contents of the entire Item table are returned. This isn't good. We call over Brendan, the database administration (DBA) expert on the team, and ask for his help. He suggests two strategies. The first one is to first submit the query to the database and ask it to estimate the result size, if the estimation is too big then we simply return a message

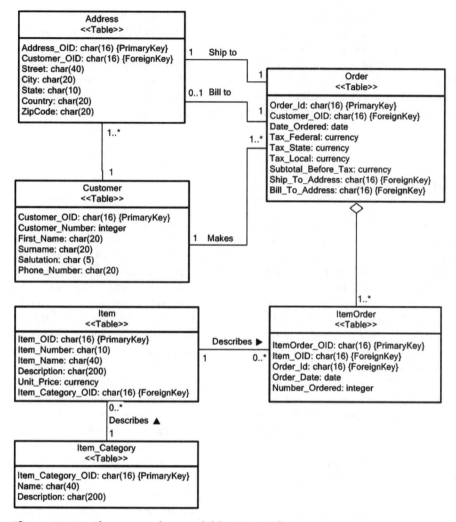

Figure 26.13 The current data model for SWA Online.

asking the customer to tighten up their criteria. Otherwise we submit the query to the database and return the results. The second approach is to work with database cursors, returning a block of 20 items at a time and allowing the customer to scroll up and down through the blocks as they see fit. This is more complicated as it requires us to handle scroll up and scroll down requests. More importantly, because our requirements do not specify what we should do, we need guidance from our project stakeholders. So, once again we iterate back to the Requirements discipline, explaining to Wendy what the issue is and what the options are. We quickly estimate the effort for each approach and ask her to decide, and she chooses to go with the cursor approach because it's more user friendly.

We rework our code to reflect this new approach, testing it as we work, and finally decide to commit our work to our version control system. Because we're following the practice *Collective Ownership* we want to update our shared artifact repository on a regular basis. This includes source code, any permanent models such as our class diagram and data model, and any permanent documentation that we've decided to maintain. Once we've resolved any conflicts, for example someone else may have also made changes to the Item class that we need to reconcile with our own work, we continue working on the Place Order use case. Your version control process is described by your instantiation of the Configuration and Change Management discipline (see Chapter 23).

Embracing Change

The next step is to write the code to build the shopping cart page for placing orders. In Figure 26.9 you can see that the current approach is to indicate the customer number at the top of the page. We had discussed this issue with Wendy a couple of days ago, suggesting the use of email address instead, and she had promised to consider it although we hadn't heard back from her yet. Once again we track down Wendy; she was working with a few other developers on the team so we had to wait until she was free to help us. While we waited for her we took a look at our existing models to identify potential changes that we needed to make. Regardless of Wendy's decision regarding using email addresses as unique customer IDs for customers we would still need to handle email addresses to support the functionality of emailing an order summary to the customer. The implication was that we may want to record the email address where the order summary was sent and we may even want to record a default email address for each customer to make their ordering process easier. Both of these decisions hinged on new requirements—if we're storing the email address for order summaries then we should do something with it and if we're maintaining a default email address for customers then our customer information editing page will need to include this functionality. More things to talk to Wendy about.

Wendy drops by to answer our questions. She agrees with our idea of having customers identify themselves using their email addresses but she still wants us to maintain a unique customer number for them. She wants to allow customers to change their email addresses over time; she recently changed her own email address and wants to make sure that our system is flexible enough to handle this change. She likes our idea of using the person's email address as the default to which to send the order summary although doesn't see a need to keep a record in the database of where the summary was sent.

These new requirements force the team to rework existing functionality that we had already worked on. As agile modelers we follow the principle *Embrace Change* so this isn't as frustrating to us as it would have been in the past. We realize that the initial logon page and the customer information page both need updating as do the corresponding EJBs. The Customer table in Figure 26.13 also needs to have an email address column added to it. This functionality then needs to be tested and placed under version control. Brendan offers to update the data model and to update the database schema for us and we decide to make the other changes. Luckily the code that generates the HTML pages and that performs the system logon is currently baselined so we check that out and get to work. Other team members are working on the Customer class so we ask them to let us know when it's available to work on; in the mean time we make a copy of the latest version and begin making our changes. A few hours later the new version of the Customer class, fully tested, becomes available so we check it out of version control and apply our changes to it. Once we're done we test our code and put it back into the version control system.

How Does This Work in Practice?

The principles and practices of AM are clearly applicable to your Analysis and Design discipline efforts, which shouldn't be a surprise considering the focus of this discipline is on modeling. However, you need to consciously decide to model in an agile manner, something that we may have slipped on a bit in this chapter. It happens to the best of us, which is why I choose to deviate a bit with the examples presented in this chapter. When you do find yourself modeling in a less-than-agile manner, as we did working on the use case realization, you want to stop yourself and ask why this has happened to learn from your experiences.

As you would imagine, feedback from implementers and testers is clearly important to your design effort, a concept that we focused on with the development of the design-level UML class diagram and data model. Both of these models are very close to your code, in fact many developers actively program using a combination of modeling CASE tool and IDE, so source code is often a good option when we want to *Iterate To Another Artifact(s)*. Developers that follow AM's *Rapid Feedback* principle as well as its *Prove it With Code* practice find that their design efforts become far more agile than their previous approach of creating more comprehensive models up front.

Not only should we be prepared to iterate to other artifacts, we should also be prepared to iterate to other disciplines. Several times we needed to "fall back" and work on requirements with one of our project stakeholders. This is to be expected because we're not going to get our requirements models perfectly right in the first place, and as work progresses we'll often discover that we need more information from our stakeholders. We also iterated several times into the C&CM discipline to baseline our work.

An important part of the Analysis and Design discipline is the identification and evolution of a working architecture for your system. This architecture must reflect the requirements for your system as well as the constraints placed on it by your organization's existing infrastructure. Furthermore, because agile modelers follow the practice *Reuse Existing Resources* you want to take advantage of the existing infrastructure in your modeling efforts within this discipline. One goal of the Infrastructure Management discipline, described in Chapter 27, "Agile Infrastructure Management," is to produce, support, and evolve enterprise architecture models that development teams within your organization can take advantage of.

Agile Infrastructure Management

Danger Will Robinson, Danger!

—Robbie the Robot

The Infrastructure Management discipline focuses on the activities required to develop, evolve, and support your organization's infrastructure artifacts, such as your organization/enterprise-wide models, your software processes, standards, guidelines, and your reusable artifacts. Your program management efforts, where you manage your portfolio of software projects, are also performed as part of this discipline. In short, infrastructure management is a cross-project effort.

Why is this discipline important to you as an agile modeler? Because in most large organizations you are very likely to have teams of professionals focused on various development support functions such as data administration, security administration, or software process support. The goal of these groups is to support reuse and consistency between development projects in order to reduce the overall costs to your organization for the systems that it develops and maintains. Your team will need to interact with these groups, ideally taking advantage of what they have to offer and minimally either conforming to their standards or finding a way to work around them. In this chapter we will discuss:

- Infrastructure models
- Infrastructure modeling
- Setting standards and guidelines
- Core infrastructure teams

■ Scaling AM with core architecture teams

■ How to make this work in the real world

WARNING **Infrastructure Management Often Becomes Very Non-Agile**
As you will learn in this chapter, it is possible to take an agile approach to
Infrastructure Management. However, most organizations that currently have a
process in place typically do so in a very non-agile manner, and most
organizations prefer to take a command-and-control approach to this discipline
instead of a guiding/mentoring approach. Be very careful because this
discipline treads on very dangerous grounds from the point of view of agility.

Infrastructure Models

There are three major models that your organization should develop to describe their
shared infrastructure:

1. **Enterprise requirements model.** This model reflects your organization's high-
   level requirements (Jacobson, Griss, and Jonsson 1997), and describes the
   services that your organization performs within its external environment. In an
   UP environment your best option is to develop a high-level use case diagram as
   the primary artifact, supported by high-level essential/business use cases that
   are technology-independent (and thus long lived), referencing other
   requirements artifacts such as critical business rules and constraint definitions.
   For example, I was once involved with developing an enterprise-requirements
   model that described the business of a large insurance company—a model
   comprised of less than 20 high-level use cases such as "Purchase Financial
   Instrument," "Make Claim," and "Verify Claim." This model, although clearly
   high-level, described the requirements sufficiently so that we could plan what
   systems needed to be developed and tie them directly back to the business of
   the organization. An interesting aspect of the model was that we believed it was
   long-lived. It described the insurance business of today, of 50 years ago, and
   potentially of 50 years from now. Even though the way that the insurance
   business is conducted has evolved over time, and continues to evolve, the
   fundamentals are still the same. Instead of a use-case–based approach, you may
   decide to use a Data Flow Diagram (DFD) as your main artifact, particularly if
   such a model is already in place.

2. **Domain architecture model.** This model depicts the high-level business
   structure of your systems that depicts the shared components or services
   available to your organization's business systems. This model indicates to
   development teams what domain functionality is available for reuse, and
   provides guidance as to how to architect their systems into the existing
   infrastructure so that other project teams may potentially reuse their work. In a
   component/object environment, a UML component diagram is often used that

depicts the large-scale, reusable domain components that are evolved over time by your project teams. These components, such as Order and Customer within SWA Enterprises, would be accessed by any application that needs the functionality that they provide. Although our focus so far has been on a single application, SWA Online, it is easy to see how the business components depicted in Figure 27.1 could potentially be applicable to other applications in the future. Yes, you'd need to include additional functionality required by those applications and you would likely need to refactor existing functionality, but there is clearly an opportunity for reuse here. More on this later. The individual components would in turn be described by other more detailed UML component diagrams or UML class diagrams (if modeled at all). If you're taking a data-oriented approach, then an enterprise data model is best suited for this. Ideally, this model should only show high-level data subject areas, the data equivalent of domain components, which in turn could be modeled (if at all) with detailed data models. Organizations that take a services-based approach would be best served by identifying categories of services, perhaps representing the categories as components or even more simply as a text list, potentially supported by a list of shared services.

3. **Technical architecture model.** This model depicts the high-level technical infrastructure that supports your business. Network diagrams are often used to depict your existing/legacy application, hardware, and network environment, although free-form diagrams are also common. Component/object-based approaches will often produce a high-level component diagram that shows technical infrastructure components for security, persistence, and audit control to name a few. Some organizations will indicate both their domain components and their technical infrastructure components on the same diagram, an approach taken in Figure 27.1. Services-based approaches, such as Web Services or legacy CICS environments, would once again model categories of services potentially supported by a list of shared services.

Infrastructure Modeling

Now let's consider the process of infrastructure modeling. Figure 27.2 depicts a high-level overview of relationships between organization/enterprise-level models and project-level models. The lines between each model represent "drives" or "affects" relationships. For example, the information contained in your enterprise requirements model can be used to drive or affect information in your project's requirements model, and vice versa (it's a two-headed arrow). Your enterprise requirements model has much greater breadth, that of your entire organization, than your project level requirements model, although far less detail. The enterprise model provides the overall context; the project-level model fills in the details. Considering your project-level design model, it is likely to take advantage of the functionality described by both your domain architecture model and your technical architecture model. Furthermore, as you explore the design of your system, you may feed back potentially reusable func-

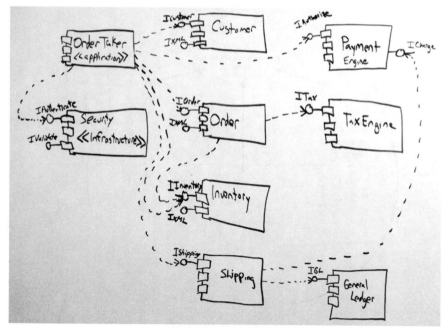

Figure 27.1 A UML component diagram for SWA Online.

tionality to the team(s) responsible for the architecture models. Let's consider the process implied by Figure 27.2 from both a top-down and bottom-up perspective.

Top-Down Modeling

Taking a top-down approach to development, you would start with the development of an enterprise requirements model that's then analyzed to formulate your domain and technical architecture models. The initial effort, infrastructure modeling, is a continual process, that can take anywhere from several days to several months, depending on how much detail you wish to go into. Once these models are in place, your organization will be in a position to understand what its mission is, as well as the architectural landscape to support those requirements.

Individual project teams enter and start by scoping out a portion of the enterprise requirements model, a goal of the Requirements discipline during the Inception phase, and typically choose small slices of the functionality implied by several enterprise-level use cases. The project team proceeds to work through the other UP disciplines as they usually would, the only difference being that they also provide feedback to the owners of the infrastructure models as appropriate to help evolve the models over time. Existing functionality should obviously be reused. Functionality identified in your models but that still remains unimplemented needs to be scheduled for development (work which would be developed by one or both of the project team and/or your infrastructure group). The previously unidentified functionality falls into one of three

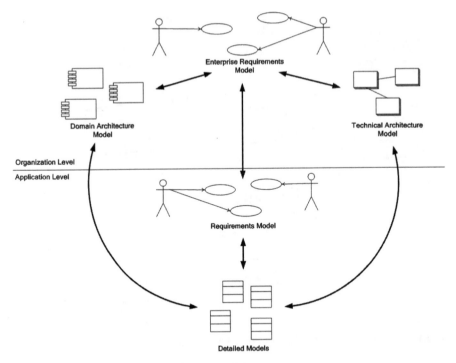

Figure 27.2 The infrastructure-driven modeling process.

categories: behavior that belongs at the enterprise level to be shared by several applications, behavior that belongs within a single business unit that is applicable to several applications in that business unit, or behavior that belongs within a single business and that is specific to a single application. Following a component approach, this behavior then needs to be added to either an enterprise-level domain component, a business-unit specific domain component, or to the specific application code respectively. Categorizing and scheduling this work is naturally a change-control activity of the Configuration and Change Management discipline. Development work can then proceed appropriately.

Bottom-Up Modeling

Following a bottom-up approach, your project team would iterate through each discipline appropriately, and at some point during the project someone would try to cull enterprise-level information from your team's efforts. Perhaps several of the components that your team develops can be evolved by other project teams to meet their specific needs. Better yet, your work could be harvested and reworked by specialized developers called "reuse engineers" and placed in a common repository available to all of your organization's developers. The domain architecture and technical architecture models could be evolved over time to depict the current resources available for reuse as well as your legacy infrastructure. The enterprise requirements model can also be developed by summarizing the information contained in the detailed require-ments models.

Comparing the Two Approaches

Which approach works best? The answer depends on your organization's culture, the resources available to you, and your desire to work towards a consistent enterprise vision. Table 27.1 compares the two approaches. Both of these approaches require sup-port from enterprise-level groups, discussed later in this chapter, so if your organiza-tion isn't willing to invest the necessary resources for such a group(s), then infrastructure modeling and related reuse efforts aren't a realistic option for you.

Setting Modeling Standards and Guidelines

An important aspect of the Infrastructure Management workflow is the creation, evo-lution, and support of corporate standards and guidelines. This is important to agile modelers because they follow the practice of *Reuse Existing Resources* and will adopt, and modify when appropriate, existing standards and guidelines applicable to the *Apply Modeling Standards* practice. The types of standards and guidelines that your organization may wish to support include but are not limited to:

- User interface design conventions
- Modeling guidelines
- Data/component/service naming standards
- Programming standards and guidelines

Once again, you may choose to take either a top-down or bottom-up approach to this aspect of the Infrastructure Management discipline, each of which has trade-offs similar to those listed in Table 27.1. My preferred strategy is that when I realize the need for standards, I will first try to identify existing industry standards and reuse those. With respect to modeling, the UML (Object Management Group 2001a) is a well-defined industry standard for the notation and semantics for object modeling. Stan-dards exist in practice for most procedural techniques such as data modeling and data flow diagrams (DFDs). A quick search on the Internet will lead to user interface design guidelines for most major computing platforms, even for the design of Web pages. When I can't find industry-recognized guidelines, my next step is to look for applica-ble documents on the Web that I can modify to meet my own needs. Worst case sce-nario is that I write the guidelines myself when I need to.

TIP **If You Write Guidelines Well, Developers Will Adopt Them**
A common problem that I see in many organizations are enterprise groups that have defined a set of standards and guidelines only to discover that development teams choose not to follow them. These groups will then futilely try to enforce these standards and guidelines through review-based quality

Table 27.1 Comparing the Two Approaches to Modeling

APPROACH	ADVANTAGES	DISADVANTAGES	ORGANIZATIONAL FIT
Top-Down Modeling	Ensures that a consistent enterprise vision exists. Models exist that agile modelers can use as input into their efforts (they *Reuse Existing Artifacts*).	Enterprise architectural models may not evolve with the times. Infrastructure models often used as a management mechanism to control development teams. Easily becomes non-agile when teams slip into a big modeling up front (BMUF) approach. Requires complex configuration management and development processes.	Culture permissive of hierarchical organizational structure. Enterprise-level group(s) exist that actively support and evolve the models.
Bottom-Up Modeling	Enterprise models reflect actual and current needs of developers. Components/functionality harvested for reuse is actually required (they are already in use in at least one application).	Enterprise models can easily become application-specific. Separate development teams that work in parallel may inadvertently develop the same functionality.	Culture is development-team–centric. Enterprise-level group(s) exist to harvest and refactor reusable items.

gates or by management edict. The most common result is it encourages animosity towards their group, often without increasing the adoption level of their guidelines. It doesn't have to be this way. For example, at www.ambysoft. com/javaCodingStandards.html I have a PDF document that describes Java coding conventions that you can download free of charge (at this page I also provide URLs to other coding standards pages, many of them for other languages). Developers are free to adopt these standards as they see fit. There has been over a quarter of a million downloads of the document and a large number of firms have purchased the rights to the source document, so I know it's being adopted. The advantages of this document are that it includes a summary of the conventions and, more importantly, it describes why the conventions are a good idea. Many developers will chaff at following a convention when it is presented at face value, but when the reasoning behind the convention is explained, they are much more likely to adopt it. My belief is that if you want to be successful at corporate standards, you should make them easy to use and the reasoning behind them clear.

Core Infrastructure Teams

The term Core Infrastructure Team (CIT) refers to any team with an enterprise-wide scope whose mission is to support development teams. Examples of CITs include data administration teams, security administration teams, process-support groups, and reuse engineering teams. Some organizations have a single CIT responsible for all aspects of the Infrastructure Management discipline, whereas others will have teams specializing in one or two activities. CITs will develop, maintain, and support infrastructure artifacts such as the infrastructure models discussed in this chapter—corporate standards and guidelines, and reusable artifacts. It's possible for CITs to be agile, unfortunately many existing CITs are not. This has given the concept a bad image within the development community.

Let's examine two ways that you may choose to implement CITs, starting with an approach that is not very agile and then one that is. Naturally your organization will be somewhere between these two extremes if it chooses to implement CITs at all. The least agile approach is based on the concept that CITs are corporate quality gates through which all systems must pass. These CITs will mandate the standards, guidelines, and infrastructure models that development teams must conform to and then will focus their efforts on formal reviews to verify that the development teams have done so. They are also given the authority to stop projects from proceeding to their next project phase, such as release of your system into production, until the project teams meet corporate standards. CIT members are often perceived as being a cut above the rest of your organization's development staff and your only hope to prevent the chaos that would result if development teams were to be set loose on their own. The advantage of this approach is that it requires a minimal number of people to make it work because the CITs only set the enterprise approach and then verify that they are followed. The main disadvantage is that the relationship between the CITs and development teams is often strained due to the adversarial nature of this approach. The CITs view the developers as being lower-skilled than they are (often a self-fulfilling prophecy) and as people that cannot be trusted. The ill will often goes both ways, with the development teams perceiving the CITs as out-of-touch bureaucrats who stand in the way of progress. Dysfunctional politics are very common in these situations.

Luckily, CITs can be agile. First and foremost, agile CITs are customer-oriented support groups to the development teams. The CITs may initiate a new standard within your organization, or initiate work on a model, but will seek feedback regarding their work by applying it on a development project. The main function of CIT members is as active participants on development teams. They are simply another type of project stakeholder from the point of view of the development team and therefore follow the practice *Active Stakeholder Participation*. CIT members work closely with their immediate customers, primarily developers, although CITs have non-developer stakeholders as well, to provide needed support. For example, a CIT specializing in data administration would loan a database administrator (DBA) to your development team. The DBA would not only help you to evolve your data models but they would also ensure that your team follows your organzation's data-naming conventions and development standards. Similarly, a CIT responsible for evolving your technical architecture would provide guidance to your development team regarding what computing facilities exist within your organization, and actively helps you to work with and even evolve those facilities. The advantages of this approach are:

- Your corporate infrastructure, including standards, guidelines, models, and reusable assets, is evolved as part of your project efforts, ensuring that they meet your actual needs.

- The relationship between developers and CIT members is much more positive, increasing the chance that developers will actually take advantage of your corporate infrastructure and will conform to your corporate standards.

- Reviews to ensure conformance to standards are minimized, if not removed entirely, because the CIT members working with your team are responsible for that effort.

The main disadvantage of this approach is that it is difficult to achieve. Critical issues that you need to overcome include:

- This approach requires a high level of trust within your IT department. CIT members must trust developers to do the right thing and developers must trust that the advice provided by CIT members reflects what is best for your organization and therefore should be followed. Furthermore, project stakeholders must trust that CIT members and developers can work together effectively to find a way to meet both immediate project needs as well as corporate needs.

- CIT members need the skills required to help project teams, including both hard technical skills as well as soft people and communication skills. Unfortunately, these are the exact skills required of highly paid consultants, which makes sense, because CIT members are in effect internal consultants to project teams, implying that CIT members must be well compensated if you wish to retain them as employees.

- CIT members still need to look at the bigger picture to ensure that the long-term needs of your organization are identified and met. The implication is that they need to meet on a regular basis to consolidate their work. This can be difficult because project teams soon come to rely on them. Schemes where individual CIT members are assigned to a project X percent of the time but are expected to focus on enterprise issues (100-X) percent of the time often devolve into the CIT member working 100 percent of the time on the project and a little bit of overtime on their enterprise responsibilities.

- It is very difficult for existing, non-agile cultures to adopt this approach. They often can't even conceive that this will work, which makes sense, because in their current situation it often won't. I have seen an agile approach to CITs work in an organization involving several hundred people, an organization where a culture of trust and teamwork had been grown since its founding. Existing organizations, particularly those with thousands of developers, must be prepared to evolve their cultures slowly over time to where it is possible for CITs and developers to work together effectively.

Scaling AM with Core Architecture Teams

A similar concept to CITs is Core Architecture Teams (CATs) that support the efforts of mid- and large-size project teams of 20 or more developers. A CAT is specific to a single project, its goal is to identify, evolve, and support an architecture for your project. Your core architecture team should be comprised of developers experienced in the technologies that your organization is working with and have the ability to work on architecture spikes to explore new technologies. They should also have a good understanding of the business domain and have the necessary skills to communicate the architecture to developers and to other project stakeholders.

To organize an effective CAT at the beginning of a large project, you should identify your most experienced developers and abstract thinkers, as well as a few people that you want to see get some architectural experience, and invite them to be members of your CAT. You should do this for two reasons. First, you want good people on this team. Second, when you organize the large project team into smaller subteams, each focusing on developing one or more subsystems, you want to ensure that each subteam includes one or two members of the core architecture team. This helps to increase the chance that each subteam learns and follows the architecture as well as increases the chance that the core architecture team will not ignore portions of the system. Furthermore, it ensures that each subteam has some senior people on it.

The core architecture team is responsible for identifying the initial architecture and then bringing it to the rest of the project team for feedback and subsequent evolution. Similar to agile CIT members, your CAT members will take active roles on the various subteams on the project, communicating the architecture to the subteams and working with them to prove portions of the architecture via concrete experiments. A CAT will work along the same lines as depicted in Figure 27.2, the difference being that the scope of the models on the top part of the diagram are for the project as a whole and the scope of the models on the bottom half are for individual subteams.

The CAT will find that they need to meet occasionally to evolve the architecture as the project progresses, negotiating changes to the architecture and updating their architectural model(s) as appropriate. These architecture-modeling sessions will be frequent at the beginning of a project and needed less and less as the architecture solidifies. It will be common for members of the development subteams, who may not be members of the core architecture team, to attend some architecture modeling sessions to present information. Perhaps they were involved with some technical prototyping and have findings to share with the architects. As you saw in Chapter 13, "Agile Modeling Sessions," the best modeling sessions are short, often no more than half an hour in length, and are typically held standing up around a whiteboard. Everyone should come prepared to the sessions, willing to present and discuss their issues as well as to work together as a team to quickly come to resolutions. Having said that, at the beginning of the project you may decide to have longer architectural modeling sessions, on the order of a day or two, to help you to define your initial candidate architecture.

How to Make This Work in the Real World

I'd like to leave you with a few words of advice to help increase your effectiveness adopting the techniques of the Infrastructure Management discipline:

1. **Recognize that it is very difficult to make this discipline work effectively.** First and foremost, your organization needs to be realistic. If you are having difficulties being successful at individual development projects, attempting to succeed at supporting collections of projects is likely unrealistic. The Infrastructure Management discipline is appropriate for organizations that are reasonably adept at software development projects (yes, they are likely to still have some hiccups), and are now looking for further productivity increases.

2. **Keep it simple.**

3. **Don't blur roles between enterprise teams and development teams.** Although CIT members actively work on project teams, and may be on loan to those teams for a period of time, they are still part of the CIT and have responsibilities beyond those of the single project.

4. **Keep it simple.**

5. **Educate, educate, educate.** Developers need to understand that their work must reflect and support your organization's infrastructure and environment. Project stakeholders must recognize that the needs of the overall enterprise may have greater priority over their personal preferences. CIT members must understand that their role is to support and guide project team efforts, not to control them.

6. **Keep it simple.**

7. **Recognize that you likely need to change.** If your existing Infrastructure Management efforts are not working well, if your CITs and developers are not working together effectively, then you should consider taking a new approach. This new approach will likely require a culture change for everyone involved, something that will take time and effort.

8. **Keep it simple.**

CHAPTER 28

Adopting AM on an UP Project

In this chapter, I explore the issues that surround the adoption of Agile Modeling principles and practices on a Unified Process (UP) project (Jacobson, Booch, & Rumbaugh 1999; Kruchten 2000; Ambler 2001b). The issues addressed in this chapter are specific to organizations that have adopted the UP, whereas Chapter 29 addresses strategies for overcoming general adversities that are pertinent beyond UP efforts.

An UP/AM project team will need to overcome the common misconceptions that developers have about the UP as well as several cultural barriers that are common within organizations that instantiate the UP. Strategies that are likely to help you to do this include:

1. **Avoid the term *use-case driven.*** Yes, it's a wonderful marketing term but the reality is that use cases aren't sufficient to drive much of anything. Use cases are a good technique to document behavioral requirements but that's only a small part of the functional requirements picture and an even smaller part of the total requirements picture. They aren't very good at documenting business rules, user interface requirements, constraints, or non-functional requirements, which is why the UP includes something called a supplementary specification to contain all of these other things. Requirements drive things, use cases don't. Your modeling efforts will always remain hobbled if you don't separate the UP's software-engineering wheat from its marketing-rhetoric chaff.

2. **Recognize that there are more modeling artifacts than those described by the UML.** AM's principle *Multiple Models* tells you that you have many modeling

artifacts at your disposal—change cases, user stories, business rules, UML Activity diagrams, UML Class diagrams, data models, and external interface specifications—to name a few (these artifacts and more are described in Appendix A of this book). An interesting implication of this principle is that you have far more than just the UML diagrams at your disposal, a topic discussed in detail in Chapter 15, "The UML and Beyond." The good news is that the UP recognizes that a wide range of models is needed to explore the complexities of modern software. Recent versions do in fact include data modeling and user interface design activities that are currently outside the scope of the UML. (At the time of this writing v1.4 of the UML is the current standard.) The bad news is that many people erroneously perceive that the UP is simply a process for using the UML.

3. **Recognize that the UP is not inherently documentation centric.** The UP is actually very clear that you should only develop the artifacts that you actually need. However, this good message is something that often gets missed by many software professionals. It is something worth repeating here. You should question every single model that the UP suggests creating because it purposely describes a wide variety of artifacts, many of which your project simply doesn't need. The UP includes three major sets of modeling-oriented artifacts: the business modeling set, the requirements set, and the analysis and design set. Each of these sets in turn is composed of several detailed artifacts. For example, the business modeling set includes a business use-case model, business rules, a business architecture document, and a business supplementary specification. Do you actually need all of these things? Likely not. If you do need them, do you need them as formal documentation? Likely not. Communicate AM's *Travel Light* and *Model With a Purpose* principles to your project stakeholders, as well as the practices *Update Only When It Hurts* and *Discard Temporary Models*.

4. **Build a common process vision between developers and project stakeholders.** Managers often lean toward a prescriptive software process, something that appears well defined and comprehensive such as the UP, one with a perceived focus on control. Developers, on the other hand, gravitate towards agile techniques such as eXtreme Programming (XP) (Beck 2000) and AM due to their perceived focus on what's important to developers: building software. Because management holds the purse strings, many developers find themselves in a situation where their managers have chosen to adopt the UP and are now required to follow it. Luckily the UP is flexible enough so that it can be tailored to be reasonably agile, but to do so, developers and project stakeholders need to come to an agreement as to the extent of the tailoring.

5. **Actively promote iterative and incremental development.** AM's practices of *Model in Small Increments*, *Iterate to Another Artifact*, and *Create Models in Parallel* can be tough ones for experienced modelers to adopt. In addition, chances are that your experienced modelers are already chaffing at the UP's concepts of iterations, let alone an even greater emphasis on iterative and incremental modeling. Traditional modeling techniques often promote a single-artifact approach, such as use-case modeling or user-interface prototyping sessions. Also, they often promoted a Big Design Up Front (BDUF), or more accurately Big Modeling Up Front (BMUF), approach where you modeled everything in

detail before you started coding. These concepts were great in theory, focusing on a single artifact at a time should have allowed the modelers to get it right quickly, but unfortunately practice shows this not to be the case. A good way to ease into these practices is instead of use-case modeling sessions, run requirements modeling sessions where you work on use cases, CRC cards, business rules, and user-interface prototypes simultaneously. Similarly, hold analysis sessions where you are use case modeling, sequence diagramming, user interface prototyping, and class modeling. Include design sessions where you are class modeling, state chart modeling, data modeling, component modeling, user interface prototyping, and hopefully even developing business code. Once you are comfortable with these practices, the next step is to then merge your modeling efforts in with your implementation efforts and apply multiple artifacts including all of your potential models, source code, and test cases as needed-truly iterative development. While you do this, keep their focus on the requirements that you implement in the current iteration, resulting in an incremental delivery of functionality each iteration.

6. **Actively promote simplicity.** *Simplicity* is a fundamental value of AM, one that motivates several critical principles that can dramatically improve the effectiveness of your modeling efforts. Many experienced modelers want to specify everything that they possibly can. For example, not only do they wish to model the overall structure of their software in UML Class diagrams, they also want to specify the scaffolding code needed to implement that structure. This is a lot of effort that provides very little actual value. A better approach is to create a Class diagram that is just barely good enough for your purpose, to depict the likely structure of your classes, and then to start coding from there. Agile modelers assume that the programmers, often themselves, can figure out the details at the time and instead will focus on issues that may not be so obvious. This approach implies less work for the modeler and less modeling noise for the actual programmer to wade through. When an agile modeler creates a class diagram they realize that they don't need to model all of the classes required to build the software, instead they focus on getting the core classes right and assume that the programmers are competent enough to handle the rest.* By keeping your models simple you are likely to work faster while at the same time creating something that is actually of value to your programmers—models that focus on critical issues and are devoid of fluff.

7. **Staff projects with skilled generalists.** Many organizations have separate positions for modelers, motivating their staff to focus on specialties, a practice that in my experience reduces your ability to be agile. Although the UP is very clear that individual developers can and should take multiple roles on a project,

---

*If this isn't the case then you have a serious human resources issue that you need to deal with appropriately. Excessively complex models aren't going to help address this situation in practice, and their creation will help management avoid making the hard decisions regarding the quality of their staff.

my experience has been that this is advice that falls on deaf ears within many organizations. Instead what happens is that organizations that adopt the UP tend to introduce positions along the lines of UP's modeling roles such as Requirements Specifier, System Analyst, User-Interface Designer, and Database Designer and slot people into individual roles, going against the advice of both AM and the UP. If your only job on a software project is to produce models then there is a tendency for you to over model things, first because you naturally want to do a good job and second because if it's your job to model then that means it's likely someone else's job *not* to model (for example, their job is to program). Because there is a hand-off there is now greater motivation to add more detail into your model; details that likely wouldn't be needed if the people writing the code also developed the models that helped them to identify what needed to be coded in the first place.

8. **Live AM's principle of *Open and Honest Communication*.** I've run into several situations where a development team was reluctant to follow the *Display Models Publicly* practice, one way to promote open and honest communication with people external to your team, often because they were afraid of what another political faction within the organization would do with the information. However, when they finally worked up the courage to display their models publicly they quickly discovered that the politicos they were so afraid of couldn't find much to criticize. If they did criticize, it provided valuable input that the developers quickly acted on and benefited from.

Something that is important to understand is that for AM to be successful the culture of your organization must be open to the concepts, values, and principles of agile software development. The problem is that the UP is often adopted by organizations that either implicitly or explicitly do not accept the values of agile software development. Their focus is often on following processes and using tools. The RUP product (Rational Corporation 2001) clearly defines many processes and describes how to apply Rational's tools effectively on software projects, and therefore the RUP is clearly attractive to them. Unfortunately this goes against the agile value of preferring individuals and interactions over processes and tools. When the culture of an organization is documentation centric they may find the UP appealing because you can instantiate it in such a way as to result in the creation of significant amounts of documentation (you can also instantiate it to result in very little documentation. Remember, the UP is flexible). If an organization is documentation centric then this aspect of its culture goes against agile software development's value of preferring working software over comprehensive documentation. This organization may still successfully adopt, tailor, and instantiate the UP but be unable to follow many of AM's principles and practices effectively because it does not have an agile culture (see Chapter 1, "Introduction," for a discussion of when adoption of AM makes sense). My point is that how well AM and UP fit together in your organization *depends largely on your organization's culture* and not so much on the UP itself. You can easily use the techniques of AM to improve your UP modeling efforts, but to be effective you will find that you need to overcome cultural challenges within your organization.

How Does This Work?

You have seen in this part of the book that it is clearly possible to tailor the Unified Process with the practices of Agile Modeling. To succeed, your organization's culture must be receptive to both the UP and to AM, and therein lies the rub—the goal of organizations that adopt the UP is often to instantiate it as a fairly rigid and prescriptive process, whereas organizations that adopt AM typically want to work in a more fluid manner. In fact, to be truly effective, AM requires such an environment. Luckily the UP is flexible enough so that it can be instantiated to be reasonably agile, as Robert Martin (2001), Gary Evans (2001), and Craig Larman (2002) show with their instantiations of the UP. When this is the case, when you have instantiated a light-weight version of the UP, then the UP and AM fit together well. Both the UP and AM are based on the idea that the majority of software is best delivered iteratively and incrementally. Because the UP explicitly includes modeling disciplines it is very easy to identify where AM practices should be used to enhance your own tailoring of the UP. This works when your project team and your project stakeholders choose to make it work.

PART

Five

Looking Ahead

This part describes important organizational and management issues that pertain to Agile Modeling. This section includes the following chapters:

- **Chapter 29: Adopting Agile Modeling or Overcoming Adversity.** This chapter discusses proven ways to bring the AM methodology into your organization. It presents a straightforward approach for organizations that already have an agile mindset, as well as strategies for overcoming common challenges that you may experience.

- **Chapter 30: Conclusion: Choose to Succeed.** This chapter looks at AM from a manager's perspective and examines how AM can help your organization. I also recap with a quick retrospective of the methodology as a whole.

CHAPTER 29

Adopting Agile Modeling or Overcoming Adversity

Do, or do not. There is no try.

—Yoda

If you've read this far in the book, then you are likely interested in adopting Agile Modeling within your organization. This chapter presents the strategies for doing exactly that. As a consultant who specializes in helping organizations to improve their internal software processes, and just as important, aiding my co-workers in doing the same for the clients they work for, I've been lucky enough (or unfortunate enough, depending on your point of view) to gain a reasonably broad range of experience with software process improvement (SPI). Recently, much of this experience has been in helping organizations adopt the principles and practices of AM, as well as the enhancements of the Enterprise Unified Process (Ambler 2001b), and before that, in my collecting of process patterns (Ambler 1998; Ambler 1999). At the same time, I've been active in Internet newsgroups and mailing lists, providing people with advice as well as simply observing the problems that people have adopting other methodologies such as the Rational Unified Process (Kruchten 2000; Rational Corporation 2001) and eXtreme Programming (Beck 2000). My goal in this chapter is to aid your efforts in successfully adopting AM by sharing my experiences with you, as well as to help you to avoid the problems and misunderstandings that people seem to run into with other methodologies.

This chapter is organized into the following sections:

- Evaluate the fit
- Keep it simple
- Overcome organizational and cultural challenges

- Overcome project-related challenges
- Consider alternatives to full adoption of AM
- How to make this work in practice

Evaluate the Fit

In this section my basic assumption is that your organization is capable of making decisions in a sensible and coherent manner, and is willing to consider and try new techniques based on their merit. Wait! Don't skip to the next section; there actually is some good material in this section, even if your organization suffers from some of the common adversities that I describe later in this chapter. My experience has been that you need to do two fundamental things to adopt AM successfully. First, you must determine whether AM makes sense for your situation, and that means you need to recognize when AM will and will not work for you. Second, you must decide to keep your adoption efforts as simple as possible—if you make it hard to adopt AM, then you very likely will fail at the effort. If you are unable to adopt AM successfully, at least not yet, I argue that you may want to consider alternatives to full adoption.

Recognize when Agile Modeling Can Work for You

AM isn't going to work for everybody; it isn't a panacea that works in every situation. Nor is it guaranteed to work even in situations where conditions are perfect. You can still make mistakes implementing AM within your organization. Having said that, my experience has been that AM has the potential to be very effective when the following factors hold true:

You take an agile approach to software development. AM isn't a complete methodology, as you saw in Chapter 1, "Introduction." The assumption is that it will be applied within the scope of another process such as XP or an instantiation of the Unified Process (UP) (Jacobson, Booch, and Rumbaugh 1999). For this to work successfully, there must be a conceptual fit between AM and this other process, otherwise you will be forced to hobble one or more of AM's techniques and therefore not truly be doing AM. Part 3 of this book explored how AM can be used with XP and Part 4 explored how to use AM with agile instantiations of the UP.

You are willing to adopt the core principles and practices of AM. For you to truly claim to be doing AM, you must minimally adopt the core principles (Chapter 3, "Core Principles") and core practices (Chapter 5, "Core Practices") of AM. Yes, you can still benefit from adopting only some of AM's principles and practices. However, you will not achieve the synergy inherent in full AM adoption (see Chapter 7, "Order from Chaos: How the AM Practices Fit Together") and could potentially put your modeling efforts at risk because your adopted practices do not have the support they require from the missing practices.

You work iteratively and incrementally. The AM value *Communication*, and in particular, its principle *Rapid Feedback*, both require an iterative and incremental approach to software development to work.

You face uncertain or volatile requirements. Martin Fowler (2001a) points out that if your project is exploratory in nature, and many are, then it is very likely that an agile approach to development is the best fit. When your requirements aren't certain, or are actively changing, then you need to follow a software process that reflects this fact. AM deals with changing requirements by embracing change, by promoting an incremental approach to development, by seeking rapid feedback, and by insisting on active participation from project stakeholders so that the requirements may be quickly and effectively explored. Note that AM still works in environments where your requirements are not volatile, although a more document-centric approach may be preferable in this case.

Your primary goal is to develop software. This is one of AM's core principles (Chapter 3), something that is not always the case for many projects. For example, sometimes a project team's primary goal is to make money from your customers (often the case in outsourcing, contracting, and consulting situations) or simply to specify the system so it can be given to another team to implement. Even worse, some development efforts are simply a political exercise with no intention of delivering anything more than a perception that something is being done. The goal of software development should be to produce systems that meet the needs of their users in an effective manner. If you are doing anything less, then AM is not for you.

You must have active stakeholder support and involvement. Fowler (2001a) also believes that for agile software development efforts to be successful, you should have the active support and involvement of your project stakeholders. As I've discussed throughout this book, a project stakeholder is anyone potentially affected by the development and/or deployment of a software project. This includes direct users, indirect users, managers, senior managers, operations staff members, support (help desk) staff members, testers, developers working on other systems that integrate or interact with this one, and maintenance professionals. To be successful with AM you need to know who your project stakeholders are, you must have access to stakeholders on a daily basis who are able to provide information and make decisions in a timely manner, and have full management support for your project. Full management support implies having sufficient resources, including but not limited to work space (see Chapter 11, "Agile Work Areas"), equipment, and staff (see Chapter 12, "Agile Modeling Teams").

Your development team has authority commensurate with your responsibilities. Agile software development, and Agile Modeling is particular, is new to most organizations. Adopting agile approaches will be difficult at best for many organizations because it is a significantly new way to work for most people. To be successful, my experience is that project teams must be given the opportunity to succeed or fail on their own merits. They must be in a position to try new techniques and be given the resources, including time, to let them run their course. Ideally, your organizational environment must have minimal politics, more on this later, implying that both senior management and other groups within your organization need to get out of your way whenever appropriate.

You require responsible and motivated developers. Fowler (2001a) points out that agile software development requires developers that have the discipline to work together to develop quality software. The implication is that you need a healthy team environment, one in which people trust one another and help each other to succeed. Contrary to what many of the detractors of agile development will tell you, my experience is that you don't need people that can walk on water—you simply need people who want to get the job done and who have the ability to work with others effectively. By including teams of these kinds of people, you increase the chance that your organization will give your team the opportunity to be in control of its own destiny. Agile modeling teams are discussed in Chapter 12.

You have someone willing to champion AM within your organization. Whenever you adopt something new, there will always be challenges. People don't like to change; they are often happy working in the non-agile way that they are used to. Others see things differently than you, or simply don't recognize the problems that you are trying to address by adopting AM. Perhaps they are promoting their own pet approaches to development, approaches that don't fit well with AM. Perhaps AM threatens the current power structure within your organization. Regardless of the situation, there will always be people who will fight change. To be successful at change someone must exist that champions the new cause, in this case adoption of AM, someone willing to garner support of project stakeholders and to protect and nurture AM efforts as they take root within your organization. Change takes time, and champions buy you that time.

You have adequate resources available to you. You will see that agile modeling requires people to work together closely. The implication is that you need "co-location space(s)," such as a dedicated modeling room, to work in, a public wall to display your models on, and ideally, even shared workstations for pair development efforts. Furthermore, you need access to modeling tools such as whiteboards, index cards, markers, and CASE tools as necessary. I've seen the lack of basic resources such as decent chairs, tables, food, drink, and top-notch workstations dramatically hamper software development efforts. If your project team is being nickel-and-dimed to death, then I have to question if your project is important to your organization—if it isn't, cancel it now and invest your efforts on something more productive. This includes environments where people are forced to wait for system administration to set up their working environment. I once worked on an eight-week contract where it would have taken six weeks from the first day I physically arrived on site to have my workstation fully configured, the normal time it took for full-time employees.

Recognize when Agile Modeling Won't Work for You

I suspect that you are likely to run into trouble with Agile Modeling in the following situations:

1. One or more of the factors listed in the previous section is missing.

2. Your organizational culture is geared towards prescriptive processes. There are many organizations that simply aren't interested in taking an agile approach to software development. These organizations are happy with the status quo and that's fine by them. This likely includes organizations such as Government agencies, large established firms (some banks, insurance companies, telecommunications firms, and so on), and consulting firms that specialize in serving these organizations. This isn't to say that it's impossible to adopt AM in these organizations, but it is likely that an extraordinary effort such as an off-site/skunkworks effort will be required to be successful.

3. You have a large and/or distributed team. Agile modeling works very well on teams that are co-located in the same work area, particularly when the developers are co-located in a shared work room (often called a "tiger team" room). You can attempt to apply AM on large or distributed teams, but you will find that communication challenges quickly get in the way. This problem is addressed later in this chapter.

I would also be leery of applying agile modeling to develop life-critical systems, such as an air traffic control system or patient-monitoring system, simply because I don't work on such projects and have no insights into how well AM will work on these. That doesn't imply that AM won't work, but I suspect that the documentation needs of these types of projects will motivate you to take a less agile approach than AM would prefer (and there's nothing wrong with that). Similarly, I don't work on embedded software and therefore have never had a chance to apply AM techniques on these types of projects. I highly suspect that AM is applicable to embedded software development, but this is just speculation at the moment. I look forward to hearing about your experiences in these situations on the Agile Modeling mailing list (visit www.agilemodeling.com/feedback.htm for details).

Keep It Simple

So what do you do when your situation isn't ideal? Less-than-ideal environments are the norm from what I can tell, having personally never seen an ideal situation yet. My advice is to focus on keeping things as simple as possible—live the principles and practices of AM as best you can. A good start is to educate people in AM, including both developers and project stakeholders, perhaps by sharing this book with them or by giving a short overview presentation. Start talking with them, working together to determine where AM (or a subset thereof) might fit in well. You don't need to create a formal software-process engineering group (SEPG), also known as a process improvement group (PIG), when a couple of reasonable discussions over a beer or two will suffice.

Second, recognize that the decision to adopt AM (or any other process) is a difficult one to make. You need to have courage to change your environment,* and to do this

---

*As Ron Jeffries likes to say, "Change your organization or change your organization."

you must garner support from your project stakeholders, in particular, senior management. Identify a problem that is critical to their success, such as developing high-quality software quickly that meets their needs, and show that AM can help to address this problem. You need to convince them that there are better ways to work; ask them to give you a chance to prove it to them.

Overcome Organizational and Cultural Challenges

When you introduce AM into your organization, there are several very common organizational and cultural challenges that you may run into. These challenges are:

- Skeptical developers
- Overzealous process police
- Paper pushers with power
- Cookbook philosophy
- Inability to accept blame
- Excessive documentation due to fear of losing everyone

Skeptical Developers

Many people are skeptical of new techniques, and as far as I'm concerned, this is a very good thing because a little bit of skepticism is healthy. However, too much skepticism will often hinder your ability as a software professional. Here are some of the more common issues that skeptics will raise regarding AM, as well as my responses:

1. **I've seen this before.** They're right. They've seen much of this before. As I described in Chapter 1, and I hope as you've seen throughout the book, the individual principles and practices have been around for quite a long time. What is new about AM is the packaging of these principles and practices into a chaordic, synergistic methodology. Don't let this skepticism dissuade you from adopting AM. Many developers chose to ignore the object-oriented paradigm shift for much longer than they should have for this very same reason.

2. **It's just another fad.** I hope this isn't true, but only time will tell. I suspect that AM isn't a fad for several reasons. First, it's based on existing principles and practices, many of which you likely follow already but were unwilling to admit to publicly because it just didn't seem like proper software engineering. Second, as you've seen in this book, it works well in practice with leading methodologies, particularly XP and UP, and in fact enhances them. Third, my own organization has been field testing AM for a while now and, more importantly, AM has received significant attention by modelers worldwide through public discussions on the AM mailing list.

3. **It's not software engineering.** I guess this depends on how you define software engineering, and the jury is clearly still out on this issue, but from the point of view of people who are familiar with traditional/prescriptive forms of software engineering, this is a fair statement. So what? There are a lot of commonly accepted software engineering techniques that provide little benefit in practice (Jones 2000), so perhaps this isn't such a bad thing. The real issue isn't whether AM is software engineering or not; it's whether AM offers the potential to improve your productivity as a software developer. A good strong cup of coffee has improved my own productivity more than once, and that has nothing to do with software engineering.

4. **It's not proven.** That's true. The only proof that AM works is anecdotal. Once again, so what? Most aspects of object-oriented (OO) development theory remain unproven, yet OO is the dominant development paradigm within the software development community. This skepticism, like the software engineering issue, is a red herring: This is simply a convenient excuse to not try something new. Organizations that wait for proof that techniques work are almost guaranteed to remain 10 to 15 years behind the rest of the industry. From this point of view, it may be more risky to not try AM than it is to try it.

Overzealous Process Police

Many organizations have well-defined software processes in place, processes that they have been following (theoretically, at least) for years. This is particularly true in organizations that are working towards, or have already earned, accreditation in industry standards such as ISO 900X and the Capability Maturity Model (CMM) of the Software Engineering Institute (SEI) (1995). These processes are often prescriptive and very well documented. In these organizations it is quite common for a software process group to exist whose mission is to support and evolve your software process over time. Part of their "support" efforts may include inspections to ensure that development teams follow the process. The people doing this work are often disparagingly referred to as "process police." These people may not be fully aware of AM, or agile software development approaches in general, and may have difficulty grasping that a practices-based methodology can be just as effective as a prescriptive methodology. Instead of considering new ways of doing things, even ways that are potentially far more efficient, they instead declare that you may not follow AM practices at all. In these situations I would:

- Work with your "process police" to discover their reservations regarding adoption of AM practices. Try to identify any misconceptions that they may have (see Chapter 30, "Conclusion: Choose to Succeed").

- Ease into AM by adopting a few practices at a time within the existing scope of your process.

- Identify potential problems with your existing process and suggest AM practices that address them.

- Give an overview presentation to your process group and senior managers that describes AM.

Paper Pushers with Power

In large organizations it is common to discover IT professionals who haven't been directly involved with software development—programming, modeling, testing, or managing—for years. Often these people are in infrastructure support roles such as software process management, reuse management, or program management, and over time their roles have devolved to the point where their focus is on "pushing paper." These people often demand status reports from individuals or teams which they review and provide feedback on, hold status meetings to be apprised of how the project is progressing, and require metrics or evaluations of a project team with regards to their specialized area of focus such as reuse metrics, security evaluations, or data standards conformance evaluations. This isn't to say that all people in these roles are paper pushers. I've had many good experiences with reuse, security, and data professionals who were able to actively support my project teams. However, I've also had very bad experiences as well. I've found that the fundamental difference is that the people who are willing and able to roll up their sleeves and help my project team were of great value to me. The paper pushers that simply required documents or that scheduled review meetings were of little value and often a great hindrance.

Unfortunately, the ones that are a hindrance often can't be easily ignored because they are in positions of power. Refusal to fill out their forms can often result in their manager pushing a complaint up the corporate organization structure and then back down again to your project team. Whenever I come across a paper pusher with power, I apply the following strategies in order:

1. **Communicate.** I first try to talk with the person(s) to identify their priorities and to negotiate a more effective way of conforming to their request. I find that this rarely works because many people are set in their ways, but it's worth trying anyway.

2. **Deflect.** Talk with my (other) project stakeholders to make them aware of the impact the paper pusher's requests are having on the team and ask them to deal with the issue for me.

3. **Flight or fight.** Decide whether the team should acquiesce to the paper pusher's request or fight it out with them politically. The problem with fighting it out is you invest energy and political capital doing so. You are likely to make political enemies, and paper pushers are often more politically savvy than you.

Cookbook Philosophy

People who are not actively involved with software development, in particular senior management, may have what is called a "cookbook philosophy" towards development. The basic idea is that if your organization had a well-defined software process in place that prescribed in excruciating detail the steps for each development activity, then all your IT problems would be solved. This is founded on the belief that software development is a science, that if the "right" procedures were developed that they could hire low-skilled people that would simply follow the procedures and perfect software would be churned out on time and within budget. This belief is based on the underlying concept that software development is a science. My experience is that this isn't true.

AM reflects the belief that software development is more of an art than a science, an art that requires skilled craftsmen. AM doesn't tell you how to create a use case model. In fact, it doesn't even tell you to create one. It only tells you to create the right model that makes sense for that situation, for example, *Apply The Right Artifact(s)*, and trusts you to judge what's right. AM's approach is antithetical to the cookbook philosophy. Therefore, anyone who believes in it is not likely to support the adoption of AM. Whenever I encounter someone with this mindset, I will point out that:

- Software development requires skilled professionals.

- Most developers are unlikely to follow a highly detailed process, no matter how well it is written.

- Software process is needed, but it should support and enhance the efforts of developers, not restrict and burden them.

- Developers shouldn't be expected to have every skill, but they should be expected to learn new skills over time.

- AM can be used to enhance prescriptive processes, as Part 4 showed with the Unified Process (arguably the most popular prescriptive process).

Inability to Accept Blame

A problem that I have seen with other processes, including both XP and the UP, are people that blame project failures on the process they (mis-)followed instead of accepting the blame themselves. Yes, they may have made a process-related mistake, but that doesn't mean that the process is at fault. It means that they are. The common process-related mistakes that I often see are:

1. **Right process, wrong situation.** People will try to apply a process in a situation that it isn't well suited for. This problem was a primary motivator for the *Recognize When Agile Modeling Won't Work For You* section earlier in this chapter. Hopefully your team can avoid applying AM in the wrong situations.

2. **Right name, wrong process.** A common problem within the XP community is project teams that do not adopt all of XP's practices; thus, they are not truly doing XP. They fail because they have missed addressing a fundamental aspect of software development supported by that practice. This is why I am so adamant about the need to adopt the core principles and practices of AM in order to claim that you're doing AM. You could still run into trouble, but it won't be because you've missed a critical aspect of the methodology.

3. **Right process, wrong instantiation.** A common problem within the UP community is organizations that adopt the Rational Unified Process (RUP) (Rational Corporation 2001) right out of the box, not realizing that they need to tailor it to their own environment. It is possible to make the same mistake with

AM, particularly when you do not follow the advice of the principle, *Local Adaptation.*

Many organizations are successful with AM and it is reasonable to expect that AM isn't going to work for everyone. If your team fails with AM, please don't blame AM. To paraphrase America's National Rifle Association (NRA)—processes don't kill projects; people kill projects.

Excessive Documentation Due to Fear of Losing Everyone

Many organizations fear the loss of their software development teams because when all or most of the team leaves, very important and often undocumented knowledge goes with them. There are several common reasons why you may lose your team:

- A competitor hires the team away from you to kick-start their own projects.
- Some developers job hop on a regular basis, never staying long at any one company.
- You purposely disband a team once they've completed their project.

To counteract this problem, a common strategy is for senior management to request significant amounts of documentation in the belief that if they lose the team, then they can simply form another team and hand them the documentation. This approach sounds good but often proves impotent in practice. First, although the documentation may help the situation, the new development team is unlikely to trust it, preferring instead to use it to get a "lay of the land" with respect to the system and then dive into the code to get at the details. In other words, they're only likely to use it for the small subset of overview documentation that your detailed documentation contains. Second, this strategy often becomes a self-fulfilling prophecy. You force your developers to write excessive amounts of documentation because you fear they'll leave, and then they decide to leave because of your organizational bureaucracy, lack of trust in them, and lack of focus on software development.

In this situation I will work with the people that request the documentation and try to negotiate a more agile approach. My experience is that high-quality source code supported by succinct overview documentation and appropriate contract models provides an adequate system description for the developers who need to maintain and enhance it in the future. Chapter 14, "Agile Documentation," presents strategies for writing agile documentation.

Overcoming Project-Related Challenges

In addition to the organizational challenges described in the previous section, many project teams will confront issues that are specific to them. These situations include:

■ Distributed development

■ Hand-offs to other teams

■ Fixed-price contracts

TIP **Your Project Isn't Different**
I often hear the refrain, "We'd love to adopt XYZ but unfortunately we're different." Poppycock! I regret to inform you that there is nothing special about your project. Yes, there are very likely some challenges that you need to overcome. Yes, it will be difficult to do so. No, that isn't an excuse for not trying to be as effective as you possibly can. Stop looking for reasons why you can't adopt AM and start looking for ways to do so.

Distributed Development

Many projects, large and small, involve distributed teams of people. Perhaps your organization has instituted a flex-time arrangement with some developers that allows them to work from home part or all of the time. Perhaps your project is a multi-
division effort that involves sub-teams throughout your organization. Perhaps your project is a multi-organization effort with teams distributed across the globe. In all of these situations, it is unlikely that you will be able to co-locate developers and project stakeholders in a communication-rich environment in which AM thrives.

When faced with this situation, I will often try the following strategies:

1. **Co-locate the team.** Sometimes a distributed approach is taken for less than logical reasons; perhaps there's a political desire to spread the work out between locations (common on government projects and multi-organization efforts) or perhaps someone has simply jumped to the erroneous conclusion that you can't co-locate. It's worth questioning why a project team is distributed on the chance that you can change the situation and avoid this problem all together. Does this project actually need to be performed in a distributed manner? Is it an option to co-locate your team temporally to deliver the project? Can it be reorganized into one co-located team that brings in expertise as needed from the other locations?

2. **Choose an underlying process that supports distributed development.** Your overall process must support distributed development; this isn't just an AM issue. Your chosen process will typically describe how to organize and manage your project as a collection of smaller sub-projects, and it is on these sub-projects that it may be possible to take an AM approach. Chapter 27, "Agile Infrastructure Management," overviewed the modeling aspects of the Infrastructure Management discipline of the Enterprise Unified Process (EUP), a discipline that describes programmer-management activities applicable to distributed development efforts.

3. **Use collaborative tools.** Many tools exist—including collaborative modeling tools, collaborative writing tools, discussion tools, conferencing tools, and virtual meeting tools—that can be used to support distributed development efforts. These tools were described in Chapter 8, "Communication."

4. **Have some travelers.** A "traveler" is someone who moves back and forth between locations, perhaps spending a certain amount of their time at a "home location" and portions at other locations, to facilitate communication between the groups. They'll participate as active members of the groups when they are there on site, often bringing insights regarding the project from the other teams. Travelers are often actively involved with the practice *Formalize Contract Models* when the various subteams are defining interfaces to their work. This is a role often taken on by people who have a high-level view of the project. Although the traveler role sounds romantic at first, particularly to people who have never spent much time traveling for business, it is often very difficult on a personal level for many people. It strains relationships and recovering from time-zone differences can be very demanding on your body—regardless of what you may have heard, you never get used to it. At best, you get good at fooling yourself that you're handling it as you stifle a yawn.

Hand-Offs to Other Teams

Many project teams find that they need to hand-off (deliver) their work to another team. Perhaps you're working on a development team within an organization, or on a team within an outsourcing company, with the intention that you'll deliver it to another team that focuses on maintaining and enhancing systems over time. Similarly, perhaps you're a consultant or contractor who has been brought into an organization for a specific time with the expectation that you will provide "fully-documented" work to hand-off when you leave. Your hand-off is facilitated by the inclusion of the people whom you are delivering your work to. These people are among your project stakeholders, so follow the practice of *Active Stakeholder Participation* to ensure that you've met their actual needs and that they understand what it is that you're building. This will help to reduce the need for extensive documentation because they won't require it. Furthermore, by actively involving your project's stakeholders, you've turned your situation into something where AM is likely to fit much better.

Another problematic situation is when you're working on a "piece-meal project" that focuses on a single aspect of a project. For example, a common approach taken by the U.S. Federal Government is to award a firm the requirements engineering part of a project, the goal often being to create a formal Software Requirements Specification (SRS) that describes the system that should be built. The SRS is handed-off to the firm that wins the bid for the construction phase of the project, which may be the same firm that created the SRS to begin with. A similar approach is often taken for other phases, such as architectural or design modeling. This situation clearly goes against several fundamentals of agile software development. First, the team is taking a serial approach instead of an iterative one. Second, the primary goal is to produce documentation, not work on software. Assuming that you can't avoid this situation to begin with, your best strategy is to partially adopt AM principles and practices as appropriate. Practices that likely won't work well in this situation are:

- *Depict Models Simply* because you'll still want to keep your models as simple as possible, but your need for comprehensive documentation will constrain your efforts.

- *Model in Small Increments* and *Prove It With Code* will both be problematic because you don't have the opportunity to move beyond your current serial phase.

- *Update Only When It Hurts* likely isn't applicable because of the need for consistent and thorough documentation. Another way to look at it is that the practice is still applicable, although you have a spectacularly low pain threshold.

- *Use The Simplest Tools* will likely be constrained by the need to produce "professional" documentation.

Fixed-Price Contracts

Several years ago I spoke at a conference in Brazil. During my talk, one person asked me how I would go about estimating a fixed-price contract where the requirements weren't well defined yet. My response was that I didn't do fixed-priced contracts, but that I would provide an estimate for the next two to three months of effort instead of the eighteen to twenty-four months he was asking for. My estimate would have a range instead of a fixed amount. This wasn't the answer he was looking for. This person then asked the same question of other speakers throughout the conference and they gave him similar advice. The speakers were all very experienced software developers, most of whom had been in the industry for over 20 years. They had a wide variety of backgrounds and development philosophies, yet from what I could tell, no one believed the fixed-price contract was a good idea.

Fixed-price contracts commonly occur because your project stakeholders, often senior management, want to impose financial constraints on your project team to avoid having them go over budget. This is something that the XP community would refer to as "playing not to lose" (Beck 2000). Fixed price contracts are often imposed on outsourcing and contracting firms that take over the development of the project with little or no direct management by members of your organization, although there will be indirect oversight of the effort. Internal fixed-price efforts are also common, particularly in organizations with strict budgeting processes or that have experienced significant cost overruns in the past.

There is nothing inherently wrong with a fixed-price contract, as long as you're allowed to vary another aspect of your work. Project managers will often refer to the "iron triangle" of planning—cost, scope, and quality—you can only fix two of these three aspects on your project. Because your contract fixes the cost of the project and AM fixes quality through its *Quality Work* principle, the implication is that you need to be flexible on scope, the amount of functionality that you can deliver for that fixed amount of money. Unfortunately, the real world is rarely that simple because the people who define the contract also want to fix all three of these variables: They want to know exactly what they're getting for their money and naturally they want high-quality work. Your best option is to educate people in this fundamental concept and try to move them towards a less-dysfunctional situation such as one or more of the following:

- A ranged estimate, for example $500,000 +/- $100,000
- A series of smaller phases/iterations which you estimate as you reach them
- A low time and materials rate that covers costs plus bonuses for meeting performance-based goals

Consider Alternatives to Full Adoption of AM

It is very likely that your project team will face several challenges when taking an AM approach, some of which you will be able to overcome and others that you'll need to learn to live with. You may discover that even after changing what you can, you're still not in a position to fully adopt AM. Therefore you need to choose one of the following options:

1. **Partially adopt AM.** You can adopt as many of the principles and practices of AM as possible; you won't be truly doing AM but you will likely be more productive as a developer. Once your organization discovers that there are better ways to develop software, perhaps they will be more willing to change the factors required to fully adopt AM. In other words, just as you want to *Apply Patterns Gently*, you should consider the practice, *Apply Methodologies Gently* as well.

2. **Give up on AM within your organization.** Personally, I don't like this option but I have to admit that it's a valid one. The reality is that AM isn't for everyone and perhaps your organization is one where AM simply isn't a good fit.

3. **Start looking for employment elsewhere.** There are a lot of organizations out there that are choosing to succeed at the software development game— organizations that are more than willing to hire motivated software developers.

How to Make This Work in Practice

The best advice that I can give you is to look for ways to make AM work for you instead of looking for ways that it won't work.

Conclusion: Choose to Succeed

Small shifts in deeply held beliefs and values can massively alter societal behavior and results. In fact, may be the only things that ever have.

—Dee Hock

Many people think of a conclusion as an ending, but I'd rather think of it as a beginning. A beginning? By reading this book I hope that you have gained valuable new insights into effective modeling practices as well as effective development practices. This is a beginning because you can now start to apply these insights on a daily basis in your job.

Before you put this book down and get to work, let's wrap up several very important loose ends. First, I want to address several misconceptions that you or your co-workers may have regarding Agile Modeling. Second, I want to provide some guidelines to help you determine when you are in fact agile modeling. Third, I want to introduce you to several important resources to help you adopt and apply AM within your organization. Finally, I have a few parting words that I want to share with you.

Common Misconceptions Regarding Agile Modeling

Through discussions on public mailing lists and newsgroups as well as working closely with my company's clients, I have already met several people who held some disturbing misconceptions regarding AM. To be fair, my description of AM at the time often wasn't complete and this book obviously wasn't available yet. However, I'm still concerned

Table 30.1 Potential Misconceptions Regarding AM

MISCONCEPTION	REALITY
Business analysts, architects, and other specialized modelers are disallowed	AM does in fact prefer that developers be generalists with one or more specialties, see Chapter 12, but does not require it. Specialists such as business analysts can be quite effective when you need someone to work with project stakeholders at a site distant from the development team and architecture experts can be useful at the beginning of a project to help you identify a candidate architecture.
You can't/don't review agile models	Although this book didn't touch on the topic of reviews, there is no reason why you cannot review an agile model or document for that matter. The reviewers need to set their expectations accordingly, remembering that *Content Is More Important Than Representation*, and you want to organize the review meeting itself in much the way that Chapter 13 suggests to organize modeling sessions.
AM is carved in stone	This is partially true because at a minimum you need to adopt AM's core practices to claim an AM approach to development, as you learned in Chapter 29. However, there is significant leeway in the way that you follow these practices. For example AM suggests that you *Apply The Right Artifact(s)* but doesn't tell you what the right artifacts are. (Some *suggestions* are provided in Appendix A.)
You don't use CASE tools	Agile modelers follow the practice *Use The Simplest Tools*, and sometimes the simplest tool for the job is in fact a CASE tool, as Chapter 10 describes in detail.
Agile modelers are highly skilled "super developers"	Having a wide range of modeling experience certainly helps, but it isn't a requirement. It can be your first day on the job as a developer and you can still follow the principles and practices of AM. It's far more important to be willing to work with others and to learn new skills—anyone willing to do so can become an agile modeler.

enough to address these misconceptions here because I suspect they will continue to crop up. The misconceptions that I have observed are summarized in Table 30.1.

When Is(n't) it Agile Modeling?

One of the biggest challenges that all development methodologies face is from those developers who claim to follow the method, but in reality they don't. This is because they often run into trouble and then proceed to blame the method that they weren't following properly to begin with. As I described in Chapter 29, "Adopting Agile Modeling or Overcoming Adversity," we've seen this problem within both the XP (Beck 2000) and UP (Jacobson, Booch, and Rumbaugh 1999) communities. I would like to try and avoid this problem with AM. Although your primary test is to determine whether or not you've adopted all of AM's core practices as described in Chapter 4, "Supplementary Principles," it may not always be clear to you whether or not you are indeed following them. To make this clearer, Table 30.1 provides a factor checklist (all of which must be true) that identifies when you are truly performing agile modeling. Table 30.2 provides a factor checklist (only one of which needs to be true) that identifies when you're not agile modeling.

It's important to note that although you may not be agile modeling, often due to environmental circumstances beyond your control, you can still apply many of the principles and practices of AM to your project. However, just because you're sketching on a whiteboard, doesn't necessarily imply that you are agile modeling. All it implies is that you're sketching on a whiteboard.

Table 30.2   Factors to Determine If You're Engaged in Agile Modeling

X	FACTOR
	Your customers/users are active participants in your requirements and/or analysis modeling efforts.
	Changing requirements are welcomed and acted upon accordingly; there is no "requirements freeze."
	You work on the highest-priority requirements first, as prioritized by your project stakeholders, and in turn focus on the highest-risk issues as work progresses.
	You take an iterative and incremental approach to modeling.
	Your primary focus is on the development of software, not documentation or the models themselves.
	You model as a team where everyone's input is welcome.
	You actively try to keep things as simple as possible. You use the simplest tools available to you and create the simplest model(s) to do the job.
	You discard most, if not all, of your models as development progresses.
	Customers/business owners make business decisions; developers make technical decisions.
	The model's content is recognized as being significantly more important than the format/representation of that content.
	How you test what you describe with your model(s) is a critical issue continually considered as you model.

Table 30.3   Factors to Determine If You're Not Engaged in Agile Modeling

X	FACTOR
	Your goal is to produce documentation, such as a requirements document, for sign-off by one or more project stakeholders or to deliver to another team.
	You use a CASE tool to specify the architecture and/or design of your software BUT don't use that specification to generate part or all of your software.
	Your customers/users have limited involvement with your efforts. For example, they are involved with the initial requirement's development, perhaps are available on a limited basis to answer questions, and at a later date will be involved in one or more acceptance reviews of your work.
	You focus on a single model at a time. Common examples are "use case modeling sessions," "class modeling sessions," or "data modeling sessions." The root cause of this problem is typically "one artifact developers" such as people specialized in data modeling or user interface modeling. With AM, generalists lead the effort.
	You work towards a freeze of one or more of your models. In other words, you take a serial approach.

Agile Modeling Resources

This book isn't the only source of information regarding AM. There are several web-based resources also available to you:

The Agile Modeling Web site. At www.agilemodeling.com I continue to describe the AM methodology and provide links to other agile software development and model resources on the Web.

The Agile Modeling mailing list. Everyone is free to join and get involved with the AM mailing list. Visit www.agilemodeling.com/feedback.htm for details.

The Agile Modeling Workshop. In this three-day workshop students work on a real-world case study where they apply the principles and practices of AM to create a wide range of modeling artifacts. Visit www.ronin-intl.com/services/agileModeling.htm for details.

Furthermore, I openly invite other authors, and budding authors for that matter, to write about their experiences applying AM in practice. Ideas that currently come to mind include books that describe how to use AM with software processes other than XP or the UP, or how to apply AM's principles and practices with other modeling methodologies such as ICONIX (Rosenberg and Scott 1999) or Catalysis (D'Souza and Wills 1999).

A Few Parting Thoughts . . .

I can only show you the door. You're the one that has to walk through it.

-Morpheus, in *The Matrix*

My experience has been that one of the hardest choices that you will ever have to make is to choose to succeed. AM asks you to do some very difficult things:

- Work closely with your project stakeholders and fight to have them actively involved, even when they may not want to or when it is hard to gain access to them.

- Work closely with other developers, ideally within a shared workspace, even when your existing environment promotes individual efforts.

- Learn how to create a wide variety of models and be willing to continue to learn new techniques, even if you prefer to specialize in only one or two.

- Iterate between those models and other artifacts (including source code), even when pressure exists to focus on a single model in order to "complete it."

- Focus on software development, even when other people within your organization coerce you to write excessive documentation or to create more paperwork than what is absolutely required.

- Embrace change by acting on it appropriately, even when you desperately want to "freeze" your requirements so you can know exactly what you need to build.

- Create and accept models that are just good enough, models built with simple tools that often aren't perfect, even when other teams within your organization invest their time creating more "professional looking" models with sophisticated electronic tools.

AM can be a little overwhelming at first. Many people are taken aback with AM's brutal honesty regarding the number of modeling artifacts that you need to learn over time. (There are over 30 modeling artifacts described in Appendix A, "Modeling Techniques.") Don't worry, you don't need to know every one of them to start and you're likely to find that you are effective with only a subset. If you keep an open mind and are willing to learn new techniques, you will discover that your intellectual toolbox slowly grows over time.

You'll also find that AM requires discipline at first, particularly the discipline to stop modeling once you have fulfilled the model's purpose and to iterate to another artifact once you've become stuck working on the current model. The reason why you need this discipline isn't because AM is difficult; it's because you're building new modeling habits and that takes time and effort. Once you've internalized these modeling habits AM will become quite easy for you; you just need patience until then. A good analogy is learning how to walk: at first walking is quite difficult for young children, requiring great focus, yet after gaining some experience walking and even running quickly, it becomes something that you just do without any conscious thought. If you choose to succeed, you will very quickly find that you can run with Agile Modeling where you used to crawl.

Modeling Techniques

This is a reference section that summarizes common modeling techniques that agile modelers may choose to apply to their projects. While reading the material presented in this section, please keep the following in mind:

1. **This is only a subset of the techniques available to you.** Although the list is fairly robust and includes a wide range of techniques, it is not complete, nor is it meant to be. There are hundreds of modeling techniques that you may use on your project; I am merely describing some of the more common ones. The important thing to understand is that there is a much wider variety of modeling techniques than many methodologies or modeling language standards will lead you to believe, so keep an open mind when a co-worker wants to try a new or *non-standard* technique.

2. **The techniques are merely summarized.** My goal for this section is to summarize each modeling technique and then point you in the right direction for more information about it. *It is not my intention to teach you how to become proficient at each technique.* Table A.1 overviews how each modeling artifact is described. Table A.2 presents the different modeling techniques.

3. **You need to understand a wide range of techniques.** The more types of modeling artifacts that you know, the greater the chance that you will be able to *Apply the Right Artifact(s)* for the job at hand.

4. **The descriptions reflect common experiences.** The descriptions reflect my experiences and those of my colleagues at Ronin International over many years working on a wide range of projects. Having said that, the one consistent aspect of each of these projects is that they are unique and therefore we applied a subset of these techniques in a different way on each project. In other words, expect to locally adapt these techniques to meet your exact needs.

Table A.1　How the Artifact Summaries Are Organized

SECTION	EXPLANATION
Description	A description of the modeling artifact.
Common applications	Common uses for the modeling artifact, with a focus on the development of business applications.
Common misapplications	Common misuses specific to the artifact that often lead to busy work or rework because the concept could be better captured using another development artifact. Generic misapplications, such as investment in unnecessary detail or complexity, are not included as they pertain to all types of modeling artifacts. When it isn't obvious what to do, advice is presented for addressing the misapplication.
Iterate to	Potential artifacts to work on after the given artifact, providing insights for following the practice *Iterate to Another Artifact*.
Suggested media	An ordered list of media that can be used to support the artifact. Possible alternatives include: • Diagramming tool (for example, Microsoft Visio or Corel Draw) • Hand-drawn sketch (for example, on a whiteboard) • Index cards • Modeling tool (for example, Together from TogetherSoft or Cittera from Canyon Blue) • Paper • PostIt notes
When to keep it	Advice for situations when it may make sense for this model to be a "keeper." However, never forget the principle of *Travel Light*—don't keep something unless you desperately need it. This section also includes a rating (High, Medium, Low) of the likeliness that keeping the artifact will actually prove of value to your future efforts.

Table A.2 Modeling Techniques

ARTIFACT	DESCRIPTION	COMMON APPLICATIONS	COMMON MISAPPLICATIONS	ITERATE TO	SUGGESTED MEDIA	WHEN TO KEEP IT
Activity Diagram (UML)	A UML activity diagram (Rumbaugh, Jacobson, and Booch 1999; Fowler and Scott 1999; Ambler 2001a) is used to model high-level business processes or the transitions between states of a class. Activities can either be business processes or technical processes, such as collections of operations implemented by classes or components.	Analysis or design of a business process or business rule. Design of the logic flow of a complex operation. Depiction of the logic of a use case, usage scenario, or user story.	None known	• Acceptance test case. • Class diagram. • Essential use case. • Organization chart. • Source code. • System use case. • Usage scenario. • Use case diagram. • User story.	1. Hand-drawn sketch 2. Drawing tool 3. CASE tool	(Low Value) To provide a high-level overview of the logic for a business process.

Table A.2 continued

ARTIFACT	DESCRIPTION	COMMON APPLICATIONS	COMMON MISAPPLICATIONS	ITERATE TO	SUGGESTED MEDIA	WHEN TO KEEP IT
Business Rule Definition	A business rule (Ross 1997; Wiegers 1999; Ambler 2001a) is an operating principle or policy that your software must satisfy. Business rules often describe access control issues, business calculations, or the policies of your organization.	Requirements identification	Documentation of technical requirements	• Acceptance test case. • Class diagram. • CRC model. • Essential use case. • Flowchart. • Glossary. • Source code. • System use case. • Usage scenario.	1. Word processor 2. Index card 3. CASE tool	(Medium value) When exact definitions of business rules are required in a stakeholder-readable format.
Change Case	Change cases (Bennett 1997; Ambler 2001a) are used to describe new potential requirements for a system or modifications to existing requirements.	Exploration of future potential requirements	Justification to overbuild software to meet "potential" requirements	• Constraint. • CRC model. • Technical requirement. • Usage scenario. • Use case. • User story.	1. Index card 2. Word processor	(Low value) When you need to justify design or architecture decisions to project stake holders AND they require documentation.

continues

Table A.2 Modeling Techniques (continued)

ARTIFACT	DESCRIPTION	COMMON APPLICATIONS	COMMON MISAPPLICATIONS	ITERATE TO	SUGGESTED MEDIA	WHEN TO KEEP IT
Class Diagram (UML)	UML class diagrams (Rumbaugh, Jacobson, and Booch 1999; Fowler and Scott 1999; Ambler 2001a) depict classes, their static inter-relationships (including inheritance, aggregation, and association), and the operations and attributes of the classes.	Conceptual modeling. Domain modeling. Design of the structure of object-oriented software. Detailed design of the internals of a component.	Physical database modeling. Domain model documentation for users (they often don't understand the notation). Only design diagram for OO software (use multiple models).	• Collaboration diagram. • Component diagram. • CRC model. • Data model. • Glossary. • Sequence diagram. • Source code. • State chart diagram. • Usage scenario. • User story.	1. Hand-drawn sketch 2. CASE tool 3. Index cards connected by string	(Low value) You need to communicate the internal structure of your software to others.

Table A.2 continued

ARTIFACT	DESCRIPTION	COMMON APPLICATIONS	COMMON MISAPPLICATIONS	ITERATE TO	SUGGESTED MEDIA	WHEN TO KEEP IT
Class Responsibility Collaborator (CRC) Cards	A Class Responsibility Collaborator (CRC) model (Beck 2000; Ambler 2001a) is a collection of standard index cards, each of which have been divided into three sections indicating: the name of the class, the responsibilities of the class, and the collaborators of the class.	Domain modeling with project stakeholders. Conceptual modeling with project stakeholders. Exploration of the design of the structure of object-oriented software.	None known	• Acceptance test case. • Business rule. • Change case. • Constraint. • Class diagram. • Essential use case. • Glossary. • Organization chart. • Source code. • System use case. • Usage scenario. • Use case diagram. • User story.	1. Index cards	Typically discarded after use.

continues

Table A.2 Modeling Techniques (continued)

ARTIFACT	DESCRIPTION	COMMON APPLICATIONS	COMMON MISAPPLICATIONS	ITERATE TO	SUGGESTED MEDIA	WHEN TO KEEP IT
Collaboration Diagram (UML)	UML collaboration diagrams (Rumbaugh, Jacobson, and Booch 1999; Fowler and Scott 1999; Ambler 2001a) provide a birds-eye view of a collection of collaborating objects that work together to fulfill a common purpose. Collaboration diagrams show message flow between objects in an object-oriented application, and also imply the basic associations (relationships) between classes.	Exploration of the dynamic nature of complex object or component interactions	To explore the sequence of object interactions (use a sequence diagram instead)	• Class diagram. • Component diagram. • Deployment diagram. • Robustness diagram. • Source code. • System use case. • Usage scenario. • User interface flow diagram. • User interface prototype. • User story.	1. Hand-drawn sketch 2. CASE tool	(Low value) Typically discarded after use, although may be kept to show design of a complex portion of software.

Table A.2 continued

ARTIFACT	DESCRIPTION	COMMON APPLICATIONS	COMMON MISAPPLICATIONS	ITERATE TO	SUGGESTED MEDIA	WHEN TO KEEP IT
Component Diagram (UML)	A UML component diagram (Rumbaugh, Jacobson, and Booch 1999; Fowler and Scott 1999; Ambler 2001a) depicts the software components of a system, their interfaces, and the relationships between the components.	Design of the high-level structure of business architecture for a component-based system. Design of the high-level structure of technical software components or subsystems.	None known	• Collaboration diagram. • Class diagram. • Deployment diagram. • Sequence diagram. • Source code.	1. Hand-drawn sketch 2. Index cards connected by string 3. CASE tool	(Medium value) To provide an overview diagram of your software architecture.
Constraint Definition	A constraint (Wiegers 1999; Ambler 2001a) is a restriction on the degree of freedom you have in providing a solution.	Definition of a business or technical constraint.	Definition of a business rule. Definition of a technical requirement.	• Acceptance test case. • Change case. • CRC model. • Deployment diagram. • Essential use case.	1. Index card 2. Word processor	(Medium value) Kept as part of official definition of requirements.

continues

Table A.2 Modeling Techniques (continued)

ARTIFACT	DESCRIPTION	COMMON APPLICATIONS	COMMON MISAPPLICATIONS	ITERATE TO	SUGGESTED MEDIA	WHEN TO KEEP IT
Constraint Definition	Constraints are effectively global requirements for your project. Constraints can be economic, political, technical, or environmental and pertain to your project resources, schedule, target environment, or to the system itself.			• Glossary. • Source code. • System use case. • Technical requirement. • Usage scenario.		
Data Diagram	A data diagram/model (Reingruber and Gregory 1994; Ambler 2001a) depicts data entities and their inter-relationships.	Physical database design. Conceptual or domain modeling for a data warehouse. Explore relationships between several entities.	Conceptual modeling of OO software (use a class diagram instead). Domain modeling for OO software (use a class diagram instead). Exploration of structure of OO software (use a class diagram instead). A primary driver of the structure of a class diagram.	• Acceptance test case. • Class diagram. • Data flow diagram. • Deployment diagram. • Source code. • System use case. • Usage scenario. • User story.	1. Hand-drawn sketch 2. CASE tool	(Very High) To document physical database design. (Very High) As a contract model between the database owners and other systems accessing the database.

Table A.2 continued

ARTIFACT	DESCRIPTION	COMMON APPLICATIONS	COMMON MISAPPLICATIONS	ITERATE TO	SUGGESTED MEDIA	WHEN TO KEEP IT
Deployment Diagram (UML)	A UML deployment diagram (Rumbaugh, Jacobson, and Booch 1999; Fowler and Scott 1999; Ambler 2001a) depicts a static view of the run-time configuration of processing nodes and the components that run on those nodes. This includes the hardware for your system, the software that is installed on that hardware, and the middleware used to connect the disparate machines to one another.	Identification of the physical architecture for a system. Identification of how software components are and/or will be deployed to physical architecture.	To show dependences between software components (use a component diagram instead).	• Acceptance test case. • Activity diagram. • Collaboration diagram. • Component model. • Constraint. • Data model. • External interface specification. • Sequence diagram. • Usage scenario. • User story.	1. Hand-drawn sketch 2. CASE tool	(Medium value) To document technical architecture of your system.

continues

Table A.2 Modeling Techniques (continued)

ARTIFACT	DESCRIPTION	COMMON APPLICATIONS	COMMON MISAPPLICATIONS	ITERATE TO	SUGGESTED MEDIA	WHEN TO KEEP IT
Data Flow Diagram (DFD)	A data-flow diagram (DFD) (Yourdon 1989; Gane and Sarson 1978; Ambler 1997) shows the movement of data within a system between processes, entities, and data stores.	Analysis of existing business processes. Design of new or updated business processes.	Over-specification of a system by "drilling down" into sub processes with more DFDs. Significant effort to level balance between a DFD and its sub-DFDs.	• Acceptance test case. • Change case. • Constraint. • Data model. • Deployment diagram. • Organization chart. • Structure diagram. • System Use case. • Usage scenario. • User story. • Use case diagram.	1. Hand-drawn sketch 2. Drawing tool 3. CASE tool	(Low value) To communicate overall design of a process-intensive system.

Table A.2 continued

ARTIFACT	DESCRIPTION	COMMON APPLICATIONS	COMMON MISAPPLICATIONS	ITERATE TO	SUGGESTED MEDIA	WHEN TO KEEP IT
External Interface Specification	An external interface (EI) specification (Linthicum 2000) models the interface(s) to a system that is external to yours. Because external systems can be accessed using a variety of means—perhaps via a C-API, via file access, or via calls to a shared database—the contents and format of an EI specification may vary.	As a contract model defining to interface (via an API, data feed, . . .) to a system.	None known	• Data flow diagram. • Data model. • Deployment diagram. • Glossary.	1. Word processor 2. CASE tool	(Very high) As a contract model between your system and an external one.

continues

Table A.2 Modeling Techniques (continued)

ARTIFACT	DESCRIPTION	COMMON APPLICATIONS	COMMON MISAPPLICATIONS	ITERATE TO	SUGGESTED MEDIA	WHEN TO KEEP IT
Essential User Interface Prototype	An essential user interface (UI) prototype (Constantine and Lockwood 1999; Ambler 2001a) is a low-fidelity model, or prototype, of the UI for your system. It represents the general ideas behind the UI but not the exact details.	Exploration of the requirements for the user interface of a system in a technology-independent manner.	None known	• Business rule. • Constraint. • Essential use case. • Glossary. • Usage scenario. • User interface flow diagram. • User interface prototype.	1. Paper and Post-It Notes 2. Hand-drawn sketch	Typically discarded.
Essential Use Case	A use case is a sequence of actions that provide a measurable value to an actor.	Identification of usage requirements for a system. Identification of enterprise-level requirements for an organization.	None known	• Acceptance test case. • Change case. • Constraint. • Essential user interface flow prototype.	1. Word processor 2. CASE tool	(Medium value) Part of official requirements documentation for a system.

Table A.2 continued

ARTIFACT	DESCRIPTION	COMMON APPLICATIONS	COMMON MISAPPLICATIONS	ITERATE TO	SUGGESTED MEDIA	WHEN TO KEEP IT
Essential Use Case	An essential use-case (Constantine and Lockwood 1999; Ambler 2001a) is a simplified, abstract, generalized use case that captures the intentions of a user in a technology and implementation-independent manner.			• Glossary. • System use case. • Technical requirement.		
Feature	A feature is a "small, useful in the eyes of the client result". A feature is a tiny building block for planning, reporting, and tracking.	Exploration of requirements.	None known	• Acceptance test case. • Business rule definition. • Class diagram. • Class Responsibility Collaborator (CRC) model. • Collaboration diagram.	1. Index card 2. Word processor	(Medium value). When you need a feature list describing your system.

continues

Table A.2 Modeling Techniques (continued)

ARTIFACT	DESCRIPTION	COMMON APPLICATIONS	COMMON MISAPPLICATIONS	ITERATE TO	SUGGESTED MEDIA	WHEN TO KEEP IT
Feature	It's understandable, measurable, and do-able (along with several other features) within a two-week increment (Coad, Lefebvre, and DeLuca, 1999). Features typically describe functional requirements although may also describe constraints describing performance or operational characteristics of your application.			• Constraint definition. • Essential user interface prototype. • Glossary. • Source code. • User interface prototype.		

Table A.2 continued

ARTIFACT	DESCRIPTION	COMMON APPLICATIONS	COMMON MISAPPLICATIONS	ITERATE TO	SUGGESTED MEDIA	WHEN TO KEEP IT
Flow Chart	Flow charts (Gane and Sarson 1979) depict the logic flow of a business process or software operation. Flow charts are very simple, depicting activities or processes, the logic flow from process to process, and the decision points reached.	Definition of complex logic.	Over-specification of logic (use source code or specification language instead).	• Class diagram. • Collaboration diagram. • Glossary. • Sequence diagram. • Source code. • System use case. • Usage scenario. • User story.	1. Hand-drawn sketch 2. Drawing tool 3. CASE tool	(Medium value) Description of the logic for a business rule or business process.

continues

Table A.2 Modeling Techniques (continued)

ARTIFACT	DESCRIPTION	COMMON APPLICATIONS	COMMON MISAPPLICATIONS	ITERATE TO	SUGGESTED MEDIA	WHEN TO KEEP IT
Glossary	A glossary (Jacobson, Booch, and Rumbaugh 1999; Ambler 1998) is a collection of definitions of terms that are relevant to your project. Your glossary may include both business and technical terms.	Definition of business and technical terms pertinent to the project.	Definition of business rules. Definition of all possible corporate terms.	• Business rule definition. • Class diagram. • Class Responsibility Collaborator (CRC) model. • Constraint definition. • Essential use case. • System use case. • Technical requirement. • Usage scenario. • User story.	1. Word processor 2. Index cards	(Medium value) To define critical business terms to developers. (Medium value) To define critical technical terms to project stake holders.
Network Diagram	Network diagrams depict the various types of hardware nodes and the interconnections between them.	Analysis of existing technical infrastructure. Design of proposed technical infrastructure.	None known	• Component diagram. • System use case.	1. Hand-drawn sketch 2. Drawing tool 3. CASE tool	(High value) Official description of technical infrastructure for your system or organization.

Table A.2 continued

ARTIFACT	DESCRIPTION	COMMON APPLICATIONS	COMMON MISAPPLICATIONS	ITERATE TO	SUGGESTED MEDIA	WHEN TO KEEP IT
Organization Chart	Organization charts depict the reporting structure between the people, positions, and teams within an organization.	Depiction of existing or proposed organization structure. Documentation of who is involved on a project team.	None known	• Activity diagram. • Class Responsibility Collaborator Model. • Data flow diagram. • Use case diagram.	1. Index cards & string 2. Hand-drawn sketch 3. Human resources software 4. Drawing tool	(Medium value) Official description of the organization structure of your enterprise or portion thereof.
Physical Prototype	Physical prototypes (Greenbaum, and Kyng 1991) model the actual environment in which a system is to be deployed. Physical prototypes can be as simple as a shoe box diorama to a simulated workstation of a single user to something as complex as an entire office simulation.	Explore ergonomic issues of a system. Determine physical equipment (hardware, furniture, ...) requirements.	None known	• Activity diagram. • Deployment diagram. • Network diagram. • System use case. • Usage scenario. • User story.		Typically discarded.

continues

Table A.2 Modeling Techniques (continued)

ARTIFACT	DESCRIPTION	COMMON APPLICATIONS	COMMON MISAPPLICATIONS	ITERATE TO	SUGGESTED MEDIA	WHEN TO KEEP IT
Robustness Diagram	Robustness diagrams (Rosenberg and Scott 1999) depict the major objects–classified into boundary/ interface objects, entity objects, or control/process objects–that participate in fulfilling an actor's interaction with a system as defined by a usage scenario.	Analyze use cases to identify candidate business classes and major user interface elements (screens, reports, ...). To perform a sanity check on the logic of a behavioral requirement (use case, user story, ...). To do a preliminary design of your system.	To design user interface flow for a system (use an interface flow diagram instead). To design the static structure of OO software (use a class diagram instead).	• Acceptance test case. • Business rule definition. • Collaboration diagram. • Constraint definition. • Glossary. • Sequence diagram. • System use case. • Usage scenario. • User interface flow diagram. • User interface prototype. • User story.	1. Hand-drawn sketch 2. CASE tool	Typically discarded.

Table A.2 continued

ARTIFACT	DESCRIPTION	COMMON APPLICATIONS	COMMON MISAPPLICATIONS	ITERATE TO	SUGGESTED MEDIA	WHEN TO KEEP IT
Sequence Diagram (UML)	Sequence diagrams (Rumbaugh, Jacobson, and Booch 1999; Fowler and Scott 1999; Ambler 2001a) are used to model the logic of usage scenarios. A *usage scenario* is exactly what its name indicates—the description of a potential way that your system is used.	Modeling the logic of a usage scenario or a path through one or more use cases, user stories, or usage scenarios (or part(s) thereof). Modeling the logic of a complex transaction to explore its design.	Modeling of the logic for every single path through all the usage requirements for your system (model just the complicated paths instead).	• Class diagram. • Robustness diagram. • System use case. • Usage scenario. • User story.	1. Hand-drawn sketch 2. CASE tool	Typically discarded.
Specification Language	Specification language (Gane and Sarson 1979) is used to describe logic in a structured, formal manner.	Define precise logic of a process, operation, constraint, or business rule. Define constraints or rules that appear on diagrams.	Over-specification on diagrams (write documentation or record as comments in source code instead).	• Acceptance test case. • Business rule. • Class diagram. • Collaboration diagram.	1. CASE tool 2. Word processor	

continues

Table A.2 Modeling Techniques (continued)

ARTIFACT	DESCRIPTION	COMMON APPLICATIONS	COMMON MISAPPLICATIONS	ITERATE TO	SUGGESTED MEDIA	WHEN TO KEEP IT
Specification Language	The industry standard specification language is the Object Constraint Language (OCL) (Warner and Kleppe 1999).	Specification of constraints or invariants on classes, components, or operations.	Detailed documentation for project stakeholders (they likely don't understand the language so use diagrams such as flowcharts instead)	• Component diagram. • Dataflow diagram.		
State Chart Diagram (UML)	UML state chart diagrams (Rumbaugh, Jacobson, and Booch 1999; Douglass 1999; Fowler and Scott 1999; Ambler 2001a) depict the various states that an object may be in and the transitions between those states. A state represents a stage in the behaviour pattern of an object and a transition is a progression from one state to another.	Design the behavior of a complex class or component. Design the functionality of a hardware component. Analyze a complex business process.	Model process flow (use a data flow diagram instead). Design the behavior of a simple class and/or one without interesting behavior based on state.	• Acceptance test case. • Business rule. • Class diagram. • Source code. • System use case. • Usage scenario.	1. Hand-drawn sketch 2. Index cards and string 3. CASE tool	(Low value) Part of your design documentation for complex class. (Medium value) Part of your requirements documentation to describe a complex business process.

Table A.2 continued

ARTIFACT	DESCRIPTION	COMMON APPLICATIONS	COMMON MISAPPLICATIONS	ITERATE TO	SUGGESTED MEDIA	WHEN TO KEEP IT
Structure Diagram	Structure diagrams (Gane and Sarson 1979; Page-Jones 1988; Yourdon 1989) show the modules of procedure-based code and the invocation relationships between those modules.	Explore the "call" hierarchy within the design of procedural software. Explore the invocation of (web) services.	Internal design of object-oriented software (use sequence or collaboration diagrams instead).	• Dataflow diagram. • Source code.	1. Hand-drawn sketch 2. Drawing tool 3. CASE tool	(Very low) High-level design of structured software
System Use Case	A system use case (Cockburn 2001a; Ambler 2001a) is a use case in which high-level implementation decisions are reflected, such as the specific type of user interface (GUI, HTML, ...) and your physical environment.	Analysis of usage requirements. High-level design of implementation of usage requirements.	Identification of usage requirements for a system. The ONLY source of system specification for a system (for example, you should question use-case driven [INSERT TERM HERE]).	• Acceptance test case. • Collaboration diagram. • Essential use case. • Flowchart. • Glossary. • Robustness diagram. • Sequence diagram. • State chart diagram. • Usage scenario. • Use case diagram. • User interface prototype.	1. Word processor 2. CASE tool	(Medium value) Part of your design documentation for your system.

continues

Table A.2 Modeling Techniques (continued)

ARTIFACT	DESCRIPTION	COMMON APPLICATIONS	COMMON MISAPPLICATIONS	ITERATE TO	SUGGESTED MEDIA	WHEN TO KEEP IT
Technical Requirement	A technical requirement (Wiegers 1999; Ambler 2001a) pertains to a non-business-related aspect of your system, such as a performance-related issue, a reliability issue, or technical environment issue.	Requirements identification.	Identification of business requirements. Identification of "gold plate" requirements that the technical staff wants to implement.	• Acceptance test case. • Change case. • Constraint. • Deployment diagram. • Glossary. • Network diagram.	1. Index card 2. Word processor	(Medium value) As part of your official requirements definition.
Usage Scenario	A usage scenario (Greenbaum and Kyng 1991; Ambler 2001a) describes a single path of logic through one or more use cases or user stories.	Exploration of the usage of a system.	None known.	• Acceptance test case. • Activity diagram. • Business rule. • Change case. • Constraint. • CRC model.	1. Index card 2. Word processor	Typically discarded.

Table A.2 continued

ARTIFACT	DESCRIPTION	COMMON APPLICATIONS	COMMON MISAPPLICATIONS	ITERATE TO	SUGGESTED MEDIA	WHEN TO KEEP IT
Usage Scenario	A usage scenario could represent the basic course of action, the happy path, through a single use case, a combination of portions of the happy path replaced by the steps of one or more alternate paths through a single use case, or a path spanning several use cases or user stories.			• Deployment diagram. • Essential use case. • Flowchart. • Glossary. • Network diagram. • System use case. • Technical requirement.		

continues

Table A.2 Modeling Techniques (continued)

ARTIFACT	DESCRIPTION	COMMON APPLICATIONS	COMMON MISAPPLICATIONS	ITERATE TO	SUGGESTED MEDIA	WHEN TO KEEP IT
Use Case Diagram (UML)	A use-case diagram (Cockburn 2001a; Fowler and Scott 1999; Rumbaugh, Jacobson, and Booch 1999; Ambler 2001a) depicts a collection of use cases, actors, their associations, and optionally a system boundary box.	System overview diagram indicating major usage requirements. System context diagram indicating project scope. Analysis of usage requirements of an existing system. Summary overview of essential or system use cases.	Process diagramming (use a data flow diagram or activity diagram instead). Diagramming without supporting use cases.	• Activity diagram. • Essential use case. • Organization chart. • Robustness diagram. • System use case.	1. Hand-drawn sketch 2. CASE tool 3. Drawing tool	(Medium Value) Overview of your usage requirements.

Table A.2 continued

ARTIFACT	DESCRIPTION	COMMON APPLICATIONS	COMMON MISAPPLICATIONS	ITERATE TO	SUGGESTED MEDIA	WHEN TO KEEP IT
User Interface Flow Diagram	A user interface (UI) flow diagram (Constantine and Lockwood 1999; Page-Jones 2000; Ambler 2001a) enables you to model the high-level relationships between major user interface elements, depicting a birds-eye view of the user interface of your system.	Exploration of user interface requirements. High-level architectural view of an application's user interface. High-level design of the user interface to support a use case or usage scenario (often called storyboarding)	None known	• Essential use case. • Essential user interface prototype. • Robustness diagram. • System use case. • User interface prototype. • User story.	1. Hand-drawn sketch 2. Index cards connected by string 3. Drawing tool 4. CASE tool	(Medium value). Part of official design documentation to provide overview of your user interface design. (Medium value) Part of your user documentation to provide an overview of the system.

continues

Table A.2 Modeling Techniques (continued)

ARTIFACT	DESCRIPTION	COMMON APPLICATIONS	COMMON MISAPPLICATIONS	ITERATE TO	SUGGESTED MEDIA	WHEN TO KEEP IT
User Interface Prototype	User interface (UI) prototyping (Constantine and Lockwood 1999; Raskin 2000; Mayhew 1992; Ambler 2001a) is an iterative analysis technique in which users are actively involved in the mocking-up of the UI for a system. UI prototyping typically involves exploration of the requirements for the UI, creation or update of a prototype that fulfills those requirements, and the evaluation of the prototype against the requirements.	Exploration of the problem space. Detailed design of a user interface.	The ONLY source of system specification. Identification of user interface requirements (use an essential user interface prototype instead).	• Business rule. • Constraint. • Essential use case. • Glossary. • Robustness diagram. • Source code. • System use case. • User interface flow diagram.	1. Hand-drawn sketch 2. User interface prototyping tool 3. Programming environment (for example Java)	Typically discarded or evolved into working system.

Table A.2 continued

ARTIFACT	DESCRIPTION	COMMON APPLICATIONS	COMMON MISAPPLICATIONS	ITERATE TO	SUGGESTED MEDIA	WHEN TO KEEP IT
User Story	A user story (Newkirk & Martin 2001; Beck and Fowler 2001) is a reminder to have a conversation with your project stakeholders. User stories capture high-level requirements, including behavioral requirements, business rules, constraints, and technical requirements.	Exploration of requirements. Reminder to have a conversation with a project stakeholder.	None known	• Acceptance test case. • Collaboration diagram. • Deployment diagram. • Glossary. • Robustness diagram. • Sequence diagram. • Source code.	1. Index card 2. Word processor	

Glossary of Definitions and Abbreviations

The following list of terms and abbreviations are described as I have used them in this book. They may deviate from usage in other publications and that's okay; I'm not attempting to write a dictionary.

Accessor   An operation that is used to either modify or retrieve a single attribute. Also known as getter and setter operations.

Agile developer   Someone who develops software that follows an agile approach to software development.

Agile model   A model that is just barely good enough. This means that it fulfills its purpose and no more; is understandable to its intended audience; is simple, sufficiently accurate, consistent, and detailed; and investment in its creation and maintenance provides positive value to your project.

Agile modeler   Someone who follows the Agile Modeling methodology.

Agile Modeling (AM)   A chaordic, practice-based methodology for effectively modeling software-based systems.

API   Application programming interface.

Agile modeling session   A modeling session where you follow the principles, and apply the practices, of AM.

Analysis modeling session   A modeling session where your focus is on fleshing out the requirements for your system.

Analysis paralysis   The fear of moving forward until your models are perfect.

Analyst   A developer responsible for working directly with project stakeholders to potentially gather/elicit information from them, document that information, and/or validate that information.

Architecture modeling session   A modeling session where your focus is on identifying a high-level strategy for how your system will be built.

Architecture spike   An XP concept that refers to just enough code to show that a candidate architecture will work.

Artifact   A deliverable or work product.

Baseline   A tested and certified version of a deliverable that represents a conceptual milestone which thereafter serves as the basis for further development and that can be modified only through formal change control procedures. A particular version becomes a baseline when a responsible group decides to designate it as such.

BDUF   Big design up front.

Behavioral requirement   A requirements category that describes how a user will interact with a system, how someone will use a system, or how a system fulfills a business function.

Boundary object   An object that represents user interface elements such as screens, reports, HTML pages, or emails.

Business rule   An operating principle or policy that your software must satisfy.

Cardinality   Represents the concept "how many?" in associations.

CASE   Computer-aided system engineering.

CASE tool   Software that supports the creation and manipulation of models of software-oriented systems.

Catalysis   A next-generation software process for the systematic, business-driven development of component-based systems.

C&CM   Configuration and Change Management.

Change case   An artifact used to describe a potential requirement for a system or a potential modification to existing requirements.

Chaordic   The behavior of a self-governing organism, organization, or system that harmoniously blends chaos and order.

Class diagram   A UML diagram that depicts classes, their static inter-relationships (including inheritance, aggregation, and association), and the operations and attributes of those classes.

Class Responsibility Collaborator (CRC) card   A standard index card that has been divided into three sections, one indicating the name of the class that the card represents, one listing the responsibilities of the class, and the third listing the names of the other classes that this one collaborates with to fulfill its responsibilities.

Class Responsibility Collaborator (CRC) model   A collection of CRC cards.

CMM   Capability Maturity Model.

Cohesion   The degree of relatedness within an encapsulated unit (such as a component or a class).

Collaboration diagram   A UML diagram that shows instances of classes, their interrelationships, and the message flow between them. Collaboration diagrams provide a birds-eye view of a collection of collaborating objects working together to fulfill a common purpose.

Collaborative modeling tool   A CASE tool that enables several developers to simultaneously work on one or more models with real-time updates of those models.

Collaborative writing tool   A word processing tool that enables several people to simultaneously write a document with real-time updates of that document.

Communication   The act of transmitting information between individuals.

Component diagram   A UML diagram that depicts the software components of a system, their interfaces, and the relationships between the components.

Connascence   Between two software elements, A and B, the property by which a change in A would require a change to B to preserve overall correctness within your system.

Context diagram   A diagram that shows how your system fits into its overall environment. It is common to develop high-level data flow diagrams or deployment diagrams for this.

Contract model   A model that defines an agreement between two or more parties. A contract model is something that the parties should mutually agree to and mutually change over time if required. Contract models are often required when an external group controls an information resource that your system requires, such as a database, legacy application, or information service.

Control object   An object that serves as the glue between boundary/interface objects and entity objects, implementing the logic required to manage the various objects and their interactions.

Constraint   A restriction on the degree of freedom you have in providing a solution.

CORBA   Common Object Request Broker Architecture.

Core infrastructure team (CIT)   Any team with an enterprise-wide scope whose mission is to support development teams.

COTS   Commercial off-the-shelf.

Data definition language (DDL)   Commands supported by a database that enable the creation, removal, or modification of structures (such as relational tables or classes) within it.

Data domain   A collection of related data entities and the relationships between those entities. Most data domains are based on a common theme or concept within your business domain, such as customer, account, brokerage, and insurance within a financial institution.

Data manipulation language (DML)   Commands supported by a database that enable the access of data within it, including the creation, retrieval, update, and deletion of that data.

Data model   A diagram that depicts data entities and their inter-relationships.

Data-flow diagram (DFD)   A diagram that shows the movement of data between processes, entities, and data stores within a system.

Death march   A doomed software project, without any apparent hope of success, where the developers carry on anyway.

Deliverable   An artifact that is delivered as part of your overall system. Examples include source code, user documentation, and technical system documentation for operations and maintenance personnel.

Deployment diagram   A diagram that depicts a static view of the run-time configuration of processing nodes and the components that run on those nodes.

Design modeling session   A modeling session where your focus is on identifying a detailed strategy for building a portion of your system.

Developer   Anyone directly involved in the creation of a software development artifact. People in the roles of programmer, modeler, and tester are examples of developers.

Development team   Developers and the active project stakeholders.

Document   Any artifact external to source code whose purpose is to convey information in a persistent manner.

Documentation   Persistent information written for people that describes a system, including both documents and comments in source code.

Documentation handoff   This occurs when one group or person provides documentation to another group or person.

Domain model   A model that depicts major business classes or entities and the relationships between them. It is common to use a class diagram or data diagram for this purpose.

Drawing tool   A software tool that supports the ability to draw diagrams. Drawing tools are effectively low-end CASE tools.

DSDM   Dynamic Systems Development Method.

Enterprise architectural modeling The act of creating and evolving models that depict the business and technical infrastructure of your organization.

Enterprise requirements modeling The act of creating and evolving models that reflect the high-level requirements of your organization.

Entity object An object that is typically found in your domain model, such as Order and Item in an inventory control system.

Essential use-case A simplified, abstract, generalized use case that captures the intentions of a user in a technology and implementation-independent manner.

Essential user interface prototype A low-fidelity model for a portion of the user interface for a system in a technology-independent manner.

EUP Enterprise Unified Process.

Evil wizard A code generator that produces code that you do not understand.

Executable UML A strategy in which systems are modeled using the artifacts of the UML and a formal language such as the OCL from which working software is generated.

Executive overview A definition of the vision for the system and a summary of the current cost estimates, predicted benefits, risks, staffing estimates, and scheduled milestones.

Facilitator Someone responsible for planning, running, and managing modeling sessions.

FDD Feature-Driven Development.

Flow chart A diagram that depicts the logic flow of a business process or software operation. Flow charts are a primary artifact of structured/procedural modeling.

Formal model A model that is based on a language that has a well-defined syntax and semantics and possibly a defined way to show the validity of its constructs such as rules of analysis, inference, or proof.

Getter An operation that obtains the value of a data attribute, or calculates the value, of an object or class.

Glossary A collection of definitions of terms that are relevant to your project.

Gold owner The person or organization that funds your project.

Graphical user interface (GUI) A style of user interface composed of graphical components such as windows and buttons.

Hardware node A computer, switch, printer, or other hardware device.

IDE Integrated Development Environment.

Increment The difference between two releases of a system.

Information radiator   A display of information posted on the wall where passersby can see it.

Interface   In Java, a collection of zero or more operation signatures that a class implements in whole.

Interface object   See boundary object.

Iron triangle   A planning concept that you can only fix two of three aspects—cost, scope, and quality—on your project.

IRUF   Initial requirements up front.

IT   Information Technology.

Iterate   To move on to the next step/task, often in a repetitious manner, taking small steps each time.

Iteration   A Unified Process term that refers to a distinct sequence of activities with a baselined plan and valuation criteria that results in a release (either internal or external).

Ivory tower architecture   An architecture developed in isolation from the developers, or teams of developers, responsible for following it.

Joint application development (JAD)   A structured, facilitated meeting in which modeling is performed by a group of people. JADs are often held for gathering requirements or for modeling candidate architecture(s).

KISS   Keep it simple stupid.

Landscape model   See overview model.

Layering   The organization of software collections (layers) of classes or components that fulfill a common purpose.

Level-0 DFD   A DFD used model used as a context diagram.

Major user interface element   A large-grained item such as a screen, HTML page, or report.

Message-invocation box   The long, thin, vertical boxes that appear on sequence diagrams which represent invocation of an operation on an object or class.

Minor user interface element   A small-grained item such as a user input field, menu item, list, or static text field.

Model   An abstraction that describes one or more aspects of a problem or a potential solution to that problem. Traditionally, models are thought of as zero or more diagrams plus any corresponding documentation. However, non-visual artifacts such as collections of CRC cards, a textual description of one or more business rules, or the structured English description of a business process are also considered to be models.

Model Document Architecture (MDA)   Part of the OMG's vision to support interoperability with specifications, defining the relationships among OMG standards and how they can be used together in a coordinated manner.

Modeling session   An activity where one or more people focus on the development of one or more models.

Multiplicity   The UML combines the concepts of cardinality and optionality into the single concept of multiplicity.

Network diagram   A model that depicts the various types of hardware nodes and the interconnections between them.

Non-behavioral requirement   A category of requirements that describe technical features of a system, features typically pertaining to availability, security, performance, interoperability, dependability, and reliability.

Normalization (data)   A data modeling technique, the goal of which is to organize data elements in such a way that they are stored in one place and one place only.

Normalization (object)   An object modeling technique, the goal of which is to organize behavior in such a way that it is implemented in one place and one place only.

Note   A modeling construct for adding free-form text to UML diagrams.

Object Constraint Language (OCL)   The industry standard specification language defined by the Object Management Group (www.omg.org).

Object lifeline   Represents, in a sequence diagram, the life span of an object during an interaction.

OOA&D   Object-oriented analysis and design.

Optionality   Represents the concept "do you need to have it?" in associations.

Operations documentation   This documentation typically includes an indication of the dependencies that your system is involved with; the nature of its interaction with other systems, databases, and files; references to backup procedures; a list of contact points for your system and how to reach them; a summary of the availability/reliability requirements for your system; an indication of the expected load profile of your system; and troubleshooting guidelines.

Organization chart   A model that depicts the reporting structure between the people, positions, and/or teams within an organization.

Osmotic communication   Indirect information transfer through overhearing conversations or simply noticing things that happen around you.

Overview diagram   A high-level depiction of one aspect of your system's architecture. Any type of diagram, such as a UML class diagram or a data model, may be used as an overview diagram when appropriate for the given view.

Phase modeling sessions   A modeling session where your focus is on creating models pertinent to the major phases of traditional development. This includes but is not limited to requirements, analysis, architecture, and design modeling sessions.

Physical prototype   A physical model of the actual environment in which a system is to be deployed.

Platform Independent Model (PIM)   A type of MDA model that specifies a system in a manner that abstracts away technical details.

Platform Specific Model (PSM)   A type of MDA model that realizes a portion, one, or several PIMs to take into account technical considerations.

PIG   Process improvement group (the pun is intended).

Process object   See control object.

Project overview   A document that summarizes critical information such as the vision for the system, primary user contacts, technologies and tools used to build the system, the critical operating processes (some applicable to development, such as how to build the system, and some applicable to production, such as how to back up data storage), and references to critical project artifacts such as the source code, the permanent models, and other documents. This document serves as a starting point for anyone new to the team.

Project Stakeholder   A direct user, indirect user, manager, senior manager, operations staff member, support (help desk) staff member, testers, developers working on other systems that integrate or interact with this one, or maintenance professionals potentially affected by the development and/or deployment of a software project. For the sake of Agile Modeling, developers working on the project shall be excluded whenever the term "project stakeholder" is used, even though they clearly have an important stake in the projects that they work on.

Referential integrity   The assurance that a reference from one entity to another entity is valid. If entity A references entity B, then entity B exists. If entity B is removed, then all references to entity B must also be removed.

Relational database (RDB)   A permanent storage mechanism in which data is stored as rows in tables.

Release   The deployment of a working version of a system. Releases may be internal, available only to the development team, or external, available to some or all of the users for the system.

Requirements   A description of what your project stakeholders want a system to do, including the functionality that it should exhibit within a defined set of constraints.

Requirements document   This document defines what the system will do, summarizing or composed of requirements artifacts such as business rule definitions, use cases, user stories, or essential user interface prototypes (to name a few).

Requirements modeling   The act of identifying and exploring the requirements for a system.

Requirements modeling session   A modeling session where your focus is on defining what your project stakeholders want your system to do.

Requirements traceability matrix   The artifact used to record traceability relations between artifacts.

Reverse engineering   The generation of a model based on the information contained in source code.

Robustness diagram   A model that depicts the major objects—classified into boundary/interface objects, entity objects, or control/process objects—that participate in fulfilling an actor's interaction with a system as defined by a usage scenario.

RUP   Rational Unified Process.

Scaffolding   Additional code, including both operations and attributes, required to make your design work. Programmers often introduce scaffolding code or it is automatically generated by a CASE tool; it is not modeled as part of analysis and often not even as part of design.

Scribe   A person responsible for recording information during a modeling session.

SEI   Software Engineering Institute.

SEPG   Software engineering process group.

Sequence diagram   A UML diagram used to explore the logic of usage scenarios.

Setter   An operation that sets the value of a data attribute of an object or class. Also known as a mutator.

Simple tools   Manual item that you use to model systems, including but not limited to flipchart paper, Sticky Notes, paper napkins, sheet paper, string, thumb tacks, whiteboards, and index cards.

Software development artifact.   See artifact.

Source code   A sequence of instructions, including comments that describe those instructions, for a computer system. Also known as program code, program source code, or simply as code.

Specification language   A style of writing, such as Object Constraint Language (OCL) and Structured English, used to describe logic in a structured/formal manner.

SPI   Software process improvement.

Spike   See architecture spike.

SRS   Software Requirements Specification.

State chart diagram   A UML diagram used to depict the various states that an object may be in and the transitions between those states.

Stereotype   A UML stereotype denotes a common usage of a modeling element. Stereotypes are used to extend the UML in a consistent manner.

Structure diagram A diagram that depicts the modules of procedure-based code and the invocation relationships between those modules.

Structured English A traditional, easy to read, style of specification language.

Support documentation This documentation includes training materials specific to support staff; all user documentation to use as reference when solving problems; a trouble-shooting guide; escalation procedures for handling difficult problems; and a list of contact points within the maintenance team.

System The software, documentation, hardware, middleware, installation procedures, and operational procedures.

System documentation The purpose of this document is to provide an overview of the system and to help people understand the system. Common information in this document includes an overview of the technical architecture, the business architecture, and the high-level requirements for the system.

System use case A use case in which high-level implementation decisions are reflected, such as the specific type of user interface and your physical environment.

Trigger An operation that is automatically invoked as the result of data manipulation language (DML) activity within a database.

Technical requirement A requirement pertaining to a non-business-related aspect of your system, such as a performance-related issue, a reliability issue, or a technical environment issue.

Traceability The ease with which the features of one artifact—perhaps a document, model, or source code—are related/traced to the features of another.

Truck insurance The assurance that if the development team leaves, or gets hit by a truck, that critical information about the project is left behind in the form of documentation.

Truck number An estimate of the minimum number of people you would need to lose from your team before you find yourself in trouble (for example, the number of people that would need to be hit by a truck).

UML Unified Modeling Language.

UP Unified Process.

Usage scenario A description of a single path of logic through one or more use cases or user stories.

Use case A sequence of actions that provide a measurable value to an actor.

Use case diagram A UML diagram used to depict a collection of use cases, actors, their associations, and optionally a system boundary box.

Use case model The combination of one or more use case diagrams and their supporting use cases and actor definitions.

Use case realization An artifact of the Rational Unified Process (RUP) that is a collection of one or more models that describes the implementation of a single use case.

User documentation Documents that describe how to work with your system, including reference manuals, usage guides, support guides, and training materials.

User interface (UI) The portion of the software that a user directly interacts with.

User interface element See major user interface element and minor user interface element.

User interface flow diagram A diagram that enables you to model the high-level relationships between major user interface elements, depicting a birds-eye view of the user interface of your system.

User story A reminder to have a conversation with your project stakeholders that captures a behavioral requirement, a business rule, a constraint, or a technical requirement.

Version control tool A software tool used to check in/out, define, and manage versions of project artifacts.

Virtual meeting tool A tool that enables communication between several people in different physical locations.

Work product A type of artifact, such as a model or project schedule, that you create during development that you can discard or evolve into an actual deliverable.

Working software Software that has been tested, accepted by its users, and then released.

XP eXtreme Programming.

YAGNI You Ain't Gonna Need It Anyway.

ZFR Zero-feature release.

References and Suggested Reading

Agile Alliance (2001a). *Manifesto for Agile Software Development.* www.agilealliance.org

Agile Alliance (2001b). *Principles: The Agile Alliance.* www.agilealliance.org/principles.html

Ambler, S. W. (1995). *The Object Primer: Application Developer's Guide to Object Orientation.* New York, NY: Cambridge University Press.

Ambler, S. W. (1997). *Building Object Applications That Work: Your Step-By-Step Handbook for Developing Robust Systems with Object Technology.* New York, NY: Cambridge University Press. www.ambysoft.com/buildingObjectApplications.html

Ambler, S. W. (1998). *Process Patterns: Building Large-Scale Systems Using Object Technology.* New York, NY: Cambridge University Press. www.ambysoft.com/processPatterns.html

Ambler, S. W. (1999). *More Process Patterns: Delivering Large-Scale Systems Using Object Technology.* New York, NY: Cambridge University Press. www.ambysoft.com/moreProcessPatterns.html

Ambler, S. W. (2001a). *The Object Primer, Second Edition: The Application Developer's Guide to Object Orientation.* New York, NY: Cambridge University Press. www.ambysoft.com/theObjectPrimer.html.

Ambler, S. W. (2001b). *Enterprise Unified Process White Paper.* www.ronin-intl.com/publications/unifiedProcess.htm

Ambler, S. W. (2001c). *Agile Modeling Home Page.* www.agilemodeling.com

Ambler, S. W. (2001d). *The Design of a Robust Persistence Layer.* www.ambysoft.com/persistenceLayer.html

Ambler, S. W. (2001e). *Mapping Objects to a Relational Database.* www.ambysoft.com/mappingObjects.html

Ambler, S. W. (2001f). *Agile Modeling Mailing List Instructions.* www.agilemodeling.com/feedback.htm

Ambler, S. W. and Constantine, L. L. (2000a). *The Unified Process Inception Phase.* Gilroy, CA: CMP Books. www.ambysoft.com/inceptionPhase.html

Ambler, S. W. and Constantine, L. L. (2000b). *The Unified Process Elaboration Phase.* Gilroy, CA: CMP Books. www.ambysoft.com/elaborationPhase.html

Ambler, S. W. and Constantine, L. L. (2000c). *The Unified Process Construction Phase.* Gilroy, CA: CMP Books. www.ambysoft.com/constructionPhase.html

Ambler, S. W. and Constantine, L. L. (2002). *The Unified Process Transition and Production Phases.* Gilroy, CA: CMP Books. www.ambysoft.com/transitionProductionPhase.html

Bass, L., Clements, P., and Kazman, R. (1998). *Software Architecture in Practice.* Reading, MA: Addison Wesley Longman, Inc.

Beck, K. (2000). *Extreme Programming Explained: Embrace Change.* Reading, MA: Addison Wesley Longman, Inc.

Beck, K. and Cunningham, W. (1989). *A Laboratory for Teaching Object-Oriented Thinking.* Proceedings of OOPSLA'89, pp. 1-6.

Beck, K. and Fowler, M. (2001). *Planning Extreme Programming.* Boston, MA: Addison Wesley.

Beedle, M. and Schwaber, K. (2001). *Agile Software Development With SCRUM.* Upper Saddle River, NJ: Prentice Hall, Inc.

Bennett, D. (1997). *Designing Hard Software: The Essential Tasks.* Greenwich, CT: Manning Publications Co.

Boehm, B. W. (1988). *A Spiral Model Of Software Development and Enhancement.* IEEE Computer, pp. 61-72, 21(5).

Booch, G. (1994). *Object-Oriented Analysis and Design with Applications.* Reading, MA: Addison Wesley Publishing Company.

Bremer, M. (1999). *UnTechnical Writing: How to Write About Technical Subjects and Products So Anyone Can Understand.* Concord, CA: UnTechnical Press.

Brooks, F. P. (1995). *The Mythical Man Month: Essays on Software Engineering Anniversary Edition.* Reading, MA: Addison Wesley Publishing Company.

Brown, W. J., McCormick, H. W. III, and Thomas, S. W. (2000). *AntiPatterns in Project Management.* New York, NY: John Wiley & Sons, Inc.

Buschmann, F., Meunier, R., Rohnert, H., Sommerlad, P., and Stal, M. (1996). *Pattern-Oriented Software Architecture: A System of Patterns*. New York, NY: John Wiley & Sons Ltd.

Christel, M. G. and Kang, K. C. (1992). *Issues in Requirements Elicitation*. Software Engineering Institute (SEI) Technical Report CMU/SEI-92-TR-12. www.sei.cmu.edu

Coad, P., Lefebvre, E., and DeLuca, J. (1999). *Java Modeling in Color with UML: Enterprise Components and Process*. Upper Saddle River, NJ: Prentice Hall, Inc.

Cockburn, A. (1998). *Surviving Object-Oriented Projects: A Manager's Guide*. Reading, MA: Addison Wesley Longman, Inc.

Cockburn, A. (2001a). *Writing Effective Use Cases*. Boston, MA: Addison Wesley.

Cockburn, A. (2001b). *Crystal Clear: A Human-Powered Software Development Methodology for Small Teams*. http://members.aol.com/humansandt/crystal/clear/

Cockburn, A. (2001c). *Characterizing People as Non-Linear, First-Order Components in Software Development*. members.aol.com/humansandt/papers/nonlinear/nonlinear.htm

Cockburn, A. (2002). *Agile Software Development*. Reading, MA: Addison Wesley Longman, Inc.

Constantine, L. L., and Lockwood, L. A. D. (1999). *Software For Use: A Practical Guide to the Models and Methods of Usage-Centered Design*. New York, NY: ACM Press.

Coplien, J. and Harrison, N. (2001). *Organizational Patterns Site*. www.bell-labs.com/cgi-user/OrgPatterns/OrgPatterns

Davis, A. M. (1995). *201 Principles of Software Development*. New York, NY: McGraw Hill Inc.

Douglass, B. P. (1999). *Doing Hard Time: Developing Real-Time Systems With UML, Objects, Frameworks, and Patterns*. Reading, MA: Addison Wesley Longman, Inc.

D'Souza, D. F., Wills, A. C. (1999). *Objects, Components, and Frameworks with UML: The Catalysis Approach*. Reading, MA: Addison Wesley Longman, Inc.

Evans, G. (2001). *Palm Sized Process: Point of Sale Gets Agile*. Software Development, September 2001.

Fowler, M. (1997). *Analysis Patterns: Reusable Object Models*. Menlo Park, CA: Addison Wesley Longman, Inc.

Fowler, M. (1999). *Refactoring: Improving the Design of Existing Code*. Menlo Park, CA: Addison Wesley Longman, Inc.

Fowler, M. (2001a). *The New Methodology*. www.martinfowler.com/articles/newMethodology.html

Fowler, M. (2001b). *Is Design Dead?* www.martinfowler.com/articles/designDead.html

Fowler, M. & Scott, K. (1999). *UML Distilled Second Edition: A Brief Guide to the Standard Object Modeling Language*. Reading, MA: Addison Wesley Longman, Inc.

Gane, C., Sarson, T. (1979). *Structured Systems Analysis: Tools and Techniques*. Englewood Cliffs, NJ: Prentice Hall, Inc.

Gamma, E., Helm, R., Johnson, R., and Vlissides, J. (1995). *Design Patterns: Elements of Reusable Object-Oriented Software*. Reading, MA: Addison-Wesley Publishing Company.

Gilb, T. & Graham, D. (1993). *Software Inspection*. Harrow, England: Addison Wesley Longman Limited.

Gottesdiener, E. (2001). *Specifying Requirements With a Wall of Wonder*. http://www .therationaledge.com/content/nov_01/t_wallOfWonder_eg.html

Graham, I., Henderson-Sellers, B., and Younessi, H. (1997). *The OPEN Process Specification*. New York, NY: ACM Press Books.

Greenbaum, J. and Kyng, M., editors (1991). *Design At Work: Cooperative Design of Computer Systems*. Hillsdale, NJ: Lawrence Erlbaum Associates, Publishers.

Highsmith, J. A. III (2000). *Adaptive Software Development: A Collaborative Approach to Managing Complex Systems*. New York, NY: Dorset House Publishing.

Hock, D. W. (2000). *Birth of the Chaordic Age*. San Francisco, CA: Berrett-Koehler Publishers, Inc.

Hohmann, L. (1996). *Journey of the Software Professional: The Sociology of Computer Programming*. Upper Saddle River, NJ: Prentice Hall PTR.

Hunt, A. & Thomas, D. (2000). *The Pragmatic Programmer: From Journeyman to Master*. Reading, MA: Addison Wesley Longman, Inc.

Jacobson, I., Booch, G., and Rumbaugh, J. (1999). *The Unified Software Development Process*. Reading, MA: Addison Wesley Longman, Inc.

Jacobson, I., Christerson, M., Jonsson, P. and Overgaard, G. (1992). *Object-Oriented Software Engineering: A Use Case Driven Approach*. Wokingham, England: ACM Press.

Jacobson, I., Griss, M., and Jonsson, P. (1997). *Software Reuse: Architecture, Process, and Organization for Business Success*. New York, NY: ACM Press.

Jeffries, R., Anderson, A., and Hendrickson, C. (2001). *Extreme Programming Installed*. Boston, MA: Addison-Wesley.

Jeffries, R. (2001a). *Essential XP: Card, Conversation, Confirmation*. www.xprogramming.com/xpmag/expCardConversationConfirmation.htm

Jeffries, R. (2001b). *Essential XP: Documentation*. www.xprogramming.com/xpmag/ expDocumentationInXp.htm

Jeffries, R. (2001c). *Natural XP: Documentation*. www.xprogramming.com/xpmag/ natural.htm

Jeffries, R. (2001d). *Essential XP: Emergent Design*. www.xprogramming.com/xpmag/ expEmergentDesign.htm

Jeffries, R. (2001e). *Much Ado About Nothing: Documentation*. www.xprogramming.com/xpmag/FussAboutDocumentation.htm

Jones, C. (2000). *Software Assessments, Benchmarks, and Best Practices*. Boston, MA: Addison Wesley Longman Inc.

Kerievsky, J. (2001). *Patterns and XP. Extreme Programming Examined*. pp. 207-220, Eds. Succi, G. and Marchesi, M. Boston, MA: Addison Wesley.

Kerth, N. (2001). *Project Retrospectives: A Handbook for Team Reviews*. New York, NY: Dorset House Publishing.

Kruchten, P. (1995). *The 4+1 View Model of Architecture. IEEE Software*. 12(6), November 1995. pp. 42-50.

Kruchten, P. (2000). *The Rational Unified Process, Second Edition: An Introduction*. Reading, MA: Addison Wesley Longman, Inc.

Larman, C. (2002). *Applying UML and Patterns: An Introduction to Object-Oriented Analysis and Design and the Unified Process*. Upper Saddle River, NJ: Prentice Hall PTR.

Leuf, B. and Cunningham, W. (2001). *The Wiki Way: Quick Collaboration on the Web*. Reading, MA: Addison Wesley Longman, Inc.

Linthicum, D. S. (2000). *Enterprise Application Integration*. Reading, MA: Addison Wesley Longman, Inc.

Martin, R. (2001). *The Process*. www.objectmentor.com/publications/RUPvsXP.pdf

Mayhew, D. J. (1992). *Principles and Guidelines in Software User Interface Design*. Englewood Cliffs, NJ: Prentice Hall.

McConnell, S. (1993). *Code Complete: A Practical Handbook of Software Construction*. Redmond, WA: Microsoft Press.

Microsoft Corporation (1995). *The Windows Interface Guidelines for Software Design: An Application Design Guide*. Redmond, WA: Microsoft Press.

Microsoft Corporation (2001). The Microsoft Solutions Framework (MSF). www.microsoft.com/business/services/mcsmsf.asp

Naiburg, E. J. and Maksimchuk, R. A. (2001). *UML for Database Design*. Boston, MA: Addison Wesley.

Newkirk, J. and Martin, R. C. (2001). *Extreme Programming in Practice*. Boston: Addison Wesley.

Object Management Group (2001a). *The Unified Modeling Language (UML) Specification*. www.omg.org/technology/documents/formal/uml.htm

Object Management Group (2001b). Model Drive Architecture (MDA). ftp.omg.org/pub/docs/ormsc/01-07-01.pdf.

Page-Jones, M. (1988). *Practical Guide to Structured Systems Design 2/e*. Upper Saddle River, NJ: Prentice-Hall, Inc.

Page-Jones, M. (2000). *Fundamentals of Object-Oriented Design in UML*. New York, NY: Dorset-House Publishing.

Raskin, J. (2000). *The Human Interface: New Directions for Designing Interactive Systems*. Reading, MA: Addison Wesley.

Rational Corporation (2001). *Rational Unified Process Home Page*. www.rational.com/products/rup/index.jsp

Reingruber, M. C. and Gregory, W. W. (1994). *The Data Modeling Handbook: A Best-Practice Approach to Building Quality Data Models*. New York, NY: John Wiley & Sons, Inc.

Roman, E., Ambler, S. W., Jewell, T., and Marinescu, F. (2002). *Mastering Enterprise Java Beans, Second Edition*. New York, NY: John Wiley & Sons, Inc.

Rosenberg, D. and Scott, K. (1999). *Use Case Driven Object Modeling With UML: A Practical Approach*. Reading, MA: Addison Wesley Longman, Inc.

Ross, R. G. (1997). *The Business Rule Book, Second Edition*. Houston, TX: Business Rules Solutions, Inc.

Rumbaugh, J., Blaha, M., Premerlani, W., Eddy, F., and Lorensen, W. (1991). *Object-Oriented Modeling and Design*. Englewood Cliffs, NJ: Prentice Hall, Inc.

Rumbaugh, J., Jacobson, I., and Booch, G. (1999). *The Unified Modeling Language Reference Manual*. Reading, MA: Addison Wesley Longman, Inc.

Software Engineering Institute. (1995). *The Capability Maturity Model: Guidelines for Improving the Software Process*. Reading, MA: Addison-Wesley Publishing Company, Inc.

Stapleton, J. (1997). *DSDM: Dynamic Systems Development Method*. Harlow, England: Addison Wesley.

Vermeulen, A., Ambler, S. W., Bumgardner, G., Metz, E., Misfeldt, T., Shur, J., and Thompson, P. (2000). *The Elements of Java Style*. New York, NY: Cambridge University Press.

Wake, W. C. (2002). *Extreme Programming Explored*. Boston, MA: Addison Wesley.

Warmer, J. and Kleppe, A. (1999). *The Object Constraint Language: Precise Modeling With UML*. Reading, MA: Addison Wesley Longman, Inc.

Weiss, E. H. (1991). *How To Write Usable User Documentation*. Phoenix, AZ: The Oryx Press.

Wells, J. D. (2001). *Extreme Programming: A Gentle Introduction*. www.extremeprogramming.org

Wiegers, K. (1999). *Software Requirements*. Redmond, WA: Microsoft Press.

Wilkinson, N. M. (1995). *Using CRC Cards: An Informal Approach to Object-Oriented Development*. New York, NY: Cambridge University Press.

Williams, L., Kessler, R. R., Cunningham, W., and Jeffries, R. (2000). *Strengthening the Case for Pair Programming*. IEEE Software, July/August 2000, pp. 19-25.

Wood, J. and Silver, D. (1995). *Joint Application Development Second Edition*. New York, NY: John Wiley & Sons, Inc.

Xerox (2001). *Aspect-Oriented Programming*. http://www.parc.xerox.com/csl/projects/aop/

Yourdon, E. (1989). *Modern Structured Analysis*. Upper Saddle River, NJ: Prentice-Hall, Inc.

Yourdon, E. (1997). *Death March: The Complete Software Developer's Guide to Surviving "Mission Impossible" Projects*. Upper Saddle River, NJ: Prentice-Hall, Inc.

Index

A

acceptance testing, 23, 216–217
accuracy of AM, 13–14
activity diagram, UML, 45–46
ad hoc teams, 131
adaptation, local (*See* local adaptation)
adaptive software development (ASD), 72
Adobe Illustrator, 105
Agile Modeling defined, 11–15, 326–328
Agile Software Development Alliance, 6
analysis and design modeling, 227, 234–240, 269–272
applying AM, 9–10
applying right artifacts, 45–47, 94, 96
   in AM modeling sessions, 137
   in design-class modeling and, 286
   in extreme programming and, 181–183, 196, 198, 219
   in Unified Process and, 228, 234, 249, 261–262, 272–273
   tools and, 117
   Unified Modeling Language (UML) and, 171

architectural modeling, 272–277
artifacts, 4

B

big design up front (BDUF) principles, 51
   extreme programming and, 187
   in nurturing AM culture, 90–91
   Unified Process and, 305–306
big modeling up front (BMUF) principles, 59
   design class modeling and, 287
   extreme programming and, 198
   Unified Process and, 268, 305–306
blame placing versus AM, 319–320
bottom up modeling, infrastructure management, 296–298
business architecture document in Unified Process, 235
business glossary in Unified Process, 235
business modeling discipline, 227, 233–234, 246–253
business object model, 235, 248–249

business process, Unified Modeling Language (UML), 170
business rules, 9, 236
business use case modeling, 236, 247–248
   business object model in, 248–249
   business vision modeling in, 252–253
   future requirements and, 251
   goals in, 253
   iterative modeling in, 252
   logical data model (LDM) in, 249
   specifications in, 249–252
   supplementary business specification in, 249–252
business vision modeling, 252–253

C

C#, 5, 41
Canyon Blue (*See also* CASE tools), 101
capability maturity model (CMM), 317
CASE tools, 17, 39–42, 58, 70, 85, 87, 92, 101, 104, 107–115, 117, 120, 172, 326